Closely Held Organizations

Closely Held Organizations

Shawn J. Bayern

Carolina Academic Press
Durham, North Carolina

Library of Congress Cataloging-in-Publication Data

Bayern, Shawn.
Closely held organizations / Shawn J. Bayern.
pages cm
Includes bibliographical references and index.
ISBN 978-1-61163-364-1 (alk. paper)
1. Business enterprises--Law and legislation--United States. 2. Close corporations--United States. 3. Partnership--United States. I. Title.

KF1355.B39 2013
346.73'0668--dc23 2013027054

Carolina Academic Press
700 Kent Street
Durham, North Carolina 27701
Telephone (919) 489-7486
Fax (919) 493-5668
www.cap-press.com

2014 Printing

Printed in the United States of America

For my students (literally)

Contents

Table of Cases

Table of Codes, Restatements, and Statutes

Model Business Corporation Act

Uniform Limited Liability Company Act (ULLCA)

Uniform Limited Partnership Act (2001)

Uniform Partnership Act (1914)

Restatement (Second) of Agency

Restatement (Second) of Torts

Restatement (Third) of Agency

Revised Uniform Limited Partnership Act (1976)

Revised Uniform Partnership Act (RUPA) (1997)

Revised Uniform Unincorporated Nonprofit Association Act

Author's Note and Acknowledgments

Cases have been edited liberally, with footnotes and citations often removed without comment. Remaining footnotes are generally renumbered.

Thanks to Rob Atkinson, Jay Kesten, Mark Seidenfeld, Manuel Utset, and Don Weidner for many interesting discussions (and to Don for his wonderful support as dean). Thanks also to Kat Klepfer, Katrina Miller, and Zach Lombardo for very helpful research assistance.

Thanks also to the law reviews and other publishers that provided permission to reprint several short excerpts.

Closely Held Organizations

Chapter 1

Agency: Basic Matters

Section 1: Basic Contractual Authority

Note on the Purposes of Agency Law

The word *agency* just means "acting," and agency law is the law that governs the questions that arise when one person acts on behalf of another. It could just as appropriately be called the law of delegation or the law of vicarious activity. It is important not to confuse this area of law with *administrative* agencies; agency law has little to do with those.

People act for each other all the time. For example, a college student might authorize her roommate to sign a lease. A former politician with a side career as a speaker for hire might say to a speaker's bureau, "Get me as many high-paying engagements as you can find for me this summer. Just set them up and tell me where to go; I don't want to be bothered with the administrative details." And, of course, organizations often have to delegate individual people or departments to sign their contracts and take care of their other business—which is one reason most studies of business law and organizations start with agency law.

Consider a simple question: if you want to enter a contract, do you have to sign a document or make an oral agreement yourself, or can you delegate someone else to do it? For example, suppose a homeowner says to a real-estate agent, "I'd like you to arrange for the sale of my home, but I'm going to be out of the country for a few months. Please enter into a contract on my behalf to sell the home to the first prospective buyer who offers more than $240,000." When such a buyer appears, suppose that the agent purports to sign a contract on behalf of the homeowner to sell the home for $240,000 on a particular date in the future. On that date, the buyer wants to enforce the contract against the homeowner. Is the contract valid because the agent was acting under the homeowner's instructions, or is it invalid because the homeowner has made no specific promise to the buyer?

Without some kind of agency law permitting one person to act for another, there would be no contract between the homeowner and the buyer; after all, the homeowner hasn't personally made any promise or representation to the buyer. It is easy to imagine, hypothetically, a legal system that had no agency law.[1] In such a system, everyone would

1. It is often said that ancient Rome had no general law of agency and that contracts ordinarily had to be made personally, but Rome had other mechanisms—dependent more than modern law on personal and family relationships—to deal with the same questions. For example, in ancient Rome, the leader of a family couldn't delegate contractual powers arbitrarily, but he would be bound to the contracts that some of his family members, and slaves, entered. *See* Paula J. Dalley, *A Theory of Agency Law*, 72 U. Pitt. L. Rev. 495 (2011); William Gordon, *Agency and Roman Law* in Roman Law, Scots Law and Legal History, Selected Essays 54 (2007).

simply need to make his or her own promises personally in order to enter contracts. Although it's possible to imagine a complex commercial world in which people needed to sign their own contracts, such a system would be extremely cumbersome. To put it into economic terms, it would increase the transaction costs of commerce. For example, in the example involving the traveling homeowner, the homeowner might have to cut her overseas trip short in order to sell her home, or delay the sale—or at least use cumbersome and expensive international courier services or faxes to exchange and execute legal documents. Or perhaps the homeowner could sell the home temporarily to the agent, who in turn could sell it to the eventual buyer, but this would require that the agent take more of a risk in laying out his own money for the home; perhaps some real-estate agents would be willing to do this, but they would probably charge more for their services if they had to do so. In any event, it's much simpler if the homeowner can simply hire the agent to take care of the contract for her.[2]

Accordingly, common-law systems adopt the principle that people can choose to let others act for them, on their behalf and subject to their control. Most of agency law addresses the problems that follow from the basic decision to permit that kind of delegation. For example, what happens if I hire someone to be my agent and that person carelessly hurts someone else in trying to do what I asked him to do? (That is one problem addressed by the area of agency law called *respondeat superior*, which most first-year Torts classes cover briefly.) What happens if I issue confusing orders about who my agents are, and a third party enters a contract with someone reasonably thinking he's my agent when in fact he isn't? What if my agent betrays me by accepting a bribe; what remedies do I have for that kind of breach of trust?

Economists call many of these types of problems *agency costs*—the costs of your agents getting your instructions wrong or betraying you. As a matter of economic terminology, agency costs also include the expenses involved in selecting and monitoring your agents.

Note on Terminology in Agency Law

Agency law uses a distinct terminology. People who act for other people are called *agents*; this is a similar use of the term as in the phrase "real-estate agent" or "sports agent." The people who hire agents, and for whom agents act, are called *principals*. (This is a roughly similar—but only a roughly similar—use of the term as in the phrase "high-school principal.") The word *principal* basically means "first," and the idea is that the principal is the chief actor—someone who takes the lead and sets things in motion.[3]

A typical pattern is that a principal hires an agent to enter into contacts with others, called "third parties." For example, a small businessperson (the principal) may hire someone (an agent) to find new customers (the "third parties"). Most of agency law concerns the relationships between these three different types of parties:

---

2. For ease of discussion, this book generally refers to agents with masculine pronouns and others with feminine pronouns.

3. See, for example, Alexander Pope's *An Essay on Man*, which argues poetically that humanity might not always know its own purpose:

> So man, who here seems principal alone,
> Perhaps acts second to some sphere unknown,
> Touches some wheel, or verges to some goal;
> 'Tis but a part we see, and not a whole.

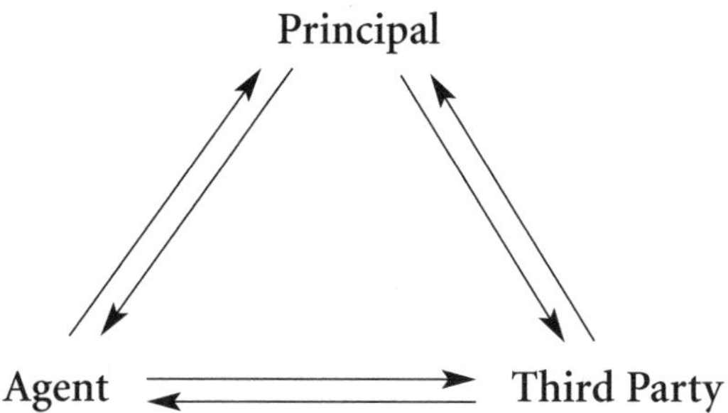

One of the fundamental questions of agency law is: when can an agent put a principal and a third party in a contract with each other, and thus make them liable to each other for breach of contract? Agency law uses the term "authority" to discuss this question: that is, it describes an agent who can enter into contracts as having "authority" to do so. The first questions we will consider concern (1) how authority arises and (2) what it means for an agent to have authority.

There are two types of authority: *actual* and *apparent.*

Restatement (Third), Agency, § 2.01: Actual Authority

An agent acts with actual authority when, at the time of taking action that has legal consequences for the principal, the agent reasonably believes, in accordance with the principal's manifestations to the agent, that the principal wishes the agent so to act.

Restatement (Third), Agency, § 2.02(1): Scope of Actual Authority

An agent has actual authority to take action designated or implied in the principal's manifestations to the agent and acts necessary or incidental to achieving the principal's objectives, as the agent reasonably understands the principal's manifestations and objectives when the agent determines how to act.

Note on Actual Authority

If everything goes well between a principal and an agent—that is, if the principal's instructions are clear and the agent properly interprets them—the agent simply does what the principal wants, and the agent is said to have *actual authority* to do so.

Though it may be a confusing term for cases beyond that simple one, "actual" authority also includes cases where the principal does *not* subjectively intend to give the agent authority but the agent reasonably thinks she did. That is, if *P* issues confusing instructions to *A*, whether *A* has actual authority or not is decided from the perspective of a reasonable person in *A*'s position. This is broadly similar to deciding whether something counts as an offer, in contract law, based on the perspective of a reasonable person receiving the offer.

Note that under Restatement § 2.02(1), above, the reasonableness of the agent's interpretation of his authority is judged at the moment "when the agent determines how to act." This means that the agent's authority is an ongoing and potentially changing question; it's not fixed at the time the agent signs a contract with the principal. If the agent learns something new about the principal's intentions, it starts to matter immediately.[4] This rule is designed to protect principals and make sure that agents can't unreasonably act for them given new information that they have learned. So, for example, if *P* says to *A*, "Please find and register a web address for my new company, using up to $5,000 to procure an advantageous name for me," but *A* learns two days later that *P* has suddenly decided on a name and registered it herself, *A* probably does not have actual authority to continue to look for an address or to spend $5,000 to acquire one.

Restatement (Third), Agency § 2.03: Apparent Authority

Apparent authority is the power held by an agent or other actor to affect a principal's legal relations with third parties when a third party reasonably believes the actor has authority to act on behalf of the principal and that belief is traceable to the principal's manifestations.

...

Illustrations

1. P owns a granary and employs A to manage it. A's employment agreement with P states that A's authority to purchase grain is limited to transactions that do not exceed $5,000; larger purchases require P's express approval. This limit is unusual in the granary business. P directs A to tell T, a seller of grain, that A's unilateral authority to purchase is unlimited because P believes this will induce T to give priority to orders placed by A. A represents to T that A's authority to purchase is unlimited and enters into a contract on P's behalf with T to buy $10,000 of grain. P is bound by the contract with T. A has actual authority to make the representation to T. A has apparent authority to enter into the contract with T because T reasonably believes A has authority to bind P to a contract to buy the grain.

Note on Apparent Authority

As the Restatement suggests, an agent has *apparent authority* when a third party reasonably believes (based on things the principal has said or done) that an agent has actual authority, even though the agent lacks actual authority. Apparent authority typically arises where the agent has made a mistake of some kind. The usual pattern, as the Restatement suggests, is that an agent with some authority exceeds his authority, but a third party reasonably thinks nothing is amiss. If that happens, the agent is said to have apparent authority.

---

4. This kind of changing obligation is not a significant departure from modern contract law; there are many areas of contract law in which modern courts recognize that not all rights and duties of the parties are fixed at the time a contract is formed. But the idea that contracts are static still has power, particularly among academics, and so a typical first-year Contracts course may leave the impression that the obligations of the parties cannot change once a contract is formed (unless there's formally a modification, novation, excuse, or something similar). On that static, older view of contract law, this rule in agency law is an exception.

For a discussion of related questions in contract law, see Melvin Aron Eisenberg, *The Emergence of Dynamic Contract Law*, 88 CALIF. L. REV. 1743 (2000).

Whereas actual authority is determined from the perspective of a reasonable *agent*, apparent authority is determined from the perspective of a reasonable *third party*.

Note on Agency by Estoppel

A doctrine very similar to apparent authority is called *agency by estoppel*, under which a third party may hold a principal liable if (1) the third party reasonably believes that an agent is acting for the principal and suffers a loss as a result, (2) the principal has notice of this, and (3) the principal doesn't take reasonable steps to correct the third party's misimpression.

Though agency by estoppel and apparent authority are very similar and the distinction between them is sometimes collapsed, there are two main differences.

First, agency by estoppel can cause a principal to be liable even if the principal gave no affirmative indication to the third party that the agent was authorized—something that is normally required for apparent authority. (As the Third Restatement puts it above, apparent authority requires that the third party's reasonable belief that an agent is authorized be "traceable to the principal's manifestations." Agency by estoppel does not require this.)

Second, agency by estoppel lets injured parties recover only for their loss in reliance on the misunderstanding. Essentially, it lets them recover reliance damages rather than expectation damages.[5] By contrast, if there is apparent authority, the third party can recover expectation damages from the principal.

Note on the Consequences of Authority

If an agent has authority—actual or apparent—then the agent has the legal power to put a principal and a third party into a contract with each other. That is, even though *A* and *T* are the only ones to sign a contract, *P* is a party to that contract and is liable to *T* if she breaches it. Similarly, *T* is ordinarily liable to *P* on the contract. If the principal breaches, the third party can recover from her—and vice-versa.

If an agent acts with *apparent* but not *actual* authority, as in Illustration 1 to Restatement § 2.03 above, the principal is liable to the third party on the contract that the agent has made, but the agent may also be liable to the principal for any losses the principal suffers as a result of the agent's error. So, for example, the third party may recover from the principal for the third party's contract damages, but the principal may then recover those same damages from the agent. It was, after all, the agent's unreasonable mistake that led to the principal's damages. (If the agent had been acting reasonably, the agent would have had actual authority in addition to apparent authority.)

Thus, agents can enter principals into contracts with third parties. Are the agents also liable on these contracts? For example, if the third party does not receive what she is promised, can she recover from the agent instead of the principal? On one hand, the third party signed a contract with the agent, so it might seem as if the agent should be liable; on the other hand, in many situations, the third party's real intent is to enter into a contract with the principal, and the agent is just a broker.

---

5. Doctrines called "estoppel," in the context of contract law, usually work similarly to reimburse parties for losses in reasonable reliance on a belief; they are tied closely to reliance-based losses and reliance damages. Thus, promissory estoppel lets promisees recover reliance damages even for non-bargain promises. Equitable estoppel, covered in some Contracts courses, similarly allows recovery of some reliance losses.

The law answers this question by asking how much information the third party had about the principal. First, there is the case of the *disclosed principal.* If an agent with authority tells the third party whom he's working for—that is, if the agent "discloses" the identity of the principal to the third party—then the agent is not considered a party to the contract and is not ordinarily liable if the principal breaches. For example, if a real-estate agent signing a contract for sale says to the buyer, "This home is owned by Charlie Merton, and the contract for sale will be between you and him," then by default the agent is not a party to the contract, and if Merton fails to sell the home, the third party cannot hold the agent liable.

Second, there is the case of the *undisclosed principal.* If the agent doesn't inform the third party that he's working for a principal—for example, if the agent pretends that the agent is operating on his own behalf instead of acting for someone else—then the agent is a party to the contract, and the third party can recover against him. This is only fair to the third party, who thought she was dealing directly with an ordinary contracting partner. For example, if a real-estate agent pretends to own a home himself, why shouldn't the law let an innocent third party seek damages against that agent if the real owner doesn't in fact sell the home to the third party?[6]

Third, there is a case between these other two—the case of the *partially disclosed principal.* (The Third Restatement updates the terminology of this case, calling such principals "unidentified.") An agent is said to *partially disclose* a principal when he informs the third party that he's acting for someone else but doesn't say who.[7] This case normally works similarly to cases of undisclosed principals: both the agent and the principal can be liable to the third party. Is this the right rule? The Third Restatement argues for it as follows:

> Without notice of a principal's identity, a third party will be unable to assess the principal's reputation, assets, and other indicia of creditworthiness and ability to perform duties under the contract. If an agent provides reassurances about the principal's soundness only generally or describes the principal, the third party will be unable to verify such claims without notice of the principal's identity.
>
> It is possible that a third party would view the fact that a principal is represented by a particular agent as a reliable proxy for the principal's reliability, if for example the agent is known to select among prospective principals carefully and to represent only those who warrant a high degree of confidence. Although this is possible, it does not typify the larger run of agency relationships.

Restatement (Third), Agency § 6.02 cmt. b.

---

6. Moreover, "a third party may avoid a contract made by an agent acting for an undisclosed principal if the agent or the principal knows or has reason to know that the third party would not have dealt with the principal as a party to the contract." Restatement (Third) Agency § 6.03, cmt. d.

7. This pattern, infused with mystery, arises often in fiction. Charles Dickens's *Great Expectations* has a memorable example of a partially disclosed principal:

> "My name," he said, "is Jaggers, and I am a lawyer in London. I am pretty well known. I have unusual business to transact with you, and I commence by explaining that it is not of my originating. If my advice had been asked, I should not have been here. It was not asked, and you see me here. What I have to do as the confidential agent of another, I do. No less, no more."

Note that Jaggers is trying to be careful not to exceed his actual authority.

This is just a default rule; the parties can agree otherwise. That is, the agent and the third party can agree that the third party has no contractual claims against the agent.

Curto v. Illini Manors, Inc.

940 N.E.2d 229 (Ill. App. 2010)

LYTTON, J.

Plaintiff, Marilee Curto, filed a complaint against defendant, Illini Manors, Inc., and Pekin Manors (Pekin Manors), under the Illinois Nursing Home Care Act (Nursing Home Care Act) (210 ILCS 45/1-101 et seq. (West 2008)) for personal injuries her husband suffered while a resident at Pekin Manors and his wrongful death. Defendant moved to dismiss the complaint and compel arbitration. The trial court denied the motion, and we affirm.

On August 9, 2007, Marilee entered into a contract with Pekin Manors, a residential nursing home, to admit and care for her husband, Charles. The contract named Charles as the resident and Marilee as the "Guardian/Responsible Party." Marilee signed the form on the preprinted signature line which designated her as the "Legal Representative." Charles did not sign the contract.

The parties also entered into a separate arbitration agreement, which provided that "any and all disputes arising hereunder shall be submitted to binding arbitration and not to a court for determination." In the arbitration agreement, each party waived its right to a trial by jury. Marilee signed the arbitration agreement above the line that stated "Signature of Resident Representative." Charles did not sign the arbitration agreement.

On August 13, 2009, Marilee filed a complaint against Pekin Manors pursuant to the Nursing Home Care Act for personal injuries Charles sustained while he was a resident. The complaint also sought damages suffered by Charles' next of kin under the Wrongful Death Act (740 ILCS 180/1 et seq. (West 2008)). It further alleged that Charles suffered pain and anguish, which subjected defendant to liability under the Survival Act (755 ILCS 5/27-6 (West 2008)), and that his heirs incurred expenses, which they were entitled to recover under the Rights of Married Persons Act (Family Expense Act) (750 ILCS 65/15 (West 2008)).

Pekin Manors filed a motion to dismiss and to compel arbitration, asserting that the estate was contractually bound by the arbitration agreement Marilee signed when Charles was admitted. After a thorough examination of authority supporting both positions, the trial judge denied the motion. The judge found that "the spouse is not an agent for the other spouse for purposes of an agreement to arbitrate." He concluded that the arbitration agreement was not valid and enforceable because there was no indication that Marilee had the authority to bind Charles to the mandatory arbitration terms of the contract.

Standard of Review

Initially, the parties dispute the standard of review. Generally, the issue we are asked to consider on an interlocutory appeal is whether there was a sufficient showing to sustain the order of the trial court granting or denying the relief sought. However, where the trial court does not make any factual findings, or the underlying facts are not in dispute and the court's decision is based on a purely legal analysis, we review the trial court's denial of a motion to stay the proceedings and compel arbitration de novo. Here, the trial court based its decision on the undisputed facts in the record.

Thus, our review of the issue is de novo.

Analysis

Pekin Manors claims that Marilee was Charles' agent and thus the agreement to arbitrat[e] is enforceable against him. It contends that the evidence permitted a finding of agency based on (1) actual authority and (2) apparent authority.

I. Agency

Whether a nonsignatory party is bound to an arbitration agreement is dictated by the ordinary principles of contract and agency. Johnson v. Noble, 240 Ill. App. 3d 731, 608 N.E.2d 537, 181 Ill. Dec. 464 (1992). The spouse's signature on an arbitration agreement may bind a nursing home resident if the spouse has the authority to sign the document as the resident's agent. The status of the parties as husband and wife, by itself, does not create an agency relationship. Capital Plumbing & Heating Supply Co. v. Snyder, 2 Ill. App. 3d 660, 275 N.E.2d 663 (1971). The agency of the spouse is a question of fact to be proved by direct or circumstantial evidence; there is no presumption that the wife has authority to act for the husband. Fettes, Love & Sieben, Inc. v. Simon, 46 Ill. App. 2d 232, 196 N.E.2d 700 (1964). The scope and extent of an agency relationship depend on the terms of the agreement between the principal and the agent and the intention of the parties. Brown v. Kerber Packing Co., 342 Ill. App. 474, 97 N.E.2d 117 (1951). The party claiming an agency relationship must prove it by a preponderance of the evidence. Granite Properties Ltd. Partnership v. Granite Investment Co., 220 Ill. App. 3d 711, 581 N.E.2d 90, 163 Ill. Dec. 139 (1991).

A. Actual Authority

Pekin Manors first argues that Marilee had actual authority to bind Charles to the arbitration agreement because she signed the admission contract and the arbitration agreement as her husband's "representative."

In any agency relationship, the principal can be legally bound by action taken by the agent where the principal confers actual authority on the agent. Granite Properties, 220 Ill. App. 3d at 714. Actual authority may be express or implied. Buckholtz v. MacNeal Hospital, 337 Ill. App. 3d 163, 785 N.E.2d 162, 271 Ill. Dec. 511 (2003). Express authority is directly granted to the agent in express terms by the principal and extends only to the powers the principal confers upon the agent. United States v. Schaltenbrand, 930 F.2d 1554 (11th Cir. 1991). Such authority may be granted through a written contract, a power of attorney or a court-ordered guardianship. Amcore Bank, N.A. v. Hahnaman-Albrecht, Inc., 326 Ill. App. 3d 126, 759 N.E.2d 174, 259 Ill. Dec. 694 (2001) (power of attorney explicitly listed powers given to the attorney-in-fact); 755 ILCS 5/11a-17(a) (West 2006) (guardian has authority as provided in court order under provisions of Probate Act). Implied authority, on the other hand, is actual authority circumstantially proved. Buckholtz, 337 Ill. App. 3d at 172. It arises when the conduct of the principal, reasonably interpreted, causes the agent to believe that the principal desires him to act on the principal's behalf. See Restatement (Second) of Agency § 26 (1958). For example, implied authority may be established from the circumstances of a case based on prior course of dealing of a similar nature between the alleged agent and principal or from a previous agency relationship. Hartshorn v. State Farm Insurance Co., 361 Ill. App. 3d

731, 838 N.E.2d 211, 297 Ill. Dec. 724 (2005); Linowiecki v. Wisniewski, 249 Ill. App. 474 (1928).

In this case, Marilee's signature on the nursing home documents did not confer express or implied authority on her. First, nothing in the record suggests that Charles gave Marilee express authority to make legal decisions on his behalf. The terms of the admission contract and the arbitration agreement did not give Marilee authority to act as Charles' agent, nor did Charles execute a power of attorney appointing Marilee as his agent for that purpose. Second, Pekin Manors failed to demonstrate any implied authority. No evidence indicates that Charles was present and directed Marilee to sign the arbitration agreement as his representative, nor is there any indication in the record that Charles knew Marilee signed the agreement and agreed to or adopted her signature as his own. Thus, Marilee's signature as a representative does not establish that she had actual authority to sign the arbitration agreement on Charles' behalf.

We recognize that this issue is one of first impression in Illinois. However, several other jurisdictions have addressed the authority of a spouse to bind a nursing home resident to an arbitration agreement and have reached similar dispositions. In Dickerson v. Longoria, 414 Md. 419, 995 A.2d 721 (Md. 2010), a personal representative signed an arbitration agreement on the resident's behalf when he was admitted to the nursing home. The Maryland Court of Appeals held that the representative, Dickerson, did not have actual authority to sign the arbitration agreement. The court concluded that Dickerson's reference to herself as the resident's "legal power of attorney" did not expand her authority absent some evidence that the resident, Bradley, authorized, adopted or acquiesced to the statement. The court specifically noted: "The fact that Dickerson signed the arbitration agreement at issue in this case certainly does not alter Dickerson's authority, as there is no evidence suggesting that Bradley authorized Dickerson to make this type of decision on his behalf." Dickerson, 995 A.2d at 740.

The majority of jurisdictions have followed Dickerson's reasoning and have concluded that a spouse or other family member did not have actual authority to sign an arbitration agreement on the resident's behalf. Koricic v. Beverly Enterprises-Nebraska, Inc., 278 Neb. 713, 773 N.W.2d 145 (Neb. 2009) (decedent's son did not possess authority necessary to sign arbitration agreement); Mississippi Care Center of Greenville, LLC v. Hinyub, 975 So. 2d 211 (Miss. 2008) (daughter did not have authority to enter arbitration agreement where there was no declaration of resident's inability to manage his affairs and no power of attorney in the record); Mt. Holly Nursing Center v. Crowdus, 281 S.W.3d 809 (Ky. Ct. App. 2008) (spouse lacked authority to bind resident to arbitration agreement); Goliger v. AMS Properties, Inc., 123 Cal. App. 4th 374, 19 Cal. Rptr. 3d 819 (Cal. Ct. App. 2004) (daughter was not acting as mother's agent when she signed arbitration agreement without some evidence of authority beyond merely signing admission contracts).

Even where a health care power of attorney was present, courts have concluded that the spouse lacked authority to sign the arbitration agreement. Those cases have held that a health care power of attorney granted for medical decisions does not confer authority to sign an arbitration agreement waiving legal rights. See Life Care Centers of America v. Smith, 298 Ga. App. 739, 681 S.E.2d 182 (Ga. App. 2009) (power of attorney granted to daughter for medical decisions did not grant authority to waive legal rights under arbitration agreement); Lujan v. Life Care Centers of America, 222 P.3d 970 (Colo. Ct. App. 2009) (health care proxy's decision to agree to arbitrate was unauthorized); Texas Cityview Care Center, L.P. v. Fryer, 227 S.W.3d 345 (Tex. Ct. App. 2007) (medical power of attorney did not indicate that it was intended to confer authority to sign arbitration agreement). See also Monticello Community Care Center, LLC v. Estate of Martin, 17 So. 3d 172 (Miss. Ct. App. 2009); Moffett v. Life Care Centers of America, 187 P.3d 1140 (Colo. App. 2008); Blankfeld v. Richmond Health Care, Inc., 902 So. 2d 296 (Fla. Dist. Ct. App. 2005). But see Owens v. National Health Corp., 263 S.W.3d 876 (Tenn. 2007) (attorney-in-fact authorized to enter into arbitration agreement as part of contract admitting nursing home resident).

As the trial court said in denying the motion to compel arbitration: "[T]he agreement to submit to binding arbitration is ultra vires[8] of a power of attorney for health care and the duty/power to provide for the nursing home spouse's medical needs."

These cases support our conclusion that a spouse's signature on an arbitration agreement as the resident's representative does not demonstrate actual authority to bind a nursing home resident to the agreement. An actual agency relationship is controlled by the express authorization of the principal or implied conduct of the principal and agent. The principal's conduct is crucial to establish actual authority. Such authority is not dictated by an independent act or signature of the agent. Thus, absent some evidence that the resident gave the agent spouse authority to sign the agreement to arbitrate on his behalf, the resident is not bound by its terms. By our decision today, we join the majority of states reviewing this issue.

Nevertheless, Pekin Manors urges us to consider the decisions of a minority of courts that have enforced nursing home arbitration agreements signed by a family member. Those cases follow the reasoning of Sovereign Healthcare of Tampa, LLC v. Estate of Huerta, 14 So. 3d 1033 (Fla. Dist. Ct. App. 2009). In Sovereign Healthcare, the Florida appellate court held that a daughter-in-law had the authority to sign a contract for admission on the resident's behalf, including the arbitration agreement, in reliance on a durable power of attorney. The durable power of attorney in that case included a catch-all provision giving the attorney-in-fact the authority "to sign any and all releases or consent required." Sovereign Healthcare, 14 So. 3d at 1035; see also Triad Health Management of Georgia, III, LLC v. Johnson, 298 Ga. App. 204, 679 S.E.2d 785 (Ga. 2009) (signature of patient's son on arbitration agreement was enforceable where son had general power of attorney executed by father); Five Points Heath Care, Ltd v. Mallory, 998 So. 2d 1180 (Fla. Dist. Ct. App. 2008) (daughter had durable power of attorney to prosecute, defend and settle all actions or other legal proceedings and to "do anything" regarding resident's estate). These cases, however, are distinguishable. In each case, there is at least some evidence of actual authority granting general powers of attorney to the spouse or family representative. Here, Pekin Manors has produced neither a general or property power of attorney, nor an order of guardianship authorizing Marilee to administer her husband's legal affairs. Thus, Marilee lacked actual authority to sign the arbitration agreement on Charles' behalf.

B. Apparent Authority

Pekin Manors also claims that the arbitration agreement is valid because Marilee acted as her husband's apparent agent at the time of his nursing home admission. Pekin Manors argues that since Marilee made a health care decision for her husband to be placed in the nursing home and Charles remained in the nursing home, Charles consented to Marilee's authority to sign the arbitration agreement.

---

8. We will encounter this term again later in the book; *ultra vires* is just a Latin phrase that means "beyond the powers" [—ed.]

rule = agent is liable to 3rd party if they act as if they had apparent authority

In the absence of actual authority, a principal can be bound by the acts of a purported agent when that person has apparent authority to act on behalf of the principal. Amcore Bank, 326 Ill. App. 3d at 137. Apparent authority arises when a principal creates a reasonable impression to a third party that the agent has the authority to perform a given act. Crawford Savings & Loan Ass'n v. Dvorak, 40 Ill. App. 3d 288, 352 N.E.2d 261 (1976). To prove apparent authority, the proponent must show that (1) the principal consented to or knowingly acquiesced in the agent's exercise of authority, (2) based on the actions of the principal and agent, the third party reasonably concluded that the agent had authority to act on the principal's behalf, and (3) the third party justifiably relied on the agent's apparent authority to his detriment. Career Concepts, Inc. v. Synergy, Inc., 372 Ill. App. 3d 395, 404, 865 N.E.2d 385, 310 Ill. Dec. 61 (2007) (company's sales manager had apparent authority to sign contract with employee-placement agency where company authorized manager to enter other contracts and interview potential employees). In establishing apparent authority, it is critical to find some words or conduct by the principal that could reasonably indicate consent. Emmenegger Construction Co. v. King, 103 Ill. App. 3d 423, 431 N.E.2d 738, 59 Ill. Dec. 237 (1982). An agent's authority may be presumed by the principal's silence if the principal knowingly allows another to act for him as his agent. Elmore v. Blume, 31 Ill. App. 3d 643, 647, 334 N.E.2d 431 (1975).

The record before us demonstrates that Charles never acted or conducted himself in a way that would indicate to Pekin Manors that Marilee was his apparent agent for purposes of the arbitration agreement. There is no evidence showing that Charles was present when Marilee signed the agreement or that Charles understood Marilee was signing an agreement waiving his legal rights. The record contains no words or conduct by Charles that would reasonably indicate consent. Thus, Pekin Manor failed to establish that Marilee had apparent authority to sign the arbitration agreement on her husband's behalf. As a result, Marilee cannot be required to arbitrate Charles' claims against the nursing home.

Pekin Manors attempts to analogize this case to Strino v. Premier Healthcare Associates, P.C., 365 Ill. App. 3d 895, 850 N.E.2d 221, 302 Ill. Dec. 784 (2006). In that case, parents of a newborn filed a medical negligence case against the obstetrician that delivered the baby Cesarian section. The jury found the mother was contributorily negligent due to the father's decision to decline the use of forceps for a vaginal delivery. On appeal, the parents claimed that the agency instruction was error. The reviewing court disagreed, finding an agency relationship based on the father's blatant refusal to allow the doctor to use forceps, the mother's presence in the operating room and her silence when the doctor requested her permission to use forceps. Strino, 365 Ill. App. 3d at 902.

The facts in this case are dissimilar. The record does not indicate that Charles was present when Marilee signed the contracts on his behalf. And neither party suggests that the nursing home staff asked Charles to agree to the terms of the arbitration agreement. Without some evidence of an agency relationship, he cannot be bound by the arbitration agreement.

II. Marilee's Personal Claims

In the alternative, Pekin Manors argues that Marilee is obligated to arbitrate her personal claims for wrongful death and medical expenses because she had the authority to bind herself to the agreement. We disagree.

Marilee signed the arbitration agreement as "Resident Representative." Marilee did not sign the agreement in her individual capacity. She signed the agreement as a representative of the beneficiary, Charles. Thus, Marilee's signature carries no legally binding weight regarding the arbitration of her personal claims against the nursing home under the Wrongful Death Act or the Family Expense Act. See Ward v. National Healthcare Corp., 275 S.W.3d 236 (Mo. 2009) (arbitration clause signed by daughter did not preclude daughter's personal wrongful death claim); Goliger, 19 Cal. Rptr. 3d at 821.

Conclusion

Because Marilee lacked authority to enter into the arbitration agreement on behalf of Charles, the arbitration agreement is invalid. Therefore, Marilee is not required to arbitrate her claims against Pekin Manors. In light of our holding on the issue of agency, it is unnecessary for this court to address the remaining issues raised on appeal.

The judgment of the circuit court of Tazewell County denying the motion to dismiss and compel arbitration is affirmed. The cause is remanded to the circuit court for further proceedings consistent with this opinion.

Affirmed and remanded.

Restatement (Third), Agency § 2.01 cmt. c

Most conferrals of [actual] authority combine two elements. The first, always present, is a manifestation, however general or specific, by a principal as to the acts or types of acts the principal wishes to be done. The second, less invariably present, consists of instructions or directives that specify how or within what constraints acts are to be done. A principal's communications to an agent begin with an initial expression granting authority, followed in many instances by instructions or directions that clarify matters, prescribe in more specific terms what the principal wishes the agent to do, or reduce or enlarge the scope of the agent's authority. A principal's manifestations may raise questions—at one end, as to whether the principal wishes the agent to move beyond the acts explicitly specified in order to fulfill the principal's implicit purpose and, at the other end, as to whether implicit restrictions apply in addition to the limits the principal has stated. An agent must interpret the principal's manifestations and determine how to act. The context in which the relationship is situated, including the nature of the principal's objectives and the custom generally followed in such circumstances, affects how the agent should interpret the principal's manifestations....

If a principal states directions to an agent in general or open-ended terms, the agent will have to exercise discretion in determining the specific acts to be performed to a greater degree than if the principal's statement specifies in detail what the agent should do. It should be foreseeable to the principal that an agent's exercise of discretion may not result in the decision the principal would make individually. Regardless of the detail in a principal's statements or other conduct, an agent's duty is to interpret them reasonably to further purposes of the principal that the agent knows or should know, in light of facts that the agent knows or should know when the agent acts. When a principal's instructions are ambiguous, or if circumstances change, it will often be reasonable for the agent to seek clarification from the principal rather than speculating about the principal's wishes.... If an agent's interpretation is reasonable at the time the agent acts, the agent is not subject to liability to the principal even if, after the fact, the principal can demonstrate that the agent's interpretation was erroneous.

Note on Agency Creation

The hallmark of an agency relationship is that an agent agrees to act on behalf of, and subject to the control of, a principal. There needn't be a written contract, or indeed a contract of any kind, but there often is. (The simplest example of an agency relationship without a contract involves a principal and agent who agree that the agent will act for the principal for free; this is an agreement, but it may lack consideration and thus not be a contract.) If one exists, a contract's terminology is not dispositive; thus, a contract can explicitly say that it doesn't create an agency relationship but still create one. The substance of the relationship—whether a reasonable agent would believe he has the power to act for a principal, based on the principal's manifestations—is the law's focus.

Note on Inherent Authority

The Second Restatement defined a third kind of authority called *inherent authority* or *inherent agency powers* to include "the power of an agent which is derived not from authority, apparent authority or estoppel, but solely from the agency relation" and suggested that it "exists for the protection of persons harmed by or dealing with a servant or other agent." Restatement (Second), Agency § 8A. The Third Restatement drops this concept on the thought that it overlaps with other doctrines and is unnecessary.

The core idea behind inherent authority is that it handles inevitable errors that arise when agents are involved. A principal might expressly forbid an agent from doing something, but complex commercial relationships are messy enough that a principal might still expect the agent to commit hard-to-avoid errors. When the agent is an employee and the errors lead to torts within the scope of employment, the result is vicarious tort liability (respondeat superior), which we will study later in the book. But the Second Restatement suggests that a similar concept can apply to contractual liability. For example, suppose corporate policy prevents a store's employees from accepting a return of merchandise (so that the employees have no actual authority to do so), and suppose the customer was told at the time of sale that there will be no refunds (so that there is arguably no apparent authority for the employee to accept a refund). If a store manager (misunderstanding her corporate policy) says to a customer, "As a courtesy, because we value your business, we'll let you make a return just this once," the manager's inherent authority may explain why the return is binding.

On appropriately general understandings of actual authority (the manager might have reasonably thought she was permitted to vary slightly from a strict corporate policy in the interest of serving customers) or apparent authority (the customer may have reasonably believed the store authorized managers to veer from the same strict policies), the Third Restatement suggests the concept of inherent authority is unnecessary. In particular, the Third Restatement makes an allowance for situations in which it is "reasonable for the agent to believe that the principal wishes the agent to construe the instructions in light of changed circumstances." Restatement (Third) Agency, § 2.02 cmt. e. Compare the following two illustrations:

> 20. P retains A, directing A to buy Blackacre but to offer no more than $250,000. A then learns that Blackacre has increased substantially in value and, if purchased for $300,000, would represent a bargain. As A knows, it is financially feasible for P to pay $300,000 for Blackacre. A does not have actual authority to offer more than $250,000 for Blackacre.

> 22. Same facts as Illustration 20, except that P owns and operates a golf course on land that almost entirely surrounds Blackacre. A has notice of P's long-term business plan to enhance the aesthetic and athletic qualities of the course and thereby make it more profitable. At the auction of Blackacre, A learns for the first time that there will be one other bidder, B. A also learns that B's plan for using Blackacre is to construct a cement factory on it. A is unable to contact P to relay this information and receive further instructions. A succeeds in purchasing Blackacre for P by bidding $260,000. A acted with actual authority.

Id. cmt. e. illus. 20, 22. The Second Restatement would likely have treated this case as one of "inherent authority" instead of "actual authority."

ICC v. Holmes Transp., Inc., 983 F.2d 1122 (1st Cir. 1993). "Although, under Massachusetts law, the 'general powers' of an attorney to represent a client do not entail the authority either to settle a case or to make substantial modifications to an existing contract, the principal's consent to be bound may be implied by showing the agent's actual or apparent authority to act in the principal's behalf. An agent's actual authority to bind his principal may be implied ... in circumstances where the principal has acquiesced in or adopted conduct by the agent which is reasonably considered to encompass the authority to undertake the subject conduct on the principal's behalf. See LaBonte v. White Constr. Co., 363 Mass. 41, 292 N.E.2d 352, 355 (1973) (superintendent of schools held to be 'agent' of school district for purposes of receiving plaintiff's statement of claim, where superintendent was familiar with contract involved in litigation, and school district had acquiesced in superintendent's acceptance of other plaintiffs' claims on several prior occasions); Hurley v. Ornsteen, 311 Mass. 477, 42 N.E.2d 273 (1942) (existence of agency relationship may be implied from "course of conduct showing that a principal has repeatedly acquiesced therein and adopted acts of the same kind"); Restatement (Second) Agency § 43. In light of its finding that the private escrow agreement and the consent decree were 'symbiotic' documents designed to serve the identical function, viz., providing an indemnity fund for settling the ICC refund claims against HTI, the court supportably ruled that Seder's authority to negotiate and execute the escrow agreement in behalf of the Holmes parties implied the authority to modify the escrow agreement as necessary to implement settlement of the ICC refund claims in litigation."

Note on Ratification

Suppose an agent purports to enter a principal into a contract but does not have authority to do so. Normally, the principal will not be a party to that contract and will not have any liability as a result of it. Even without authority, however, a principal can become bound through a process known as *ratification*. The concept of ratification is simple: for reasons of convenience and simplicity, a principal can take responsibility for a contract made by a purported agent even after it is signed. Ratification is probably justified by commercial norms and convenience; in most cases, ratification is probably cheaper for the parties than having to conclude a new contract from scratch. Ordinarily, it is just a way to eliminate doubt—to take a potential disagreement and source of legal uncertainty off the table when the principal wants to do so.

The simplest sort of ratification essentially corrects a minor legalistic deficiency; the doctrine of ratification lets a third party and a principal move forward with a contract if a principal says "I'm going to honor that contract you signed on Thursday with my agent, even though the agent didn't really have my authority to enter into it." Ratification effectively rewrites history; it "retroactively creates the effects of actual authority." Restatement (Third), Agency § 4.05.

Ratification does not require consideration to be effective, and it probably does not even need to be communicated to anyone, although the cases supporting that idea are mostly English. See Restatement (Third), Agency § 4.01 cmt d. Signing a piece of paper in the dark saying "I ratify Thursday's contract" is probably enough for ratification in theory, although courts do not permit a principal to use this possibility as a way to speculate (on, for example, changes in market price) at a third party's expense. In particular, ratification becomes unavailable after a third party makes any attempt to withdraw from the transaction or after "any material change in circumstances that would make it inequitable to bind the third party, unless the third party chooses to be bound." *Id.* § 4.05.

Most of the practical problems concerning ratification involve interpretations of factual situations: did a principal, through her actions, ratify a purported agent's actions? Absent the sort of "express" ratification just described, are there situations in which a principal's conduct can amount to implicit ratification? The basic answer to this question is that a principal can ratify a purported agent's actions by either "manifesting assent" (as in the example above) or by engaging in "conduct that justifies a reasonable assumption that the person so consents." Restatement (Third), Agency, § 4.01. The Restatement's comment offers perhaps a better formulation than "conduct that justifies a reasonable assumption" of ratification: it suggests that a principal "may ratify the act through conduct justifiable only on the assumption that the person consents to be bound by the act's legal consequences. For example, knowing acceptance of the benefit of a transaction ratifies the act of entering into the transaction." *Id.* cmt. d. The comment makes clear a weighty justification for allowing implicit ratification: it is unfair for someone to act in a way that they could justify only if there were a contract and yet still try to disclaim the contract. Thus, for example, if I run a small business and my employee, lacking strict authority, purchases a laptop for $1,200 on my business's credit card and then arrives back at my office with the laptop and tells me what he's done, what basis would I have for using the laptop except that I had intended to honor its purchase? Otherwise, why would I even be entitled to use the laptop?

Johnson v. Hospital Service Plan

25 N.J. 134 (N.J. 1957)

WACHENFELD, J.

On April 11, 1955 Alfreida Johnson, infant daughter of plaintiff William Johnson, was struck by an automobile and suffered a severe fracture of the hip. She was conveyed by ambulance to the Newark City Hospital, now known as Martland Medical Center, where she was admitted as an emergency case. The hospital, a public institution owned by the municipality, is principally dedicated to the charitable care of indigents, but by virtue of an ordinance enacted in 1937, persons may be accepted for emergency treatment although they possess the financial resources to secure adequate care elsewhere. Section 9.2 of the ordinance under consideration provides:

> "Any person who shall receive emergency treatment and who is not indigent, shall be charged and pay the cost of such care and treatment at rates to be fixed by the director."

Alfreida Johnson required hospitalization and medical treatment for a total of 70 days. Her hospital bill, computed at the normal rates for non-indigent patients as established by the medical director of the hospital, amounted to $1,190. Only $100 of this sum was ever paid to the city, however, and this fact is at the heart of the present litigation.

During 1955 William Johnson was a subscriber to the Hospital Service Plan of New Jersey, also known in common parlance as the New Jersey Blue Cross Plan. Under the terms of his individual contract with the Plan, his daughter was eligible for the benefits of his subscription.

The Department of Institutions and Agencies of the State of New Jersey in 1944 had approved the Newark City Hospital as a possible participant in the Hospital Service Plan. Thereafter, negotiations were commenced for the inclusion of the Newark City Hospital as a cooperating member of the Plan. These discussions eventuated in a purported agreement signed by the then Medical Director of the City Hospital, Dr. Earl Snavely, whereby certain fixed rates were to be paid the hospital by the Plan for the hospitalization and treatment of subscribers and eligible members of their families. This agreement stipulated that payments made under its terms would constitute payment in full to the hospital.

The initial arrangement, made by Medical Director Snavely, provided for payment to the hospital at the rate of $5 per day for the first 21 days that a subscriber was hospitalized on an emergency basis, and for the payment of $3.63 per day thereafter for a period of not more than 90 days. Subsequently, this basic understanding was modified several times to increase the charges to the Plan, but the provision was always retained that the payment required of the Plan on behalf of any subscriber, or eligible member of his family, should constitute payment in full to the city.

At the time when Alfreida Johnson was injured the agreement with the Plan, signed by Medical Director Chmelnik, provided for payment of the flat sum of $100 per subscriber-patient regardless of the amount or quality of hospitalization required. Thus, if a subscriber to the Hospital Service Plan were taken into the city hospital as an emergency case and hospitalized for only one day, the Plan was nevertheless obligated to pay the full $100 to the hospital. Correspondingly, if 70 days of hospitalization and treatment were necessary, as here, the Plan was still obligated to pay only $100 as full compensation to the city.

In accordance with the alleged agreement entered into by its medical director, the city hospital billed the Plan in the amount of $100 for its care of Alfreida Johnson. This sum was paid by the Plan, and the city accepted the check. Meanwhile, the Johnsons had instituted a negligence action against the driver allegedly responsible for Alfreida's injuries, and a settlement of the suit had been effected. The insurance carrier for the putative tortfeasor refused, however, to pay over $1,090 of the settlement money to the Johnsons because the city had filed a hospital lien in that amount. Under N.J.S. 2A:44-37 such a lien attaches to the proceeds of any settlement assented to by a person who has been treated for personal injuries sustained in an accident due to the alleged negligence of another. The lien claim filed by the city represented the difference between the original hospital bill of $1,190 and the $100 sum rendered by the Plan as payment in full of the Johnsons' obligation.

As a result of the insurance company's action, William Johnson initiated this suit for a declaratory judgment absolving him of any liability to the city for his daughter's care. He contended that either the $100 paid by the Plan to the city hospital on his behalf constituted payment in full or that, if the agreement between the Plan and the city were held invalid, the Plan was obligated to pay the amount of the lien. An agreed statement of facts was drawn by the parties, and they stipulated that under no circumstances would Johnson be liable for the sum involved.

Thus, the litigation resolved itself into a contest between the City of Newark and the Hospital Service Plan, the fundamental argument of the city being that its medical director was not authorized to enter into any contract with the Plan and that the purported agreement was therefore invalid.

The court below determined that the requisite authorization was present and that, in any event, the city had ratified the original agreement and its subsequent modifications agreed to by the respective medical directors. The judgment in favor of the Hospital Service Plan directed the Clerk of Essex County to cancel of record the hospital lien of the City of Newark. An appeal was taken by the city to the Appellate Division, but we certified the cause on our own motion before argument there.

[Potentially ambiguous state statutes provided various public officials with the authority to approve contracts for the hospital, and the city of Newark denied that the medical director of the city hospital was the proper agent to negotiate agreements with insurance plans. The Plan argued that the correct interpretation of the statutes was precisely that such an officer had that authority.]

We find it unnecessary, however, to resolve the true meaning of the [statutes], and to determine in which local official the authority to contract with the Plan resides. Even assuming the medical director was acting beyond the bounds of his authorization, it is clear that in light of the events succeeding the inauguration of the agreement the city has accepted it by ratification and is now estopped to deny its validity.

It is well established in this jurisdiction and generally conceded by the authorities that a municipality can ratify a contract entered into by an unauthorized agent as long as such contract is one within the corporate powers and not ultra vires in the primary sense as entirely beyond the municipal jurisdiction. The ratifying power exists when the deficiency invalidating the municipal contract consists only in the lack of proper authorization on the part of the party executing it in behalf of the municipality. The public is not disserved by this doctrine for the responsible officials who should properly have made the agreement are not bound by their subsequent acceptance of it through the means of ratification unless they were acquainted with all the material facts. Thus, the public, in large, is fully protected.

Here there was no express ratification through the adoption of an ordinance or resolution confirming the acts of the respective medical directors in making contracts with the Hospital Service Plan. The doctrine of implied ratification applies to municipalities as well as to individuals, however, and we find that the conduct of the appellant city manifests an intention to affirm the unauthorized act of its agent.

The intent to ratify an unauthorized transaction may be inferred from a failure to repudiate it. Restatement, Agency, § 94. McQuillin states a city may be bound by inaction and that mere silence, the performance of the contract, or the acceptance of benefits under it can constitute ratification. 10 McQuillin, [*Municipal Corporations* (3d ed. 1950)], at § 106. Any conduct on the part of the municipality reasonably evidencing approval of the unauthorized transaction will suffice. Thus, in *Frank v. Bd. of Education of*

Jersey City, [100 A. 211 (N.J. Ct. Err. App. 1917)], the court found an implied ratification where the board of education knew that work and materials had been furnished by the plaintiff at the direction of unauthorized agents but did not deny their authority or protest the claims presented until three years after the last work had been performed. Similarly, in *Ratajczak v. Bd. of Education, Perth Amboy*, [177 A. 880 (N.J. 1935)], it was held the school board had affirmed the unauthorized hiring of plaintiff as a janitor despite the absence of a formal resolution when for approximately three years it had paid him a salary, assigned him to janitorial duties and in every other respect treated him as a regularly employed custodian.

We think the facts sub judice conduce more strongly to the conclusion that an implied ratification was effected than did those in the *Frank* and *Ratajczak* cases. The city permitted the contract with the Hospital Service Plan to remain in effect from 1944 through 1956, although by its very terms the contract was terminable upon 60 days' notice by either party. Prominent is it that during this entire period and, in fact, from 1922 forward no one in the city administration other than the medical director had ever established rates for hospital care. Newark cannot contend its administrative officials were ignorant of the existence of the contract or the material facts concerning its execution and terms. The very officer charged by the City of Newark with the authority to negotiate such contracts knew of its consummation in 1944 and was also familiar with the rates which the Hospital Service Plan undertook to pay.

Commissioner Brady, who was Director of the Department of Public Affairs, having under its jurisdiction the Newark City Hospital, from 1944 to 1949, admitted in his deposition that he may have directed Medical Director Snavely to enter into an agreement with the Hospital Service Plan, and further stated he had "undoubtedly" approved any rates fixed during his term of office. The conclusion is irresistible that the contract was ratified by the official who Newark contends had the authority to make it in the first instance. Furthermore, both the present Director of the Department of Health and Welfare, under the mayor-council form of local government, and Mayor Carlin admitted that in December of 1954 at the hearings upon the proposed 1955 budget they had learned of the 1944 agreement and the modifications effected thereafter, realizing that the city was collecting a flat payment of $100 for its hospitalization and treatment of subscribers to the Hospital Service Plan. Nevertheless, no steps were taken to abrogate the arrangement and the city continued to receive benefits under it. The 1954 financial report of the city hospital showed that a portion of its receipts had been collected from the New Jersey Blue Cross Plan, and the 1955 report reflected a complete breakdown of receipts, including those from the Hospital Service Plan.

The cases cited by the city in support of its argument that no ratification occurred are easily distinguishable. In *Service Commercial Body Works v. Borough of Dumont*, 5 N.J. Super. 327 (App. Div. 1949), the court held there was no ratification by virtue of the borough's receiving a fire truck, which had been painted and lettered without authorization, and using it for six weeks prior to rejecting the plaintiff's bill. The court expressly found there was no evidence that the governing body was aware the truck had been painted without authority and noted that even if there were such knowledge, the borough was compelled to accept the truck because it was needed for fire protection. The delay in notifying plaintiff that its claim had been denied was attributed to the customary time lag incident to municipal procedures. Likewise, in *N.J. Car Spring & Rubber Co. v. Jersey City*, 64 N.J.L. 544 (E. & A. 1900), there was nothing to indicate that the body authorized to purchase certain goods had any knowledge of their requisition or receipt and use. *Jersey City Supply Co. v. Jersey City*, 71 N.J.L. 631 (E. & A. 1905), simply holds there was no express ratification of an unauthorized purchase of goods where the mayor vetoed the ratifying resolutions adopted by the board of fire commissioners. His consent was an essential element in the ratifying process, and there could be no effective ratification without his concurrence. Again, the municipal body charged with the responsibility for making such purchases had no knowledge of their requisition or delivery and use before plaintiff's claims were presented, and therefore an issue as to implied ratification did not arise.

We are amply satisfied that if the medical directors of the city hospital were wanting in authority to transact agreements with the Hospital Service Plan, the city by its course of conduct has by this time rectified the deficiency through implied ratification.

Additionally, the doctrine of estoppel applies against municipal corporations. A great injustice would be perpetrated if at this late date Newark were permitted to deny its obligations to the Hospital Service Plan. The Plan has undergone a considerable change in position as a result of its reliance upon the authority of the medical director to enter into a valid cooperating hospital agreement, and the city's continued compliance with full knowledge of the agreement is directly responsible for the Plan's payment of benefits over the course of 11 years.

...

The city maintains the agreement with the Plan was exceedingly detrimental in that for the years 1953 through 1956 considerably less money was received under the $100 payment-in-full provision than would have been received if the regular rates established for non-indigents were charged to Plan subscribers. These figures ignore, however, the administrative ease of collectibility involved in having the Plan as the sole source of payment and also fail to take into account the assurance of payment which the Plan represents. If the city hospital had no agreement with the Hospital Service Plan, the results would probably be far less beneficial. The rates payable by the Plan to the city hospital would have to be established on the basis of the average payment made by all patients treated therein, and since the great majority of them are indigent, these rates would be extremely low. If the city chose to remain outside the Hospital Plan, it would be faced with the large and often unrewarding task of collecting its obligations from each individual patient. The arrangements with the Hospital Service Plan may not have established a perfect balance of quid pro quo, but there can be no doubt that they were fair and reasonable and approved by disinterested state officials.

While public money must be conserved and to this end special rules govern the validity of municipal obligations, it would be grossly unjust not to make municipalities reasonably amenable to fair standards of conduct in their transactions with outsiders. It is difficult to imagine a case which more compels the application of this general standard than the case sub judice.

The judgment below is affirmed.

P wins

Progress Printing Corp. v. Jane Byrne Political Committee, 601 N.E.2d 1055 (Ill. App. 1992). A political candidate had told the chairman of a printing company that Griffin was the person in charge of the campaign's printing arrangements. "It was to Griffin that [the printing company] sent its invoices. Thus Griffin was in the best position to discover any impropriety promptly, given that the invoices detailed the content and size of each order and thus contained sufficient information to permit repudiation even though they lacked the name of the orderer. Griffin, however, by his own admission rarely even opened the invoices and reviewed none of them. Any lack of actual knowledge of the unauthorized orders is therefore the result of his breach of the duty to gain knowledge of the transactions by simply reviewing the invoices, a breach that has the same legal effect as actual knowledge of the facts and which may be imputed to his principal. In addition, the benefits of the transactions were retained in that the campaign staff accepted the materials, which were then used without question. Thus, the circuit court's decision that the unpaid orders were ratified was not against the manifest weight of the evidence because the evidence demonstrated that defendants' designated agent had the opportunity to repudiate the orders and that defendants 'took a position inconsistent with nonaffirmation' by accepting and using the products of those transactions without objection. To hold otherwise would permit a principal to foist liability onto third parties on the basis of its lack of actual knowledge of an unauthorized transaction even when its ignorance of the facts is the direct result of its expressly designated agent's neglect."

Peter Tiersma, *The Language of Silence*

48 Rutgers L. Rev. 1 (1995)

Once an agency relationship is established, the agent may speak for, and legally bind, the principal. The power of the agent to bind the principal, however, is almost invariably limited. Thus, if an airline authorizes a travel agent to sell tickets on its behalf, the agent cannot sell one of the airline's aircraft to the highest bidder.

Unfortunately, the scope of an agent's authority is frequently not so well defined, especially from the point of view of third parties. Someone who sells refrigerators to retailers might believe that the manager of an appliance store has the power to order ten refrigerators to be sold in the store, but in fact the store's owner may not have given the manager this authority. There are, not surprisingly, various means by which a principal may nonetheless be held responsible for acts by an agent that are beyond the agent's authority, some of which involve instances of legally significant silence.

One such situation occurs when an agent does an act that could reasonably have been included within his authority, but which on closer examination may not have been. In this situation, courts have held that the principal, by remaining silent or inactive after learning of the agent's act, has acquiesced in the act, thus indicating that the conduct was authorized:

> Example 5: A salesman is given the authority to entertain customers at his company's expense without any particular limitation. The salesman later informs an officer of the company who has authority in such matters that he (the salesman) plans to use his private airplane to entertain some of the company's customers. The officer remains silent, and thus has acquiesced in the salesman's plan....

Drawing inferences from conduct and particularly silence often depends on social norms reflecting how people ought to behave. An example is the common behavioral norm that people should greet each other when they meet, especially if they know each other. Although this practice has diminished in our increasingly impersonal cities, it survives in smaller communities, as well as in many subcommunities such as places of worship or the workplace. Consequently, if you encounter someone who would ordinarily be expected to greet you but does not, you will usually try to infer why. The person might be angry or preoccupied, or may not have recognized you. The point is simply that certain behavioral norms create situations in which people are expected to speak; their failure to do so will allow observers to draw certain conclusions.

Positing the existence of a behavioral norm is critical in accounting for Example 5. If the salesman informs the officer that he is planning to engage in an unauthorized act, the officer's silence can support several inferences besides acquiescence. For example, the officer might just be thinking the plan over, he might be uncertain about whether this act is within the salesman's authority, or he might cynically intend to let the salesman use his own airplane for the jaunt and then deny reimbursement because the act was never authorized.

To consider the silence as acquiescence, we must have information that allows us to eliminate these competing inferences. In this case, there is a behavioral norm that accomplishes this goal. As the Restatement of Agency observes, "persons ordinarily express dissent to acts done on their behalf which they have not authorized or of which they do not approve." The principal's silence—failure to express such dissent—"indicates that the parties understood that such acts were authorized."

...

Admittedly, this norm is probably somewhat fictional; it is not certain that most principals and agents are aware of it. Yet it does have a basis in reality. There is a more general norm that if A obviously misconstrues something B said, B should correct the misconception, especially if it relates to an important matter. Furthermore, courts recognize this norm in order to avoid the injustices that could result if the principal were free to await the outcome of a transaction before approving or rejecting it.

Acquiescence is possible only when the agent's conduct is arguably within his authority. Yet even if the agent has clearly acted beyond his authority, his conduct can still be ratified by the principal. Ratification can take place when the principal explicitly states that he approves of conduct by the agent. But it may also occur by silence; indeed, the Restatement of Agency comments that ratification may be inferred from a failure to repudiate a transaction. This conclusion is particularly probable when, "according to the ordinary experience and habits of men, one would naturally be expected to speak if he did not consent." Typically, ratification occurs when, upon learning that an agent has exceeded her authority, the principal remains silent, as the following example illustrates:

> Example 6: After a hotel clerk is killed, the manager offers a reward to anyone who assists in locating the culprit. Joanne claims the reward for her efforts in apprehending and convicting the killer. The hotel owner, however, refuses to pay on the ground that the manager had no authority to make the reward offer. Assuming that the owner knew of the reward offer made on behalf of the hotel and did nothing about it, he will be held to have ratified the manager's actions by silence.

A commentator has noted that what is often called ratification by silence in fact reflects several distinct phenomena. In some cases the courts impose ratification upon the principal because the principal acts in a way that is inconsistent with nonaffirmance or nonratification of the transaction. For instance, the principal may act as though he had ratified the transaction by receiving property to which he would be entitled only if the transaction had been authorized. In another type of case—also commonly called ratification by the courts—the operative principle is estoppel. Here, a purported principal does something that misleads a third party into believing that a transaction is authorized or ratified, or at least, does not correct the third party's obviously mistaken impression in this respect. In both of the above cases, the actual intention of the principal is not controlling.

...

Incidentally, inferring that a person agrees with something because that person remains silent, especially when that person could easily have spoken up to protect her interests, is a broad principle that is not exclusive to Anglo-American law. Among the Igbo of Nigeria, for example, a person's silence during the making of a collective community decision is deemed to be consent to that decision.

...

People can reasonably assume that when a principal learns that his agent has exceeded her authority, he will follow this behavioral norm and will repudiate the transaction if he does not wish to be a party to it. Once sufficient time has passed for him to do so, his silence is a strong indication that he does not wish to repudiate, but instead consents to the transaction. Consequently, this analysis is similar to the traditional legal approach: ratification is viewed as consent that is inferred from the principal's silence and failure to object. This analysis is confirmed by the fact that the law imposes no direct liability on the principal for his failure to speak, but rather simply binds him to the agent's transaction.

What has probably confused the issue is that the term "ratification" is used differently in other areas of the law. Treaties, for example, must be ratified by the Senate after they are negotiated by the President. And amendments to the federal Constitution must be "ratified" by the states before becoming effective. Both of these actions are similar to ratification in agency law in that they involve subsequent approval of an act that in broad outline has already been accomplished. Yet in agency law this approval requires no more than that the principal consent to becoming a party to the transaction, and consent can generally be inferred from actions and silence. On the other hand, Congress cannot ratify a treaty by doing nothing after it learns that the President has signed it. Indeed, the fact that the members of Congress may favor the treaty means nothing; their actual mental state is irrelevant. What matters is how they vote on the ratification issue, regardless of how they truly feel about it. In this case, therefore, ratification requires a particular speech act (i.e., voting), while in agency law the ability to infer that the principal has the proper mental state is sufficient.

Note on Terminating an Agency Relationship

As part of a pattern we'll see throughout business law, principals have the power to terminate an agency relationship even if doing so is otherwise wrongful. For example, suppose that Melissa, an actress, signs a three-year contract with a personal manager under which (1) Melissa promises to pay the manager 15% of all revenues from artistic endeavors, and (2) the manager has (actual) authority to sign Melissa up for roles, collect her employers' payments, subtract 15%, and give Melissa the rest.

If Melissa decides, a year into the contract, to breach the contract for personal or professional reasons and gives notice to the manager, the manager's authority to do anything on Melissa's behalf ends immediately. This is true even if the contract expressly provides that the term of the agency relationship is three years and that Melissa has no right to unilaterally terminate it. Thus, once hearing of the termination from Melissa, the manager would have no actual authority to sign Melissa up for new theatrical contracts; even though Melissa has breached the contract, she has the power to terminate the agency relationship. The rationale for this rule is that the agency relationship is weighty and often personal; it lets one person create new legal obligations for another. Compare the rule in contract law that specific performance is ordinarily not awarded for employment relationships; there, as here, it is seen as too intrusive to keep people in a relationship that one of them doesn't want.

Of course, because of the wrongful termination, the manager can still sue Melissa for damages—in this case, probably 15% of her artistic revenues for the remainder of the contract's term, plus whatever other incidental damages the manager may incur as a result of breach.

Though the agent's power to sign Melissa up for new contracts terminates immediately, what of his power to continue to accept money on Melissa's behalf, subtract his 15% fee, and pay Melissa the rest? This sort of power can sometimes survive termination under an exception to the general rule. The exception is that a power "given as security"—an older and somewhat narrower term is "coupled with an interest"—is not terminated merely because the principal wants it terminated.

The precise boundaries of this exception are unclear. The chief idea is that when an agency power is given as part of a contract to ensure that the promisee will be able to serve his own interests, rather than to act as a representative of the principal's interests, the principal cannot unilaterally revoke that power because doing so would undermine the contract. The typical example is that a contract gives A power to sell something of B's if B defaults on a loan; B cannot unilaterally terminate such a power. The point is that the power isn't especially personal, and A isn't really B's agent; B has simply given A the power to do something in order to compensate A for the risk of B's default in an ordinary, non-agency contract.

Because Melissa's relationship with her manager is largely an agency relationship, the manager's power to continue to accept Melissa's money directly would probably terminate once the agent receives notice of termination from Melissa. The manager's remedies are probably limited to damages.

Section 2: The Agent's Duty of Care

Restatement (Third), Agency § 8.08: Duties of Care, Competence, and Diligence

Subject to any agreement with the principal, an agent has a duty to the principal to act with the care, competence, and diligence normally exercised by agents in similar circumstances. Special skills or knowledge possessed by an agent are circumstances to be taken into account in determining whether the agent acted with due care and diligence. If an agent claims to possess special skills or knowledge, the agent has a duty to the principal to act with the care, competence, and diligence normally exercised by agents with such skills or knowledge.

...

Some exculpatory provisions are unenforceable. See, e.g., Restatement Third, The Law Governing Lawyers § 54(2) (agreement prospectively limiting lawyer's liability to client for malpractice).

...

Illustrations

...

2. P, a successful pop singer, retains A, a talent agent, to represent P in negotiations with recording companies. A has skills as an investment manager that are unusual among otherwise similarly situated talent agents. At P's request, A undertakes to manage P's investment portfolio. However, A does so ineptly, resulting in losses for P. Under applicable law, A's management of P's investment portfolio is not consistent with the exercise of competence to be expected of an investment manager. A is subject to liability to P.

3. Same facts as Illustration 2, except that A in fact lacks skills as an investment manager but represents to P that A has such skills. P does not know that A's claim is false. Same result.

4. Same facts as Illustration 3, except that A makes no representation to P that A has skills as an investment manager. A is subject to liability if A failed to act with the care, competence, or diligence normally exercised by agents who undertake to manage property of a principal.

...

5. P, who wishes to buy a used car, gives an amount of cash to P's friend, A, and asks A to select and purchase a suitable car for P. A is not employed as an auto mechanic but has substantial avocational experience in buying and selling cars and working on them. A selects and purchases a used car for P from T. A does not inspect the car or have an inspection conducted. Thus, A does not discover, nor does P, that the car has been in an accident that rendered it unsafe and without substantial value. Conducting a routine inspection, which A was competent to do, would have revealed the car's condition. A is subject to liability to P. A's failure to inspect the car or have it inspected prior to purchasing it for P was inconsistent with the exercise of competence and diligence reasonably to be expected of a person in A's position. It was reasonable for P to expect that A would exercise A's skill.

6. Same facts as Illustration 5, except that the used car selected by A has a nonobvious defect in its internal computer system. To discern the presence of such a defect requires specialized skills apart from those ordinarily associated with auto mechanics. A is not subject to liability to P. A's skills do not extend to computer technology.

Carrier v. McLlarky

693 A.2d 76 (N.H. 1997)

JOHNSON, J.

The defendant, Bruce M. McLlarky d/b/a Assured Plumbing & Heating, appeals an adverse judgment by the Derry District Court (Warhall, J.) in a small claims matter. We reverse.

The defendant installed a replacement hot water heater in the home of the plaintiff, Janet Carrier, in September 1994. The existing water heater had been installed by a different plumber approximately four years prior to its failure. When the defendant installed the new water heater, he told the plaintiff that he believed the old unit was under warranty, and that he would try to obtain a credit against the cost of the new water heater from the manufacturer. The defendant subsequently returned the defective unit to a supplier. The defendant has not given the plaintiff the desired credit and claims that he has failed to do so because he has not received payment from the manufacturer. The plaintiff sued the defendant in small claims court for the replacement value of the water heater and assorted costs. The district court rendered judgment in favor of the plaintiff, and this appeal followed.

The district court held: "The defendant in accepting the duty of returning the unit for the benefit of his [principal], the plaintiff[,] either obtained a credit or failed to pursue a credit to the detriment of the plaintiff." We interpret the court's holding as imposing liability under a theory of breach of duty on the part of an agent.

We find no error in the district court's determination that the parties had entered into an agency agreement whereby "the defendant would on behalf of the plaintiff return the old water heater for credit, which the plaintiff would [recoup]," and that "the defendant accepted the authority to act for the plaintiff and took the old water heater to return it to the manufacturer for credit." Whether an agency agreement has been created is a question of fact. An agency relationship is created when a principal gives authority to another to act on his or her behalf, and the agent consents to do so. See 93 Clearing House, Inc. v. Khoury, 415 A.2d 671, 673 (1980). The granting of authority and consent to act need not be written, but "may be implied from the parties' conduct or other evidence of intent." Id. at 349. This court will not overturn a factual finding of the trial court unless it is unsupported by the evidence. Here, both the testimony and documentary evidence submitted by the parties support a finding that an agency agreement had been formed.

The question thus becomes whether there is evidence in the record to support a finding of breach. Agents have a duty to conduct the affairs of the principal with a certain level of diligence, skill, and competence. A determination that an agent was not sufficiently diligent is a question of fact that will not be disturbed unless it can be said that no rational trier of fact could come to the conclusion that the trial court has reached.

Under ordinary circumstances, the promise to act as an agent is interpreted as being a promise only to make reasonable efforts to accomplish the directed result." Restatement (Second) of Agency § 377, comment b at 174 (1957). The court's own findings show that the defendant did make a reasonable attempt to obtain a refund for the plaintiff. Specifically, the court found that after agreeing to act on behalf of the plaintiff, "the defendant then gave the old water [heater] to [a supplier] to return it to the manufacturer." The court's subsequent statement that "the plaintiffs contacted the defendant numerous times regarding the credit and were told they would receive their money as soon as he received the credit," is insufficient to support a finding that the defendant breached his duty of diligence. This is especially true given that "the duties of an agent toward his principal are always to be determined by the scope of the authority conferred." 3 Am. Jur. 2d Agency § 209; *see* Restatement (Second) of Agency § 376. The record shows only that the defendant was charged with returning the defective water heater for a possible credit; he did not guarantee that a credit would be obtained.

In addition, the degree of skill required by an agent in pursuit of the principal's objective is limited to the level of competence which is common among those engaged in like businesses or pursuits. See Restatement (Second) of Agency § 379, comment c at 179. There is no indication from the evidence on the record that more was required of the defendant in his agent capacity beyond executing the actual return and seeking the credit. The invoices and work orders provided to the court by the plaintiff do not indicate that the defendant guaranteed a refund. Rather, he merely promised to attempt to obtain a credit from the manufacturer. The invoice drawn up by the defendant and submitted as evidence by the plaintiff stated only that a refund under a warranty may be possible. Further, the record contains a letter from a supplier stating that the defendant "acted in a normal manner as any dealer would under these circumstances," and "was right to withhold credit ... until the factory actually covered the unit."

Furthermore, an agent cannot be held liable to the principal simply "because he failed to procure for him something to which the latter is not entitled." 3 Am. Jur. 2d Agency § 215. The defendant correctly argues that any finding by the court that there was a valid warranty in place is unsupported by the record. The evidence submitted regarding the existence of a warranty included only two undated sales brochures claiming that a similar unit would be covered by a five to ten-year warranty and a letter dated approximately six months after the unit was replaced noting that a warranty currently offered to customers was valid for five to twelve years. Notably, the plaintiff did not produce a warranty for her actual unit. No evidence in the record established that the actual heater returned by the plaintiff was in fact covered by a warranty with terms identical to those described in the sales brochures or letter. Moreover, the defendant's supplier stated in a letter that the unit in question was not covered under a valid warranty.

There is also no support in the record for the holding that the defendant failed to turn over a refund actually received from the manufacturer. As noted above, the record contains a letter from a supplier stating that "technically, the unit was out of warranty." While the court did find the defendant to be less credible than the plaintiff, there is simply no evidence on the record that the defendant ever received the credit at all. Hence, there is no evidence to support a finding that the defendant breached his duty to remit funds actually received on behalf of the plaintiff. Cf. Restatement (Second) of Agency § 427 (agent who has received money on behalf of principal has duty to deliver it to principal on demand).

Consequently, because the district court's ruling was unsupported by the evidence, we reverse.

Reversed.

All concurred.

Oxford Shipping Co. v. New Hampshire Trading Corp.

697 F.2d 1 (1st Cir. 1982)

BREYER, J.

Oxford Shipping Co., Ltd. ("Oxford"), is a subsidiary of a large Hong Kong commercial firm. Oxford's assets consist principally of one cargo ship, the "Eastern Saga." Oxford claims that it was hurt when its ship was seized by South Korean authorities as a result of a scheme to cheat a Korean firm, Yulsan. Yulsan had bought about 20,000 tons of scrap metal, which applicable bills of lading represented to be aboard the "Eastern Saga," but the ship actually contained only about 17,000 tons of metal.

Oxford brought suit to recover damages in New Hampshire federal district court. It sued Avon Trading Corporation ("Avon"), the shipper that used the "Eastern Saga" to transport the metal; New Hampshire Trading Corp. ("NHT"), a scrap dealer that sold scrap to Avon; Frederic Gendron, the president of NHT; and Tager Steamship Agency ("Tager"), an agent retained to issue bills of lading and perform other tasks associated with loading and shipping the scrap.

Since Oxford itself seems to have been innocent of wrongdoing (although the captain and crew of its ship may have known of the plot), while several of the defendants seem to have been guilty of conduct ranging from simple breach of fiduciary duty to what approaches criminal behavior, one might believe at first glance that it would be fairly easy for Oxford (the company and its shareholders) to recover for the harms suffered. The record reveals, however, a highly complicated set of legalistic arguments, made by the defendants' lawyers and by Oxford's lawyers in response, that led the district court to conclude that the defendants were entitled to judgment on all counts. Oxford appeals. Our review of the case convinces us that the law should, and does, correspond with one's elementary sense of justice: namely, as between Oxford and most of these defendants, the defendants rather than Oxford and its shareholders should pay for the damage caused.

I

The complex set of facts underlying this litigation can be simplified as follows. Avon contracted in 1978 to sell roughly 20,000 tons of scrap metal to Yulsan. Avon subchartered the "Eastern Saga" from Transamerica Steamship Corp., which had previously subchartered the vessel from several other firms which in turn had chartered it from Oxford. The evidence before the district court indicated that Avon tried to cheat Yulsan by only loading some 17,000 tons of scrap on board. In particular, after buying an initial quantity of scrap elsewhere, Avon purchased roughly 7,000 tons of scrap from NHT, but represented the amount as over 10,000 tons. Avon used various false documents to conceal the fraud, including bills of lading issued by Tager that overstated the weight of the scrap by several thousand tons. In issuing the bills of lading, Tager relied upon a letter signed by NHT's Gendron concerning the scrap weight, but Gendron testified at trial that the letter was written by Avon officials and signed by him at their behest, and that he was not aware that it misrepresented the amount of scrap sold by NHT to Avon.

The captain and first officer of the "Eastern Saga," who were agents of Oxford, probably knew that the ship was carrying too little scrap, for they were approached by Avon officials at several points with schemes to cover up the shortfall by taking on water ballast and dumping it in South Korea while the ship was being unloaded. They refused to go along with the plot, but they do not appear to have informed either their superiors at Oxford or Yulsan itself of what was going on. When the ship reached South Korea the short-weighting was quickly discovered, and Yulsan had the "Eastern Saga" seized by South Korean port authorities. The fact that Yulsan had accepted the bills of lading, however, apparently triggered automatic payment through letters of credit, so Yulsan appears to have had to pay for the missing metal. Yulsan began litigation in South Korea against Oxford and other parties to recover the value of the shortfall, and Oxford was able to extract its ship in the interim only by posting a security bond worth approximately $200,000.

Oxford began its suit in federal district court to recover for various losses incurred by the seizure of its ship and for the potential liability created by Yulsan's claims against it. Oxford sought to recover from Avon, NHT, Gendron, and Tager for breach of contract, negligence, and fraudulent misrepresentation in connection with Avon's attempted fraud against Yulsan. After a four-day bench trial, the district court entered judgment against Oxford on every claim.

...

Claims against Tager

Oxford's claims against Tager, while asserted under headings of "contract," "negligence," and "fraudulent misrepresentation," come down to an assertion that Tager, in issuing false bills of lading, breached a fiduciary duty that it owed to Oxford. In making a "contract" claim, Oxford essentially seeks to find an implied contractual term forbidding Tager from issuing a false bill of lading; in making its "tort" claim, it seeks to find a negligent act. The legal claim that Oxford asserts, however, is simply founded upon basic principles of the law of agency. Tager does not dispute that it was an agent of Oxford, hired to arrange for supplies and services for the "Eastern Saga," to prepare government documentation, to enter and clear the ship through customs, and to prepare bills of lading. As Oxford's agent Tager owed Oxford a "fiduciary" duty of care. See Restatement (Second) of Agency § 379.

[T]he court found that Tager breached its fiduciary obligations by failing accurately to determine how much scrap had been loaded before making out the bill of lading. The court went on to hold that Oxford nonetheless could not recover because of the "contributory negligence" of Oxford's captain and first officer—negligence that consisted of their failing to tell Oxford or Yulsan about the plot. We believe that, in this respect, the court erred.

The legal question presented is simply whether an innocent principal (Oxford) is barred from collecting for damages caused by one set of negligent agents (Tager) because another set of agents has also been negligent (the captain and first officer)—in other words, whether one agent's contributory negligence is to be imputed to his principal to bar the principal from recovering from another negligent agent. The courts that have faced this question have divided in their responses. Compare Buhl v. Viera, 328 Mass. 201, 102 N.E. 2d 774 (1954) (contributory negligence of one agent not imputed to bar recovery by principal against second agent); Brown v. Poritzky, 30 N.Y.2d 289, 283 N.E.2d 751, 332 N.Y.S.2d 872 (1972) (same); and Zulkee v. Wing, 20 Wis. 408 (1866) (same), with Insurance Co. of North America v. Anderson, 92 Idaho 114, 438 P.2d 265 (1968) (contributory negligence imputed), and Capitola v. Minneapolis, S.P. & S.S.M. Railroad Co., 258 Minn. 206, 103 N.W.2d 867 (1960) (same). We believe that the better reasoned cases are those that would allow recovery in these circumstances. We also believe that those are the cases that the New Hampshire Supreme Court would follow.

Our conclusion rests on our view that in the cases in which the contributory negligence of one agent has been held to bar an innocent principal from recovering against another, the courts have simply reasoned by analogy from a different situation without recognizing the difference. The different situation is that in which the principal seeks to recover from a third party, such as when Firm A seeks to recover from a driver of a car who negligently collides with Firm A's truck. In such circumstances, courts often have held that the contributory negligence of Firm A's driver, if sufficient to bar the driver's own recovery, is sufficient to bar recovery by Firm A as well. The servant's or agent's contributory negligence is "imputed" to the master or principal. See Restatement (Second) of Agency § 317 (principal-agent); Restatement (Second) of Torts § 486 (master-servant).

This general rule of imputation presumably is grounded in the desire to require the principal to recover from his agent, rather than allowing him to pursue the third party as well. If so, that rationale is defeated rather than furthered if two negligent agents are allowed to impute each other's negligence and bar recovery against either: instead of being remitted to his agents for relief, the principal is barred from recovering against them altogether. We have not found any other plausible rationale underlying the imputing of contributory negligence that would require imputation in this case. Given the basic legal rule that a principal can recover for damages caused by an agent's breach of his duties of trust and care, we see no reason why the principal should be barred by the fact that injuries were caused by two agents or two sets of agents. To allow each to set up that breach of duty of the other as a defense to the principal's claim is, in effect, to disallow the principal's recovery where more than one agent defaults in his duty. We see no rational basis for such a distinction.

Given the lack of a rational basis for imputing the agents' contributory negligence to the principal here, and the New Hampshire Supreme Court's flat statement that the 'waning defense of contributory negligence' should not be extended by imputation," Glidden v. Butler, 288 A.2d 695, 696, 112 N.H. 68 (1972), we believe that the New Hampshire courts would follow Buhl, Brown, and Zulkee here, and would not impute the captain's or first officer's negligence to Oxford to bar Oxford's recovery against its agent Tager. In light of this holding we need not reach Oxford's claim based on "fraudulent misrepresentation," for Oxford already had an adequate basis for recovering against Tager.

Section 3: The Agent's Duty of Loyalty

Restatement (Third), Agency § 8.01: General Fiduciary Principle

An agent has a fiduciary duty to act loyally for the principal's benefit in all matters connected with the agency relationship.

Restatement (Third), Agency § 8.02: Material Benefit Arising Out of Position

An agent has a duty not to acquire a material benefit from a third party in connection with transactions conducted or other actions taken on behalf of the principal or otherwise through the agent's use of the agent's position.

...

[**Illustration**] **1.** P, who owns a racehorse, Grace, engages A, a jockey, to ride Grace in an upcoming race. P agrees to pay A a fee of $500. T, who has made a large bet that Grace will win the race, promises to pay A $5000 if Grace wins the race. T asks A not to tell P about T's promise. Neither A nor T tells P about T's promise. Grace, ridden by A, wins the race. T pays A $5000. A and T are subject to liability to P. A's receipt of $5000 from T breached A's duty to P. T knowingly provided substantial assistance and encouragement to A in A's breach of duty to P.

...

[**Comment**] **e. Remedies.** When an agent breaches the duty stated in this section, the principal may recover monetary relief from the agent and, in appropriate circumstances, from any third party who participated in the agent's breach. A principal may avoid a contract entered into by the agent with a third party who participated in the agent's breach of duty. The principal may recover any material benefit received by the agent through the agent's breach, the value of the benefit, or proceeds of the benefit retained by the agent. The principal may also recover damages for any harm caused by the agent's breach. If an agent's breach of duty involves a wrongful disposal of assets of the principal, the principal cannot recover both the value of the asset and what the agent received in exchange. If a principal recovers damages from a third party as a consequence of an agent's breach of fiduciary duty, the principal remains entitled to recover from the agent any benefit that the agent improperly received from the transaction.

Note on Remedies for an Agent's Breach of Fiduciary Duties

As the comment to Restatement (Third) Agency § 8.02 makes clear, a principal may recover from an agent even when the agent's breach does not harm her—that is, even if she is not materially worse because of the agent's breach.

There are other ways that remedies for breaches of fiduciary duties can be quite broad. As potential remedies, Restatement (Third) Agency § 8.01, cmt. d lists injunction, rescission of contracts, tort damages (including punitive damages), and early termination of the agent's contract with the principal.

A further potential remedy, unusual in other contexts, is the forfeiture of the disloyal agent's salary or other compensation. The Restatement explains:

> An agent's breach of fiduciary duty is a basis on which the agent may be required to forfeit commissions and other compensation paid or payable to the agent during the period of the agent's disloyalty. The availability of forfeiture is not limited to its use as a defense to an agent's claim for compensation.
>
> Forfeiture may be the only available remedy when it is difficult to prove that harm to a principal resulted from the agent's breach or when the agent realizes no profit through the breach. In many cases, forfeiture enables a remedy to be determined at a much lower cost to litigants. Forfeiture may also have a valuable deterrent effect because its availability signals agents that some adverse consequence will follow a breach of fiduciary duty.
>
> Although forfeiture is generally available as a remedy for breach of fiduciary duty, cases are divided on how absolute a measure to apply. Some cases require forfeiture of all compensation paid or payable over the period of disloyalty, while others permit apportionment over a series of tasks or specified items of work when only some are tainted by the agent's disloyal conduct. The better rule permits the court to consider the specifics of the agent's work and the nature of the agent's breach of duty and to evaluate whether the agent's breach of fiduciary duty tainted all of the agent's work or was confined to discrete transactions for which the agent was entitled to apportioned compensation. For the general principle permitting denial of restitution to a party in default whose default involved fraud or inequitable conduct, see Restatement Third, Restitution and Unjust Enrichment § 36(d) (Tentative Draft No. 3, 2004). For the application of the principle to compensation otherwise due a lawyer, see Restatement Third, The Law Governing Lawyers § 37.

Restatement (Third) Agency § 8.01 cmt. d.

Restatement (Third), Agency § 8.03: Acting as or on Behalf of an Adverse Party

An agent has a duty not to deal with the principal as or on behalf of an adverse party in a transaction connected with the agency relationship.

...

[**Illustration**] **4.** P, who owns Blackacre, lists it for sale with A, telling A that P would consider selling Blackacre in exchange for installment payments over 15 years, with a down payment of at least $7,500. P agrees to pay A a 5% commission. A presents P with an offer from T for $210,000 but does not tell P that A has agreed to lend T the $7,500 required for the down payment. P accepts T's offer. A has breached A's duty to P. A has a substantial economic interest in T.

Restatement (Third), Agency § 8.04: Competition

Throughout the duration of an agency relationship, an agent has a duty to refrain from competing with the principal and from taking action on behalf of or otherwise assisting the principal's competitors. During that time, an agent may take action, not otherwise wrongful, to prepare for competition following termination of the agency relationship.

Restatement (Third), Agency § 8.05: Use of Principal's Property; Use of Confidential Information

An agent has a duty

(1) not to use property of the principal for the agent's own purposes or those of a third party; and

(2) not to use or communicate confidential information of the principal for the agent's own purposes or those of a third party.

...

Illustrations:

1. P, who owns a stable of horses, employs A to take care of them. While P is absent for a month, and without P's consent, A rents the horses to persons who ride them. Although being ridden is beneficial to the horses, A is subject to liability to P for the amount A receives for the rentals.

2. Same facts as Illustration 1, except that A permits A's friends to ride P's horses for free during P's absence. A is subject to liability to P for the value of the use made of the horses.

Reading v. Regem

[1948] 2 KB 26 (King's Bench)

DENNING, J.

The suppliant joined the army in 1936, and at the beginning of 1944 he was a sergeant in the Royal Army Medical Corps stationed at the general hospital in Cairo, where he was in charge of the medical stores.

The suppliant had not had any opportunities, in his life as a soldier, of making money, but in March, 1944, there were found standing to his credit at banks in Egypt, several thousands of pounds, and he had more thousands of pounds in notes in his flat. He had also acquired a motor car worth £1,500. The Special Investigation Branch of the army looked into the matter, and he was asked how he came by these moneys. He made a statement, from which it appears that they were paid to him by a man by the name of

Manole in these circumstances. A lorry used to arrive loaded with cases, the contents of which were unknown. Then the suppliant, in full uniform, boarded the lorry, and escorted it through Cairo, so that it was able to pass the civilian police without being inspected. When it arrived at its destination, it was unloaded, or the contents were transferred to another lorry. After the first occasion when this happened, the suppliant saw Manole in a restaurant in Cairo. Manole handed him an envelope which he put in his pocket. On examining it when he arrived home, he found that it contained £2,000. Two or three weeks later, another load arrived, and another £2,000 was paid. £3,000 was paid after the third load, and so it went on until eventually some £20,000 had gone into the pocket of the suppliant.[9] The services which he rendered for that money were that he accompanied this lorry from one part of Cairo to another, and it is plain that he got it because he was a sergeant in the British army, and, while in uniform, escorted these lorries through Cairo. It is also plain that he was clearly violating his duty in so doing. The military authorities took possession of the money. The money in the bank was taken under a military proclamation then in force, the military governor of the Cairo area ordering the banks to place the money at the disposal of the headquarters of the British Middle East Forces. The money in the suppliant's flat was taken possession of by the special investigation branch.

In this petition of right, the suppliant alleges that these moneys are his and should be returned to him by the Crown. In answer, the Crown say: "These were bribes received by you by reason of your military employment, and you hold the money for the Crown. Even if we were wrong in the way in which we seized them, we are entitled to recover the amount of them, and to set off that amount against any claim you may have." In these circumstances, it is not necessary to dwell on the form of the claim. The question is whether or not the Crown is entitled to the money. It is not entitled to it simply because it is the Crown—moneys which are unlawfully obtained are not ipso facto forfeited to the Crown. The claim of the Crown rests on the fact that at the material time it was the suppliant's employer.

There are many cases in the books where a master has been held entitled to the unauthorised gains of his servant or agent. At law, the action took the form of money had and received. In equity it was put on the basis of a constructive trust due to a fiduciary relationship. Nowadays it is unnecessary to draw a distinction between law and equity. The real cause of action is a claim for restitution of moneys which, in justice, ought to be paid over. In my judgment, it is a principle of law that, if a servant takes advantage of his service and violates his duty of honesty and good faith to make a profit for himself, in the sense that the assets of which he has control, the facilities which he enjoys, or the position which he occupies, are the real cause of his obtaining the money as distinct from merely affording the opportunity for getting it, that is to say, if they play the predominant part in his obtaining the money, then he is accountable for it to his master. It matters not that the master has not lost any profit nor suffered any damage, nor does it matter that the master could not have done the act himself. If the servant has unjustly enriched himself by virtue of his service without his master's sanction, the law says that he ought not to be allowed to keep the money, but it shall be taken from him and given to his master, because he got it solely by reason of the position which he occupied as a servant of his master. Instances readily occur to mind. Take the case of the master who tells his servant to exercise his horses, and while the master is away, the servant lets them out and makes a profit by so doing. There is no

9. Determining the values of currency across time is problematic and controversial for a variety of reasons, but this value in 1944 would by some measures be worth about £700,000 in 2014, or at modern exchange rates roughly $1.1 million. [—ed.]

loss to the master, the horses have been exercised, but the servant must account for the profits he makes. The Attorney-General put in argument the case of a uniformed policeman who, at the request of thieves and in return for a bribe, directs traffic away from the site of the crime. Is he to be allowed to keep the money? So, also, here, the use of the facilities provided by the Crown in the shape of the uniform and the use of his position in the army were the only reason why the suppliant was able to get this money. It was solely on that account that he was able to sit in the front of these lorries and give them a safe conduct through Cairo. There was no loss of profit to the Crown. The Crown would have been violating its duty if it had undertaken the task, but the suppliant was certainly violating his duty, and it is money which must be paid over to his master—in this case, the Crown.

Attorney General v Goddard, where a police sergeant was ordered to hand over bribes which he had received, is paroled to this case, but it does not cover it, because Rowlatt J put his decision on the ground that Sergeant Goddard got the money in the course of making confidential enquires. The present case goes a step further. There was not, in this case, a fiduciary relationship. The suppliant was not acting in the course of his employment. In my opinion, however, those are not essential ingredients of the cause of action. The uniform of the Crown and the position of the suppliant as a servant of the Crown were the only reasons why he was able to get this money, and that is sufficient to make him liable to hand it over to the Crown. The case is to be distinguished from cases where the service merely gives the opportunity of making money. A servant may, during his master's time, in breach of his contract, do other things to make money for himself, such as gambling, but he is entitled to keep that money himself. The master has a claim for damages for breach of contract, but he has no claim to the money. So, also, the fact that a soldier is stationed in a certain place may give him the opportunity, contrary to the King's Regulations, of engaging in trade and making money in that way. In such a case, the mere fact that his service gave the opportunity for getting the money would not entitle the Crown to it, but if, as here, the wearing of the King's uniform and his position as a soldier is the sole cause of his getting the money and he gets it dishonestly, that is an advantage which he is not allowed to keep. Although the Crown, has suffered no loss, the court orders the money to be handed over to the Crown, because the Crown is the only person to whom it can properly be paid. The suppliant must not be allowed to enrich himself in this way. He got the money by virtue of his employment, and must hand it over.

Note on *Reading v. Regem*

The case was appealed to the House of Lords, which then functioned as the United Kingdom's highest court. The House of Lords affirmed the judgment. The following is a brief excerpt from the high-court case:

LORD PORTER:

...

It is often convenient to speak of money obtained as received in the course of the servant's employment, but strictly speaking I do not think that expression accurately describes the position where a servant receives money by reason of his employment but in dereliction of his duty. In Attorney-General v. Goddard the bribes given to Sergeant Goddard were received by reason of his employment but not in the course of it, except in the sense that his employment afforded the opportunity by which the gain was made. Just as in the often-quoted instance of a servant letting out his own services and the use of his master's horses for private gain, he is not acting in the course of his employment, he is taking advantage of the position which his employment gives him and for reward so gained he is answerable to his master none the less, as Attorney-General v. Goddard shows, though the obtaining of the money is a criminal act. It is true that the right of the master to demand payment of the money is often imputed to a promise implied from his relationship to the servant. I doubt whether it is necessary to raise such an implication in order to show that the money has been received to the master's use, but even if it were it may well be contended that there is no illegality in a servant promising to hand over to his master any sums he gains by use of his position. Nor would the master be affirming any criminal act committed by the servant in earning the sum claimed; he would only be saying that as between himself and the servant the servant could not set up his own wrong as a defence. Any third party's claim to the money would not be affected....

Restatement (Third), Agency § 8.04, cmt. e.

Post-termination competition; preparations to compete. Once a relationship of agency has terminated, unless the agent has agreed otherwise the agent has the right to compete with the now-former principal. A former agent may use skills and more general knowledge, although learned in the course of work done for the former principal, in such competition. However, a former agent's right to compete with the principal is not absolute and does not privilege conduct that would be tortious if committed by a third party. A former agent remains subject to duties concerning confidential information and property of the principal. See § 8.05. If a former agent continues to have a confidential relationship with the principal, for example by furnishing advice to the principal on which the principal relies, the former agent may owe fiduciary duties to the principal derived from their confidential relationship that prohibit competition on that ground.

Town & Country House & Home Service v. Newbery

147 N.E.2d 724 (1958) (N.Y. App. 1958)

VAN VOORHIS, J.

This action was brought for an injunction and damages against appellants on the theory of unfair competition. The complaint asks to restrain them from engaging in the same business as plaintiff, from soliciting its customers, and for an accounting and damages. The individual appellants were in plaintiff's employ for about three years before they severed their relationships and organized the corporate appellant through which they have been operating. The theory of the complaint is that plaintiff's enterprise "was unique, personal and confidential", and that appellants cannot engage in business at all without breach of the confidential relationship in which they learned its trade secrets, including the names and individual needs and tastes of its customers.

The nature of the enterprise is house and home cleaning by contract with individual householders. Its "unique" quality consists in superseding the drudgery of ordinary house cleaning by mass production methods. The house cleaning is performed by a crew of men who descend upon a home at stated intervals of time, and do the work in a hurry after the manner of an assembly line in a factory. They have been instructed by the housewife but work without her supervision. The householder is supplied with liability insurance, the secrets of the home are kept inviolate, the tastes of the customer are served and each team of workmen is selected as suited to the home to which it is sent. The complaint says that the customer relationship is "impregnated" with a "personal and confidential aspect".

The complaint was dismissed at Special Term on the ground that the individual appellants were not subjected to negative covenants under any contract with plaintiff, and that the methods and techniques used by plaintiff in conducting its business are not confidential or secret as in the case of a scientific formula; that house cleaning and housekeeping "are old and necessary chores which accompany orderly living" and that no violation of duty was involved in soliciting plaintiff's customers by appellants after resigning from plaintiff's employ. The contacts and acquaintances with customers were held not to have been the result of a confidential relationship between plaintiff and defendants or the result of the disclosure of secret or confidential material.

By a divided vote the Appellate Division reversed, but on a somewhat different ground, namely, that while in plaintiff's employ, appellants conspired to terminate their employment, form a business of their own in competition with plaintiff and solicit plaintiff's customers for their business. The overt acts under this conspiracy were found by the Appellate Division to have been that, in pursuance of this plan, they formed the corporate appellant and bought equipment and supplies for their operations—not on plaintiff's time—but during off hours, before they had severed their relations as employees of plaintiff. The Appellate Division concluded that "it is our opinion that their agreement and encouragement to each other to carry out the course of conduct thus planned by them, and their consummation of the plan, particularly their termination of employment virtually en masse, were inimical to, and violative of, the obligations owed by them to appellant as its employees; and that therefore appellant was entitled to relief."

The Duane Jones case involved unusual facts. There the defendants appropriated overnight upwards of 50% of the business of their previous employer, and 90% of its skilled employees as well as a majority of the entire working force. There the findings were in favor of the plaintiff in the trial court, whereas in this case the findings of the trial court were in favor of defendants, and those of its findings which remain untouched by the Appellate Division stand in favor of defendants. The dominating purpose in the Duane Jones case was to damage and paralyze the plaintiff corporation to enable the defendants to seize it or force a sale to them on their own terms. There the employees were all executives, whereas in this simpler organization (although Newbery is called a key man) the formation and supervision of teams for house cleaning was not complicated and could be done by others. Moreover in Duane Jones there had been solicitation of the customers of plaintiff while the defendants were still employed; there was an attempt to panic and break the morale of the employees, again with the over-all purpose of paralyzing the plaintiff in order to seize it. Here, although these three employees and their wives left at the same time, there was no abrupt departure of most of the key men and nothing in reference to the interruption or paralysis of plaintiff's business. In fact, at the time of the trial, Mrs. Rossmoore testified that they had 280 customers and 8 crews, which were 40 more customers and 1 more crew than at the time when appellants departed.

Although the Appellate Division implied more relief than we consider to have been warranted, we think that the trial court erred in dismissing the complaint altogether. The only trade secret which could be involved in this business is plaintiff's list of customers. Concerning that, even where a solicitor of business does not operate fraudulently under the banner of his former employer, he still may not solicit the latter's customers who are not openly engaged in business in advertised locations or whose availability as patrons cannot readily be ascertained but "whose trade and patronage have been secured by years of business effort and advertising, and the expenditure of time and money, constituting a part of the good-will of a business which enterprise and foresight have built up" (Witkop & Holmes Co. v. Boyce, 61 Misc. 126, 131, affd. 131 App. Div. 922). In the latter case it was pointed out by the Appellate Division that although there was no evidence that the former employee had a written customers list, "There was in his head what was equivalent. They were on routes, in streets and at numbers revealed to him through his service with plaintiff. Their faces were familiar to him, and their identity known because of such employment." That case was not overruled by Scott & Co. v. Scott (186 App. Div. 518, 525), as is clear from the opinion by Justice Callahan in Kleinfeld v. Roburn Agencies (270 App. Div. 509, 511), where it is said: "A distinction is made in the cases between a former employee soliciting customers of his former employer who are openly engaged in business in advertised locations and his soliciting unadvertised customers who became known to the employee only because of information obtained during his employment." (People's Coat, Apron & Towel Supply Co. v. Light, 171 App. Div. 671, affd. 224 N. Y. 727; Scott & Co., Inc., v. Scott, 186 App. Div. 518.)

That case points the way toward the solution of this lawsuit.... Boosing distinguishes Witkop by stating ... that it there appeared that the plaintiff had obtained a customers list, the names of which "could only be secured by the expenditure of a large amount of time, effort and money in gathering together such a vast list of consumers who desired to do business in this peculiar way. These customers were not classified as likely customers in any public directory. They were not discoverable by any public display of their willingness to deal on the trading-stamp basis. They were not congregated together in any well-known place where thousands of people gathered daily to purchase supplies."

The testimony in the instant record shows that the customers of plaintiff were not and could not be obtained merely by looking up their names in the telephone or city directory or by going to any advertised locations, but had to be screened from among many other housewives who did not wish services such as respondent and appellants were equipped to render, but preferred to do their own housework. In most instances housewives do their own house cleaning. The only appeal which plaintiff could have was to those whose cleaning had been done by servants regularly or occasionally employed, except in the still rarer instances where the housewife was on the verge of abandoning doing her own work by hiring some outside agency. In the beginning, prospective customers of plaintiff were discovered by Dorothy Rossmoore, wife of plaintiff's president, by telephoning at random in "sections of Nassau that we thought would be interested in this type of cleaning, and from that we got directories, town directories, and we marked the streets that we had passed down, and I personally called, right down the list". In other words, after selecting a neighborhood which they felt was fertile for their kind of business, they would telephone to all of the residents of a street in the hope of discovering likely prospects. On the first day Mrs. Rossmoore called 52 homes. If she enlisted their interest, an appointment would be made for a personal call in order to sell them the service. At the end of the first year, only 40 to 50 customers had thus been secured. Two hundred to three hundred telephone calls netted 8 to 12 customers. Moreover, during the first year it was not possible to know how much to charge these customers with accuracy, inasmuch as the cleaning requirements of each differed from the others, so that special prices had to be set. In the beginning the customer usually suggested the price which was paid until some kind of cost accounting could demonstrate whether it should be raised or lowered. These costs were entered on cards for every customer, and this represented an accumulated body of experience of considerable value. After three years of operation, and by August, 1952, when the individual appellants resigned their employment by plaintiff, the number of customers amounted to about 240. By that time plaintiff had 7 or 8 crews doing this cleaning work, consisting of 3 men each.

Although appellants did not solicit plaintiff's customers until they were out of plaintiff's employ, nevertheless plaintiff's customers were the only ones they did solicit. Appellants solicited 20 or 25 of plaintiff's customers who refused to do business with appellants and about 13 more of plaintiff's customers who transferred their patronage to appellants. These were all the people that appellants' firm solicited. It would be different if these customers had been equally available to appellants and respondent, but, as has been related, these customers had been screened by respondent at considerable effort and expense, without which their receptivity and willingness to do business with this kind of a service organization could not be known. So there appears to be no question that plaintiff is entitled to enjoin defendants from further solicitation of its customers, or that some profits or damage should be paid to plaintiff by reason of these customers whom they enticed away.

For more than this appellants are not liable. The order and opinion of the Appellate Division do not express the particular relief to which plaintiff was deemed to be entitled. The nature and extent of the injunction and of the accounting or damages were not passed upon but were remitted to Special Term. The order and memorandum of decision do state that judgment is "directed to be entered in favor of Appellant". Inasmuch as the complaint asks that appellants be enjoined, severally and jointly, from engaging directly or indirectly in the business of house and home cleaning in any manner, shape or form adopted by the plaintiff, it is necessary for us to point out that plaintiff is not entitled to that much relief. The business of plaintiff has not been found to be unique either by Special Term or the Appellate Division and the evidence demonstrates that it is not so. No trade secrets are involved, as has been stated, except the customers list. The theory on which the Appellate Division implied that such relief should be granted is that of Duane Jones Co. v. Burke (supra). The alleged similarity to the Duane Jones case stems from the circumstance that appellant Percy Newbery was second in command of plaintiff's business under president Howard Rossmoore, that he had worked there for three years during which time he had been assigned important duties by Rossmoore; that in June, 1952 (about three years after plaintiff went into business), appellants Newbery, Colagrande, Bordini, and their wives conferred about starting a new competing business after Rossmoore had declined to increase their remuneration or to give them greater security in the business (it does not appear how much their wages were except that the two who were highest paid received about $1,700 during half a year); that while still on plaintiff's payroll but outside of business hours, they met upon a number of occasions to plan the organization of a company of their own, and purchased some equipment for that purpose (Bordini was to buy a truck, Newbery to get supplies and Colagrande to buy a vacuum cleaner, and someone was to get a waxing machine for their projected operations). The appellant corporation was organized August 19, 1952; Newbery quit on August 29, 1952, and the others, including their wives, at about the same time. They went to work on the night shift at Fairchild Engineering Company at Farmingdale, Long Island, after leaving plaintiff, and started operating their small personal service corporation during the daytime. That forms an insufficient basis on which to invoke the relief that was granted in Duane Jones Co. v. Burke (306 N. Y. 172, supra).

It would have been courteous of appellants to have given Rossmoore advance notice that they were going to leave plaintiff's employ and engage in a competing business, but their employment was at will, which legally required no notice to be given, and rendered the employments terminable at any time at the option of either party. Plaintiff is entitled to enjoin appellants from soliciting its former customers, and to recover such damages or loss of profits as may be established to have resulted from those that have been solicited to date. Further than that the complaint is dismissed.

The order appealed from should be affirmed, without costs, and the case remitted to the Special Term under the order of the Appellate Division for proceedings not inconsistent with this opinion. The question certified should be answered in the affirmative.

Order affirmed, etc.

Section 4: The Principal's Duty of Indemnification

Restatement (Third), Agency § 8.14: Duty to Indemnify

A principal has a duty to indemnify an agent

(1) in accordance with the terms of any contract between them; and

(2) unless otherwise agreed,

(a) when the agent makes a payment

(i) within the scope of the agent's actual authority, or

(ii) that is beneficial to the principal, unless the agent acts officiously in making the payment; or

(b) when the agent suffers a loss that fairly should be borne by the principal in light of their relationship.

...

[**Illustration**] **1.** P retains A, an import broker, to handle importation of a large quantity of herbicide. A learns that the amount of duty payable on the herbicide will exceed a prior estimate given by the customs service because the herbicide contains various chemicals not listed on its label. Fearing forfeiture of the security bond A has posted for the duty, A pays the additional amount under protest and seeks indemnity from P. P has a duty to indemnify A. A acted with actual authority in making the payment.

Admiral Oriental Line v. United States

86 F.2d 201 (2nd Cir. 1936)

L. HAND, Circuit Judge.

These appeals are from decrees dismissing two libels in personam in the admiralty. In the first the libellant, the Admiral Oriental Line, alleged that it had been employed by the respondent, the Atlantic Gulf & Oriental Company, as ship's agent in the Philippines, and had had charge of fitting out the steamship, "Elkton," on a voyage out of Pulupandan, on which she was lost with all hands in a typhoon. The "Elkton" was owned by the United States, and had been entrusted to the Atlantic Gulf & Oriental S.S. Co. as ship's agent under an operating contract. The "Elkton's" cargo owners sued the Admiral Oriental Line for its loss, and the Line was put to certain expenses in defending the suit, in which it was however successful. It claimed these expenses on the theory that as agent it had paid them upon its principal's account. The Atlantic Gulf & Oriental S.S. Co. answered and attempted to bring in the United States under the Fifty-Sixth Rule (28 U.S.C.A. following section 723). It alleged that the United States was the principal in the whole venture and as such responsible to its immediate agent, the Atlantic Gulf & Oriental S.S. Co. not only for any expenses to which it was put in its own defense, but for any which it might be compelled to pay to the sub-agent, the Admiral Oriental Line, under decree in the main suit. The second suit was filed directly under the Suits in Admiralty Act (46 U.S.C.A. §741 et seq.) against the United States by the Atlantic Gulf & Oriental S.S. Co. for its own expenses in defending itself in the suit by the "Elkton's" cargo, to which it too had been made a party. Each libellant appealed, and the Atlantic Gulf & Oriental S.S. Co. filed assignments of error in the suit of the Admiral Oriental Line.

An agent, compelled to defend a baseless suit, grounded upon acts performed in his principal's business, may recover from the principal the expenses of his defense. We considered the question in Cory Bros. & Co. v. United States, 51 F.(2d) 1010, where we did not have to rule upon it; but the cases are unanimous, so far as we have found. In Howe v. Buffalo, etc., R.R. Co., 37 N.Y. 297, and Clark v. Jones, 16 Lea (Tenn.) 351, notwithstanding that the agent had lost the suit brought by the third party against him, he recovered of the principal because his conduct was within the scope of his authority, though it was wrongful. The right of recovery in all these instances is only an example of the general doctrine that an agent may recover any expenditures necessarily incurred in the transaction of his principal's affairs. The United States urges that there is a distinction between general and special agents, but we can see nothing in principle to justify one; it is indeed true that the implications from the two kinds of agency are often different, but they always depend upon the whole setting, like other implications, and there is no reason for saying that a general agent's defense of a suit laid upon his conduct of the principal's affairs is not an incident of the business. The doctrine stands upon the fact that the venture is the principal's, and that, as the profits will be his, so should be the expenses. Since by hypothesis the agent's outlay is not due to his mismanagement, it should be regarded only as a loss, unexpected it is true, but inextricably interwoven with the enterprise. The Atlantic Gulf & Oriental S.S. Co. insists, on its part, that the Admiral Oriental Line should have given it notice to defend the suit on its behalf. We can see no reason for this and none is suggested; the Atlantic Gulf & Oriental S.S. Co. was itself a party to the suit, and the Admiral Oriental Line had a separate interest of its own to defend; certainly until the Atlantic Gulf & Oriental S.S. Co. volunteered to defend that interest, it was justified in protecting it itself. No doubt the amount of its expenditures is always open to contest, but their necessity is undoubted and it is that which imposes the liability.

The contract between the Admiral Oriental Line and the Atlantic Gulf & Oriental S.S. Co. appointed the Line "General Freight Agents" for all ships which the principal was operating on behalf of the United States in the "Far East." The Line agreed to have subagents at all ports where it had no offices of its own, and to perform all the principal's duties under its contract with the United States; it was to receive for its services a commission on the gross freights with brokerage. Thus, if Atlantic Gulf & Oriental S.S. Co. was an agent of the United States, the Line was an agent of the Atlantic Gulf & Oriental S.S. Co. We therefore turn to the relations between that company and the United States. These were set forth in a contract whose substance was as follows. The Shipping Board appointed the company "its Agent to manage, operate and conduct the business of such vessel as it * * * may assign to the Agent", and the company agreed to act as such "in accordance with the directions" of the Board. The company was to "man, equip, victual and supply" the vessels as the Board required, and to pay all expenses and maintain them in seaworthy condition, all on the Board's account. It was to issue all documents on the Board's form, appoint sub-agents, collect freights which it must deposit in a bank approved by the Board and in the Board's name, and for which it was to account on forms prescribed by the Board. For this the company was to be paid in percentages on the gross receipts including salvage; out of these it was to bear its "administrative and general expenses of every nature," not including brokerage however, or commissions "for agency services rendered at foreign ports." The company was to furnish a bond for faithful performance of its duties and was forbidden to profit in any way from the services rendered. We find it difficult to see how this contract can be construed as creating anything but a straight agency for operating the Board's ships. As we have already said, the question at bar turns chiefly upon whose the venture is; upon who stands to win or lose. The United States not only described itself throughout as owner, but was in that position, letter for letter. It chose, not to charter its ships to the company, but to put them in trade on its own account; why it should not bear the hazard of defending unwarranted suits we cannot see. We have so construed almost identical contracts. So has the Third Circuit. The argument of the United States that the conduct of the parties put another interpretation on their relations is wholly unsupported by the evidence, and would in any event have been irrelevant. Had the Atlantic Gulf & Oriental S.S. Co. paid the Admiral Oriental Line, it would therefore have been in position to recover of the United States, for there is no difference between payment by an agent of his sub-agent's recovery against him, and payment of his own expenses. Obviously the same considerations apply to the suit of the Atlantic Gulf & Oriental S.S. Co. against the United States.

...

Decrees reversed; causes remanded with instructions to proceed according to the foregoing.

Note on Subagents and Coagents

As *Admiral Oriental Line* shows, agents can hire their own agents, called *subagents*. As the Restatement makes clear, agents can hire subagents only if they have the actual or apparent authority to do so. Restatement (Third), Agency § 3.15(2). The Restatement's comment adds: "A subagent acts subject to the control of the appointing agent, and the principal's legal position is affected by action taken by the subagent as if the action had been taken by the appointing agent. Thus, a subagent has two principals, the appointing agent and that agent's principal. Although an appointing agent has the right and duty to control a subagent, the interests and instructions of the appointing agent's principal are paramount." *Id.* cmt. b.

Often, an agent is empowered to find new, parallel agents for a principal. These parallel agents need not be subagents; they need not work for the agent and can instead work directly for the principal. Such parallel agents are called *coagents*. This structure may at first seem abstract and unfamiliar, but it is very common; it is indeed the way most organizations work. While people often refer to their managers within an organization as "bosses," employees do not ordinarily work *for* their managers; the managers simply supervise their work on behalf of the principal organization. Thus, the boss and the junior employee are usually coagents of the same company. One simply has a dominant position with a greater scope of authority—including, perhaps, the authority to hire new coagents. By contrast, if a small company is engaged as an agent for a principal, the agent's employees are subagents of the principal.

Coagency and subagency are functionally very similar, but they can occasionally have different consequences. The Restatement explains:

> As among a principal, an appointing agent, and a subagent, the fact that action is taken by a subagent may carry different or additional legal consequences than if the action were taken directly by the appointing agent or by a coagent of the appointing agent. The legal consequences of subagency reflect the distinct significance of (1) the relationship between an appointing agent and a subagent; (2) the relationship between a principal and an appointing agent; and (3) the relationship between a principal and a subagent. An appointing agent is responsible to the principal for the subagent's conduct. This may subject an appointing agent to liability for loss incurred by the principal as a consequence of misconduct by a subagent. A contract between the principal and the appointing agent that requires or permits the appointment of subagents will often delineate the extent of the appointing agent's liability and will require indemnification by the principal of the appointing agent. In contrast, an agent is subject to liability stemming from a coagent's conduct only when the agent's own conduct subjects the agent to liability.

Restatement (Third), Agency § 3.15. Note that this means that, all else equal, an agent might prefer to create coagents rather than subagents in order to reduce its own liability. If a boss hires a bad employee, the boss is not liable on that basis alone for the bad employee's bad contracts (or, as we will see later, his torts). If an agent hires a bad subagent, the agent *is* responsible for that subagent's actions.

Section 5: Notice and Imputation of Knowledge

Note on Imputation of Knowledge to a Principal

In various areas of law, whether a party has *notice* or knowledge of some fact can be legally significant. For example, local real-estate law may let homebuyers recover from sellers if the sellers failed to notify the buyer of certain defects. One significant, though somewhat formal, interaction between agency law and the rest of the law involves a simple question: when does notifying an agent have the same legal effect as notifying a principal?

This area of agency law is probably inappropriately formalistic. It is not clear in the first place that general rules of agency law, rather than more contextual principles underlying whatever substantive considerations of policy and morality motivate the areas of law that depend on whether a principal has notice of some fact, should be used to determine whether the law assumes a principal knows or should know some fact. For example, whether a homebuyer should be able to demand that a seller repair part of a house should probably depend more on local real-estate customs and business practices than on general propositions about agency law.

The general, formal rules of agency law concerning notice are somewhat complicated. The simplest, most general rule is that an agent's knowledge, however acquired, will be imputed to the principal if the fact is "material to the agent's duties to the principal." Restatement (Third), Agency § 5.03. There is, however, a basic exception to avoid a technicality: if the agent is acting adversely to the principal's interest, the agent's knowledge will not be imputed to the principal. So, for example, a third party cannot collude with an agent to make a show of giving the agent notice, knowing the agent will not repeat the information to the principal, in order to cause the law to treat a principal incorrectly as having received notice.[10]

In Cromer Fin. Ltd. v. Berger, 245 F. Supp. 2d 552, 560 (S.D.N.Y. 2003), the court justified the general rule as follows:

> The law presumes that it is fair to find that that which the agent knows, the principal knows as well, because it is also presumed that in the normal course of their relationship, the agent will have a duty to disclose information acquired in the course of the agency. The Restatement puts it this way: "the liability of a principal because of the knowledge of the agent is based upon the existence of a duty on the part of the agent to act in light of the knowledge which he has." Restatement (Second) of Agency § 272, cmt. a (1958); see also Torres v. Pisano, 116 F.3d 625, 637 (2d Cir. 1997). Agency law therefore creates vicarious liability not out of a legal fiction, but from a recognition of how business is actually to be conducted between a principal and its agent.

This justification is questionable. If the law's presumption about the principal's knowledge does indeed depend on reality, it would probably be better simply for the court to ask whether the parties expected—or should reasonably have expected—that the principal, in reality, received notice. The underlying question is simply: Who must bear the risk of confusion or factual errors, the principal or the third party? Presumably concrete business norms, rather than abstract and possibly overly general agency rules, can provide the most desirable answers to that question in various contexts.

There is a further exception that shows the brittleness of the general rule: an agent's knowledge is not imputed to a principal if the agent "is subject to a duty to another not to disclose the fact to the principal." Restatement (Third) Agency, § 5.03. This rule causes legal outcomes concerning notice to depend on whether a court finds the presence or absence of an agency relationship, what the agent's precise duties are to others (even if those duties were not known to the third party or the principal), and other potentially irrelevant factors.

Note on Legal Notification to Agents

The Third Restatement elaborates the basic rule about imputation of knowledge by developing a special notion called *notification*. The Restatement defines a notification—the word is a term of art in this context—as "a manifestation that is made in the form required by agreement among parties or by applicable law, or in a reasonable manner in the absence of an agreement or an applicable law, with the intention of affecting the legal rights and duties of the notifier in relation to rights and duties of persons to whom the notification is given." Restatement (Third), Agency § 5.01(1). The idea behind this definition is that, in order to facilitate the interpretation of basic duties, contracts, and statutes, it may be useful to have a general rule about what parties must do in order to give formal notice to each other. The Restatement's specific rule as to notification is much narrower than its general rule about the imputation of knowl-

10. There is an exception to the exception, which is that the agent's knowledge will be imputed to the principal anyway—even if the agent is acting adversely to the principal—when fairness so dictates. *See* Restatement (Third), Agency § 5.04(a).

edge discussed above: formal notifications given to an agent are effective as to the agent's principal only if the agent has actual or apparent authority to receive the notification (unless the third party knows or should know that the agent is acting adversely to the principal).

The purpose of this rule is to give parties a specific way to authorize agents to receive certain formal legal communications—or, to put it more simply, to let principals designate those who can receive their legal communications. The operation of this rule is usually simple and unproblematic. Consider, for example, the following illustration from the Restatement:

> P, who owns a garden center, employs A to manage it. P enters into a contract with T providing that T shall supply the garden center's requirements for mulch for five years. The contract provides that either party may cancel by giving the other 60 days' written notice and further provides that any notice to P shall be given to A. T mails a written notice canceling the contract to A. A opens and reads T's notification but does not tell P. T's notification is effective against P.

Restatement (Third), Agency § 5.02 cmt. b. illus. 1.

Section 6: Temporary and Ambiguous Principals, and the Flexibility of Agency Law

Norby v. Bankers Life Company of Des Moines, Iowa

231 N.W.2d 665 (Minn. 1975)

PETERSON, J.

Important issues in the administration of group insurance programs for the benefit of employees are raised in this appeal.

The issues arise out of an uncomplicated factual situation. Hoffman Brothers, Inc. (hereafter Hoffman), third-party defendant, is a member of the Upper Midwest Employers Association. The association is named as policyholder in a group accident and sickness policy issued by The Bankers Life Company of Des Moines, Iowa (hereafter Bankers Life), defendant. The policy provides for reimbursement of a portion of the medical bills incurred by covered employees of the association's employer members, including dependents of employees. Plaintiff, Fred G. Norby, is an employee of Hoffman, and claims benefits for the expense of medical care for his injured child in the undisputed amount of $3,460.49.

Plaintiff commenced his employment with Hoffman in August 1970. He completed an application for coverage under the policy in September 1970, which was thereupon delivered to his employer, Hoffman. If Hoffman had transmitted the application to Bankers Life, plaintiff's insurance coverage would have begun immediately and his subsequent claim would have been paid. But, through oversight or neglect, Hoffman failed to forward the application.

Plaintiff, on discovering Hoffman's error, completed a second application on December 31, 1970, which was promptly transmitted to Bankers Life. Because of an intervening period of temporary layoff, plaintiff's coverage, under the terms of the policy, was not effective until January 20, 1971—that is, unless the initial, untransmitted application was binding upon Bankers Life. Plaintiff's child, for whom the claim is made, was injured on January 19, 1971.

Bankers Life denied the claim, asserting that plaintiff was not effectively covered until it had received his application form from Hoffman. Plaintiff then brought this action on the policy against Bankers Life, which in turn instituted a third-party action against Hoffman for indemnity or contribution. The trial court ordered judgment for plaintiff, finding and concluding that Hoffman stood in the relationship of agent to Bankers Life with authority to accept the application, thus binding Bankers Life at the time of plaintiff's initial application. The court ordered the third-party complaint dismissed. This appeal followed, raising the primary issue of whether such an agency relationship existed and secondary issues concerning plaintiff's standing as a real party in interest and Bankers Life's claimed right of indemnity from Hoffman....

The principal issue for determination is whether an employer may be held to be acting as an agent of a group insurer for the purpose of accepting insurance applications from eligible employees. If, as the trial court here found, Hoffman acted as the agent of Bankers Life with respect to plaintiff's timely initial application, Bankers Life is bound by Hoffman's action, since a principal is bound by the acts of its agent. Restatement, Agency 2d, § 144. We hold that it was.

Conventional wisdom has been that the employer functions in the administration of a group insurance policy solely for its own interests or for the benefit of its employees, rather than serving the purposes of the insurer, and that the employer and the employees are allied in their interests adverse to the insurer. Judicial precedent, including the older precedents, are numerically weighted against finding the existence of an employer-insurer agency relationship.

Pragmatic, as well as theoretical, considerations induce us to undertake, as others have, a reappraisal of these concepts. Group insurance is today a widespread and most significant form of insurance protection, particularly for employee groups, as shown by data published by the Institute of Life Insurance, Life Insurance Fact Book (1974). Group life insurance coverage amounted to over 708 billion dollars in 1973, which is nearly 40% of all life insurance in force in this country. Over 86% of group life insurance is of the employer-employee type. It may not be an impermissible assumption that data for the general category of health insurance in the private sector of the economy would parallel those for life insurance.

The growth of group insurance in labor-management situations undoubtedly relates to the advantages inherent in it. The advantage to the employee is that it permits insured protection, generally without necessity of physical examination, at little or no cost. The advantage to the employer is that it is able, at moderate cost, to satisfy the felt needs of its employees, thereby reducing the labor unrest or turnover that impairs productivity. The advantage to insurers is that the mass sale and administration of group insurance involves a low rate of lapse and low per capita expense of administration, the efficiency and economy of which are profitable to the insurer.

Administration of group insurance policies entails some rather routine functions, such as enrolling employees through their completing applications for themselves and dependents; collecting employee contributions, if any, and remitting premiums to the insurer; terminating and reinstating insurance; and assisting in the processing of claims. Employers may have a role in determining eligibility for coverage, at least to the extent that the classification and employment status of employees relates to whether or not an employee is within the insured group. There may be situations where the insurer performs all these functions itself, in which case the plan is wholly "insurer-administered," and in which case no issue of agency between the employer and insurer arises. There are the other situations, as in this case, in which the employer performs such a number of these functions that, at least as a shorthand expression, it may be considered, in whole or in part, to be "employer-administered." To the extent the employer, with the consent of the insurer, performs the functions of the insurer, it may properly be considered the insurer's agent.

An agency relationship is based upon consent by one person that another shall act in his behalf and be subject to his control. Restatement, Agency 2d, § 1. These aspects of the relationship in employer-sponsored insurance plans should be realistically viewed from the various perspectives of the insurer, the employer, and the employee. The insurer has an obvious choice as to whether or not to authorize the performance of administrative functions by the employer and, if it does so, is in a position to exercise effective control over the performance of those functions; the employer, likewise, has a choice of whether or not to purchase an insurance policy under those conditions, recognizing that the choice may have an effect upon the premium it pays. The employee-beneficiary, however, ordinarily has no choice with respect to the policy purchased or the manner of its implementation. He usually knows only that he is entitled to stated insurance benefits. He does not ask whether the insurance plan is "insurer-administered" or "employer-administered." He may reasonably assume that his employer and the insurer will, in their dealings with each other, do that which is necessary to provide him with the promised benefits. It is, therefore, unreasonable and inequitable to frustrate the employee's expectations because of an employer's negligence in administering the insurance agreement.

This is substantially the rationale of that minority of the courts which hold that the employer, in circumstances similar to these, acts as the agent of the insurer. This view was most thoroughly articulated in Elfstrom v. New York Life Ins. Co., 432 P. 2d 731 (1967). An abbreviated version of the facts in Elfstrom will serve to indicate some similarities in that case to the case at bar. There, the insurer of an employer's group insurance policy delegated to the employer the function of enrolling employees, adding and deleting dependents, terminating and reinstating insurance, reporting details of coverage, indicating the amounts of premiums paid, determining eligibility matters, and issuing certificates of insurance. The insurer provided the employer with an instruction manual for determining eligibility matters, and the insurer's group representative was available for consultation. The group representative made an annual review of the employer's records. Here, as the trial court found, the employer was to take applications of employees on forms supplied by the insurer and to forward them directly to the insurance company, with no intermediaries and with no agents of the insurer calling upon the employer for the purpose of taking such applications. The employee had no contact with the defendant insurer. The employer processed the insurance applications and paid for all premiums....

We now hold that the employer policyholder may, in appropriate circumstances, be found to be the agent of the group insurer of employees and affirm the trial court's finding that third-party defendant, Hoffman, was in this case the agent of defendant, Bankers Life.

We do not undertake to anticipate what may constitute appropriate circumstances to support a finding of agency in any future case, except to make two clarifying points about our reliance on *Elfstrom* and our commentary on it in *Bowes*. First, the use of the terms, "employer-administered" and "insurer-administered" is not necessarily of determinative significance, for it would seem that few insurance plans for employee groups are likely to be wholly one or the other. The focus, instead, should be on which specific and relevant administrative functions are performed by the employer on behalf of the insurer, with respect to the particular ground asserted for noncoverage or nonpayment under the policy. An employer may be considered an agent of an insurer for some purposes but not for others. Here, the employee was plainly eligible for coverage but was denied coverage only because the function of enrollment, clearly delegated to the employer by the insurer, was mishandled. The delegated act was specifically relevant to the particular ground upon which the insurer denied coverage. Whether the insurance plan was or was not "employer-administered" in other respects, is, in this situation, of little relevance. That is, in essence, the basis upon which the trial court made its finding and is the basis upon which it is affirmed.

Second, we take anticipatory note of the danger of collusion between an employer and employee to defeat the insurer for each other's benefit. Circumstances tending to show collusion were apparent in both *Elfstrom* and *Bowes*, but were neither alleged nor apparent in this case. Those courts which have rejected a finding of agency have done so on the assumption that the interests of both the employer and employee are adverse to the insurer. Although we depart from those precedents, we agree that whenever it is established that the employer and employee have colluded adversely to the insurer, no agency may be found to exist. Any authority of an agent clearly terminates if, without knowledge of the principal, he acquires adverse interests or if he is otherwise guilty of a breach of loyalty to the principal. A principal is not bound by an agent's actions where the agent acts adversely to the principal and the party with whom the agent deals is aware of such adverse dealing. Restatement, Agency 2d....

Chapter 2

Agency and Tort: Respondeat Superior

Section 1: Agents and Employees

Restatement (Third), Agency §2.04: Respondeat Superior

An employer is subject to liability for torts committed by employees while acting within the scope of their employment.

Note on the Justifications of Respondeat Superior

Most modern Torts courses cover the basic doctrine of respondeat superior, a Latin label meaning "let the superior respond"—i.e., let the employer answer for the torts of the employee. The idea is simple: employers are responsible for torts that employees commit within the scope of their employment. The area, however, is rife with confusion, both in broad justifications and in many details.

Respondeat superior is a settled part of the common law, but its precise justifications have long been in dispute. Respondeat superior is a form of strict tort liability—employers are liable even if they have done nothing wrong—yet it depends on employees' negligence. As a result, those who study the justifications of respondeat superior face a puzzle: what principle of strict liability makes it appropriate to hold employers strictly liable for employees' negligence but not strictly liable for other harms that the employer's activity causes? Recall that the ordinary principle in the common law of torts is one of negligence, although strict liability has made inroads in other areas, such as for defectively manufactured products.

Given its complex and rough contours, respondeat superior is probably justified on complex, pragmatic grounds rather than by any analytically clean theory. (In the real world, this is not necessarily a drawback.) There are at least three plausible justifications. First, in our society, few employees have sufficient assets or even insurance to provide needed tort compensation for victims, so without respondeat superior, tort cases would far more frequently be frustrated by insolvent defendants. Second, employers also have opportunities to take systematic precautions and make general operational decisions that would be hard to judge by a negligence standard; respondeat superior fills that gap without entirely replacing a negligence standard with a strict-liability standard. Third, employers get the benefits from good employees' work and thus seem a salient—and morally appropriate?—target when things go wrong.

Though strict liability for *all* risks created by an enterprise has strong analytical reasons in favor of it—large enterprises are excellent spreaders of cost, and it is arguably both moral and efficient to cause enterprises to internalize the costs they force onto others—strict liability also faces a variety of conceptual and practical problems. For example, strict liability based on simple causation might identify far too many implausible defendants; if I fall while walking on a sidewalk and talking on a mobile phone, it seems unlikely that all the but-for causes are appropriate defendants: the mobile carrier, the phone manufacturer, the city that commissioned the sidewalk, the construction company that built the sidewalk, the manufacturer of my shoes, the designer of my shoes, and so on. Part of the reason that these defendants are not all appropriately liable is that there was probably little most of them could have done to prevent my fall, and so both moral blame and a need for incentives are absent (or at least extremely attenuated). Similarly, if I can recover for all my damages in strict liability, then at least as a matter of economic theory, I may have less incentive to take precautions against my own injuries.

In any case, full enterprise liability has not taken hold as a general principle of the common law of torts. Nevertheless, employee negligence probably serves as a useful rough indicator of the sorts of risks that an enterprise can predict and perhaps readily prevent. It also serves as an administratively useful focal point for a case: No longer are we faced with dozens of potential defendants to hold strictly liable; we have instead identified one—the one that employed the negligent person.

Consider these potential justifications of respondeat superior when reading the cases that follow.

Note on Terminology

The terminology in this area has changed significantly over the years. Until recently, law books predominantly used the archaic terms "master" and "servant" to refer to employers and employees, respectively. The Third Restatement uses the simple terms "employer" and "employee," although it is important to keep in mind that in the context of agency law, these words are terms of art. Thus, there are legal "employees" whom we would never call employees in casual conversation. *See Heims v. Hanke*, *infra*. And there are people we informally call employees who are not actually employees under agency law.

Legally speaking, every employee is an agent. That is, employees are a special kind of agent. What makes them special is the subject of several cases below; for now it is important just to understand the relationship between the terms *agent* and *employee*.

You may already have encountered the term "independent contractor." It is worth observing that this term is ambiguous. It can sometimes refer to agents who are not a principal's (e.g., client's) employees, as in the case of most lawyers and real-estate agents. It can also refer to mere contracting partners who are not agents at all, such as those remodeling one's house or cutting one's hair.

Figure 1

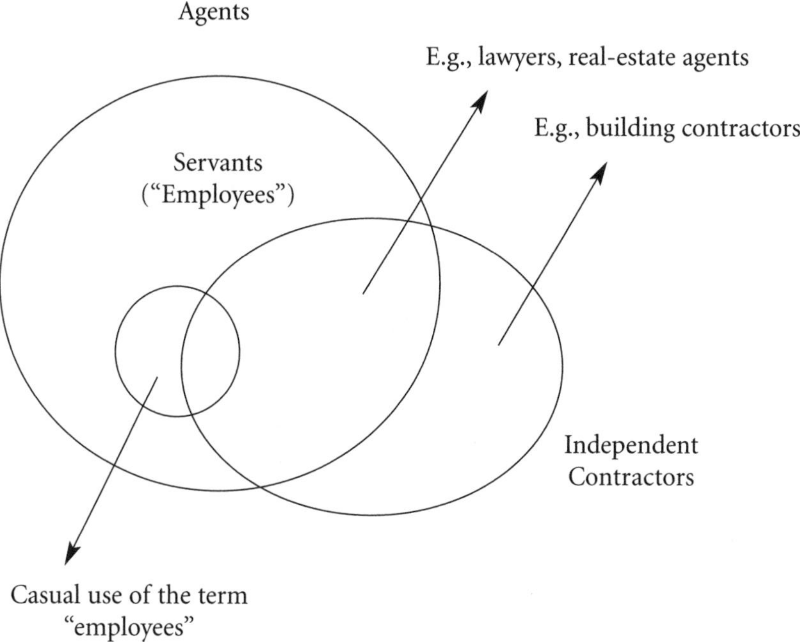

See Figure 1 for a graphical demonstration of the relationship between these various terms.

This book uses the modern terms. Thus, it uses "employee" to mean the sort of agent who can generate ordinary respondeat superior liability for an employer.

The first basic question to consider is what distinguishes employees from nonemployee agents (and indeed from people who are not agents at all).

Heims v. Hanke

93 N.W.2d 455 (Wis. 1958)

Action for personal injuries sustained when plaintiff slipped and fell on a patch of ice on a sidewalk. The case was tried by the court without a jury, and on findings that both parties were causally negligent, and that defendant's negligence was 90% of the total negligence, judgment was entered for the plaintiff. Defendant appeals.

The accident occurred about 11:00 A.M. on April 3, 1954, when the temperature was below freezing. A few minutes before the accident, defendant had finished washing his car at the street curb across the sidewalk from a house which he owned. His 16 year old nephew, William Hanke, helped him as an unpaid volunteer. Defendant washed the street side of the car and William the side next to the curb. Water was obtained by the pailful from a faucet on the outside of the house across the sidewalk. The court found on sufficient evidence that defendant several times requested or directed William to get more water, and William did so, and that in carrying the water from the faucet to the automobile some of it was spilled on the sidewalk, where it froze. After the car washing was finished and defendant and William had left and the water had frozen, plaintiff walked along the sidewalk in an easterly direction, failed to see the ice, and slipped and fell on it.

WINGERT, Justice.

Appellant contends that there was no evidence of actionable negligence on his part, that William's negligence, if any, could not properly be imputed to defendant, that no nuisance was established, that plaintiff's negligence was the sole cause of the accident, and that the trial court erred in excluding certain evidence....

The finding that the icy condition of the sidewalk was caused by the negligence of the defendant is supported by sufficient evidence.

The court could properly find that William, the nephew, was negligent in spilling water on the sidewalk in freezing weather and doing nothing to prevent the formation of ice or to remove or sand it, or to warn pedestrians of it. While the day was not too cold for washing a car bare-handed, the car was in the bright sunlight while the sidewalk where the water as spilled was then or soon would be in the shade of the house. The court could well infer that one in the exercise of ordinary care would have foreseen the formation of a slippery condition and would have done something to protect users of the sidewalk.

It was also permissible to conclude from the evidence that defendant was liable for injuries resulting from William's negligence, on the principle respondeat superior. Probably William was defendant's servant in carrying the water. A servant is one employed to perform service for another in his affairs and who, with respect to his physical conduct in the performance of the service, is subject to the other's control or right to control. Restatement 1 Agency, 2d §220. The evidence permits the inference that William was in that category, although he was an unpaid volunteer. One volunteering service without any agreement for or expectation of reward may be a servant of the one accepting such services. Restatement 1 Agency, 2d §225. The illustration given in Comment a under that section is pertinent:

> 'A, a social guest at P's house, not skilled in repairing, volunteers to assist P in the repair of P's house. During the execution of such repair, A negligently drops a board upon a person passing upon the street. A may be found to be a servant of P.'

If William was not the employee or servant of the defendant in the strict sense, he was certainly defendant's agent in fetching water from the faucet, although he received no compensation. Restatement 1 Agency, 2d §§1(1) and 16; Krzysko v. Gaudnyski, 207 Wis. 608, 615, 242 N.W. 186. A principal is subject to liability for physical harm to the person of another caused by the negligence of an agent who is not a servant, where the principal is under a duty to have care used to protect others and he confides the performance of the duty to the agent. Restatement 1 Agency, 2d §§251(a) and 214; Schmidt v. Leary, 213 Wis. 587, 590, 252 N.W. 151.

When defendant sent his agent to carry water across the sidewalk in freezing weather, he was under a duty to have care used to protect users of the sidewalk from ice, and since he confided the performance of that duty to William, he was responsible for William's negligence in the premises....

Judgment affirmed.

Lazo v. Mak's Trading Co., 644 N.E.2d 1350 (N.Y. 1994). "Plaintiff, the operator of a tractor trailer, delivered a shipment of rice to defendant, a wholesale and retail grocer in New York City. Defendant grocer engaged three neighborhood men to help unload the trailer. During the unloading, one of the three individuals got into an altercation with plaintiff, resulting in personal injuries.

"The alleged tortfeasor came and went as he and his companion pleased, worked at their own convenience, were free to hold other employment, were never placed on defendant's payroll, received no fringe benefits, and had no taxes withheld from the flat rate, single payment for all three. Defendant paid $80 in cash to one of the three workers and left it up to them to divide the payment. While they had performed other unloading tasks for defendant previously, they did so on a random, on-inquiry-for-work basis. In the circumstances of this case, defendant did not exercise actual or constructive control over the performance and manner in which the work of these unloaders was performed. We agree with the Appellate Division that this record does not support the existence of any question of fact that could lead to the conclusion that defendant supervised these day laborers' activities for vicarious liability purposes. Also, in the circumstances of this case, there is no duty to conduct background inquiries in the selection of individuals for this as-needed task."

Section 2: Employees Versus Independent Contractors

Nonemployee agents, often called independent contractors, do not ordinarily cause employers to be liable in respondeat superior (but see section 5, *infra*, for some other ways their use can lead to vicarious liability for employers). Essentially, you can think of nonemployee agents as having no "scope of employment."

The boundary between nonemployee agents and employees is not precise. All agents work for principals' benefit and subject to their control. Past a certain level of control, or subject to particular social conventions, agents become employees.

Using the archaic terms "master" and "servant" instead of "employer" and "employee," the Second Restatement provides a long list of factors that courts have used to distinguish employees from independent contractors:

(a) the extent of control which, by the agreement, the master may exercise over the details of the work;

(b) whether or not the one employed is engaged in a distinct occupation or business;

(c) the kind of occupation, with reference to whether, in the locality, the work is usually done under the direction of the employer or by a specialist without supervision;

(d) the skill required in the particular occupation;

(e) whether the employer or the workman supplies the instrumentalities, tools, and the place of work for the person doing the work;

(f) the length of time for which the person is employed;

(g) the method of payment, whether by the time or by the job;

(h) whether or not the work is a part of the regular business of the employer;

(i) whether or not the parties believe they are creating the relation of master and servant; and

(j) whether the principal is or is not in business.

Restatement (Second), Agency §220.

In general, factors (a) and (c) are probably the most important.[1] Most cases that decide whether an agent is an employee or not can be explained by asking two questions. First, did the employer control the agent's *output* only, or did the employer also control the details of the *method* the employee used? Second, do popular convention and business norms dictate that a particular kind of agent is ordinarily thought of as an employee? The second question, when it has a simple answer, is usually dispositive. So, for example, people who show up every weekday from 9:00 to 5:00 at an office where there is only one organizational employer are almost invariably employees, even if the employer doesn't control the details of the work. For example, even though law schools control very little of the methods that law professors use in their teaching and research, law professors are almost certainly employees of their law schools.

The parties' intent—and their use of labels in a contract—does not determine alone whether an agent is an employee or not. For example, just as with the creation of agency relationships in general, even if a contract clearly says "This is not an employment contract, and any agent created by this contract is an independent contractor," the contract might still create an employment relationship; third parties' rights under tort law are not so easily abridged. As with the creation of agency relationships in general, the law looks at the substance of the relationship, not what it is called.

Nonetheless, there is nothing illegitimate in a principal's decision to use independent contractors instead of employees, and the law obviously does not prevent that decision. So, for example, a savvy principal who wants to avoid liability in respondeat superior can choose to structure her affairs so that she has no employees, using independent contractors when necessary. The law simply requires that parties who seek not to create an employment relation not actually do so, and it doesn't let them avoid tort liability with an artificial contract.

Section 3: Scope of Employment

Christensen v. Swenson

874 P.2d 125 (Utah 1994)

DURHAM, J.:

This case is before the court on a petition for a writ of certiorari to the Utah Court of Appeals. Plaintiffs Jeff Christensen and Kyle James Fausett claim that the court of appeals erred when it concluded that defendant Burns International Security Services ("Burns") was not liable under the doctrine of respondeat superior for the actions of its employee, Gloria Swenson. The court of appeals determined that Swenson was acting outside the scope of her employment at the time of her automobile accident with Christensen and Fausett and therefore affirmed the trial court's grant of summary judgment. We reverse.

---

1. Almost any list of ten factors is likely to be diffuse and unhelpful. As the computer scientist Alan Perlis put it in the context of computer programming, "If you have a procedure with 10 parameters, you probably missed some." Alan Perlis, *Epigrams in Programming*, 17 ACM SIGPLAN NOTICES 7 (1982).

Burns provides security services for the Geneva Steel Plant ("Geneva") in Orem, Utah. Burns employed Swenson as a security guard in June 1988. On the day of the accident, July 26, 1988, Swenson was assigned to guard duty at Gate 4, the northeast entrance to the Geneva property. Security guards at Gate 4 worked eight-hour continuous shifts, with no scheduled breaks. However, employees were permitted to take ten- to fifteen-minute unscheduled lunch and restroom breaks.

When taking their lunch breaks, Gate 4 guards generally ate a bag lunch but occasionally ordered take-out food from the sole restaurant within close physical proximity to Gate 4, the Frontier Cafe. The Frontier Cafe was located directly across the street from the Geneva plant, approximately 150 to 250 yards from Gate 4. The cafe's menu was posted near the telephone at Gate 4. Aside from vending machines located within a nearby Geneva office building, the Frontier Cafe provided the sole source of food accessible to Gate 4 guards within their ten- to fifteen-minute breaks. Indeed, the Frontier Cafe was the only restaurant in the immediate area. Whether they brought their lunches or ordered from the cafe, Gate 4 guards were expected to eat at their posts.

Shortly after 11:00 A.M. on the day of the accident, Swenson noticed a lull in the traffic at Gate 4 and decided to get a cup of soup from the Frontier Cafe. She placed a telephone order for the soup from Gate 4 and then drove her automobile to the cafe. She intended to pick up the soup and return to Gate 4 to eat at her post. She expected the round trip to take approximately ten to fifteen minutes, as permitted by Burns' unscheduled break policy. On her return trip, however, she collided with plaintiffs' motorcycle at a public intersection just outside Geneva's property. Both Christensen and Fausett were injured.

Christensen and Fausett filed a negligence action against Swenson and Burns. After answering the complaint, Burns moved for summary judgment, claiming that it was not liable under the doctrine of respondeat superior because Swenson was not acting within the scope of her employment at the time of the accident. The trial court granted Burns' motion, and Christensen and Fausett appealed. The court of appeals affirmed the trial court's decision, concluding that reasonable minds could not disagree that Swenson was acting outside the scope of her employment at the time of the accident. We granted plaintiffs' petition for certiorari....

Under the doctrine of respondeat superior, employers are vicariously liable for torts committed by employees while acting within the scope of their employment. Whether an employee is acting within the scope of her employment is ordinarily a question of fact. The question must be submitted to the jury "'whenever reasonable minds may differ as to whether the [employee] was at a certain time involved wholly or partly in the performance of [the employer's] business or within the scope of employment.'" [citation omitted]. However, when the employee's activity is so clearly within or outside the scope of employment that reasonable minds cannot differ, the court may decide the issue as a matter of law.

In Birkner, we stated that acts falling within the scope of employment are "'those acts which are so closely connected with what the servant is employed to do, and so fairly and reasonably incidental to it, that they may be regarded as methods, even though quite improper ones, of carrying out the objectives of employment.'" 771 P.2d at 1056 (quoting W. Page Keeton et al., Prosser and Keeton on the Law of Torts §70, at 502 (5th ed. 1984)). We articulated three criteria helpful in determining whether an employee is acting within or outside the scope of her employment. First, the employee's conduct must be of the general kind the employee is hired to perform, that is, "the employee must be about the employer's business and the duties assigned by the employer, as opposed to being wholly involved in a personal endeavor." Id. at 1056-57. Second, the employee's conduct must occur substantially within the hours and ordinary spatial boundaries of the employment. Id. at 1057. Finally, "the employee's conduct must be motivated, at least in part, by the purpose of serving the employer's interest." Id.

The court of appeals held that Swenson was not substantially within the ordinary spatial boundaries of her employment because the accident did not occur on Geneva property. Christensen and Fausett argue that the court of appeals erred in its application of the second criterion identified in Birkner. Burns responds that the court of appeals properly construed the second Birkner criterion in holding that Swenson was acting outside the scope of her employment at the time of the accident.

Because the court of appeals concluded that Swenson failed to satisfy the second Birkner criterion, it did not address the first and third criteria. However, our review of the record indicates that reasonable minds could differ on all three criteria. Thus, to avoid a second summary judgment on remand, we address all three of the Birkner criteria.

The first Birkner criterion requires that the employee's conduct be of the general kind the employee is hired to perform, that is, "the employee must be about the employer's business and the duties assigned by the employer, as opposed to being wholly involved in a personal endeavor." Birkner, 771 P.2d at 1056-57. Reasonable minds could differ as to whether Swenson was about Burns' business when she was involved in the traffic accident between Gate 4 and the Frontier Cafe.

We base this conclusion on two disputed issues of material fact. First, Swenson claims that Burns employed her as a security guard to "see and be seen" on and around the Geneva plant. Thus, traveling the short distance to the Frontier Cafe in uniform arguably heightened the secure atmosphere that Burns sought to project. Burns, on the other hand, claims that Swenson was not hired to perform that function. Burns' position is supported by the deposition of another security guard who stated that he considered lunch trips to the Frontier Cafe to be entirely personal in nature.

A second material issue of fact remains as to whether Burns tacitly sanctioned Gate 4 guards' practice of obtaining lunch from the Frontier Cafe. Burns expected its Gate 4 guards to work eight-hour continuous shifts and to remain at their posts as much as possible. However, because Burns also recognized that the guards must at times eat meals and use the restroom, the company permitted them to take ten- to fifteen-minute paid breaks. The record indicates that Burns was aware that its employees occasionally traveled to the Frontier Cafe during these unscheduled breaks but had never disciplined them for doing so. Indeed, Swenson asserts that a menu from the Frontier Cafe was posted in plain view at Gate 4. Thus, reasonable minds could differ as to whether Burns tacitly sanctioned, or at least contemplated, that its guards would satisfy their need for nourishment by obtaining meals from the Frontier Cafe.

The second Birkner criterion states that the employee's conduct must occur substantially within the hours and ordinary spatial boundaries of the employment. Birkner, 771 P.2d at 1057. It is undisputed that Swenson's action occurred within the hours of her employment. She was at her post and in uniform when she decided to take advantage of a lull in plant traffic to eat lunch.

With respect to spatial boundaries, we find that reasonable minds might differ as to whether Swenson was substantially within the ordinary spatial boundaries of her employment when traveling to and from the Frontier Cafe. Again, the court of appeals concluded that Swenson did not pass this criterion because the accident did not occur on Geneva property. Christensen, 844 P.2d 992 at 995. While it is true that Swenson was not on Geneva property when the accident occurred, she was attempting to obtain lunch from a restaurant within the geographic area accessible during her ten- to fifteen-minute break. Given the other facts of this case, reasonable minds could differ as to whether Swenson's trip to the Frontier Cafe fell substantially within the ordinary spatial boundaries of her employment.

Furthermore, Burns could not point to specific orders barring guards from leaving the facility in their own vehicles to go to the Frontier Cafe on break, although two managers opined that such behavior was prohibited. This dispute alone presents a genuine issue of material fact. If guards were expressly forbidden to drive to the Frontier Cafe to pick up lunch during their break, a jury could find that Swenson was substantially outside the ordinary spatial boundaries of her employment; if they were not so forbidden, a jury might find her to have been acting substantially within the ordinary spatial boundaries of her employment.

Under the third criterion of the Birkner test, "the employee's conduct must be motivated, at least in part, by the purpose of serving the employer's interest." Birkner, 771 P.2d at 1057. Applying this criterion to the instant case poses the question of whether Swenson's trip to the Frontier Cafe was motivated, at least in part, by the purpose of serving Burns' interest. Reasonable minds might also differ on this question.

First, two Burns managers admitted in their depositions that employee breaks benefit both the employee and the employer. Employees must occasionally eat meals and use the restroom, and employers receive the corresponding benefit of productive, satisfied employees. Reasonable minds could differ as to whether Swenson's particular break fell into this mutual-benefit category.

Second, given the continuous-shift nature of the job and the comparatively brief breaks permitted, Burns' break policy obviously placed a premium on speed and efficiency. Swenson claimed that traveling to the Frontier Cafe enabled her to obtain lunch within the allotted period and thus maximize the time spent at her post. In this respect, reasonable minds might conclude that Swenson's conduct was motivated, at least in part, by the purpose of serving Burns' interest. Evidence indicating that Swenson tried to save time on her lunch break by phoning her order ahead, driving instead of walking, and attempting to return immediately to her post is also relevant in this regard.

In sum, we hold that reasonable minds could differ as to whether Swenson was acting within or outside the scope of her employment when she collided with plaintiffs' motorcycle. Thus, summary judgment is inappropriate. We reverse and remand for further proceedings.

HOWE, J., concurring:

I concur. I write to address the concerns of the court of appeals when, in affirming the summary judgment in favor of Burns, it wrote:

Holding otherwise would unduly expand the scope of employment. Every off-site location regularly patronized by an employee for personal purposes could potentially be considered within the ordinary spatial boundaries of the employment. Such a holding would also blur the rule that conduct occurring during an employee's off-premises lunch hour is outside the scope of employment. See, e.g., 1 Arthur Larson, The Law of

Workmen's Compensation §15.51 (1992). Christensen v. Burns Int'l Sec. Servs., 844 P.2d 992, 995 (Utah Ct. App. 1992).

Larson in his treatise recognizes exceptions to the general rule relied on by the court of appeals. One such exception is where the employee is paid during the time taken out for lunch or coffee and to suit the employer's convenience, the employee rushes out to "get a quick bite to eat, and [hurries] back because of the pressure of work....Here the very making of a lightning excursion for lunch is an effort expended in the employer's interest to conserve his time." 1 Arthur Larson, The Law of Workmen's Compensation, §15.52 (1993). Larson cites many cases where the exception was relied on. Only one need be mentioned. In Shoemaker v. Snow Crop Marketers Division of Clinton Foods, Inc., 74 Idaho 151, 258 P.2d 760 (1953), an employee was awarded compensation when he was injured while retrieving his packed lunch from a building adjoining his employer's premises. He was on paid time and under orders of his employer to hurry back.

Although the case presently before the court is not a workers' compensation case, I believe that this well-recognized exception may be applicable here, as the majority opinion correctly opines.

Fiocco v. Carver

137 N.E. 309 (N.Y. 1922)

CARDOZO, J. The defendants, engaged in business in the city of New York, sent a truckload of merchandise from Manhattan to Staten Island. The duty of the driver when he had made delivery of the load was to bring the truck back to the garage at Twenty-third street and Eleventh avenue on the west side of the city. Instead of doing that, he went, as he tells us, to Hamilton street on the east side, to visit his mother. A neighborhood carnival was in progress in the street. A crowd of boys, dressed in fantastic costumes, as Indians, Uncle Sam, cowboys, and the like, were parties to the frolic. They asked the driver for a ride, and in response to the request, he made a tour of the district, going from Hamilton street to Catherine, then through other streets, and back again to Catherine. At this point he stopped in front of a pool room, and left his truck for a moment to say a word to a friend. It is here that the plaintiff, a child of eleven years, arrived upon the scene. The merrymakers were still crowding about the truck. The plaintiff with a playmate tried to join them. While he was climbing up the side, the driver came back and three times ordered him to get off. As the third order was given, the plaintiff started to come down, but before he could reach the ground, the truck, as he tells us, was started without warning, and his foot was drawn into a wheel. The driver gives a different story, insisting that the boy ran after the moving truck and climbed on the side when it was impossible to see him. All the witnesses agree that the truck as it left Catherine street was still carrying the boys. The driver adds that his purpose then was to go back to the garage. Upon these facts a jury has been permitted to find that he was in the course of his employment. The ruling was upheld at the Appellate Division by a divided court.

We think the judgment may not stand.

The plaintiff argues that the jury, if it discredited the driver's narrative of the accident, was free to discredit his testimony that there had been a departure from the course of duty. With this out of the case, there is left the conceded fact that a truck belonging to the defendant was in the custody of the defendant's servant. We are reminded that this without more sustains a presumption that the custodian was using it in the course of his employment. But the difficulty with the argument is that in this case there is more, though credit be accorded to the plaintiff's witnesses exclusively. The presumption disappears when the surrounding circumstances are such that its recognition is unreasonable. We draw the inference of regularity, in default of evidence rebutting it, presuming, until otherwise advised, that the servant will discharge his duty. We refuse to rest upon presumption, and put the plaintiff to his proof, when the departure from regularity is so obvious that charity can no longer infer an adherence to the course of duty.

Such a departure is here shown, apart altogether from the narrative put before us by the driver. The plaintiff's testimony, confirmed by the testimony of his witnesses, breaks the force of the presumption that might otherwise be indulged, and leaves his case unproved unless something is in the record, in addition to the presumption, to show that the defendant's servant was in the course of the employment. The wagon was an electric truck intended for the transportation of merchandise in connection with the defendants' business. At the time of the accident it was crowded with boys, "packed as thick as sardines," whom the driver was taking on a frolic. They filled, not only its body, but also the roof and sides and box. Plainly on proof of these facts the presumption vanishes that the driver was discharging his duty to the master. The character of the transaction is so extraordinary, the occupation of the truck by the revellers so dominant and exclusive, as to rebut the inference that the driver was serving his employer at the same time that he was promoting the pleasure of his friends. The dual function, if it existed, can no longer rest upon presumption. Regularity will no longer be taken for granted when irregularity is written over the whole surface of the picture. We will no longer presume anything. What the plaintiff wishes us to find for him, that he must prove.

We turn, then, to the driver's testimony to see whether anything there, whether read by itself or in conjunction with the plaintiff's narrative, gives support for the conclusion that the truck was engaged at the moment of the accident in the business of the master. All that we can find there, when we view it most favorably to the plaintiff, is a suggestion that after a temporary excursion in streets remote from the homeward journey, the servant had at last made up his mind to put an end to his wanderings and return to the garage. He was still far away from the point at which he had first strayed from the path of duty, but his thoughts were homeward bound. Is this enough, in view of all the circumstances, to terminate the temporary abandonment and put him back into the sphere of service? We have refused to limit ourselves by tests that are merely mechanical or formal. Location in time and space are circumstances that may guide the judgment, but will not be suffered to control it, divorced from other circumstances that may characterize the intent of the transaction. The dominant purpose must be proved to be the performance of the master's business. Till then there can be no resumption of a relation which has been broken and suspended.

We think the servant's purpose to return to the garage was insufficient to bring him back within the ambit of his duty. He was indisputably beyond the ambit while making the tour of the neighborhood which ended when he stopped at Catherine street upon a visit to a pool room. Neither the tour nor the stop was incidental to his service. Duty was resumed, if at all, when, ending the tour, he had embarked upon his homeward journey. It was in the very act of starting that the injury was done. The plaintiff had climbed upon the truck while it was at rest in front of the pool room, still engaged upon an errand unrelated to the business. The negligence complained of is the setting of the truck in motion without giving the intruder an opportunity to reach the ground. The selfsame act that was the cause of the disaster is supposed to have ended the abandonment and re-established a relation which till then had been suspended. Act and disaster would alike have been avoided if the relation had not been broken. Even then, however, the delinquent servant did not purge himself of wrong. The field of duty once forsaken, is not to be re-entered by acts evincing a divided loyalty and thus continuing the offense. Many of the illicit incidents of the tour about the neighborhood persisted. The company of merrymakers was still swarming about the truck. The servant was still using the property of the master to entertain his friends and help the merriment of the carnival. The presence of these merrymakers was the very circumstance that had prompted the little boy to jump upon the truck, and make himself a party to all the fun and frolic. Add to this that the truck was still far away from the route which it would have traveled if the servant had followed the line of duty from the beginning. We do not need to separate these circumstances and to insist that any one of them alone would be strong enough to shape the judgment. Our concern is with the aggregate. We are not dealing with a case where in the course of a continuing relation, business and private ends have been co-incidently served. We are dealing with a departure so manifest as to constitute an abandonment of duty, exempting the master from liability till duty is resumed. Viewing the circumstances collectively, we are constrained to the conclusion that at the moment of the wrong complained of, the forces set in motion by the abandonment of duty were still alive and operative. Whether we have regard to circumstances of space or of time or of causal or logical relation, the homeward trip was bound up with the effects of the excursion, the parts interpenetrated and commingled beyond hope of separation. Division more substantial must be shown before a relation, once ignored and abandoned, will be renewed and re-established.

The judgment of the Appellate Division and that of the Trial Term should be reversed, and the complaint dismissed, with costs in all courts.

Note on Scope of Employment

There is little clarity in the law concerning scope of employment, but two principles seem to explain most of the cases. The first is that the scope of liability usually extends to include actions that reflect characteristic risks that the employer should expect to arise from the employment. The second is that scope of liability is usually "sticky": once an employee begins acting within the scope of employment, it usually takes some significant deviation to take the employee outside the scope, and vice versa. Thus, commuting to work is not ordinarily within the scope of employment, but as in *Christiansen*, crossing the street for a personal errand is. In *Fiocco*, a deviation that would have been almost comical if not for the injury took the employee outside his scope of employment, but lesser deviations ordinarily do not. (The terms "frolic" and "detour" are sometimes used in discussing respondeat superior, but these terms are largely unhelpful because they are conclusory: those deviations that courts decide take employees outside the scope of employment are called frolics, and the rest are called detours, but the terms do not explain the difference.)

The second principle, concerning the "stickiness" of scope of employment, can be justified as a matter of administrative simplicity and attention to context. To deny a plaintiff recovery merely because an employee crossed the street for a few seconds is arguably both (1) needlessly harsh and formal and (2) potentially difficult to administer, as it raises extra questions about employees' motivations and precise locations that may be hard to answer reliably. (For example, is testimony likely to be reliable in such cases?)

The justification for the first principle, concerning expected harms, relates to a potential purpose of respondeat superior liability in general—namely, the notion of enterprise liability. Consider the following two cases in that light.

Ira S. Bushey & Sons, Inc. v. United States

398 F.2d 167 (2nd Cir. 1968)

FRIENDLY, Circuit Judge:

While the United States Coast Guard vessel Tamaroa was being overhauled in a floating drydock located in Brooklyn's Gowanus Canal, a seaman returning from shore leave late at night, in the condition for which seamen are famed, turned some wheels on the drydock wall. He thus opened valves that controlled the flooding of the tanks on one side of the drydock. Soon the ship listed, slid off the blocks and fell against the wall. Parts of the drydock sank, and the ship partially did—fortunately without loss of life or personal injury. The drydock owner sought and was granted compensation by the District Court for the Eastern District of New York in an amount to be determined, 276 F. Supp. 518; the United States appeals.

...

The Tamaroa had gone into drydock on February 28, 1963; her keel rested on blocks permitting her drive shaft to be removed and repairs to be made to her hull. The contract between the Government and Bushey provided in part:

(o) The work shall, whenever practical, be performed in such manner as not to interfere with the berthing and messing of personnel attached to the vessel undergoing repair, and provision shall be made so that personnel assigned shall have access to the vessel at all times, it being understood that such personnel will not interfere with the work or the contractor's workmen.

Access from shore to ship was provided by a route past the security guard at the gate, through the yard, up a ladder to the top of one drydock wall and along the wall to a gangway leading to the fantail deck, where men returning from leave reported at a quartermaster's shack.

Seaman Lane, whose prior record was unblemished, returned from shore leave a little after midnight on March 14. He had been drinking heavily; the quartermaster made mental note that he was "loose." For reasons not apparent to us or very likely to Lane, he took it into his head, while progressing along the gangway wall, to turn each of three large wheels some twenty times; unhappily, as previously stated, these wheels controlled the water intake valves. After boarding ship at 12:11 A.M., Lane mumbled to an off-duty seaman that he had "turned some valves" and also muttered something about "valves" to another who was standing the engineering watch. Neither did anything; apparently Lane's condition was not such as to encourage proximity. At 12:20 A.M. a crew member discovered water coming into the drydock. By 12:30 A.M. the ship began to list, the alarm was sounded and the crew were ordered ashore. Ten minutes later the vessel and dock were listing over 20 degrees; in another ten minutes the ship slid off the blocks and fell against the drydock wall.

The Government attacks imposition of liability on the ground that Lane's acts were not within the scope of his employment. It relies heavily on §228(1) of the Restatement of Agency 2d which says that "conduct of a servant is within the scope of employment if, but only if: *** (c) it is actuated, at least in part by a purpose to serve the master." Courts have gone to considerable lengths to find such a purpose, as witness a well-known opinion in which Judge Learned Hand concluded that a drunken boatswain who routed the plaintiff out of his bunk with a blow, saying "Get up, you big son of a bitch, and turn to," and then continued to fight, might have thought he was acting in the interest of the ship. Nelson v. American-West African Line, 86 F.2d 730 (2 Cir. 1936), cert. denied, 300 U.S. 665, 57 S. Ct. 509, 81 L. Ed. 873 (1937). It would be going too far to find such a purpose here; while Lane's return to the Tamaroa was to serve his employer, no one has suggested how he could have thought turning the wheels to be, even if—which is by no means clear—he was unaware of the consequences.

In light of the highly artificial way in which the motive test has been applied, the district judge believed himself obliged to test the doctrine's continuing vitality by referring to the larger purposes respondeat superior is supposed to serve. He concluded that the old formulation failed this test. We do not find his analysis so compelling, however, as to constitute a sufficient basis in itself for discarding the old doctrine. It is not at all clear, as the court below suggested, that expansion of liability in the manner here suggested will lead to a more efficient allocation of resources. As the most astute exponent of this theory has emphasized, a more efficient allocation can only be expected if there is some reason to believe that imposing a particular cost on the enterprise will lead it to consider whether steps should be taken to prevent a recurrence of the accident. Calabresi, The Decision for Accidents: An Approach to Non-fault Allocation of Costs, 78 Harv.L.Rev. 713, 725-34 (1965). And the suggestion that imposition of liability here will lead to more intensive screening of employees rests on highly questionable premises, see Comment, Assessment of Punitive Damages Against an Entrepreneur for the Malicious Torts of His Employees, 70 Yale L.J. 1296, 1301-04 (1961).[2] The unsatisfactory quality of the allocation of resource rationale is especially striking on the facts of this case. It could well be that application of the traditional rule might induce drydock owners, prodded by their insurance companies, to install locks on their valves to avoid similar incidents in the future,[3] while placing the burden on shipowners is much less likely to lead to accident prevention.[4] It is true, of course, that in many cases the plaintiff will not be in a position to insure, and so expansion of liability will, at the very least, serve respondeat superior's loss spreading function. See Smith, Frolic and Detour, 23 Colum.L.Rev. 444, 456 (1923). But the fact that the defendant is better able to afford damages is not alone sufficient to justify legal responsibility, see Blum & Kalven, Public Law Perspectives on a Private Law Problem (1965), and this overarching principle must be taken into account in deciding whether to expand the reach of respondeat superior.

A policy analysis thus is not sufficient to justify this proposed expansion of vicarious liability. This is not surprising since respondeat superior, even within its traditional limits, rests not so much on policy grounds consistent with the governing principles of tort

---

2. We are not here speaking of cases in which the enterprise has negligently hired an employee whose undesirable propensities are known or should have been. See Koehler v. Presque-Isle Transp. Co., 141 F.2d 490 (2 Cir.), cert. denied, 322 U.S. 764, 64 S. Ct. 1288, 88 L. Ed. 1591 (1943). [Court's footnote. —ed.]

3. The record reveals that most modern drydocks have automatic locks to guard against unauthorized use of valves. [Court's footnote. —ed.]

4. Although it is theoretically possible that shipowners would demand that drydock owners take appropriate action, see Coase, The Problem of Social Cost, 3 J.L. & Economics 1 (1960), this would seem unlikely to occur in real life. [Court's footnote. —ed.]

law as in a deeply rooted sentiment that a business enterprise cannot justly disclaim responsibility for accidents which may fairly be said to be characteristic of its activities. It is in this light that the inadequacy of the motive test becomes apparent. Whatever may have been the case in the past, a doctrine that would create such drastically different consequences for the actions of the drunken boatswain in Nelson and those of the drunken seaman here reflects a wholly unrealistic attitude toward the risks characteristically attendant upon the operation of a ship. We concur in the statement of Mr. Justice Rutledge in a case involving violence injuring a fellow-worker, in this instance in the context of workmen's compensation:

> "Men do not discard their personal qualities when they go to work. Into the job they carry their intelligence, skill, habits of care and rectitude. Just as inevitably they take along also their tendencies to carelessness and camaraderie, as well as emotional make-up. In bringing men together, work brings these qualities together, causes frictions between them, creates occasions for lapses into carelessness, and for fun-making and emotional flare-up. *** These expressions of human nature are incidents inseparable from working together. They involve risks of injury and these risks are inherent in the working environment."

Hartford Accident & Indemnity Co. v. Cardillo, 72 App.D.C. 52, 112 F.2d 11, 15, cert. denied, 310 U.S. 649, 60 S. Ct. 1100, 84 L. Ed. 1415 (1940); cf. Robinson v. Bradshaw, 92 U.S.App.D.C. 216, 206 F.2d 435 (1953). Judge Cardozo reached a similar conclusion in Leonbruno v. Champlain Silk Mills, 229 N.Y. 470, 128 N.E. 711, 13 A.L.R. 522 (1920). Further supporting our decision is the persuasive opinion of Justice Traynor in Carr v. Wm. C. Crowell Co., 28 Cal.2d 652, 171 P.2d 5 (1946) [employer liable for violent acts of servant against employee of a subcontractor working on the same construction job], followed in Fields v. Sanders, 29 Cal.2d 834, 180 P.2d 684, 172 A.L.R. 525 (1947) [employer liable for violent acts of driver against another driver in traffic dispute].

Put another way, Lane's conduct was not so "unforeseeable" as to make it unfair to charge the Government with responsibility. We agree with a leading treatise that "what is reasonably foreseeable in this context [of respondeat superior] *** is quite a different thing from the foreseeably unreasonable risk of harm that spells negligence * *. The foresight that should impel the prudent man to take precautions is not the same measure as that by which he should perceive the harm likely to flow from his long-run activity in spite of all reasonable precautions on his own part. The proper test here bears far more resemblance to that which limits liability for workmen's compensation than to the test for negligence. The employer should be held to expect risks, to the public also, which arise 'out of and in the course of' his employment of labor." 2 Harper & James, The Law of Torts 1377-78 (1956). See also Calabresi, Some Thoughts on Risk Distribution and the Law of Torts, 70 Yale L.J. 499, 544 (1961). Here it was foreseeable that crew members crossing the drydock might do damage, negligently or even intentionally, such as pushing a Bushey employee or kicking property into the water. Moreover, the proclivity of seamen to find solace for solitude by copious resort to the bottle while ashore has been noted in opinions too numerous to warrant citation. Once all this is granted, it is immaterial that Lane's precise action was not to be foreseen. Consequently, we can no longer accept our past decisions that have refused to move beyond the Nelson rule, since they do not accord with modern understanding as to when it is fair for an enterprise to disclaim the actions of its employees.

One can readily think of cases that fall on the other side of the line. If Lane had set fire to the bar where he had been imbibing or had caused an accident on the street while returning to the drydock, the Government would not be liable; the activities of the "enterprise" do not reach into areas where the servant does not create risks different from those attendant on the activities of the community in general. We agree with the district judge that if the seaman "upon returning to the drydock, recognized the Bushey security guard as his wife's lover and shot him," 276 F. Supp. at 530, vicarious liability would not follow; the incident would have related to the seaman's domestic life, not to his seafaring activity, and it would have been the most unlikely happenstance that the confrontation with the paramour occurred on a drydock rather than at the traditional spot. Here Lane had come within the closed-off area where his ship lay, to occupy a berth to which the Government insisted he have access, cf. Restatement, Agency 2d, §267, and while his act is not readily explicable, at least it was not shown to be due entirely to facets of his personal life. The risk that seamen going and coming from the Tamaroa might cause damage to the drydock is enough to make it fair that the enterprise bear the loss. It is not a fatal objection that the rule we lay down lacks sharp contours; in the end, as Judge Andrews said in a related context, "it is all a question [of expediency,] *** of fair judgment, always keeping in mind the fact that we endeavor to make a rule in each case that will be practical and in keeping with the general understanding of mankind." Palsgraf v. Long Island R.R. Co., 248 N.Y. 339, 354-355, 162 N.E. 99, 104, 59 A.L.R. 1253 (1928) (dissenting opinion).

Since we hold the Government responsible for the damage resulting from Lane's turning the wheels, we find it unnecessary to consider Bushey's further arguments that liability would attach in any event because of later inaction of Lane and others on the Tamaroa; and that in libels in rem, whose principles are here applicable by virtue of §3 of the Suits in Admiralty Act, ordinary rules of agency are inapplicable and the ship is liable for anything ship-connected persons cause it to do. Cf. The China, 74 U.S. (7 Wall.) 53, 19 L. Ed. 67 (1868); Burns Bros. v. Central R.R. of N.J., 202 F.2d 910, 914 (2 Cir. 1953).

Affirmed.

Lisa M. v. Henry Mayo Newhall Memorial Hospital

907 P.2d 358 (Cal. 1995)

WERDEGAR, J.

Plaintiff Lisa M. was injured in a fall and sought treatment at defendant Henry Mayo Newhall Memorial Hospital (Hospital). Under the pretense of conducting an ultrasound imaging examination, a technician sexually molested her. In plaintiff's action against Hospital and others, the trial court granted summary judgment in favor of Hospital; the Court of Appeal reversed. The question presented is whether Hospital, even if not negligent in employing or supervising the technician, may be held vicariously liable for his misconduct under the doctrine of respondeat superior. We conclude the undisputed facts show Hospital is not vicariously liable.

Facts and Procedural Background

...

On July 9, 1989, plaintiff, 19 years old and pregnant, was injured in a fall at a movie theater and sought treatment at Hospital's emergency room. At the direction of the examining physicians, ultrasound technician Bruce Wayne Tripoli performed obstetrical and upper-right-quadrant ultrasonic imaging examinations.

Tripoli took plaintiff to the ultrasound room on a gurney. She remained in her street clothes, shorts and a maternity top. No one else was present during the examination; plaintiff had asked that her boyfriend accompany her, but Tripoli refused the request, as was his practice in conducting emergency obstetrical examinations. Tripoli turned out the room lights but left the adjacent bathroom door ajar to admit dim light.[5]

Tripoli first conducted the prescribed examinations. Plaintiff pulled up her shirt and pushed her shorts down to expose the area to be examined. The obstetrical or "general pelvic" examination requires passing an ultrasound-generating wand across the patient's lower abdomen. The sound waves must be mediated by a gel, which Tripoli testified must be worked into the skin somewhat to displace all the air. The exact placement and movement of the wand varies with the patient's body type, and on some patients the best images are obtained by passing the wand as much as an inch below the pubic hairline. Tripoli found it necessary to do so in plaintiff's case. In performing the upper right quadrant examination (to see the liver), Tripoli had to lift plaintiff's right breast, which he did through a towel with the back of his hand.

After conducting the ordered examinations, Tripoli left the room for about 10 minutes to develop the photographic results. On his return, Tripoli asked plaintiff if she wanted to know the sex of the baby, and she said she did. He told her, falsely, that to determine the sex he would need to scan "much further down," and it would be uncomfortable. With plaintiff's cooperation, Tripoli pulled plaintiff's shorts down and began to scan in her pubic hair. According to plaintiff, he also inserted the wand in her vagina. After a while he put down the wand and fondled plaintiff with his fingers. Plaintiff testified he moved his fingers "around everywhere down there." While fondling plaintiff, Tripoli said he needed to excite her to get a good view of the baby. Plaintiff found the touching uncomfortable, but Tripoli testified he thought she was getting pleasure from it because she said it tickled. Tripoli eventually stopped molesting plaintiff and returned her to the emergency room.

At the time of the misconduct, plaintiff thought it was part of a "regular procedure," albeit "kind of weird." Later that day, however, she began to suspect Tripoli's actions were improper, a suspicion confirmed the next morning when she talked to her regular obstetrician. Tripoli was criminally prosecuted and pleaded no contest to a felony charge arising out of his molestation of plaintiff.

Plaintiff's suit named Tripoli, Hospital and others as defendants, and contained causes of action for professional negligence, battery and intentional and negligent infliction of emotional harm. In opposition to Hospital's motion for summary judgment, plaintiff maintained triable issues of fact existed as to whether Hospital was vicariously liable for the battery as a tort committed within the scope of Tripoli's employment, or was directly liable for its own negligence in failing to have a third person present during the examination. The superior court granted the summary judgment motion, rejecting both arguments.

The Court of Appeal reversed. The court relied only on the theory of respondeat superior and expressly declined to reach the question of Hospital's negligence. We granted Hospital's petition for review in order to decide the vicarious liability question.

---

5. Tripoli's deposition testimony was inconsistent as to whether the door to the ultrasound room was open or closed; although he testified he usually left the door slightly open, and did so on this occasion, he also testified the room door's magnetic latch was not working properly, and the door closed instead of remaining ajar. [Court's footnote. —ed.]

Discussion

I. Review of Pertinent Law on Respondeat Superior

The rule of respondeat superior is familiar and simply stated: an employer is vicariously liable for the torts of its employees committed within the scope of the employment.[6] Equally well established, if somewhat surprising on first encounter, is the principle that an employee's willful, malicious and even criminal torts may fall within the scope of his or her employment for purposes of respondeat superior, even though the employer has not authorized the employee to commit crimes or intentional torts. What, then, is the connection required between an employee's intentional tort and his or her work so that the employer may be held vicariously liable?

It is clear, first of all, that California no longer follows the traditional rule that an employee's actions are within the scope of employment only if motivated, in whole or part, by a desire to serve the employer's interests. (See Rest.2d Agency, § 228, subd. 1(c) [conduct must be "actuated, at least in part, by a purpose to serve the master"].) Our departure from that limiting rule dates at least from [*Carr v. Wm. C. Crowell Co*, 171 P.2d 5 (Cal. 1946)].

In *Carr*, this court held a building contractor liable for injuries caused when an employee, angry at a subcontractor's employee for interfering in his work, threw a hammer at the other worker's head. We rejected the defendant's claim its employee was not acting within the scope of employment because he "could not have intended by his conduct to further" the employer's interests: "It is sufficient, however, if the injury resulted from a dispute arising out of the employment.... 'It is not necessary that the assault should have been made "as a means, or for the purpose of performing the work he (the employee) was employed to do." ' " (28 Cal. 2d at p. 654, []) [that tortious act "was not committed in order to further the interests of the principal" does not preclude vicarious liability]; Perez v. Van Groningen & Sons, Inc.,...41 Cal. 3d at p. 969 ["The plaintiff need not demonstrate that the assault was committed for the purpose of accomplishing the employee's assigned tasks."]; Rodgers v. Kemper Constr. Co.,..., 50 Cal. App. 3d at p. 621 ["[T]he 'motive test,' though still the 'majority rule,' has been abandoned in California."].)[7]

While the employee thus need not have intended to further the employer's interests, the employer will not be held liable for an assault or other intentional tort that did not have a causal nexus to the employee's work. This rule, too, can be traced to *Carr*.... There the court acknowledged that "[i]f an employee inflicts an injury out of personal malice, not engendered by the employment, the employer is not liable." We further ex-

6. [California] Civil Code section 2338, which has been termed a codification of the respondeat superior doctrine, is not limited to employer and employee but speaks more broadly of agent and principal; it makes the principal liable for negligent and "wrongful" acts committed by the agent "in and as part of the transaction of such [agency] business."

Tripoli was not formally employed by Hospital, but by Mediq Imaging Services, Inc., with which Hospital contracted for his services. Hospital, however, concedes it did not seek summary judgment on the ground Tripoli was not its employee, did not argue that issue in the Court of Appeal, and does not rely on it in this court. For purposes of reviewing the ruling on summary judgment, therefore, we will treat Tripoli as Hospital's employee, without considering or deciding whether Tripoli was Hospital's nonemployee agent or ostensible agent. [Court's footnote. —ed.]

7. See also Ira S. Bushey & Sons, Inc. v. United States (2d Cir. 1968) 398 F.2d 167, 171 (discussing "inadequacy" of the motivation-to-serve test generally); LeGrand & Leonard, Civil Suits for Sexual Assault: Compensating Rape Victims (1979) 8 Golden Gate L.Rev. 479, 507 (the "motive-benefit" test, which would preclude respondeat superior liability for most sexual assaults, has been "abandoned" in California). [Court's footnote. —ed.]

plained that in the case under consideration the attack was, indeed, "an outgrowth" of the employee's work: "Not only did the altercation leading to the injury arise solely over the performance of [the employee's] duties, but his entire association with plaintiff arose out of his employment on the building under construction."

In Rodgers v. Kemper Constr. Co.,..., 50 Cal. App. 3d 608, 614–616, off-duty employees, who had been drinking beer at the jobsite, assaulted workers for another contractor after requesting and being refused a ride on a bulldozer driven by one of the victims. Applying the analysis developed in [*Carr*], the Court of Appeal found substantial evidence the attack—in which the victims were seriously injured and permanently disabled—was within the scope of the assailants' employment. The assailants and victims, the court noted, were "complete strangers" until their work brought them together; thus the dispute could not have derived from "personal malice unrelated to the employment." Rather, a work-related dispute was the "proximate cause" of the attack.

Because an intentional tort gives rise to respondeat superior liability only if it was engendered by the employment, our disavowal of motive as a singular test of respondeat superior liability does not mean the employee's motive is irrelevant. An act serving only the employee's personal interest is less likely to arise from or be engendered by the employment than an act that, even if misguided, was intended to serve the employer in some way.

The nexus required for respondeat superior liability—that the tort be engendered by or arise from the work—is to be distinguished from "but for" causation. That the employment brought tortfeasor and victim together in time and place is not enough. We have used varied language to describe the nature of the required additional link (which, in theory, is the same for intentional and negligent torts): the incident leading to injury must be an "outgrowth" of the employment; the risk of tortious injury must be " 'inherent in the working environment' " or " 'typical of or broadly incidental to the enterprise [the employer] has undertaken' ".

Looking at the matter with a slightly different focus, California courts have also asked whether the tort was, in a general way, foreseeable from the employee's duties. Respondeat superior liability should apply only to the types of injuries that " 'as a practical matter are sure to occur in the conduct of the employer's enterprise.' " The employment, in other words, must be such as predictably to create the risk employees will commit intentional torts of the type for which liability is sought.

...

II. Application to This Case

Was Tripoli's sexual battery of Lisa M. within the scope of his employment? The injurious events were causally related to Tripoli's employment as an ultrasound technician in the sense they would not have occurred had he not been so employed. Tripoli's employment as an ultrasound technician provided the opportunity for him to meet plaintiff and to be alone with her in circumstances making the assault possible. The employment was thus one necessary cause of the ensuing tort. But, as previously discussed, in addition to such "but for" causation, respondeat superior liability requires the risk of the tort to have been engendered by, "typical of or broadly incidental to," or, viewed from a somewhat different perspective, "a generally foreseeable consequence of," Hospital's enterprise.

At the broadest level, Hospital argues sex crimes are never foreseeable outgrowths of employment because they, unlike instances of nonsexual violence, are not the product of "normal human traits." Hospital urges us not to "legitimize" sexual misconduct by treating it on a par with mere fights. These generalized distinctions are not, however, compelling. Neither physical violence nor sexual exploitation is legitimate, excusable or routinely expected in the workplace. In [Carr], this court did not "legitimize" the act of the construction worker who, on trivial provocation, threw a carpenter's hammer at the plaintiff, "striking him on the head and seriously injuring him," any more than we excused, condoned or otherwise "legitimized" a police officer's forcible rape of a detainee in Mary M. v. City of Los Angeles, supra, 54 Cal. 3d 202. Nor did the Court of Appeal in Rodgers v. Kemper Constr. Co., supra, 50 Cal. App. 3d 608, 615-616, indicate any inclination to approve of or excuse the intoxicated off-duty workers' brutal attack on two other workers—kicking and beating them with fists, rocks and a hardhat, rendering one unconscious and permanently injuring the other's eyesight. The references in certain cases to " 'the faults and derelictions of human beings' " and "normal human traits" thus must be taken in context to include not only minor character flaws, but also the human tendency toward malice and viciousness. We are not persuaded that the roots of sexual violence and exploitation are in all cases so fundamentally different from those other abhorrent human traits as to allow a conclusion sexual misconduct is per se unforeseeable in the workplace.

Focusing more specifically on the type of sexual assault occurring here, we ask first whether the technician's acts were "engendered by" or an "outgrowth" of his employment. They were not.

Nonsexual assaults that were not committed to further the employer's interests have been considered outgrowths of employment if they originated in a work-related dispute. (E.g., Fields v. Sanders,..., 29 Cal. 2d at pp. 839-840 [employee truck driver's assault on another motorist following dispute over employee's driving]. "Conversely, vicarious liability [has been] deemed inappropriate where the misconduct does not arise from the conduct of the employer's enterprise but instead arises out of a personal dispute (e.g., Monty v. Orlandi (1959) 169 Cal. App. 2d 620, 624 [337 P.2d 861] [bar owner not vicariously liable where on-duty bartender assaulted plaintiff in the course of a personal dispute with his common law wife]), or is the result of a personal compulsion (e.g., Thorn v. City of Glendale (1994) 28 Cal. App. 4th 1379, 1383 [35 Cal. Rptr. 2d 1] [city not vicariously liable where fire marshal set business premises on fire during an inspection].)" (Farmers Ins. Group v. County of Santa Clara, supra, 11 Cal. 4th 992, 1006.)

As with these nonsexual assaults, a sexual tort will not be considered engendered by the employment unless its motivating emotions were fairly attributable to work-related events or conditions. Here the opposite was true: a technician simply took advantage of solitude with a naive patient to commit an assault for reasons unrelated to his work. Tripoli's job was to perform a diagnostic examination and record the results. The task provided no occasion for a work-related dispute or any other work-related emotional involvement with the patient. The technician's decision to engage in conscious exploitation of the patient did not arise out of the performance of the examination, although the circumstances of the examination made it possible. "If... the assault was not motivated or triggered off by anything in the employment activity but was the result of only propinquity and lust, there should be no liability."

Our conclusion does not rest on mechanical application of a motivation-to-serve test for intentional torts, which would bar vicarious liability for virtually all sexual misconduct.[8] Tripoli's criminal actions were, of course, unauthorized by Hospital and were not

8. Because we do not apply a motivation-to-serve test as the sole standard of vicarious liability, our rationale differs from that of most other courts that have considered factually similar cases, al-

motivated by any desire to serve Hospital's interests. Beyond that, however, his motivating emotions were not causally attributable to his employment. The flaw in plaintiff's case for Hospital's respondeat superior liability is not so much that Tripoli's actions were personally motivated, but that those personal motivations were not generated by or an outgrowth of workplace responsibilities, conditions or events.

Analysis in terms of foreseeability leads to the same conclusion. An intentional tort is foreseeable, for purposes of respondeat superior, only if "in the context of the particular enterprise an employee's conduct is not so unusual or startling that it would seem unfair to include the loss resulting from it among other costs of the employer's business." The question is not one of statistical frequency, but of a relationship between the nature of the work involved and the type of tort committed. The employment must be such as predictably to create the risk employees will commit intentional torts of the type for which liability is sought.

In arguing Tripoli's misconduct was generally foreseeable, plaintiff emphasizes the physically intimate nature of the work Tripoli was employed to perform. In our view, that a job involves physical contact is, by itself, an insufficient basis on which to impose vicarious liability for a sexual assault. (Accord, Boykin v. District of Columbia (App.D.C. 1984) 484 A.2d 560, 562 "[[T]hat physical touching was necessarily a part of the teacher-student relationship" held insufficient to impose liability on employer for teacher's molestation of deaf and blind student, who could be taught only through touch.].) To hold medical care providers strictly liable for deliberate sexual assaults by every employee whose duties include examining or touching patients' otherwise private areas would be virtually to remove scope of employment as a limitation on providers' vicarious liability. In cases like the present one, a deliberate sexual assault is fairly attributed not to any peculiar aspect of the health care enterprise, but only to "propinquity and lust".

Here, there is no evidence of emotional involvement, either mutual or unilateral, arising from the medical relationship. Although the procedure ordered involved physical contact, it was not of a type that would be expected to, or actually did, give rise to intense emotions on either side. We deal here not with a physician or therapist who becomes sexually involved with a patient as a result of mishandling the feelings predictably created by the therapeutic relationship (see, e.g., Simmons v. United States (9th Cir. 1986) 805 F.2d 1363, 1369-1370; Doe v. Samaritan Counseling Center (Alaska 1990) 791 P.2d 344, 348-349), but with an ultrasound technician who simply took advantage of solitude, access and superior knowledge to commit a sexual assault.

Although the routine examination Tripoli was authorized to conduct involved physical contact with Lisa M., Tripoli's assault on plaintiff did not originate with, and was not a generally foreseeable consequence of, that contact. Nothing happened dur-

---

though several courts have reached the same result as we do: sexual assault by a medical technician is not within the scope of employment. (Compare Hendley v. Springhill Memorial Hosp. (Ala. 1990) 575 So.2d 547, 551 [technician " 'acted from wholly personal motives'"], Mataxas v. North Shore University Hosp. (1995) 211 A.D.2d 762 [621 N.Y.S.2d 683, 684] [radiology technician's molestation of patient "committed . . . for purely personal motives"], and Taylor v. Doctors Hosp. (West) (1985) 21 Ohio App.3d 154 [486 N.E.2d 1249, 1251] [radiology orderly's sexual assault on patient committed "from intensely personal motives" and "in no way served to further or promote the business of the employer-hospital"], with Samuels v. Southern Baptist Hosp. (La.Ct.App. 1992) 594 So.2d 571, 574 [vicarious liability imposed for rape of patient by nursing assistant] and Stropes v. Heritage House Children's Ctr. (Ind. 1989) 547 N.E.2d 244, 249-250 [same for molestation of disabled child by nurse's aide].) [Court's footnote. —ed.]

ing the course of the prescribed examinations to provoke or encourage Tripoli's improper touching of plaintiff. (See Alma W. v. Oakland Unified School Dist., supra, 123 Cal. App. 3d at p. 141 [contrasting assault cases, in which a work-related quarrel preceded the assault, with school custodian's rape of student, which was held unrelated to custodian's duties]; Wiersma v. City of Long Beach (1940) 41 Cal. App. 2d 8, 11, 15 [106 P.2d 45] [producer of wrestling exhibition not vicariously liable for injuries caused by wrestler who "suddenly and, apparently without provocation," attacked spectator].) The assault, rather, was the independent product of Tripoli's aberrant decision to engage in conduct unrelated to his duties. In the pertinent sense, therefore, Tripoli's actions were not foreseeable from the nature of the work he was employed to perform.

Plaintiff contends the battery in this case, like the police officer's rape of a detainee in Mary M. v. City of Los Angeles, supra, 54 Cal. 3d 202, "arose from an abuse of job-created authority." More accurately, Tripoli abused his position of trust, since he had no legal or coercive authority over plaintiff. Assuming an analogy can be fully maintained between authority and trust, Mary M. still provides less than compelling precedent for liability here. In Mary M., we held a police officer's assault was a generally foreseeable consequence of his position. "In view of the considerable power and authority that police officers possess, it is neither startling nor unexpected that on occasion an officer will misuse that authority by engaging in assaultive conduct." (Mary M. v. City of Los Angeles, supra, 54 Cal. 3d at p. 217.) We expressly limited our holding: "We stress that our conclusion in this case flows from the unique authority vested in police officers. Employees who do not have this authority and who commit sexual assaults may be acting outside the scope of their employment as a matter of law." (Id. at p. 218, fn. 11.)

While a police officer's assault may be foreseeable from the scope of his unique authority over detainees, we are unable to say the same of an ultrasound technician's assault on a patient. Hospital did not give Tripoli any power to exercise general control over plaintiff's liberty. He was not vested with any coercive authority, and the trust plaintiff was asked to place in him was limited to conduct of an ultrasound examination. His subsequent battery of the patient was independent of the narrow purpose for which plaintiff was asked to trust him. Whatever costs may be fairly attributable to a police officer's public employer in light of the extraordinary scope of authority the community, for its own benefit, confers on the officer, we believe it would not be fair to attribute to Hospital, which employed Tripoli simply to conduct ultrasound examinations, the costs of a deliberate, independently motivated sexual battery unconnected to the prescribed examination.

In reaching our conclusion we have consulted the three identified policy goals of the respondeat superior doctrine—preventing future injuries, assuring compensation to victims, and spreading the losses caused by an enterprise equitably—for additional guidance as to whether the doctrine should be applied in these circumstances. In this case, however, we have drawn no firm direction from consideration of the first two policy goals. Although imposition of vicarious liability would likely lead to adoption of some further precautionary measures, we are unable to say whether the overall impact would be beneficial to or destructive of the quality of medical care. Hospital and its amici curiae predict imposition of respondeat superior liability would lead health care providers to overreact by monitoring, for possible sexual misconduct, every interaction between patient and health care worker. Published research, on the other hand, indicates providers have available several other approaches to preventing sexual misconduct by employees.

As for ensuring compensation, the briefing does not enable us to say with confidence whether or not insurance is actually available to medical providers for sexual torts of employees and, if so, whether coverage for such liability would drastically increase the insurance costs—or, if not, the uninsured liability costs—of nonprofit providers such as Hospital. The second policy consideration is therefore also of uncertain import here; imposing vicarious liability is likely to provide additional compensation to some victims, but the consequential costs of ensuring compensation in this manner are unclear.

Third and finally, we attempt to assess the propriety of spreading the risk of losses among the beneficiaries of the enterprise upon which liability would be imposed. As Hospital points out, this assessment is another way of asking whether the employee's conduct was "so unusual or startling that it would seem unfair to include the loss resulting from it among other costs of the employer's business." For reasons already discussed, we conclude the connection between Tripoli's employment duties—to conduct a diagnostic examination—and his independent commission of a deliberate sexual assault was too attenuated, without proof of Hospital's negligence, to support allocation of plaintiff's losses to Hospital as a cost of doing business. Consideration of the respondeat superior doctrine's basis in public policy, therefore, does not alter our conviction that an ultrasound technician's sexual assault on a patient is not a risk predictably created by or fairly attributed to the nature of the technician's employment.

Although, as we have concluded, Tripoli's criminal acts were not engendered by or broadly incidental to his work so as to render Hospital vicariously liable, Hospital's duty of due care to its patient obliged it to take all measures dictated by ordinary prudence to protect against even such unusual sources of injury. The Court of Appeal declined to decide whether plaintiff's cause of action for negligence could survive summary judgment. The court therefore did not decide whether Hospital fulfilled its duty of care under the circumstances nor did it resolve any issue as to the adequacy of, or necessity for, plaintiff's expert declaration. Consequently, we consider it appropriate to remand the matter to the Court of Appeal for decision in the first instance on plaintiff's negligence cause of action.

...

Lucas, C. J., Arabian, J., Baxter, J., and George, J., concurred.

GEORGE, J., Concurring.

I concur in the result and reasoning of the majority, and I have signed the majority opinion. I write separately because...I would go further and overrule the decision in Mary M. v. City of Los Angeles.

Lucas, C. J., concurred.

MOSK, J.

I dissent. Justice Kennard demonstrates that the Court of Appeal's decision is without error and hence that its judgment should be affirmed. I join in her opinion.

I write separately to emphasize the unsoundness of the majority's reasoning and the incorrectness of their result.

In its narrowest scope, the doctrine of respondeat superior declares that "the employer's responsibility for the torts of his employee extends beyond his actual or possible control of the servant to injuries which are 'risks of the enterprise.'" For its firmest basis, the doctrine rests on the premise that such injuries are costs that the employer's business imposes on the community—costs that the employer may equitably be required to avoid if he can or to cover if he cannot: "'We are not here looking for the master's fault but rather for risks that may fairly be regarded as typical of or broadly incidental to the enterprise he has undertaken....Further, we are not looking for that which can and should reasonably be avoided, but with the more or less inevitable toll of a lawful enterprise.'"

The majority recognize, as they must, that "[n]onsexual assaults" come within the doctrine of respondeat superior "if they originate[] in a work-related dispute," as when an "employee truck driver[] assault[s]...another motorist following [a] dispute over [the] employee's driving." Such an attack, of course, falls beyond the doctrine's bounds if " 'the misconduct...arises out of a personal dispute,' " as when an "'on-duty bartender assault[s] [a bystander] in the course of a personal dispute [between the bartender and] his common law wife....'"

It follows that sexual assaults are within the doctrine of respondeat superior if they originate in work-related concupiscence, as when "a physician or therapist...becomes sexually involved with a patient as a result of mishandling the feelings predictably created by the therapeutic relationship...." Similarly, an attack of this sort is outside the doctrine's limits if the impropriety springs from a particularized lust, as when a meat cutter makes a sexual advance on a customer as he fills an order.

In my view, it is at least a question for the trier of fact whether the sexual assault in this cause comes within the doctrine of respondeat superior. The facts are undisputed that, in the course of his employment at Henry Mayo Newhall Memorial Hospital, Bruce Wayne Tripoli, an ultrasound technician, was required to have intimate physical contact with female patients, like Lisa M., which involved the touching of their breasts and the rubbing of their pubic areas—all without a chaperon. The facts are also undisputed that Tripoli had no acquaintance whatever with Lisa apart from the event with which we are here concerned. In a word, it is certainly arguable that the itch that Tripoli improperly scratched arose from intimate physical contact that was altogether proper to his work. The majority claim to discern a particularized lust rather than work-related concupiscence. They blink reality. Worse still, they ignore the undisputed facts. The "[h]ospital," they admit, "may have set the stage for [Tripoli's] misconduct...." "[B]ut the script," they assert "was entirely of his own, independent invention." On that point, perhaps they are right. They are wrong, however, in refusing to acknowledge that his inspiration arose from the mise-en-scene established by the hospital.

In conclusion, having found no error in the Court of Appeal's decision, I would affirm its judgment.

KENNARD, J.

I dissent.

The majority holds that, as a matter of law, a hospital employee was not acting within the scope of his employment when he sexually molested a pregnant woman while purportedly conducting an ultrasound examination necessitating that he have physical contact with intimate areas of the woman's body. I disagree. Scope of employment in this case, as in most cases, is a question of fact to be resolved by the trier of fact.

The scope-of-employment question presented here is very similar to one this court addressed just a few weeks ago in Farmers Ins. Group v. County of Santa Clara. In that case, an employee had sexually harassed coemployees, whereas here an employee sexually assaulted a nonemployee, but both cases pose the question whether an employee's on-the-job sexual misconduct arises in the scope of employment. In Farmers, as here, the majority concluded, as a matter of law, that the sexual misconduct was outside the scope of employment. In Farmers, as here, I have concluded that because reasonable minds may differ as to the proper resolution of the issue, it should not be resolved as a matter of law.

...

True, there is no dispute as to the predicate facts underlying the question whether ultrasound technician Tripoli acted in the scope of his employment; that is, the parties agree on where, when, and how Tripoli molested plaintiff, and they agree that defendant was Tripoli's employer. But the absence of a dispute regarding the predicate facts does not necessarily mean that the ultimate question—that is, whether Tripoli's conduct fell within the scope of employment—is one of law, to be decided on summary judgment. As I shall explain, whether Tripoli's acts arose within the scope of his employment is itself a disputed factual question, notwithstanding the parties' agreement on the predicate facts.

This court has long held that whether an employee's tortious conduct falls outside of the scope of employment is generally a question of fact, even when the facts underlying that determination are not in dispute. In Westberg v. Willde, a truck driver making deliveries for the Reliable Delivery Service stopped at his home for lunch, then left to deliver a letter to his father's place of employment before returning to his office. On the way, he negligently collided with another car, killing the driver. The decedent's heirs sued the owner of the delivery service, contending that the accident occurred in the scope of employment, and that the owner was therefore liable for the damages arising from his employee's negligence. This court affirmed a jury verdict for the plaintiffs, rejecting the defendant's contention that the accident occurred, as a matter of law, outside the scope of employment. The court explained: "'Whether there has been a deviation so material or substantial as to constitute a complete departure is usually a question of fact. In some cases the deviation may be so marked, and in others so slight relatively, that the court can say that no conclusion other than that the act was or was not a departure could reasonably be supported; while in still others the deviation may be so uncertain in extent and degree in view of the facts and circumstances as to make the question of what inferences should be drawn from the evidence properly one for the jury....'"

...

In this case, as shown below, the parties dispute the inferences that may reasonably be drawn from ultrasound technician Tripoli's conduct when he sexually molested plaintiff; that is, they dispute whether that conduct was so closely related to the performance of his duties that it may reasonably be inferred that the conduct occurred in the scope of his employment.

The majority asserts that ultrasound technician Tripoli's conduct fell outside the scope of employment because Tripoli molested plaintiff, a patient, for personal reasons unrelated to Tripoli's employment at defendant hospital. In the words of the majority: "[T]here is no evidence [here] of emotional involvement, either mutual or unilateral, arising from the medical relationship," and "[n]othing happened during the course of the prescribed examinations to provoke or encourage Tripoli's improper touching of plaintiff." Thus, the majority concludes, Tripoli's sexual assault on plaintiff "is fairly attributed not to any peculiar aspect of the health care enterprise, but only to 'propinquity and lust' [citation]."

Perhaps. But a trier of fact might also reasonably conclude that Tripoli's employment as an ultrasound technician did have certain "peculiar aspects" that played a not insignificant role in the sexual assault. To perform an ultrasound examination on a pregnant woman, a technician rubs a gel on the woman's exposed lower abdomen. This intimate contact, inherent in the job, put plaintiff in a vulnerable position and permitted Tripoli to dupe plaintiff into believing that his sexual assault was actually part of a standard medical procedure, thereby giving Tripoli a basis to hope that his misconduct would remain undetected. Moreover, it is not unreasonable to infer that the intimate contact inherent in the job contributed to Tripoli's sexual arousal and incited him to engage in the misconduct. In short, a reasonable trier of fact could conclude that this sexual assault would never have occurred had Tripoli been employed by defendant in a capacity other than ultrasound technician, and that therefore the misconduct may fairly be attributed to risks arising from, and inherent in, the "peculiar aspects" of Tripoli's employment

When an employee's personal motivations are so enmeshed with the employee's performance of occupational duties that reasonable minds can differ as to whether the employee's tortious act is incidental to those duties, the issue of whether the act arose in the scope of employment should be resolved by the trier of fact, rather than a trial court acting on a motion to dismiss....

I do not suggest, by the foregoing comments, that the question whether an employee's tortious conduct is within the scope of employment may never be resolved on summary judgment. Although scope of employment is ordinarily a question of fact, it becomes a question of law "where the undisputed facts would not support an inference that the employee was acting within the scope of his employment." Thus, this court held in John R. that, as a matter of law, a junior high school teacher acted outside the scope of his employment when he molested one of his students, and that therefore no liability could be imposed on the school district that employed him. But the converse is also true: when an employee's tortious acts, although personally motivated, are so integrally entwined with his or her employment that reasonable minds can differ as to whether the acts arose in the scope of employment, then scope of employment is a question of fact, rather than one of law, and may not be decided on a motion for summary judgment. This is the case here.

I would affirm the judgment of the Court of Appeal, which held that the trial court erred when it granted plaintiff's motion for summary judgment.

Lyon v. Carey, 533 F.2d 649 (D.C. Cir. 1976). "Michael Carey was in the employment of the defendant Pep Line as a delivery man. He was authorized to make the delivery of [a] mattress and springs plaintiff's sister had bought. He gained access to the apartment only upon a showing of the delivery receipt for the merchandise. His employment contemplated that he visit and enter that particular apartment. Though the apartment was not owned by nor in the control of his employer, it was nevertheless a place he was expected by his employer to enter.

"After Carey entered, under the credentials of his employment and the delivery receipt, a dispute arose naturally and immediately between him and the plaintiff about two items of great significance in connection with his job. These items were the request of the plaintiff, the customer's agent, to inspect the mattress and springs before payment (which would require their being brought upstairs before the payment was made), and Carey's insistence on getting cash rather than a check.

"Carey threatened the plaintiff that he would rape her if she wouldn't pay cash, and he then followed through on that threat and also seriously injured the plaintiff with a knife and scissors.

"Tarman v. Southard, 92 U.S. App. D.C. 297, 205 F.2d 705 (1953) held a taxi owner liable for damages (including a broken leg) sustained by a customer who had been run over by the taxi in pursuit of a dispute between the driver and the customer about a fare. Dilli v. Johnson, 71 App. D.C. 139, 107 F.2d 669 (1939), held a restaurant owner liable to a restaurant patron who was beaten with a stick by one Propst, a restaurant employee, after a disagreement over the service."

Held, that scope of employment was a question for the jury: "We face, then, this question: Should the entire case be taken from the jury because, instead of a rod of wood (as in Dilli), in addition to weapons of steel (as in Tarman); and in addition to his hands (as in [another case]), Carey also employed a sexual weapon—a rod of flesh and blood—in the pursuit of a job-related controversy?

"The answer is, No. It is a jury's job to decide how much of plaintiff's story to believe, and how much if any of the damages were caused by actions, including sexual assault, which stemmed from job-related sources rather than from purely personal origins."

Restatement (Second) of Agency §214, cmt. e.

Voluntary relations. A master or other principal may be in such relation to another that he has a duty to protect, or to see that due care is used to protect, such other from harm although not caused by an enterprise which has been initiated by the master or by things owned or possessed by him. This duty may be created by contract, as where one agrees to protect another, or may be imposed by law as incident to a relation voluntarily entered into, as the relation of carrier and passenger, or by statute. A statement of the situations in which a duty of this sort exists and of the limits of such duty is beyond the scope of the Restatement of this Subject. In situations coming within the rule stated in this Section, the fact that the one to whom the performance of the duty is delegated acts for his own purposes and with no intent to benefit the principal or master is immaterial.

Illustrations

3. P, a railroad, employs A, a qualified conductor, to take charge of a train. A assaults T, a passenger. P is subject to liability to T.

4. P invites T to his home as a social guest. A, P's butler, steals from T. P is not liable to T, unless P was negligent in the selection of A.

5. The chambermaid at a hotel steals the clothes of a traveler stopping at the hotel. The hotel keeper is subject to liability although he reasonably believed the chambermaid to be honest.

Note on Employee Liability

An employer's liability does not ordinarily shield the employee from having to pay damages. It is a common mistake to assume, in many kinds of tort suits, that the purpose of the law is to identify one party from which the plaintiff can recover; in fact, however, whether one defendant is liable usually does not depend on whether other defendants are or aren't liable additionally. Indeed, in the ordinary case of respondeat superior, if an employee has assets, the employer can recover against those assets for damages that the employer had to pay as a result of the employee's negligence. Of course, companies rarely sue their employees in cases like this, probably because so few employees have sufficient assets to make such lawsuits worthwhile.

This general rule makes sense; indeed, why should "I was just doing my job" be a defense to an accusation that someone behaved wrongfully? If I'm a bad driver, should it matter in deciding my liability that I was driving on my own business or for my job?

Occasionally, a statute might exempt employees for individual liability within the scope of their employment. For example, as the Third Restatement points out in a comment, "the Federal Tort Claims Act, 28 U.S.C. §§2671–2680, and comparable state statutes bar actions against governmental employees for acts within the scope of their employment or require that the government be substituted as the defendant." Restatement (Third), Agency §7.01.

Problem

Should an employee whose negligence causes property damage to an employer be liable for that damage? For example, suppose an airline pilot who has accumulated significant savings makes an unreasonable mistake while taking off from a runway and causes damage to the plane that costs $900,000 to fix. Or suppose a factory worker's negligence destroys a valuable piece of factory equipment.

This problem is addressed, at least technically, by the materials we have already covered on the agent's duty of care to the principal. But when the employer is the only person to suffer from an employee's negligence, would liability match employees' and employers' expectations?

As we'll see in our discussion of business organizations, the agent's duty of care is a significant topic in business law. At least in the law governing corporations, there are rules that make it exceedingly difficult for businesses to recover against managers. Should corporate managers receive greater legal protection than airplane pilots? If so, why?

Section 4: Temporary Employees

Charles v. Barrett

135 N.E. 199 (N.Y. 1922)

CARDOZO, J.

One Steinhauser was in the trucking business. He supplied the Adams Express Company, the defendant, with a motor van and a chauffeur at the rate of $2 an hour. The defendant did the work of loading at its station and unloading at the railroad terminal. It sealed the van at the point of departure and unsealed at the point of destination. Between departure and destination, the truck remained without interference or supervision in charge of the chauffeur. While so engaged, it struck and killed the plaintiff's son. Negligence is not disputed. The question is whether the defendant shall answer for the wrong. The trial judge ruled as a matter of law that it must; the Appellate Division, holding the contrary, dismissed the complaint.

We think that truck and driver were in the service of the general employer. There was no such change of masters as would relieve Steinhauser of liability if the driver of the van had broken the seals, and stolen the contents. By the same token, there was no such change as to relieve of liability for other torts committed in the conduct of the enterprise. Where to go and when might be determined for the driver by the commands of the defendant. The duty of going carefully, for the safety of the van as well as for that of wayfarers, remained a duty to the master at whose hands he had received possession. Neither the contract nor its performance shows a change of control so radical as to disturb that duty or its incidence. The plaintiff refers to precedents which may not unreasonably be interpreted as pointing in a different direction. Minute analysis will show that distinguishing features are not lacking. Thus, in Hartell v. Simonson & Son Co. (218 N. Y. 345) the special employer used his own truck. The submission to a new "sovereign" was more intimate and general (Driscoll v. Towle, 181 Mass. 416, 418). We do not say that in every case the line of division has been accurately drawn. The principle declared by the decisions remains unquestioned. At most the application is corrected. The rule now is that as long as the employee is furthering the business of his general employer by the service rendered to another, there will be no inference of a new relation unless command has been surrendered, and no inference of its surrender from the mere fact of its division.

The judgment should be affirmed with costs.

Section 5: Tort Liability for Principals Outside the Scope of Employment

As we have seen, respondeat superior lets plaintiffs recover from employers for torts within an employee's scope of employment. The law of agency provides several additional mechanisms by which a plaintiff might recover in tort against a principal, either for actions outside an employee's scope of liability or for actions of a nonemployee agent.

In general, whenever principals are negligent in their own right and hurt others as a result, they can be liable for tort damages. This is an ordinary principle of tort law and has little to do directly with agency law. Thus, for example, the Third Restatement observes that a "principal who conducts an activity through an agent is subject to liability for harm to a third party caused by the agent's conduct if the harm was caused by the principal's negligence in selecting, training, retaining, supervising, or otherwise controlling the agent." Restatement (Third), Agency §7.05. But this means only that a principal is liable under tort law for her own negligence; just as someone might drive a truck carelessly, one might carelessly select the driver of a truck.

This section considers other doctrines on which principals may be liable as a result of the torts of their agents.

1. Principals Directing Agents' Tortious Conduct

The classical agency rule has been that principals are liable for agents' torts—even if those agents are not employees—if they personally direct the agents' actions. The Second Restatement put the rule as follows: "A person is subject to liability for the consequences of another's conduct which results from his directions as he would be for his own personal conduct if, with knowledge of the conditions, he intends the conduct, or if he intends its consequences...." Restatement (Second), Agency §212.

The Third Restatement broadens this rule in a way that may seem confusing. It says simply: "A principal is subject to liability to a third party harmed by an agent's conduct when the agent's conduct is within the scope of the agent's actual authority or ratified by the principal; and (1) the agent's conduct is tortious, or (2) the agent's conduct, if that of the principal, would subject the principal to tort liability." Restatement (Third), Agency §7.04. This rule could expand respondeat superior liability significantly. For example, an attorney might have a client's actual authority to drive to a real-estate closing in order to conclude a deal, but because the attorney is not the client's employee, the attorney's careless driving would not lead to liability for the client under respondeat superior. Should it under §7.04? Though the attorney had the authority to drive, §7.04—at least to the extent it concerns actual authority—seems to be written on the presumption that he did not have the authority to drive negligently. Of course, no reasonable principal wants her agents to drive negligently, and that desire (or even an explicit command) is not ordinarily enough to remove negligent driving from the scope of employment—but it seems to matter for the purposes of §7.04. Thus, for example, all the examples in §7.04's illustrations that involve driving cars concern specific instructions to drive under particularly dangerous conditions.

The force of §7.04, in general, appears to retain the character of the Second Restatement's arguably narrower rule. The idea is that someone who tells someone else to do something tortious is liable for the tort. Of course, telling someone to commit a tort is ordinarily tortious on its own, and that wrongfulness could be a sufficient basis for liability on its own.

Moreover, under the rule of §7.04, and given the meaning of actual authority that we have studied, a principal is liable for damages caused to third parties if the principal causes a reasonable agent to believe that he is directed to do something tortious. But isn't incorrectly leading an agent to believe that he has been asked to commit a tort negligent on its own, and shouldn't that negligence on its own be a sufficient basis for the principal's liability?

In short, there ends up being little surprising about the real operation of rules like §7.04, which simply cause principals to be liable for doing things that are ordinarily tortious anyway.

2. Ratification

In addition to "actual authority," the doctrine in §7.04 also mentions ratification as a basis for tort liability.

Just as principals can ratify the contracts of their purported agents, they can ratify the behavior of purported agents generally in ways that may have implications for tort liability. The following case demonstrates this principle and also serves as another example of the doctrine of implied ratification in general.

EEOC v. Federal Express Corp.

188 F. Supp. 2d 600 (E.D.N.C. 2000)

BOYLE, J.

This matter is before the Court on Defendant Federal Express' Motion for Summary Judgment. The underlying suit has been brought on behalf of Sheila A. Zerehi-Carter by the Equal Employment Opportunity Commission ("EEOC"), alleging sexual harassment in violation of Title VII of the Civil Rights Act of 1964, as amended, 42 U.S.C. §2000e, et seq. ("Title VII") and Title I of the Civil Rights Act of 1991, 42 U.S.C. §1981, et seq. ("Title I"). Ms. Zerehi-Carter intervened in the action, asserting state law claims of negligence and infliction of emotional distress.

Plaintiff Zerehi-Carter claims that, from her first day on the job, she was subjected to unwelcome sexual advances, conduct and language. In mid-March, 1995, Plaintiff Zerehi-Carter claims that a co-worker, Anthony Hall, touched or slapped her buttocks with his hand as they passed by one another in the ramp area. Plaintiff Zerehi-Carter asserts that she shoved Hall back and protested that he should not touch her in that way again, and also that this exchange was viewed by other RDUR workers. Plaintiff Zerehi-Carter alleges that she reported the incident immediately to her supervisor, Brenda Fitzgerald, who failed to follow standard Federal Express procedures regarding sexual harassment. There is no documentation of Fitzgerald's counseling of Hall, and Fitzgerald was later counseled by Federal Express for failure to document the incident and otherwise follow established procedures.

Plaintiff Zerehi-Carter claims that after she reported Hall's conduct to Fitzgerald, Hall labeled her a "snitch" and her fellow employees at RDUR became hostile towards her. Hall allegedly hit her with a box during a shift in which they were both assigned to work in the belly of an airplane. Plaintiff contends that six male co-workers repeatedly commented inappropriately on her anatomy, especially her breasts and buttocks, made inappropriate sexual advances, and surrounded her with lewd and inappropriate discussions of their sexual behavior. She alleges that this behavior continued throughout her employment.

Plaintiff Zerehi-Carter asserts that she reported these incidents to Fitzgerald, who failed to show any concern or take any action other than to caution Plaintiff about her poor attitude and inability to get along with her RDUR co-workers. She further claims that her efforts to seek help from Federal Express officials outside of RDUR met little success, with Personnel Representative Glendell Wilson failing to return her many phone calls. Plaintiff contends that it was only after she sent an e-mail message to Fitzgerald on October 20, 1995 that action was taken to investigate her allegations. This e-mail was sent seven months after the initial "touching" behavior that was the subject of Plaintiff's initial complaints.

While Federal Express conducted its investigation, Plaintiff Zerehi-Carter alleges that the continuing harassment made her uncomfortable and afraid to be in close quarters with certain of her male co-workers. Complaining of sleeplessness, weight loss, anxiety and bouts of crying, she sought medical and psychological treatment during October, 1995. Plaintiff Zerehi-Carter was prescribed anti-depressants and attended psychotherapy sessions. She alleges that she reported her safety concerns to Fitzgerald in early November and thereafter took a month-long leave of absence from November 17, 1995 to December 18, 1995.

Federal Express' internal investigation ended in December, 1995 with a determination that Plaintiff Zerehi-Carter had not been subjected to sexual harassment. Plaintiff claims that Federal Express failed to interview several witnesses to the events in question, despite the fact that she prepared a list of witnesses for the investigators.

In mid-December, Plaintiff learned that Federal Express had completed its investigation and had decided not to take action against her co-workers. Plaintiff alleges that she was told by Federal Express manager Gary Sheehan that he could not do anything to protect her at work since no evidence of harassment had been discovered.

Plaintiff Zerehi-Carter returned to work at Federal Express' RDUR ramp area, resuming work on the evening shift with many of the same employees whom she had previously accused of harassment. On January 3, 1996, Plaintiff was involved in an altercation with Anthony Hall, the employee who she reported as having made inappropriate contact with her buttocks in mid-March, 1995. At this time, Hall was assigned to act as a "Feeder Captain," with authority to assign handlers like Zerehi-Carter to certain tasks. While the subject of the altercation itself was work-related, and not sexual in nature, Plaintiff claims that after this altercation Hall stood behind her manager "licking his tongue out" at her. (Defendant's Exhibit 26).

Plaintiff Zerehi-Carter claims that her symptoms returned that night and that she had previously been advised by her physician and her therapist to stay away from her harassers. Thus, in her January 3 letter reporting the altercation with Hall, Plaintiff wrote that "I look forward to settle [sic] this matter and getting back in my Fed-Ex uniform to come to work." (Id.) Further, she indicated in the letter that "I can't stress the importance of not having me on an assignment with him [Hall] or any of the others that are involved in this investigation... I feel that they are trying to cause me to loose [sic] my job for what I had to do." (Id.) The next day, she wrote to Glendell Wilson, stating that "I don't have a problem doing my job at FedEx[,] the problem again is my safety and well being there." (Defendant's Exhibit 27) Plaintiff alleges that the matter was not settled, that she was not offered an acceptable accommodation away from her alleged harassers and that thereafter she decided that she could not return to work. Her February 4 letter to Wilson states that "he [Gary Sheehan] told me that it was impossible for them to put me on a different work assignment from those people that have bothered me." (Id.) She was placed on medical leave effective February 1, 1996.

On April 10, 1996, Plaintiff filed a charge of discrimination with the EEOC. On June 19, 1998, the EEOC brought the instant Complaint against Defendant Federal Express. On July 15, 1998, Plaintiff Zerehi-Carter filed a Motion to Intervene. Defendant filed its Answer to the EEOC's Complaint on August 31, 1998. This Court granted Plaintiff Zerehi-Carter's Motion to Intervene on October 2, 1998. Her Complaint was received the same day. Defendant filed its Answer to Plaintiff Zerehi-Carter's Complaint on November 23, 1998. On July 2, 1999, Defendant moved for summary judgment. Plaintiffs EEOC and Zerehi-Carter responded on July 26 and August 2, 1999, respectively. Defendant filed its Replies on August 19, 1999. All issues are fully briefed and ripe for ruling.

...

Finally, Defendant asserts that there is no basis upon which Federal Express may be held liable for the tortious conduct of its agents, and that Plaintiff cannot establish proper claims of negligent supervision and retention or negligent infliction of emotional distress.

At the outset, this Court must consider whether there is a proper basis to hold Federal Express liable for the tortious conduct of its agents. As a general rule, liability of a principal for the torts of his agent may arise in three situations: when the agent's act is expressly authorized by the principal; when the agent's act is committed within the scope of his employment and in furtherance of the principal's business; or when the agent's act is ratified by the principal. Mullis v. Mechanics & Farmers Bank, 994 F. Supp. 680, 689-90 (M.D.N.C. 1997); Hogan v. Forsyth County Country Club Co., 79 N.C. App. 483, 491, 340 S.E.2d 116, 121-122 (1986). It is the third situation, ratification by the principal, upon which Plaintiff Zerehi-Carter bases her claims.

The Courts of North Carolina have not applied a strict test for an employer's ratification of an employee's conduct. "The jury may find ratification from any course of conduct on the part of the principal which reasonably tends to show an intention on his part to ratify the agent's unauthorized acts." Equipment Co. v. Anders, 265 N.C. 393, 144 S.E.2d 252 (1965). "Such course of conduct may involve an omission to act." Brown v. Burlington Industries, 93 N.C. App. 431, 437, 378 S.E.2d 232, 236 (1989).

Here, Plaintiff Zerehi-Carter has alleged facts sufficient to raise a triable issue as to the inadequacy and untimeliness of Defendant's response to her complaints. Both its actions and its several alleged omissions would provide a jury with a reasonable basis upon which to conclude that Defendant ratified its employees' unauthorized acts.

To establish a proper claim for negligent supervision and retention, Plaintiff must further show that the employees committed a tortious act resulting in injury to her and that prior to the act, the employer knew or had reason to know of the employees' conduct. Pleasants v. Barnes, 221 N.C. 173, 19 S.E.2d 627 (1942). In Brown, a North Carolina court examining a similar case of sexual harassment found that a supervisor's "omission of action was a course of conduct which a jury could conclude reasonably tends to show ratification of [the harassing employee's] acts." 93 N.C. App. at 437, 378 S.E.2d at 236.

As discussed at length above, Plaintiff Zerehi-Carter has alleged facts which, when viewed in a light most favorable to her, are sufficient to establish (1) the existence of tortious conduct; (2) Defendant's knowledge of this conduct; and (3) that Defendant's actions or omissions served to ratify this conduct. Accordingly, Plaintiff Zerehi-Carter's claim for negligent retention and supervision survives summary judgment.

To establish a viable claim for negligent infliction of emotional distress in North Carolina, a plaintiff must show: (1) the defendant negligently engaged in conduct, (2) it was reasonably foreseeable that such conduct would cause severe emotional distress, and (3) the conduct did, in fact, cause severe emotional distress. See Johnson v. Ruark Obstetrics and Gynecology Assocs., P.A., 327 N.C. 283, 304, 395 S.E.2d 85 (1990).

With regard to the first element, this Court's analysis in Section 3 above demonstrates that Plaintiff Zerehi-Carter has alleged facts sufficient to support a conclusion that Defendant's reaction to her complaints of sexual harassment was untimely, ineffective, and failed to meet the requirements of its own policy. Should the trier of fact find Plaintiff's allegations to be truthful, they would support a finding that Federal Express acted negligently in response to her complaints. With regard to the second element, this Court further finds that failure to respond promptly and effectively to allegations of sexual harassment renders the effects of such harassment reasonably foreseeable. Plaintiff Zerehi-Carter alleges that her numerous complaints went unheeded, that she was repeatedly assigned to work with her harassers, and that no effective action was taken to protect her. These allegations, if true, would establish that any emotional distress resulting from further harassment was reasonably foreseeable.

The third and final element of the Ruark test is a much closer call. While Plaintiff alleges that her fear and anxiety resulted from her co-workers' behavior, and claims that her therapist and physician advised her not to work with her alleged harassers, Plaintiff has produced no corroborating medical records or depositions. While such material would be helpful to this Court's determination of the cause and extent of Plaintiff's emotional distress, it is not necessary. The Supreme Court of North Carolina has found that "sparse" or "limited" allegations of severe emotional distress are sufficient to state a claim of negligent infliction of emotional distress. See McAllister v. Ha, 347 N.C. 638, 646, 496 S.E.2d 577, 583 (1998).

Here, this Court finds that Plaintiff Zerehi-Carter has alleged facts which, when viewed in the light most favorable to her, are sufficient to raise a triable issue as to the cause and severity of her emotional distress. Thus, she has met the Ruark test and has stated a proper claim for negligent infliction of emotional distress under North Carolina law.

Thus, Plaintiff has alleged facts sufficient to establish viable claims for negligent supervision and retention and negligent infliction of emotional distress. Accordingly, Defendant will not be granted summary judgment as to those claims.

3. Nondelegable duties

Restatement (Third), Agency §7.06

A principal required by contract or otherwise by law to protect another cannot avoid liability by delegating performance of the duty, whether or not the delegate is an agent.

Restatement (Second), Agency §214, cmts. c, e

Highly dangerous activities. A person who directs another to enter upon an undertaking in which the risk of harm to third persons is great unless certain precautions are taken is sometimes liable to persons injured by the work through the failure of those engaging in it to take such precautions. The rule and its applications are stated more fully in the Restatement of Torts, Sections 416–429. It is not within the scope of the Restatement of this Subject to state what undertakings are so intrinsically dangerous that, although it is not negligent to engage in them, one employing another to engage in them is responsible for the incidental negligent conduct of such other in performing the work. Under the rule stated in this Section, liability exists only if some one connected with the undertaking performs it negligently and then only if the negligence is with respect to the element in the undertaking which causes it to be classed as inherently dangerous.

Illustrations

1. P employs A, a careful and competent person, to dig a hole in the street, instructing him to protect travelers therefrom, a permit therefor having been obtained from the city authorities. A digs the hole but negligently fails to illuminate it. P is subject to liability to T, a traveler hurt by falling into the hole owing to the absence of a lantern.

. . .

Note on Nondelegable Duties and Strict Liability in Tort Law

Strict liability in tort law can be seen as imposing nondelegable duties on parties who seek to achieve certain ends or purposes. That is, the ends or purposes seem to be what the law ties strict liability to. Thus, a manufacturer of products ordinarily does not escape product-defect liability by engaging a submanufacturer, for the general rule in products-liability law is that passing a defective product through the stream of commerce leads to liability for the defect. If the law imposes strict liability for the use of dynamite, one ordinarily does not escape liability by instructing someone else to use the dynamite; the familiar strict liability for blasting, then, seems to attach to the decision to order the use of dynamite—not only to the pressing of a button to detonate the dynamite. This makes sense, at least to whatever extent the underlying tort doctrines do; after all, those making the decisions are in the best position to make alternative decision that better promote public safety, and they are no less morally responsible for damage than those whom they direct (and no worse at spreading the social costs of the injuries).

4. Tortious Misrepresentations and Apparent Employees

Tortious misrepresentations made with apparent authority can subject a principal to liability, just as agents with apparent authority can subject a principal to a contract that she doesn't want.

Somewhat more broadly, if a principal gives third parties the impression that a nonemployee is actually an employee, the principal may be liable for the nonemployee's torts as if the nonemployee were really an employee. This is not, strictly speaking, a case of apparent authority, although courts often use that term in analyzing these cases.

The following two examples from the Restatements illustrate these principles:

Restatement (Third), Agency §7.08, cmt. b. illus. 1

P Numismatics Company urges its customers to seek investment advice from its retail salespeople, including A. T, who wishes to invest in gold coins, seeks A's advice at an office of P Numismatics Company. A encourages T to purchase a particular set of gold coins, falsely representing material facts relevant to their value. T, reasonably relying on A's representations, purchases the set of coins. P is subject to liability to T. A is also subject to liability to T.

Restatement (Second), Agency §267: Reliance Upon Care or Skill of Apparent Servant or Other Agent

One who represents that another is his servant or other agent and thereby causes a third person justifiably to rely upon the care or skill of such apparent agent is subject to liability to the third person for harm caused by the lack of care or skill of the one appearing to be a servant or other agent as if he were such.

. . .

Illustrations

1. P, a taxicab company, purporting to be the master of the drivers of the cabs, in fact enters into an arrangement with the drivers by which the drivers operate independently. A driver negligently injures T, a passenger, and also B, a person upon the street. P is not liable to B. If it is found that T relied upon P as one furnishing safe drivers, P is subject to liability to T in an action of tort.

2. P invites T to his house, sending to him A, who is dressed in P's livery and hence appears to be P's personal chauffeur. In fact, A is a driver operating independently. The driver is guilty of wanton conduct in driving and thereby injures T. P may be liable to T.

Chapter 3

General Partnerships

Section 1: Background and Uniform Laws

To begin to understand partnerships, it may be helpful to consider what a business organization is in the first place. Running a business doesn't require any particular legal organization. For example, suppose someone sells homemade crafts on the internet—suppose, as a small-scale entrepreneur, she buys materials with her spare change, spends some time and effort turning the materials into something that people will value more than the raw materials, and then sells them to willing buyers through a website. Although all the work and investment come from one person, it is helpful to think of what's occurring as "business" activity, as distinct from the personal activity of the "businessperson's" life. Thus, for example, if she is properly advised, our craftsperson will keep separate records for her business, accounting for business expenses and business income, because this information will be needed for her annual federal tax return.[1] Moreover, the business she sets up may have a name, a distinct website, and so on. Functionally, it presents itself to the world as a business, even though legally there's nothing more than a single person buying and selling things.

This sort of business is called, informally, a *sole proprietorship*. As a matter of organizational law, it has no special legal status. Legally, there's just an individual making a profit. This remains true even if the owner has to apply for local business licenses, and it also remains true even if she hires several employees to help her out with her work. Legally speaking, the employees work for her personally; she is the principal personally, and they are her personal contractors or employees.

The rest of this book considers a variety of organizations that have special legal status, unlike the sole proprietorship. To understand these various types of organizations, it can be helpful to consider why they exist at all. That is, why isn't every business simply a sole proprietorship? One basic answer is that, as a matter of common business experience, it has been useful for two or more people to enter into business together. There are other

1. Roughly speaking, profits made from "businesses" rather than "jobs" are usually taxed differently for individuals, and business expenses have a different tax effect from personal expenses. If a craftsperson buys a painting to hang in her house, that is simply a personal expense and likely does not affect her tax liability. If she buys a jar of paint to use in her business, however, then the cost of that paint reduces her business profits and thus may reduce her tax liability.

reasons: particular organizational forms recognized by law provide convenience, provide a variety of useful legal rules that can help the parties achieve their expectations, have tax implications, and sometimes shield the investors and operators from liability.

By default, when two or more people set up a business as co-owners but don't opt for any special legal organizational status, they automatically create an organization called a *general partnership.* In American law, the legal creation of such a partnership can occur without any formal filing of documents with the government—much like a common-law marriage. Thus, without any formal organizational filing, something operating as a business is either legally a sole proprietorship (which is to say, it's just a person acting as a business) or a general partnership (two or more people acting as a business).

Though partnership law developed as common law, since the early 1900s the law governing partnerships has been codified by uniform statutes adopted in nearly all states. The original Uniform Partnership Act (UPA) dates to 1914; a newer version of the act, commonly known as the Revised Uniform Partnership Act (RUPA), was developed in the 1990s and has been enacted by a large majority of states—with the significant exceptions of New York and a handful of other important commercial states.

In its discussion of general partnerships, this book focuses primarily on RUPA, the modern act.[2] But it provides some occasional background information on the UPA, partly as a historical contrast to aid in understanding RUPA, and partly because some significant states' laws still resemble the UPA more closely than RUPA.

Section 2: Formation of General Partnerships

Given that general partnerships can arise without any formal filing, the most commonly litigated question in partnership law is also the most foundational one: Is there a partnership at all in a particular case? Like the formation of agency relationships, the formation of partnerships depends on the substantive relationship between the parties—not what they call it.

Usually, the question of whether a partnership exists or not arises because, as a general rule of partnership law, partners are vicariously liable for the activities of other partners within the scope of the partnership. This rule, much like respondeat superior, gives third-party victims a way to recover from people who are themselves possibly blameless but related in some way to the person who engaged in harmful conduct. This liability is a topic we will consider later in detail, and it is somewhat more complicated than just described, but it is important to keep it in mind because it motivates most litigation about partnership formation. Note also how the question is similar to the materials on respondeat superior that we have studied: When should one person be liable for the acts of another?

As you consider the materials on partnership formation, consider whether it is appropriate for the law to decide whether a partnership exists in a particular case as a general matter, rather than asking a more context-specific question, like "Should *A* be liable

2. RUPA is not the official name of the statute; the current version is simply called the Uniform Partnership Act (1997). It is very commonly called RUPA by practitioners, judges, and commentators. For simplicity, when this book discusses RUPA, it refers to the 1997 version of the act; when it discusses the UPA, it refers to the 1914 version. (RUPA has a variety of earlier versions, specified by the National Conference of Commissioners on Uniform State Laws earlier in the 1990s.)

here for *B*'s injury to a third party?" More specifically, is there any good reason that the answer to the question "Are *A* and *B* in a partnership?" must be the same regardless whether the ultimate question in a proceeding is (1) liability of *A* to a third party or (2) liability between *A* and *B*? This question has too often remained unexplored in the law.

Revised Uniform Partnership Act § 101(6–7): Definitions

(6) "Partnership" means an association of two or more persons to carry on as co-owners a business for profit formed under Section 202, predecessor law, or comparable law of another jurisdiction.

(7) "Partnership agreement" means the agreement, whether written, oral, or implied, among the partners concerning the partnership, including amendments to the partnership agreement.

Revised Uniform Partnership Act § 202: Formation of Partnership

(a) Except as otherwise provided in subsection (b), the association of two or more persons to carry on as co-owners a business for profit forms a partnership, whether or not the persons intend to form a partnership.

(b) An association formed under a statute other than this [Act], a predecessor statute, or a comparable statute of another jurisdiction is not a partnership under this [Act].

(c) In determining whether a partnership is formed, the following rules apply:

(1) Joint tenancy, tenancy in common, tenancy by the entireties, joint property, common property, or part ownership does not by itself establish a partnership, even if the co-owners share profits made by the use of the property.

(2) The sharing of gross returns does not by itself establish a partnership, even if the persons sharing them have a joint or common right or interest in property from which the returns are derived.

(3) A person who receives a share of the profits of a business is presumed to be a partner in the business, unless the profits were received in payment:

(i) of a debt by installments or otherwise;

(ii) for services as an independent contractor or of wages or other compensation to an employee;

(iii) of rent;

(iv) of an annuity or other retirement or health benefit to a beneficiary, representative, or designee of a deceased or retired partner;

(v) of interest or other charge on a loan, even if the amount of payment varies with the profits of the business, including a direct or indirect present or future ownership of the collateral, or rights to income, proceeds, or increase in value derived from the collateral; or

(vi) for the sale of the goodwill of a business or other property by installments or otherwise.

Comment

1. Section 202 combines UPA Sections 6 and 7. The traditional UPA Section 6(1) "definition" of a partnership is recast as an operative rule of law. No substantive change

in the law is intended. The UPA "definition" has always been understood as an operative rule, as well as a definition. The addition of the phrase, "whether or not the persons intend to form a partnership," merely codifies the universal judicial construction of UPA Section 6(1) that a partnership is created by the association of persons whose intent is to carry on as co-owners a business for profit, regardless of their subjective intention to be "partners." Indeed, they may inadvertently create a partnership despite their expressed subjective intention not to do so. The new language alerts readers to this possibility.

As under the UPA, the attribute of co-ownership distinguishes a partnership from a mere agency relationship. A business is a series of acts directed toward an end. Ownership involves the power of ultimate control. To state that partners are co-owners of a business is to state that they each have the power of ultimate control. On the other hand, as subsection (c)(1) makes clear, passive co-ownership of property by itself, as distinguished from the carrying on of a business, does not establish a partnership.

2. Subsection (b) provides that business associations organized under other statutes are not partnerships. Those statutory associations include corporations, limited partnerships, and limited liability companies. That continues the UPA concept that general partnership is the residual form of for profit business association, existing only if another form does not.

A limited partnership is not a partnership under this definition. Nevertheless, certain provisions of RUPA will continue to govern limited partnerships because RULPA itself, in Section 1105, so requires "in any case not provided for" in RULPA. For example, the rules applicable to a limited liability partnership will generally apply to limited partnerships....

Relationships that are called "joint ventures" are partnerships if they otherwise fit the definition of a partnership. An association is not classified as a partnership, however, simply because it is called a "joint venture."

An unincorporated nonprofit organization is not a partnership under RUPA, even if it qualifies as a business, because it is not a "for profit" organization.

3. Subsection (c) provides three rules of construction that apply in determining whether a partnership has been formed under subsection (a). They are largely derived from UPA Section 7, and to that extent no substantive change is intended. The sharing of profits is recast as a rebuttable presumption of a partnership, a more contemporary construction, rather than as prima facie evidence thereof. The protected categories, in which receipt of a share of the profits is not presumed to create a partnership, apply whether the profit share is a single flat percentage or a ratio which varies, for example, after reaching a dollar floor or different levels of profits.

Like its predecessor, RUPA makes no attempt to answer in every case whether a partnership is formed. Whether a relationship is more properly characterized as that of borrower and lender, employer and employee, or landlord and tenant is left to the trier of fact. As under the UPA, a person may function in both partner and nonpartner capacities.

Paragraph (3)(v) adds a new protected category to the list. It shields from the presumption a share of the profits received in payment of interest or other charges on a loan, "including a direct or indirect present or future ownership in the collateral, or rights to income, proceeds, or increase in value derived from the collateral." ...

Martin v. Peyton

158 N.E. 77 (N.Y. 1927)

ANDREWS, J.

Partnership results from contract, express or implied. If denied it may be proved by the production of some written instrument; by testimony as to some conversation; by circumstantial evidence. If nothing else appears the receipt by the defendant of a share of the profits of the business is enough.

Assuming some written contract between the parties the question may arise whether it creates a partnership. If it be complete; if it expresses in good faith the full understanding and obligation of the parties, then it is for the court to say whether a partnership exists. It may, however, be a mere sham intended to hide the real relationship. Then other results follow. In passing upon it effect is to be given to each provision. Mere words will not blind us to realities. Statements that no partnership is intended are not conclusive. If as a whole a contract contemplates an association of two or more persons to carry on as co-owners a business for profit a partnership there is. On the other hand, if it be less than this no partnership exists. Passing on the contract as a whole, an arrangement for sharing profits is to be considered. It is to be given its due weight. But it is to be weighed in connection with all the rest. It is not decisive. It may be merely the method adopted to pay a debt or wages, as interest on a loan or for other reasons.

An existing contract may be modified later by subsequent agreement, oral or written. A partnership may be so created where there was none before. And again, that the original agreement has been so modified may be proved by circumstantial evidence—by showing the conduct of the parties.

In the case before us the claim that the defendants became partners in the firm of Knauth, Nachod & Kuhne, doing business as bankers and brokers, depends upon the interpretation of certain instruments. There is nothing in their subsequent acts determinative of or indeed material upon this question. And we are relieved of questions that sometimes arise. "The plaintiff's position is not," we are told, "that the agreements of June 4, 1921, were a false expression or incomplete expression of the intention of the parties. We say that they express defendants' intention and that that intention was to create a relationship which as a matter of law constitutes a partnership." Nor may the claim of the plaintiff be rested on any question of estoppel. "The plaintiff's claim," he stipulates, "is a claim of actual partnership, not of partnership by estoppel...."

Remitted then, as we are, to the documents themselves, we refer to circumstances surrounding their execution only so far as is necessary to make them intelligible. And we are to remember that although the intention of the parties to avoid liability as partners is clear, although in language precise and definite they deny any design to then join the firm of K. N. & K.; although they say their interests in profits should be construed merely as a measure of compensation for loans, not an interest in profits as such; although they provide that they shall not be liable for any losses or treated as partners, the question still remains whether in fact they agree to so associate themselves with the firm as to "carry on as co-owners a business for profit."

In the spring of 1921 the firm of K. N. & K. found itself in financial difficulties. John R. Hall was one of the partners. He was a friend of Mr. Peyton. From him he obtained the loan of almost $500,000 of Liberty bonds, which K. N. & K. might use as collateral to secure bank advances. This, however, was not sufficient. The firm and its members had engaged in unwise speculations, and it was deeply involved. Mr. Hall was also intimately acquainted with George W. Perkins, Jr., and with Edward W. Freeman. He also knew Mrs. Peyton and Mrs. Perkins and Mrs. Freeman. All were anxious to help him. He, therefore, representing K. N. & K., entered into negotiations with them. While they were pending a proposition was made that Mr. Peyton, Mr. Perkins and Mr. Freeman or some of them should become partners. It met a decided refusal. Finally an agreement was reached. It is expressed in three documents, executed on the same day, all a part of the one transaction. They were drawn with care and are unambiguous. We shall refer to them as "the agreement," "the indenture" and "the option."

We have no doubt as to their general purpose. The respondents were to loan K. N. & K. $2,500,000 worth of liquid securities, which were to be returned to them on or before April 15, 1923. The firm might hypothecate them to secure loans totalling $2,000,000, using the proceeds as its business necessities required. To insure respondents against loss K. N. & K. were to turn over to them a large number of their own securities which may have been valuable, but which were of so speculative a nature that they could not be used as collateral for bank loans. In compensation for the loan the respondents were to receive 40 per cent of the profits of the firm until the return was made, not exceeding, however, $500,000 and not less than $100,000. Merely because the transaction involved the transfer of securities and not of cash does not prevent its being a loan within the meaning of section 11. The respondents also were given an option to join the firm if they or any of them expressed a desire to do so before June 4, 1923.

Many other detailed agreements are contained in the papers. Are they such as may be properly inserted to protect the lenders? Or do they go further? Whatever their purpose, did they in truth associate the respondents with the firm so that they and it together thereafter carried on as co-owners a business for profit? The answer depends upon an analysis of these various provisions.

As representing the lenders, Mr. Peyton and Mr. Freeman are called "trustees." The loaned securities when used as collateral are not to be mingled with other securities of K. N. & K., and the trustees at all times are to be kept informed of all transactions affecting them. To them shall be paid all dividends and income accruing therefrom. They may also substitute for any of the securities loaned securities of equal value. With their consent the firm may sell any of its securities held by the respondents, the proceeds to go, however, to the trustees. In other similar ways the trustees may deal with these same securities, but the securities loaned shall always be sufficient in value to permit of their hypothecation for $2,000,000. If they rise in price the excess may be withdrawn by the defendants. If they fall they shall make good the deficiency.

So far there is no hint that the transaction is not a loan of securities with a provision for compensation. Later a somewhat closer connection with the firm appears. Until the securities are returned the directing management of the firm is to be in the hands of John R. Hall, and his life is to be insured for $1,000,000, and the policies are to be assigned as further collateral security to the trustees. These requirements are not unnatural. Hall was the one known and trusted by the defendants. Their acquaintance with the other members of the firm was of the slightest. These others had brought an old and established business to the verge of bankruptcy. As the respondents knew, they also had engaged in unsafe speculation. The respondents were about to loan $2,500,000 of good securities. As collateral they were to receive others of problematical value. What they required seems but ordinary caution. Nor does it imply an association in the business.

The trustees are to be kept advised as to the conduct of the business and consulted as to important matters. They may inspect the firm books and are entitled to any information they think important. Finally they may veto any business they think highly speculative or injurious. Again we hold this but a proper precaution to safeguard the loan. The trustees may not initiate any transaction as a partner may do. They may not bind the firm by any action of their own. Under the circumstances the safety of the loan depended upon the business success of K. N. & K. This success was likely to be compromised by the inclination of its members to engage in speculation. No longer, if the respondents were to be protected, should it be allowed. The trustees, therefore, might prohibit it, and that their prohibition might be effective, information was to be furnished them. Not dissimilar agreements have been held proper to guard the interests of the lender.

As further security each member of K. N. & K. is to assign to the trustees their interest in the firm. No loan by the firm to any member is permitted and the amount each may draw is fixed. No other distribution of profits is to be made. So that realized profits may be calculated the existing capital is stated to be $700,000, and profits are to be realized as promptly as good business practice will permit. In case the trustees think this is not done, the question is left to them and to Mr. Hall, and if they differ then to an arbitrator. There is no obligation that the firm shall continue the business. It may dissolve at any time. Again we conclude there is nothing here not properly adapted to secure the interest of the respondents as lenders. If their compensation is dependent on a percentage of the profits still provision must be made to define what these profits shall be.

The "indenture" is substantially a mortgage of the collateral delivered by K. N. & K. to the trustees to secure the performance of the "agreement." It certainly does not strengthen the claim that the respondents were partners.

Finally we have the "option." It permits the respondents or any of them or their assignees or nominees to enter the firm at a later date if they desire to do so by buying 50 per cent or less of the interests therein of all or any of the members at a stated price. Or a corporation may, if the respondents and the members agree, be formed in place of the firm. Meanwhile, apparently with the design of protecting the firm business against improper or ill-judged action which might render the option valueless, each member of the firm is to place his resignation in the hands of Mr. Hall. If at any time he and the trustees agree that such resignation should be accepted, that member shall then retire, receiving the value of his interest calculated as of the date of such retirement.

This last provision is somewhat unusual, yet it is not enough in itself to show that on June 4, 1921, a present partnership was created nor taking these various papers as a whole do we reach such a result. It is quite true that even if one or two or three like provisions contained in such a contract do not require this conclusion, yet it is also true that when taken together a point may come where stipulations immaterial separately cover so wide a field that we should hold a partnership exists. As in other branches of the law a question of degree is often the determining factor. Here that point has not been reached.

The judgment appealed from should be affirmed, with costs.

Note on Debt and Equity

Two sorts of arrangements have emerged as paradigms for funding a business. There is nothing magical about them; they simply reflect common patterns.

The first is called *debt* and is very straightforward: a bank or other investor may lend a business money, ordinarily to be paid back with interest to compensate the lender for its risk and for the loss of the use of the money for a period of time.

The second is called *equity* and reflects a different tradeoff between risk and reward. An equity owner often puts in money or services to a business with no promise of specific repayment. Instead, the owner agrees to share in the profits of the business.

Many arrangements other than pure debt and equity are possible and, indeed, common. But the basic pattern is typical enough that sharing profits has become the usual mark of "ownership" in a business. This is one reason that partnership law identifies partners largely by their right to share a business's profits.

Partnerships, unlike some of the other business organizations we will study later, at least usually have a group of owners who also personally have a hand in controlling and managing the business. This too is just a business norm—a pattern that characterizes many partnerships in the real world. As we will see, much of partnership law rests on a recognition of this pattern—on the idea of a small group of partners who are ordinarily both (1) equity owners and (2) business managers.

Section 3: Partnership by Estoppel

In an omitted part of *Martin v. Peyton*, Justice Andrews wrote that "only those who are partners between themselves may be charged for partnership debts by others. There is one exception. Now and then a recovery is allowed where in truth such relationship is absent. This is because the debtor may not deny the claim."

He was referring to a notion known as *partnership by estoppel.* As in agency by estoppel, people can rely to their detriment on a falsely created belief that someone is a partner in a partnership when in fact that person is not; under the right conditions, estoppel allows recovery for this loss.

RUPA preserves this doctrine, but it eliminates the older terminology of "estoppel" and speaks directly of the "liability of a purported partner." Full contractual liability—that is, damages to vindicate the expectation interest—appears to be available, but the doctrine is otherwise somewhat narrower than agency by estoppel because it requires overt conduct or consent.

Revised Uniform Partnership Act § 308: Liability of Purported Partner

(a) If a person, by words or conduct, purports to be a partner, or consents to being represented by another as a partner, in a partnership or with one or more persons not partners, the purported partner is liable to a person to whom the representation is made, if that person, relying on the representation, enters into a transaction with the actual or purported partnership. If the representation, either by the purported partner or by a person with the purported partner's consent, is made in a public manner, the purported partner is liable to a person who relies upon the purported partnership even if the purported partner is not aware of being held out as a partner to the claimant. If partnership liability results, the purported partner is liable with respect to that liability as if the purported partner were a partner. If no partnership liability results, the purported partner is liable with respect to that liability jointly and severally with any other person consenting to the representation.

(b) If a person is thus represented to be a partner in an existing partnership, or with one or more persons not partners, the purported partner is an agent of persons consenting to the representation to bind them to the same extent and in the same manner as if the purported partner were a partner, with respect to persons who enter into transactions in reliance upon the representation. If all of the partners of the existing partnership consent to the representation, a partnership act or obligation results. If fewer than all of the partners of the existing partnership consent to the representation, the person acting and the partners consenting to the representation are jointly and severally liable.

....

(e) Except as otherwise provided in subsections (a) and (b), persons who are not partners as to each other are not liable as partners to other persons.

Section 4: What Exactly Is a Partnership?

When studying legal organizations, it is important to keep in mind that they are designed, primarily, to be useful; some have called them "legal technologies" because they are innovative techniques that the law has developed for addressing legal and business problems. For example, one of the innovations in organizational law is for a court or statute to declare that a business organization can do some of the things that individual people can do—own property, file a lawsuit, be sued, pay taxes, enter into contracts, and so on. Letting an organization do these sorts of things has served as a convenient connection between organizational law and the rest of the law. Thus, modern courts don't ordinarily need a separate mechanism for processing lawsuits filed by partnerships; they can process those suits as if they had been filed by an individual.

Historically, there have been two different ways to conceive a partnership theoretically, and the differences between these conceptions have influenced the development of partnership law. Under early law (and, for the most part, the UPA), partnerships were seen as simple *aggregates* of their members. Just as a "friendship" or a "marriage" can't own property or file a lawsuit, the law's early approach to partnerships was that such organizations couldn't either. Much like the label *sole proprietorship*, to call something a *partnership* under early law was, roughly speaking, to give a loose label to a process that was occurring—and to invoke the legal rules that governed it.

The alternative view is that a partnership is a *legal entity*. On the "entity theory" of partnerships, the law should treat a partnership as being able to conduct its own business, as discussed above. Legal entities can buy and sell property, enter into contracts, and litigate—all in their own names.

In the modern world, this latter view has become dominant, largely because it is more convenient. Thus, RUPA declares up front that "A partnership is an entity distinct from its partners," RUPA § 201, and it typically adopts rules that treat partnerships as distinct legal entities.

Nonetheless, as Mel Eisenberg has put it, "It is true that generally speaking the best rule ... is one that is consistent with entity status, but it is important not to forget that an independent policy choice must still be made on each issue." Melvin Aron Eisenberg, Corporations and Other Business Organizations 42 (9th ed. 2005). That is, in deciding precisely what partnerships can and can't do under the law—or for example whether individual partners have duties to each other or just to "the partnership"—it is important to consider the benefits and drawbacks of each possibility. Nothing requires that the law follow any particular conception of the legal status of partnerships in all the decisions in makes.

Consider how taking the "aggregate theory" of partnerships too seriously may have distorted the result in the following case. Do not worry yet about the details of what it means for a partnership to dissolve, except to recognize that under the aggregate theory, a partnership between *A*, *B*, and *C* could not, by definition, be the "same" partnership if *C* left. We will discuss in later sections precisely how new members join and leave partnerships.

Fairway Development Co. v. Title Insurance Co. of Minnesota

621 F. Supp. 120 (N.D. Ohio 1985)

David D. Dowd, U. S. District Judge

Before the Court are the motions of the plaintiff, Fairway Development Company, and the defendant, Title Insurance Company of Minnesota, for summary judgment. Both parties have filed memoranda in opposition to the opposing party's motion.... For the reasons which follow, the motion of the plaintiff is denied and the motion of the defendant is granted.

Plaintiff filed this action against the defendant alleging breach of contract under a title guarantee insurance policy. Plaintiff avers that under that policy, "defendant agreed to insure plaintiff against any loss sustained by it by reason of any defects, liens or encumbrances in the title of the insured to [the real property in question]." Plaintiff avers that defendant failed to reference on the exception sheet to the title policy issued by the defendant an easement granted in favor of The East Ohio Gas Company for the purpose of maintaining a gas line over the property in question. Plaintiff claims that the easement "is a defect and encumbrance in plaintiff's title to the Property." Plaintiff avers that it gave notice to the defendant of the existence of the defect and encumbrance in the title to the property, and made a demand upon the defendant for payment of damages which it sustained as a result thereof. Plaintiff avers that defendant failed to pay plaintiff for losses sustained as a result of the defendant's material breach of the contract in question, and that defendant's "breaches and failure to pay ... were done in bad faith, with malice and in reckless disregard with the terms of the insurance policy." Plaintiff seeks compensatory and punitive damages, plus interest, costs, and any other relief the Court deems proper....

Defendant ... asserts that it is liable under the title guaranty policy in question only to the named party guaranteed. Defendant asserts that it originally guaranteed a general partnership, which it refers to as Fairway Development I, consisting of three partners: Thomas M. Bernabei, James V. Serra, Jr., and Howard J. Wenger. Defendant states that each of these three men contributed to the partnership's capital and shared in the partnership's profits and losses equally. Defendant argues that Fairway Development I commenced on October 15, 1979 and terminated on May 20, 1981, when two partners in Fairway Development I, Bernabei and Serra, sold and transferred their respective undivided one-third interests in the partnership to the remaining partner, Wenger, and a third-party purchaser, James E. Valentine. Defendant argues that a new partnership resulted from this sale, called Fairway Development II. Defendant concludes that it cannot be held liable to the plaintiff since it is not in privity with the plaintiff as the named party guaranteed. Defendant argues that the named party guaranteed was Fairway Development I, a partnership which dissolved in 1981 upon formation of Fairway Development II, and that its liability does not extend to Fairway Development II....

In response to defendant's argument that the plaintiff is not the party guaranteed under the title guaranty issued by the defendant, the plaintiff argues that under Ohio Rev. Code § 1775.26(A), the transfer of Bernabei and Serra of their partnership interests was not in itself sufficient to dissolve the partnership. Plaintiff states that in the instant case, the facts are clear that there was an intent between the partners of what defendant calls Fairway Development I and II to continue the operation of the Fairway Development Company following the sale by Bernabei and Serra of their interests to Wenger and Valentine without dissolving the partnership. Plaintiff states that in deciding this case, the Court's focus should be upon the intent of the parties. Lastly, plaintiff argues that Fairway Development II has continued to carry on the stated purpose of Fairway Development I, which is really just an expansion of the purpose set forth in the partnership agreement for Fairway Development I, the acquisition and development of real estate....

Discussion and Law

It is a fundamental principle of law that any change in the personnel of a partnership will result in its dissolution. The Court must thus determine whether the general rule has been modified by statute.

The resolution of this case is governed by the law of the forum state, Ohio. Ohio has adopted the Uniform Partnership Law, modeled after the Uniform Partnership Act enacted by the National Conference of Commissioners on Uniform State Laws in 1914. Ohio follows the common law aggregate theory of partnership, under which a partnership is regarded as the sum of the persons who comprise the partnership, versus the legal entity theory of partnership, under which the [partnership], like a [corporation], is regarded as an entity in itself....

The Court finds that the law as applicable to the facts of this case supports a finding that the named party guaranteed in the contract in question is not the plaintiff, and that the plaintiff is a new partnership which followed the termination of Fairway Development I.... Plaintiff concedes that when Fairway Development II was formed, a new partnership agreement was required under the terms of Ohio Rev. Code § 1777.03. Plaintiff states that the fact that it filed an amended partnership certificate, notwithstanding the fact that it is not in compliance with law, indicates its intent to continue the original Fairway Development partnership. However, in the section entitled "Recital" of the partnership agreement between Wenger and Valentine, the partners of Fairway Development Company recognize that they are forming and creating a new general partnership, versus continuing Fairway Development I. In Article 3 of the same agreement, under the section entitled "Term", Valentine and Wenger address the commencement of the partnership, and state that it "shall commence upon the execution of this Agreement (emphasis)." Further, the terms of the partnership agreement broadened and changed the terms of the original agreement. See e.g., Article 2, "Purpose of the Partnership", Article 8, "Management of Partnership Affairs", Article 9, "Restrictions on Transfers", and Article 10, "Default". Also, both partnership agreements provide that the partners are to own the partnership in equal shares, although an equal division of the partnership interests of

Bernabei and Serra between Wenger and Valentine under the agreement of sale would have left Wenger owning a two-thirds interest in the partnership, and Valentine owning a one-third interest in the partnership.

Additionally the Court notes, as an aside, that Fairway Development II filed income tax returns for the years of 1981, 1982, and 1983 in the name of Fairway Development II.

The Court finds it unnecessary to address the defendant's argument as to lack of notice when, for the reasons above stated, the Court finds that the provisions of the Ohio Uniform Partnership Law, together with the facts of this case, indicate that when Serra and Bernabei transferred their interests to Wenger and Valentine, the partnership known as Fairway Development I dissolved, and the partnership known as Fairway Development II, consisting of members Valentine and Wenger, was formed. Fairway Development I, being a separate entity from Fairway Development II, the current plaintiff, the Court holds that the terms of the title guaranty extended only to the named party guaranteed, that party being Fairway Development I, and that Fairway Development II therefore has no standing to sue the defendant for breach of the contract in question. Defendant's motion for summary judgment is therefore granted.

The plaintiff has filed a motion for summary judgment on grounds that no genuine issues of material fact remain for trial as to the defendant's breach of contract of title insurance which it allegedly entered into with the plaintiff herein. The Court having reviewed the plaintiff's motion, and finding it to be subsumed within the Court's disposition of the defendant's motion for summary judgment, the plaintiff's motion for summary judgment is hereby denied.

Revised Uniform Partnership Act § 201: Partnership as Entity, cmt.

RUPA embraces the entity theory of the partnership. In light of the UPA's ambivalence on the nature of partnerships, the explicit statement provided by subsection (a) is deemed appropriate as an expression of the increased emphasis on the entity theory as the dominant model. But see Section 306 (partners' liability joint and several unless the partnership has filed a statement of qualification to become a limited liability partnership).

Giving clear expression to the entity nature of a partnership is intended to allay previous concerns stemming from the aggregate theory, such as the necessity of a deed to convey title from the "old" partnership to the "new" partnership every time there is a change of cast among the partners. Under RUPA, there is no "new" partnership just because of membership changes. That will avoid the result in cases such as *Fairway Development Co. v. Title Insurance Co.*, 621 F. Supp. 120 (N.D. Ohio 1985), which held that the "new" partnership resulting from a partner's death did not have standing to enforce a title insurance policy issued to the "old" partnership.

Section 5: Authority in Partnerships

A central question in the legal study of any business organization is who has authority to act on behalf of the organization. Just as the entity theory of organizations connects organizational law to other areas of law (like property and civil procedure), rules about authority import agency-law concepts directly into the law of organizations.

The default rule in the law of general partnerships is that partners have both actual and apparent[3] authority to conduct the usual business of the partnership. Partners acting in the scope of their authority might designate other agents. But the partners are themselves a source of authority for the partnership, by default.

RUPA states the general rule, clarifies some small ambiguities in earlier law, and modifies old common-law rules by introducing the notion of a *statement of authority*, which is a document that the partnership can file with the state that may grant or revoke authority and provide notice of such decisions to the public.

Revised Uniform Partnership Act § 301: Partner Agent of Partnership

Subject to the effect of a statement of partnership authority under Section 303:

(1) Each partner is an agent of the partnership for the purpose of its business. An act of a partner, including the execution of an instrument in the partnership name, for apparently carrying on in the ordinary course the partnership business or business of the kind carried on by the partnership binds the partnership, unless the partner had no authority to act for the partnership in the particular matter and the person with whom the partner was dealing knew or had received a notification that the partner lacked authority.

(2) An act of a partner which is not apparently for carrying on in the ordinary course the partnership business or business of the kind carried on by the partnership binds the partnership only if the act was authorized by the other partners.

Comment

1. Section 301 sets forth a partner's power, as an agent of the firm, to bind the partnership entity to third parties. The rights of the partners among themselves, including the right to restrict a partner's authority, are governed by the partnership agreement and by Section 401. The agency rules set forth in Section 301 are subject to an important qualification. They may be affected by the filing or recording of a statement of partnership authority. The legal effect of filing or recording a statement of partnership authority is set forth in Section 303.

2. Section 301(1) retains the basic principles reflected in UPA Section 9(1). It declares that each partner is an agent of the partnership and that, by virtue of partnership status, each partner has apparent authority to bind the partnership in ordinary course transactions. The effect of Section 301(1) is to characterize a partner as a general managerial agent having both actual and apparent authority coextensive in scope with the firm's ordinary business, at least in the absence of a contrary partnership agreement.

Section 301(1) effects two changes from UPA Section 9(1). First, it clarifies that a partner's apparent authority includes acts for carrying on in the ordinary course "business of the kind carried on by the partnership," not just the business of the particular partnership in question. The UPA is ambiguous on this point, but there is some authority for an expanded construction in accordance with the so-called English rule. *See, e.g.*, *Burns v. Gonzalez*, 439 S.W.2d 128, 131 (Tex. Civ. App. 1969) (dictum); *Commercial Hotel Co. v. Weeks*, 254 S.W. 521 (Tex. Civ. App. 1923). No substantive change is in-

---

3. At least in effect; RUPA does not use the term "apparent authority" to describe the ostensible authority of a partner who lacks actual authority; it simply refers, in § 301, to "an act of a partner ... for apparently carrying on in the ordinary course the partnership business or business of the kind carried on by the partnership."

tended by use of the more customary phrase "carrying on in the ordinary course" in lieu of the UPA phrase "in the usual way." The UPA and the case law use both terms without apparent distinction.

The other change from the UPA concerns the allocation of risk of a partner's lack of authority. RUPA draws the line somewhat differently from the UPA.

Under UPA Section 9(1) and (4), only a person with knowledge of a restriction on a partner's authority is bound by it. Section 301(1) provides that a person who has received a notification of a partner's lack of authority is also bound. The meaning of "receives a notification" is explained in Section 102(d). Thus, the partnership may protect itself from unauthorized acts by giving a notification of a restriction on a partner's authority to a person dealing with that partner. A notification may be effective upon delivery, whether or not it actually comes to the other person's attention. To that extent, the risk of lack of authority is shifted to those dealing with partners.

On the other hand, as used in the UPA, the term "knowledge" embodies the concept of "bad faith" knowledge arising from other known facts. As used in RUPA, however, "knowledge" is limited to actual knowledge. *See* Section 102(a). Thus, RUPA does not expose persons dealing with a partner to the greater risk of being bound by a restriction based on their purported reason to know of the partner's lack of authority from all the facts they did know.

With one exception, this result is not affected even if the partnership files a statement of partnership authority containing a limitation on a partner's authority. Section 303(f) makes clear that a person dealing with a partner is not deemed to know of such a limitation merely because it is contained in a filed statement of authority. Under Section 303(e), however, all persons are deemed to know of a limitation on the authority of a partner to transfer real property contained in a recorded statement. Thus, a recorded limitation on authority concerning real property constitutes constructive knowledge of the limitation to the whole world.

3. Section 301(2) is drawn directly from UPA Section 9(2), with conforming changes to mirror the new language of subsection (1). Subsection (2) makes it clear that the partnership is bound by a partner's actual authority, even if the partner has no apparent authority. Section 401(j) requires the unanimous consent of the partners for a grant of authority outside the ordinary course of business, unless the partnership agreement provides otherwise. Under general agency principles, the partners can subsequently ratify a partner's unauthorized act. See Section 104(a).

4. UPA Section 9(3) contains a list of five extraordinary acts that require unanimous consent of the partners before the partnership is bound. RUPA omits that section.

[These five "extraordinary acts" were as follows: "(a) Assign the partnership property in trust for creditors or on the assignee's promise to pay the debts of the partnership, (b) Dispose of the good-will of the business, (c) Do any other act which would make it impossible to carry on the ordinary business of a partnership, (d) Confess a judgment, (e) Submit a partnership claim or liability in arbitration or reference."]

That leaves it to the courts to decide the outer limits of the agency power of a partner. Most of the acts listed in UPA Section 9(3) probably remain outside the apparent authority of a partner under RUPA, such as disposing of the goodwill of the business, but elimination of a statutory rule will afford more flexibility in some situations specified in UPA Section 9(3). In particular, it seems archaic that the submission of a partnership claim to arbitration always requires unanimous consent. *See* UPA § 9(3)(e).

5. Section 301(1) fully reflects the principle embodied in UPA Section 9(4) that the partnership is not bound by an act of a partner in contravention of a restriction on his authority known to the other party.

Revised Uniform Partnership Act § 303: Statement of Partnership Authority

(a) A partnership may file a statement of partnership authority, which:

(1) must include:

(i) the name of the partnership;

(ii) the street address of its chief executive office and of one office in this State, if there is one;

(iii) the names and mailing addresses of all of the partners or of an agent appointed and maintained by the partnership for the purpose of subsection (b); and

(iv) the names of the partners authorized to execute an instrument transferring real property held in the name of the partnership; and

(2) may state the authority, or limitations on the authority, of some or all of the partners to enter into other transactions on behalf of the partnership and any other matter.

(b) If a statement of partnership authority names an agent, the agent shall maintain a list of the names and mailing addresses of all of the partners and make it available to any person on request for good cause shown....

(d) Except as otherwise provided in subsection (g), a filed statement of partnership authority supplements the authority of a partner to enter into transactions on behalf of the partnership as follows:

(1) Except for transfers of real property, a grant of authority contained in a filed statement of partnership authority is conclusive in favor of a person who gives value without knowledge to the contrary, so long as and to the extent that a limitation on that authority is not then contained in another filed statement. A filed cancellation of a limitation on authority revives the previous grant of authority.

(2) A grant of authority to transfer real property held in the name of the partnership contained in a certified copy of a filed statement of partnership authority recorded in the office for recording transfers of that real property is conclusive in favor of a person who gives value without knowledge to the contrary, so long as and to the extent that a certified copy of a filed statement containing a limitation on that authority is not then of record in the office for recording transfers of that real property. The recording in the office for recording transfers of that real property of a certified copy of a filed cancellation of a limitation on authority revives the previous grant of authority.

(e) A person not a partner is deemed to know of a limitation on the authority of a partner to transfer real property held in the name of the partnership if a certified copy of the filed statement containing the limitation on authority is of record in the office for recording transfers of that real property.

(f) Except as otherwise provided in subsections (d) and (e) and Sections 704 and 805, a person not a partner is not deemed to know of a limitation on the authority of a partner merely because the limitation is contained in a filed statement.

(g) Unless earlier canceled, a filed statement of partnership authority is canceled by operation of law five years after the date on which the statement, or the most recent amendment, was filed with the [Secretary of State].

RNR Invs. Ltd. P'ship v. Peoples First Cmty. Bank

812 So. 2d 561 (Fla. App. 2002)

VAN NORTWICK, J.

RNR Investments Limited Partnership (RNR) appeals a summary judgment of foreclosure granted in favor of appellee, Peoples First Community Bank (the Bank).... RNR alleged that the Bank was negligent in lending $960,000 to RNR without consent of the limited partners when, under RNR's Agreement of Limited Partnership, the authority of RNR's general partner was limited to obtaining financing up to $650,000. Under section 620.8301(1),[4] Florida Statutes (2000), however, the Bank could rely upon the general partner's apparent authority to bind RNR, unless the Bank had actual knowledge or notice of his restricted authority. In opposing summary judgment, RNR produced no evidence showing that the Bank had actual knowledge or notice of restrictions imposed on the authority of RNR's general partner. Accordingly, no issues of material facts are in dispute and we affirm.

Factual and Procedural History

RNR is a Florida limited partnership[5] formed pursuant to chapter 620, Florida Statutes, to purchase vacant land in Destin, Florida, and to construct a house on the land for resale. Bernard Roeger was RNR's general partner and Heinz Rapp, Claus North, and S.E. Waltz, Inc., were limited partners. The agreement of limited partnership provides for various restrictions on the authority of the general partner. Paragraph 4.1 of the agreement required the general partner to prepare a budget covering the cost of acquisition and construction of the project (defined as the "Approved Budget") and further provided, in pertinent part, as follows:

> The Approved Budget for the Partnership is attached hereto as Exhibit "C" and is approved by evidence of the signatures of the Partners on the signature pages of this Agreement.... In no event, without Limited Partner Consent, shall the Approved Budget be exceeded by more than five percent (5%), nor shall any line item thereof be exceeded by more than ten percent (10%), ...

Paragraph 4.3 restricted the general partner's ability to borrow, spend partnership funds and encumber partnership assets, if not specifically provided for in the Approved Budget. Finally, with respect to the development of the partnership project, paragraph 2.2(b) provided:

> The General Partner shall not incur debts, liabilities or obligations of the Partnership which will cause any line item in the Approved Budget to be ex-

---

4. Florida is one of the many states that have adopted RUPA. In general, Florida Statute § 620.8xxx corresponds to RUPA § xxx. Thus, § 620.8301(1) corresponds to RUPA § 301(1). [—ed.]

5. Limited partnerships are a different organizational form from general partnerships; we will cover them later in the book. However, as to the particular issue of the authority of a general partner, the question for limited partnerships is governed by RUPA because the statute governing limited partnerships defers to RUPA on legal issues that it does not itself cover. [—ed.]

> ceeded by more than ten percent (10%) or which will cause the aggregate Approved Budget to be exceed by more than five percent (5%) unless the General Partner shall receive the prior written consent of the Limited Partner.

In June 1998, RNR, through its general partner, entered into a construction loan agreement, note and mortgage in the principal amount of $990,000. From June 25, 1998 through Mar. 13, 2000, the bank disbursed the aggregate sum of $952,699, by transfers into RNR's bank account. All draws were approved by an architect, who certified that the work had progressed as indicated and that the quality of the work was in accordance with the construction contract. No representative of RNR objected to any draw of funds or asserted that the amounts disbursed were not associated with the construction of the house.

RNR defaulted under the terms of the note and mortgage by failing to make payments due in July 2000 and all monthly payments due thereafter. The Bank filed a complaint seeking foreclosure. RNR filed an answer and affirmative defenses. In its first affirmative defense, RNR alleged that the Bank had failed to review the limitations on the general partner's authority in RNR's limited partnership agreement. RNR asserted that the Bank had negligently failed to investigate and to realize that the general partner had no authority to execute notes, a mortgage and a construction loan agreement and was estopped from foreclosing. The Bank filed a motion for summary judgment with supporting affidavits attesting to the amounts due and owing and the amount of disbursements under the loan.

In opposition to the summary judgment motion, RNR filed the affidavit of Stephen E. Waltz, the president one of RNR's limited partners, S.E. Waltz, Inc. In that affidavit, Mr. Waltz stated that the partners anticipated that RNR would need to finance the construction of the residence, but that paragraph 2.2(b) of the partnership agreement limited the amount of any loan the general partner could obtain on behalf of RNR to an amount that would not exceed by more than 10% the approved budget on any one line item or exceed the aggregate approved budget by more than 5%, unless the general partner received the prior written consent of the limited partners. Waltz alleged that the limited partners understood and orally agreed that the general partner would seek financing in the approximate amount of $650,000. Further, Waltz stated:

> Even though the limited partners had orally agreed to this amount, a written consent was never memorialized, and to my surprise, the [Bank], either through its employees or attorney, ... never requested the same from any of the limited partners at any time prior to [or] after the closing on the loan from the [Bank] to RNR.

Waltz alleged that the partners learned in the spring of 2000 that, instead of obtaining a loan for $650,000, Roeger had obtained a loan for $990,000, which was secured by RNR's property. He stated that the limited partners did not consent to Roeger obtaining a loan from the Bank in the amount of $990,000 either orally or in writing and that the limited partners were never contacted by the Bank as to whether they had consented to a loan amount of $990,000.

RNR asserts that a copy of the limited partnership agreement was maintained at its offices. Nevertheless, the record contains no copy of an Approved Budget of the partnership or any evidence that would show that a copy of RNR's partnership agreement or any partnership budget was given to the Bank or that any notice of the general partner's restricted authority was provided to the Bank.

A hearing on the motion for summary judgment was held, however, a transcript of that hearing is not contained in the record. Thereafter, the trial court entered a summary final judgment of foreclosure in favor of the Bank. The foreclosure sale has been stayed pending the outcome of this appeal....

Apparent Authority of the General Partner

Although the agency concept of apparent authority was applied to partnerships under the common law, see, e.g., Taylor v. Cummer Lumber Co., 59 Fla. 638, 52 So. 614, 616 (Fla. 1910), in Florida the extent to which the partnership is bound by the acts of a partner acting within the apparent authority is now governed by statute. Section 620.8301(1), Florida Statutes (2000), a part of the Florida Revised Uniform Partnership Act (FRUPA), provides:

> Each partner is an agent of the partnership for the purpose of its business. An act of a partner, including the execution of an instrument in the partnership name, for apparently carrying on in the ordinary scope of partnership business or business of the kind carried on by the partnership, in the geographic area in which the partnership operates, binds the partnership unless the partner had no authority to act for the partnership in the particular manner and the person with whom the partner was dealing knew or had received notification that the partner lacked authority.

Thus, even if a general partner's actual authority is restricted by the terms of the partnership agreement, the general partner possesses the apparent authority to bind the partnership in the ordinary course of partnership business or in the business of the kind carried on by the partnership, unless the third party "knew or had received a notification that the partner lacked authority." Id. "Knowledge" and "notice" under FRUPA are defined in section 620.8102. That section provides that "[a] person knows a fact if the person has actual knowledge of the fact." § 620.8102(1), Fla. Stat. (2000). Further, a third party has notice of a fact if that party "(a) knows of the fact; (b) has received notification of the fact; or (c) has reason to know the fact exists from all other facts known to the person at the time in question." § 620.8102(2), Fla. Stat. (2000). Finally, under section 620.8303 a partnership may file a statement of partnership authority setting forth any restrictions in a general partner's authority.

Commentators have described the purpose of these knowledge and notice provisions, as follows:

> Under RUPA, the term knew is confined to actual knowledge, which is cognitive awareness.... Therefore, despite the similarity in language, RUPA provides greater protection [than the Uniform Partnership Act (UPA)] to third persons dealing with partners, who may rely on the partner's apparent authority absent actual knowledge or notification of a restriction in this regard. RUPA effects a slight reallocation of the risk of unauthorized agency power in favor of third parties. That is consistent with notions of the expanded liability of principals since the UPA was drafted.
>
> RUPA attempts to balance its shift toward greater protection of third parties by providing several new ways for partners to protect themselves against unauthorized actions by a rogue partner. First, the partnership may notify a third party of a partner's lack of authority. Such notification is effective upon receipt, whether or not the third party actually learns of it. More significantly, the partnership may file a statement of partnership authority restricting a partner's authority.

Rule = 3rd party must have notice or knowledge of person's lack of authority to act on partnership

Donald J. Weidner & John W. Larson, *The Revised Uniform Partnership Act: The Reporters' Overview*, 49 Bus. Law 1, 31-32 (1993) (footnotes omitted). "Absent actual knowledge, third parties have no duty to inspect the partnership agreement or inquire otherwise to ascertain the extent of a partner's actual authority in the ordinary course of business, ... even if they have some reason to question it." Id. at 32 n.200. The apparent authority provisions of section 620.8301(1), reflect a policy by the drafters that "the risk of loss from partner misconduct more appropriately belongs on the partnership than on third parties who do not knowingly participate in or take advantage of the misconduct ..." J. Dennis [Hynes], *Notice and Notification Under the Revised Uniform Partnership Act: Some Suggested Changes*, 2 J. Small & Emerging Bus. L. 299, 308 (1998).

Analysis

Under section 620.8301(1), the determination of whether a partner is acting with authority to bind the partnership involves a two-step analysis. The first step is to determine whether the partner purporting to bind the partnership apparently is carrying on the partnership business in the usual way or a business of the kind carried on by the partnership. An affirmative answer on this step ends the inquiry, unless it is shown that the person with whom the partner is dealing actually knew or had received a notification that the partner lacked authority. Here, it is undisputed that, in entering into the loan, the general partner was carrying on the business of RNR in the usual way. The dispositive question in this appeal is whether there are issues of material fact as to whether the Bank had actual knowledge or notice of restrictions on the general partner's authority.

RNR argues that, as a result of the restrictions on the general partner's authority in the partnership agreement, the Bank had constructive knowledge of the restrictions and was obligated to inquire as to the general partner's specific authority to bind RNR in the construction loan. We cannot agree. Under section 620.8301, the Bank could rely on the general partner's apparent authority, unless it had actual knowledge or notice of restrictions on that authority. While the RNR partners may have agreed upon restrictions that would limit the general partner to borrowing no more than $650,000 on behalf of the partnership, RNR does not contend and nothing before us would show that the Bank had actual knowledge or notice of any restrictions on the general partner's authority. Here, the partnership could have protected itself by filing a statement pursuant to section 620.8303 or by providing notice to the Bank of the specific restrictions on the authority of the general partner....

Because there is no disputed issue of fact concerning whether the Bank had actual knowledge or notice of restrictions on the general partner's authority to borrow, summary judgment was proper.

AFFIRMED.

MINER AND WOLF, JJ., CONCUR.

Section 6: Control

Another central question in the legal study of any business organization is who can control the organization. This question is linked to questions of authority, because binding an organization to a contract does in fact reflect a significant power. But the question of control is deeper: when the partners in a general partnership disagree, who wins? Another way to conceive this problem is: When there are disputes over the *actual* authority of partners, how are those disputes resolved?

As we have seen, all partnerships are formed by some agreement to operate a business as co-owners. This agreement might be formal or informal, written or oral. It is ordinarily the starting point for questions of control, because parties can ordinarily provide in advance for potential disputes that they have foreseen.

RUPA provides a default rule that governs the partnership when the partnership agreement is otherwise silent as to questions of control.

Revised Uniform Partnership Act § 401: Partner's Rights and Duties

...

(j) A difference arising as to a matter in the ordinary course of business of a partnership may be decided by a majority of the partners. An act outside the ordinary course of business of a partnership and an amendment to the partnership agreement may be undertaken only with the consent of all of the partners....

Comment

...

11. Subsection (j) continues with one important clarification the UPA Section 18(h) scheme of allocating management authority among the partners. In the absence of an agreement to the contrary, matters arising in the ordinary course of the business may be decided by a majority of the partners. Amendments to the partnership agreement and matters outside the ordinary course of the partnership business require unanimous consent of the partners. Although the text of the UPA is silent regarding extraordinary matters, courts have generally required the consent of all partners for those matters. See, e.g., *Paciaroni v. Crane*, 408 A.2d 946 (Del. Ch. 1989); *Thomas v. Marvin E. Jewell & Co.*, 232 Neb. 261, 440 N.W.2d 437 (1989); *Duell v. Hancock*, 83 A.D.2d 762, 443 N.Y.S.2d 490 (1981).

It is not intended that subsection (j) embrace a claim for an objection to a partnership decision that is not discovered until after the fact. There is no cause of action based on that after-the-fact second-guessing.

Summers v. Dooley

481 P.2d 318 (Idaho 1971)

DONALDSON, J.

This lawsuit, tried in the district court, involves a claim by one partner against the other for $6,000. The complaining partner asserts that he has been required to pay out more than $11,000 in expenses without any reimbursement from either the partnership funds or his partner. The expenditure in question was incurred by the complaining partner (John Summers, plaintiff-appellant) for the purpose of hiring an additional employee. The trial court denied him any relief except for ordering that he be entitled to one half $966.72 which it found to be a legitimate partnership expense.

The pertinent facts leading to this lawsuit are as follows. Summers entered a partnership agreement with Dooley (defendant-respondent) in 1958 for the purpose of operating a trash collection business. The business was operated by the two men and when either was unable to work, the non-working partner provided a replacement at his own expense. In 1962, Dooley became unable to work and, at his own expense, hired an employee to take his place. In July, 1966, Summers approached his partner Dooley regarding the hiring of an additional employee but Dooley refused. Nevertheless, on his own initiative, Summers hired the man and paid him out of his own pocket. Dooley, upon discovering that Summers had hired an additional man, objected, stating that he did not feel additional labor was necessary and refused to pay for the new employee out of the partnership funds. Summers continued to operate the business using the third man and in October of 1967 instituted suit in the district court for $6,000 against his partner, the gravamen of the complaint being that Summers has been required to pay out more than $11,000 in expenses, incurred in the hiring of the additional man, without any reimbursement from either the partnership funds or his partner. After trial before the court, sitting without a jury, Summers was granted only partial relief[6] and he has appealed. He urges in essence that the trial court erred by failing to conclude that he should be reimbursed for expenses and costs connected in the employment of extra help in the partnership business.

The principal thrust of appellant's contention is that in spite of the fact that one of the two partners refused to consent to the hiring of additional help, nonetheless, the non-consenting partner retained profits earned by the labors of the third man and therefore the non-consenting partner should be estopped from denying the need and value of the employee, and has by his behavior ratified the act of the other partner who hired the additional man.

The issue presented for decision by this appeal is whether an equal partner in a two man partnership has the authority to hire a new employee in disregard of the objection of the other partner and then attempt to charge the dissenting partner with the costs incurred as a result of his unilateral decision.

The State of Idaho has enacted specific statutes with respect to the legal concept known as "partnership." Therefore any solution of partnership problems should logically begin with an application of the relevant code provision.

In the instant case the record indicates that although Summers requested his partner Dooley to agree to the hiring of a third man, such requests were not honored. In fact Dooley made it clear that he was "voting no" with regard to the hiring of an additional employee.

An application of the relevant statutory provisions and pertinent case law to the factual situation presented by the instant case indicates that the trial court was correct in its disposal of the issue since a majority of the partners did not consent to the hiring of the third man. I.C. § 53-318(8) provides:

> "Any difference arising as to ordinary matters connected with the partnership business may be decided by a *majority of the partners* * * *." (emphasis supplied)

It is the opinion of this Court that the preceding statute is of a mandatory rather than permissive nature. This conclusion is based upon the following reasoning. Whether a statute is mandatory or directory does not depend upon its form, but upon the intention of the legislature, to be ascertained from a consideration of the entire act, its nature, its object, and the consequences that would result from construing it one way or the other.

6. The trial court did award Summers one half of $966.72, which it found to be a legitimate partnership expense. [Court's footnote.—ed.]

The intent of the legislature may be implied from the language used, or inferred on grounds of policy or reasonableness. A careful reading of the statutory provision indicates that subsection 5 bestows *equal rights in the management and conduct of the partnership business* upon all of the partners.[7] The concept of equality between partners with respect to management of business affairs is a central theme and recurs throughout the Uniform Partnership law, I.C. § 53-301 et seq., which has been enacted in this jurisdiction. Thus the only reasonable interpretation of I.C. § 53-318(8) is that business differences must be decided by a majority of the partners provided no other agreement between the partners speaks to the issues.

A noted scholar has dealt precisely with the issue to be decided.

> "* * * if the partners are equally divided, those who forbid a change must have their way." Walter B. Lindley, A Treatise on the Law of Partnership, Ch. II, § III, para. 24-8, p. 403 (1924). See also, W. Shumaker, A Treatise on the Law of Partnership, § 97, p. 266.

....

In the case at bar one of the partners continually voiced objection to the hiring of the third man. He did not sit idly by and acquiesce in the actions of his partner. Under these circumstances it is manifestly unjust to permit recovery of an expense which was incurred individually and not for the benefit of the partnership but rather for the benefit of one partner.

Judgment affirmed. Costs to respondent.

National Biscuit Co. v. Stroud

249 N.C. 467 (N.C. 1959)

PARKER, J.

C. N. Stroud and Earl Freeman entered into a general partnership to sell groceries under the firm name of Stroud's Food Center. There is nothing in the agreed statement of facts to indicate or suggest that Freeman's power and authority as a general partner were in any way restricted or limited by the articles of partnership in respect to the ordinary and legitimate business of the partnership. Certainly, the purchase and sale of bread were ordinary and legitimate business of Stroud's Food Center during its continuance as a going concern.

Several months prior to February 1956 Stroud advised plaintiff that he personally would not be responsible for any additional bread sold by plaintiff to Stroud's Food Center. After such notice to plaintiff, it from 6 February 1956 to 25 February 1956, at the request of Freeman, sold and delivered bread in the amount of $171.04 to Stroud's Food Center.

In Johnson v. Bernheim, 76 N.C. 139, this Court said: "A and B are general partners to do some given business; the partnership is, by operation of law, a power to each to bind the partnership in any manner legitimate to the business. If one partner go to a third person to buy an article on time for the partnership, the other partner cannot prevent it by writing to the third person not to sell to him on time; or, if one party attempt

7. In the absence of an agreement to the contrary.... [T]here is no such agreement and thus I.C. § 53-318(5) and each of the other subsections are applicable. [Court's footnote.—ed.]

to buy for cash, the other has no right to require that it shall be on time. And what is true in regard to buying is true in regard to selling. What either partner does with a third person is binding on the partnership. It is otherwise where the partnership is not general, but is upon special terms, as that purchases and sales must be with and for cash. There the power to each is special, in regard to all dealings with third persons at least who have notice of the terms." There is contrary authority: 68 C.J.S., Partnership, pp. 578-579. However, this text of C.J.S. does not mention the effect of the provisions of the Uniform Partnership Act.

The General Assembly of North Carolina in 1941 enacted a Uniform Partnership Act, which became effective 15 March 1941. G.S. Ch. 59, Partnership, Art. 2.

G.S. 59-39 is entitled PARTNER AGENT OF PARTNERSHIP AS TO PARTNERSHIP BUSINESS, and subsection (1) reads: "Every partner is an agent of the partnership for the purpose of its business, and the act of every partner, including the execution in the partnership name of any instrument, for apparently carrying on in the usual way the business of the partnership of which he is a member binds the partnership, unless the partner so acting has in fact no authority to act for the partnership in the particular matter, and the person with whom he is dealing has knowledge of the fact that he has no such authority." G.S. 59-39(4) states: "No act of a partner in contravention of a restriction on authority shall bind the partnership to persons having knowledge of the restriction."

G.S. 59-45 provides that "all partners are jointly and severally liable for the acts and obligations of the partnership."

G.S. 59-48 is captioned RULES DETERMINING RIGHTS AND DUTIES OF PARTNERS. Subsection (e) thereof reads: "All partners have equal rights in the management and conduct of the partnership business." Subsection (h) thereof is as follows: "Any difference arising as to ordinary matters connected with the partnership business may be decided by a majority of the partners; but no act in contravention of any agreement between the partners may be done rightfully without the consent of all the partners."

Freeman as a general partner with Stroud, with no restrictions on his authority to act within the scope of the partnership business so far as the agreed statement of facts shows, had under the Uniform Partnership Act "equal rights in the management and conduct of the partnership business." Under G.S. 59-48(h) Stroud, his co-partner, could not restrict the power and authority of Freeman to buy bread for the partnership as a going concern, for such a purchase was an "ordinary matter connected with the partnership business," for the purpose of its business and within its scope, because in the very nature of things Stroud was not, and could not be, a majority of the partners. Therefore, Freeman's purchases of bread from plaintiff for Stroud's Food Center as a going concern bound the partnership and his co-partner Stroud. The quoted provisions of our Uniform Partnership Act, in respect to the particular facts here, are in accord with the principle of law stated in Johnson v. Bernheim, supra; same case 86 N.C. 339.

In Crane on Partnership, 2nd Ed., p. 277, it is said: "In cases of an even division of the partners as to whether or not an act within the scope of the business should be done, of which disagreement a third person has knowledge, it seems that logically no restriction can be placed upon the power to act. The partnership being a going concern, activities within the scope of the business should not be limited, save by the expressed will of the majority deciding a disputed question; half of the members are not a majority."

Sladen v. Lance, 151 N.C. 492, 66 S.E. 449, is distinguishable. That was a case where the terms of the partnership imposed special restrictions on the power of the partner who made the contract.

At the close of business on 25 February 1956 Stroud and Freeman by agreement dissolved the partnership. By their dissolution agreement all of the partnership assets, including cash on hand, bank deposits and all accounts receivable, with a few exceptions, were assigned to Stroud, who bound himself by such written dissolution agreement to liquidate the firm's assets and discharge its liabilities. It would seem a fair inference from the agreed statement of facts that the partnership got the benefit of the bread sold and delivered by plaintiff to Stroud's Food Center, at Freeman's request, from 6 February 1956 to 25 February 1956. But whether it did or not, Freeman's acts, as stated above, bound the partnership and Stroud.

The judgment of the court below is

Affirmed.

Section 7: Partnership Property

RUPA, along with the entity theory of partnerships, greatly simplifies the legal treatment of partnerships' ownership of property. Historically (under UPA and the aggregate theory), the precise legal status of property that was logically owned and used by a partnership—for example, a vehicle or a piece of real estate—was messy. Did the partners collectively own the property? The UPA adopted a property-law notion called "tenancy in partnership" (analogous to other joint estates, like "joint tenancy" or "tenancy by the entirety") to address this problem, laying out a series of complex interfaces between partnership law and property law in order to let partnerships function the way that partners and lawyers expected them to be able to function. See Melvin Aron Eisenberg, CORPORATIONS AND OTHER BUSINESS ORGANIZATIONS 68 (9th ed. 2005).

Under modern law, the answer is simple: partnerships simply can own real and personal property in their own name. They can buy it, possess it, and sell it just as individuals can. RUPA § 203 simply says: "Property acquired by a partnership is property of the partnership and not of the partners individually."[8] The intent of this provision is to make it clear that individual partners do not directly have any ownership rights in a partnership's property.

The major practical questions involving partnership property under modern law involve potential ambiguities concerning whether an individual partner or a partnership owns a particular piece of property. Obviously, this is less of a concern with types of property, like real estate, that are ordinarily the subject of more detailed contracts and of public recording of property rights. With personal property that is more informally purchased, however, confusion may arise. RUPA addresses potential confusions by adopting a variety of presumptions.

---

8. Perhaps somewhat redundantly, RUPA § 501 adds: "A partner is not a co-owner of partnership property and has no interest in partnership property which can be transferred, either voluntarily or involuntarily."

Revised Uniform Partnership Act (1997) § 204: When Property Is Partnership Property

(a) Property is partnership property if acquired in the name of:

(1) the partnership; or

(2) one or more partners with an indication in the instrument transferring title to the property of the person's capacity as a partner or of the existence of a partnership but without an indication of the name of the partnership.

(b) Property is acquired in the name of the partnership by a transfer to:

(1) the partnership in its name; or

(2) one or more partners in their capacity as partners in the partnership, if the name of the partnership is indicated in the instrument transferring title to the property.

(c) Property is presumed to be partnership property if purchased with partnership assets, even if not acquired in the name of the partnership or of one or more partners with an indication in the instrument transferring title to the property of the person's capacity as a partner or of the existence of a partnership.

(d) Property acquired in the name of one or more of the partners, without an indication in the instrument transferring title to the property of the person's capacity as a partner or of the existence of a partnership and without use of partnership assets, is presumed to be separate property, even if used for partnership purposes.

Comment ...

3. Ultimately, it is the intention of the partners that controls whether property belongs to the partnership or to one or more of the partners in their individual capacities, at least as among the partners themselves. RUPA sets forth two rebuttable presumptions that apply when the partners have failed to express their intent.

First, under subsection (c), property purchased with partnership funds is presumed to be partnership property, notwithstanding the name in which title is held. The presumption is intended to apply if partnership credit is used to obtain financing, as well as the use of partnership cash or property for payment. Unlike the rule in subsection (b), under which property is **deemed** to be partnership property if the partnership's name or the partner's capacity as a partner is disclosed in the instrument of conveyance, subsection (c) raises only a **presumption** that the property is partnership property if it is purchased with partnership assets.

That presumption is also subject to an important caveat. Under Section 302(b), partnership property held in the name of individual partners, without an indication of their capacity as partners or of the existence of a partnership, that is transferred by the partners in whose name title is held to a purchaser without knowledge that it is partnership property is free of any claims of the partnership.

Second, under subsection (d), property acquired in the name of one or more of the partners, without an indication of their capacity as partners and without use of partnership funds or credit, is presumed to be the partners' separate property, even if used for partnership purposes. In effect, it is presumed in that case that only the use of the property is contributed to the partnership.

4. Generally, under RUPA, partners and third parties dealing with partnerships will be able to rely on the record to determine whether property is owned by the partnership. The exception is property purchased with partnership funds without any reference to the partnership in the title documents. The inference concerning the partners' intent from the use of partnership funds outweighs any inference from the State of the title, subject to the overriding reliance interest in the case of a purchaser without notice of the partnership's interest. This allocation of risk should encourage the partnership to eliminate doubt about ownership by putting title in the partnership.

Section 8: Accounting

Note on Partnership Accounts

We have already seen that a partner, by default, has authority and a voice in the management of the partnership. Given that a general partnership is a for-profit endeavor, another significant reason to be a partner is to share in the partnership's profits. As we saw in section 2, sharing profits is often a key feature that makes someone a partner in a general partnership.

To understand how partners share profits and losses, and otherwise keep track of money, it is important to understand a basic feature of partnership accounting known as the *partnership account* (sometimes called a *capital account*). RUPA § 401 provides: "Each partner is deemed to have an account...."[9] By contributing capital to the partnership, partners can effectively deposit money into the account; under RUPA, the account is "credited with an amount equal to the money plus the value of any other property ... the partner contributes to the partnership and the partner's share of the partnership profits." RUPA § 401(a).

Such contributions, often called *capital contributions*, are often one thing that allows the partnership to start up its operations. For example, three people might get together and agree to operate a restaurant, but doing so might require $270,000 in start-up costs (for example, to purchase a franchise or to secure a lease, renovate a kitchen, and hire the initial staff). The partners can contribute the $270,000 in any manner they agree—equally or not—and each partner's contribution is simply credited to the partner's account. Thus, if *A* contributes $90,000, her partnership account starts with a positive balance of $90,000.

RUPA's default rules treat labor and capital differently. Thus, in a two-person partnership, if the "money partner" contributes $100,000 and the "labor partner" agrees to operate the business for a year, the money partner starts off with a partnership account of $100,000 and the labor partner starts off with a partnership account of $0. The parties can adjust this by agreement. When we discuss partnership dissolution, we will evaluate the degree to which this default rule comports with the parties' expectations.

---

9. Like most other provisions in RUPA, its mechanisms for partnership accounting are default provisions that the parties can override as they see fit. As the official comment to RUPA § 401 explains, "In the absence of another system of partnership accounts, these rules establish a rudimentary system of accounts for the partnership."

Note on Profit and Loss Sharing

At the end of each accounting period (usually a year), a business will have either profits or losses (unless, of course, it exactly breaks even). For example, as a simplified example, imagine that a business that starts out with $270,000 finds it has $300,000 in its bank account at the end of its first year. The business has made a profit of $30,000. Similarly, the business might experience a loss. For example, suppose it spends the full $270,000 that it started with (on commercial leases, equipment, and employees) and ends up with revenue of $230,000 after the first year. In that event, it has suffered a loss of $40,000.

Partners can agree among themselves to split profits and losses however they see fit. For example, they might decide that those who put in more money, or more effort, will receive a greater share of the profits. They might agree that one of them will, for a variety of reasons, agree to experience a greater portion of the losses.

RUPA provides two simple default rules to cover profits and losses.

First, "[e]ach partner is entitled to an equal share of the partnership profits." RUPA §401(b). Note that this default specifies equality regardless of the capital contributions, or other contributions, of the partners. If the partners want a different arrangement, they need to specify it; the presumption is that, as partners, they want this sort of equality.

Second, each partner "is chargeable with a share of the partnership losses in proportion to the partner's share of the profits." *Id.* That is, the default rule is that the partners share losses however they share gains—by default, equally, but if the partners adjust their percentages of gains, the percentages of losses follow automatically by default.

Thus, in a partnership with five partners, each partner will receive 20% of the profits and be responsible for 20% of the losses by default. If the partnership agreement says "*A* will receive 60% of the profits and *B*, *C*, *D*, and *E* will each receive 10% of the profits," under RUPA this means *A* will also be responsible for 60% of the partnership's losses and *B*, *C*, *D*, and *E* will each be responsible for 10% of the losses.

At the end of each accounting period, the partnership's profits and losses are credited to (or debited from) each partner's account.

Problem 1

Arthur Clennam and Danielle Doyce enter into a partnership to manufacture and sell custom-grown fur necklaces. They agree to split the work of the partnership equally. They will each put $50,000 cash into the business. Clennam will also contribute several computers he owns and a small piece of manufacturing equipment, together worth $18,000 in total. The parties agree that Clennam will receive 60% of the profits and Doyce will receive 40% of the profits.

After the first year, the partnership has spent the full $100,000 balance and has earned no income, largely because nobody wishes to buy custom-grown fur necklaces. What is the state of the parties' partnership accounts after the first year? What property does the partnership own?

Problem 2

Clennam and Doyce agree to form a partnership. Clennam contributes $18,000 worth of equipment; Doyce contributes nothing but agrees to work full time on partnership business. Three weeks later, the parties agree that it was a bad idea to go into business and that they should dissolve the partnership. By default, what will the parties own?

Note on Distributions

A routine business decision that partnerships need to make is whether to retain their profits or to distribute them to the partners. Economically speaking, this decision will (for theoretically rational parties) turn on the relative value of the money to the partners and the partnership. For example, if the partnership has a significant opportunity to grow and needs funds to take advantage of this opportunity, we might expect the partners to avoid distributing profits for the time being.

Money (or property) other than profits can be distributed. For example, a business may decide to distribute back to partners startup funds that it has been unable to invest or apply.

As the official comment to RUPA explains, "Absent an agreement to the contrary, ... a partner does not have a right to receive a current distribution of the profits credited to his account, the interim distribution of profits being a matter arising in the ordinary course of business to be decided by majority vote of the partners." RUPA §401 cmt. 3. Moreover, distributions need not be made equally; distributions to an individual partner may simply be deducted from that partner's capital account.

Note on the Basics of Partnership Taxation

Partnership taxation is a significant, sophisticated topic in business law. For now, it may be helpful to keep in mind two basic principles. First, taxation of a partnership depends on the partnership's actual profits and losses, not on distributions. Second, ordinarily, a partnership does not pay federal income tax on its own; it declares its profits and losses but then "passes through" that information to its partners; the income and expenses are then properly reported on the tax returns of the individual partners. Thus, a partnership that declares $20,000 in taxable profits per partner leads those partners to experience a $20,000 increase in their personal taxable incomes, regardless of what the partnership distributes.

These principles can lead to problems if partners do not negotiate a right to receive distributions associated with profits, for they may owe significant personal taxes on partnership profits and have trouble meeting this tax liability without distributions from the partnership.

Section 9: A Partner's Fiduciary Duties

As agents of the partnership, the partners have duties of loyalty, care, and good faith to the partnership and to each other.

Revised Uniform Partnership Act (1997) § 404: General Standards of Partner's Conduct

(a) The only fiduciary duties a partner owes to the partnership and the other partners are the duty of loyalty and the duty of care set forth in subsections (b) and (c).

(b) A partner's duty of loyalty to the partnership and the other partners is limited to the following:

(1) to account to the partnership and hold as trustee for it any property, profit, or benefit derived by the partner in the conduct and winding up of the partnership business or derived from a use by the partner of partnership property, including the appropriation of a partnership opportunity;

(2) to refrain from dealing with the partnership in the conduct or winding up of the partnership business as or on behalf of a party having an interest adverse to the partnership; and

(3) to refrain from competing with the partnership in the conduct of the partnership business before the dissolution of the partnership.

(c) A partner's duty of care to the partnership and the other partners in the conduct and winding up of the partnership business is limited to refraining from engaging in grossly negligent or reckless conduct, intentional misconduct, or a knowing violation of law.

(d) A partner shall discharge the duties to the partnership and the other partners under this [Act] or under the partnership agreement and exercise any rights consistently with the obligation of good faith and fair dealing.

(e) A partner does not violate a duty or obligation under this [Act] or under the partnership agreement merely because the partner's conduct furthers the partner's own interest.

(f) A partner may lend money to and transact other business with the partnership, and as to each loan or transaction the rights and obligations of the partner are the same as those of a person who is not a partner, subject to other applicable law.

(g) This section applies to a person winding up the partnership business as the personal or legal representative of the last surviving partner as if the person were a partner.

Comment

...

Arguably, the term "fiduciary" is inappropriate when used to describe the duties of a partner because a partner may legitimately pursue self-interest (see Section 404(e)) and not solely the interest of the partnership and the other partners, as must a true trustee. Nevertheless, partners have long been characterized as fiduciaries. See, e.g., *Meinhard v. Salmon*, 249 N.Y. 458, 463, 164 N.E. 545, 546 (1928) (Cardozo, J.). Indeed, the law of partnership reflects the broader law of principal and agent, under which every agent is a fiduciary. See Restatement (Second) of Agency § 13 (1957).

...

Subsection (c) is new and establishes the duty of care that partners owe to the partnership and to the other partners. There is no statutory duty of care under the UPA, although a common law duty of care is recognized by some courts. See, e.g., *Rosenthal v. Rosenthal*, 543 A.2d 348, 352 (Me. 1988) (duty of care limited to acting in a manner that does not constitute gross negligence or willful misconduct). The standard of care imposed by RUPA is that of gross negligence, which is the standard generally recognized by the courts.

. . .

Subsection (e) is new and deals expressly with a very basic issue on which the UPA is silent. A partner as such is not a trustee and is not held to the same standards as a trustee. Subsection (e) makes clear that a partner's conduct is not deemed to be improper merely because it serves the partner's own individual interest. That admonition has particular application to the duty of loyalty and the obligation of good faith and fair dealing. It underscores the partner's rights as an owner and principal in the enterprise, which must always be balanced against his duties and obligations as an agent and fiduciary. For example, a partner who, with consent, owns a shopping center may, under subsection (e), legitimately vote against a proposal by the partnership to open a competing shopping center.

Revised Uniform Partnership Act (1997) § 103: Effect of Partnership Agreement; Nonwaivable Provisions

(a) Except as otherwise provided in subsection (b), relations among the partners and between the partners and the partnership are governed by the partnership agreement. To the extent the partnership agreement does not otherwise provide, this [Act] governs relations among the partners and between the partners and the partnership.

(b) The partnership agreement may not:

. . .

(3) eliminate the duty of loyalty under Section 404(b) or 603(b)(3), but:

(i) the partnership agreement may identify specific types or categories of activities that do not violate the duty of loyalty, if not manifestly unreasonable; or

(ii) all of the partners or a number or percentage specified in the partnership agreement may authorize or ratify, after full disclosure of all material facts, a specific act or transaction that otherwise would violate the duty of loyalty;

(4) unreasonably reduce the duty of care under Section 404(c) or 603(b)(3);

(5) eliminate the obligation of good faith and fair dealing under Section 404(d), but the partnership agreement may prescribe the standards by which the performance of the obligation is to be measured, if the standards are not manifestly unreasonable....

Meinhard v. Salmon

249 N.Y. 458 (N.Y. 1928)

CARDOZO, J.

On April 10, 1902, Louisa M. Gerry leased to the defendant Walter J. Salmon the premises known as the Hotel Bristol at the northwest corner of Forty-second street and Fifth avenue in the city of New York. The lease was for a term of twenty years, commencing May 1, 1902, and ending April 30, 1922. The lessee undertook to change the hotel building for use as shops and offices at a cost of $200,000. Alterations and additions were to be accretions to the land.

Salmon, while in course of treaty with the lessor as to the execution of the lease, was in course of treaty with Meinhard, the plaintiff, for the necessary funds. The result was a joint venture with terms embodied in a writing. Meinhard was to pay to Salmon half of the moneys requisite to reconstruct, alter, manage and operate the property. Salmon was to pay to Meinhard 40 per cent of the net profits for the first five years of the lease and 50 per cent for the years thereafter. If there were losses, each party was to bear them equally. Salmon, however, was to have sole power to "manage, lease, underlet and operate" the building. There were to be certain pre-emptive rights for each in the contingency of death.

The two were coadventurers, subject to fiduciary duties akin to those of partners. As to this we are all agreed. The heavier weight of duty rested, however, upon Salmon. He was a coadventurer with Meinhard, but he was manager as well. During the early years of the enterprise, the building, reconstructed, was operated at a loss. If the relation had then ended, Meinhard as well as Salmon would have carried a heavy burden. Later the profits became large with the result that for each of the investors there came a rich return. For each, the venture had its phases of fair weather and of foul. The two were in it jointly, for better or for worse.

When the lease was near its end, Elbridge T. Gerry had become the owner of the reversion. He owned much other property in the neighborhood, one lot adjoining the Bristol Building on Fifth avenue and four lots on Forty-second street. He had a plan to lease the entire tract for a long term to some one who would destroy the buildings then existing, and put up another in their place. In the latter part of 1921, he submitted such a project to several capitalists and dealers. He was unable to carry it through with any of them. Then, in January, 1922, with less than four months of the lease to run, he approached the defendant Salmon. The result was a new lease to the Midpoint Realty Company, which is owned and controlled by Salmon, a lease covering the whole tract, and involving a huge outlay. The term is to be twenty years, but successive covenants for renewal will extend it to a maximum of eighty years at the will of either party. The existing buildings may remain unchanged for seven years. They are then to be torn down, and a new building to cost $3,000,000 is to be placed upon the site. The rental, which under the Bristol lease was only $55,000, is to be from $350,000 to $475,000 for the properties so combined. Salmon personally guaranteed the performance by the lessee of the covenants of the new lease until such time as the new building had been completed and fully paid for.

The lease between Gerry and the Midpoint Realty Company was signed and delivered on January 25, 1922. Salmon had not told Meinhard anything about it. Whatever his motive may have been, he had kept the negotiations to himself. Meinhard was not informed even of the bare existence of a project. The first that he knew of it was in February when the lease was an accomplished fact. He then made demand on the defendants that the lease be held in trust as an asset of the venture, making offer upon the trial to share the personal obligations incidental to the guaranty. The demand was followed by refusal, and later by this suit. A referee gave judgment for the plaintiff, limiting the plaintiff's interest in the lease, however, to 25 per cent. The limitation was on the theory that the plaintiff's equity was to be restricted to one-half of so much of the value of the lease as was contributed or represented by the occupation of the Bristol site. Upon cross-appeals to the Appellate Division, the judgment was modified so as to enlarge the equitable interest to one-half of the whole lease. With this enlargement of plaintiff's interest, there went, of course, a corresponding enlargement of his attendant obligations. The case is now here on an appeal by the defendants.

Joint adventurers, like copartners, owe to one another, while the enterprise continues, the duty of the finest loyalty. Many forms of conduct permissible in a workaday world for those acting at arm's length, are forbidden to those bound by fiduciary ties. A trustee is held to something stricter than the morals of the market place. Not honesty alone, but the punctilio of an honor the most sensitive, is then the standard of behavior. As to this there has developed a tradition that is unbending and inveterate. Uncompromising rigidity has been the attitude of courts of equity when petitioned to undermine the rule of undivided loyalty by the "disintegrating erosion" of particular exceptions. Only thus has the level of conduct for fiduciaries been kept at a level higher than that trodden by the crowd. It will not consciously be lowered by any judgment of this court.

The owner of the reversion, Mr. Gerry, had vainly striven to find a tenant who would favor his ambitious scheme of demolition and construction. Baffled in the search, he turned to the defendant Salmon in possession of the Bristol, the keystone of the project. He figured to himself beyond a doubt that the man in possession would prove a likely customer. To the eye of an observer, Salmon held the lease as owner in his own right, for himself and no one else. In fact he held it as a fiduciary, for himself and another, sharers in a common venture. If this fact had been proclaimed, if the lease by its terms had run in favor of a partnership, Mr. Gerry, we may fairly assume, would have laid before the partners, and not merely before one of them, his plan of reconstruction. The pre-emptive privilege, or, better, the pre-emptive opportunity, that was thus an incident of the enterprise, Salmon appropriated to himself in secrecy and silence. He might have warned Meinhard that the plan had been submitted, and that either would be free to compete for the award. If he had done this, we do not need to say whether he would have been under a duty, if successful in the competition, to hold the lease so acquired for the benefit of a venture then about to end, and thus prolong by indirection its responsibilities and duties. The trouble about his conduct is that he excluded his coadventurer from any chance to compete, from any chance to enjoy the opportunity for benefit that had come to him alone by virtue of his agency. This chance, if nothing more, he was under a duty to concede. The price of its denial is an extension of the trust at the option and for the benefit of the one whom he excluded.

No answer is it to say that the chance would have been of little value even if seasonably offered. Such a calculus of probabilities is beyond the science of the chancery. Salmon, the real estate operator, might have been preferred to Meinhard, the woolen merchant. On the other hand, Meinhard might have offered better terms, or reinforced his offer by alliance with the wealth of others. Perhaps he might even have persuaded the lessor to renew the Bristol lease alone, postponing for a time, in return for higher rentals, the improvement of adjoining lots. We know that even under the lease as made the time for the enlargement of the building was delayed for seven years. All these opportunities were cut away from him through another's intervention. He knew that Salmon was the manager. As the time drew near for the expiration of the lease, he would naturally assume from silence, if from nothing else, that the lessor was willing to extend it for a term of years, or at least to let it stand as a lease from year to year. Not impossibly the lessor would have done so, whatever his protestations of unwillingness, if Salmon had not given assent to a project more attractive. At all events, notice of termination, even if not necessary, might seem, not unreasonably, to be something to be looked for, if the business was over and another tenant was to enter. In the absence of such notice, the matter of an extension was one that would naturally be attended to by the manager of the enterprise, and not neglected altogether. At least, there was nothing in the situation to give warning to any one that while the lease was still in being, there had come to the manager an offer of extension which he had locked within his breast to be utilized by himself alone. The very fact that Salmon was in control with exclusive powers of direction charged him the more obviously with the duty of disclosure, since only through disclosure could opportunity be equalized. If he might cut off renewal by a purchase for his own benefit when four months were to pass before the lease would have an end, he might do so with equal right while there remained as many years. He might steal a march on his comrade under cover of the darkness, and then hold the captured ground. Loyalty and comradeship are not so easily abjured.

Little profit will come from a dissection of the precedents. None precisely similar is cited in the briefs of counsel. What is similar in many, or so it seems to us, is the animating principle. Authority is, of course, abundant that one partner may not appropriate to his own use a renewal of a lease, though its term is to begin at the expiration of the partnership (Mitchell v. Reed, 61 N. Y. 123; 84 N. Y. 556). The lease at hand with its many changes is not strictly a renewal. Even so, the standard of loyalty for those in trust relations is without the fixed divisions of a graduated scale. There is indeed a dictum in one of our decisions that a partner, though he may not renew a lease, may purchase the reversion if he acts openly and fairly (Anderson v. Lemon, 8 N. Y. 236; cf. White & Tudor, Leading Cases in Equity [9th ed.], vol. 2, p. 642; Bevan v. Webb, 1905, 1 Ch. 620; Griffith v. Owen, 1907, 1 Ch. 195, 204, 205). It is a dictum, and no more, for on the ground that he had acted slyly he was charged as a trustee. The holding is thus in favor of the conclusion that a purchase as well as a lease will succumb to the infection of secrecy and silence. Against the dictum in that case, moreover, may be set the opinion of Dwight, C., in Mitchell v. Read, where there is a dictum to the contrary (61 N. Y. at p. 143). To say that a partner is free without restriction to buy in the reversion of the property where the business is conducted is to say in effect that he may strip the good will of its chief element of value, since good will is largely dependent upon continuity of possession (Matter of Brown, 242 N. Y. 1, 7.) Equity refuses to confine within the bounds of classified transactions its precept of a loyalty that is undivided and unselfish. Certain at least it is that a "man obtaining his locus standi, and his opportunity for making such arrangements, by the position he occupies as a partner, is bound by his obligation to his co-partners in such dealings not to separate his interest from theirs, but, if he acquires any benefit, to communicate it to them" (Cassels v. Stewart, 6 App. Cas. 64, 73). Certain it is also that there may be no abuse of special opportunities growing out of a special trust as manager or agent (Matter of Biss, 1903, 2 Ch. 40; Clegg v. Edmondson, 8 D. M. & G. 787, 807). If conflicting inferences are possible as to abuse or opportunity, the trier of the facts must make the choice between them. There can be no revision in this court unless the choice is clearly wrong. It is no answer for the fiduciary to say "that he was not bound to risk his money as he did, or to go into the enterprise at all" (Beatty v.

Guggenheim Exploration Co., 225 N. Y. 380, 385). "He might have kept out of it altogether, but if he went in, he could not withhold from his employer the benefit of the bargain" (Beatty v. Guggenheim Exploration Co., supra). A constructive trust is then the remedial device through which preference of self is made subordinate to loyalty to others (Beatty v. Guggenheim Exploration Co., supra). Many and varied are its phases and occasions (Selwyn & Co. v. Waller, 212 N. Y. 507, 512; Robinson v. Jewett, 116 N. Y. 40; cf. Tournier v. Nat. Prov. & Union Bank, 1924, 1 K. B. 461).

We have no thought to hold that Salmon was guilty of a conscious purpose to defraud. Very likely he assumed in all good faith that with the approaching end of the venture he might ignore his coadventurer and take the extension for himself. He had given to the enterprise time and labor as well as money. He had made it a success. Meinhard, who had given money, but neither time nor labor, had already been richly paid. There might seem to be something grasping in his insistence upon more. Such recriminations are not unusual when coadventurers fall out. They are not without their force if conduct is to be judged by the common standards of competitors. That is not to say that they have pertinency here. Salmon had put himself in a position in which thought of self was to be renounced, however hard the abnegation. He was much more than a coadventurer. He was a managing coadventurer. For him and for those like him, the rule of undivided loyalty is relentless and supreme. A different question would be here if there were lacking any nexus of relation between the business conducted by the manager and the opportunity brought to him as an incident of management. For this problem, as for most, there are distinctions of degree. If Salmon had received from Gerry a proposition to lease a building at a location far removed, he might have held for himself the privilege thus acquired, or so we shall assume. Here the subject-matter of the new lease was an extension and enlargement of the subject-matter of the old one. A managing coadventurer appropriating the benefit of such a lease without warning to his partner might fairly expect to be reproached with conduct that was underhand, or lacking, to say the least, in reasonable candor, if the partner were to surprise him in the act of signing the new instrument. Conduct subject to that reproach does not receive from equity a healing benediction

A question remains as to the form and extent of the equitable interest to be allotted to the plaintiff. The trust as declared has been held to attach to the lease which was in the name of the defendant corporation. We think it ought to attach at the option of the defendant Salmon to the shares of stock which were owned by him or were under his control. The difference may be important if the lessee shall wish to execute an assignment of the lease, as it ought to be free to do with the consent of the lessor. On the other hand, an equal division of the shares might lead to other hardships. It might take away from Salmon the power of control and management which under the plan of the joint venture he was to have from first to last. The number of shares to be allotted to the plaintiff should, therefore, be reduced to such an extent as may be necessary to preserve to the defendant Salmon the expected measure of dominion. To that end an extra share should be added to his half.

Subject to this adjustment, we agree with the Appellate Division that the plaintiff's equitable interest is to be measured by the value of half of the entire lease, and not merely by half of some undivided part. A single building covers the whole area. Physical division is impracticable along the lines of the Bristol site, the keystone of the whole. Division of interests and burdens is equally impracticable. Salmon, as tenant under the new lease, or as guarantor of the performance of the tenant's obligations, might well protest if Meinhard, claiming an equitable interest, had offered to assume a liability not equal to Salmon's, but only half as great. He might justly insist that the lease must be accepted by his coadventurer in such form as it had been given, and not constructively divided into imaginary fragments. What must be yielded to the one may be demanded by the other. The lease as it has been executed is single and entire. If confusion has resulted from the union of adjoining parcels, the trustee who consented to the union must bear the inconvenience.

Thus far, the case has been considered on the assumption that the interest in the joint venture acquired by the plaintiff in 1902 has been continuously his. The fact is, however, that in 1917 he assigned to his wife all his "right, title and interest in and to" the agreement with his coadventurer. The coadventurer did not object, but thereafter made his payments directly to the wife. There was a reassignment by the wife before this action was begun.

We do not need to determine what the effect of the assignment would have been in 1917 if either coadventurer had then chosen to treat the venture as dissolved. We do not even need to determine what the effect would have been if the enterprise had been a partnership in the strict sense with active duties of agency laid on each of the two adventurers. The form of the enterprise made Salmon the sole manager. The only active duty laid upon the other was one wholly ministerial, the duty of contributing his share of the expense. This he could still do with equal readiness, and still was bound to do, after the assignment to his wife. Neither by word nor by act did either partner manifest a choice to view the enterprise as ended. There is no inflexible rule in such conditions that dissolution shall ensue against the concurring wish of all that the venture shall continue. The effect of the assignment is then a question of intention.

.... No one dreamed for a moment that the enterprise was to be wound up, or that Meinhard was relieved of his continuing obligation to contribute to its expenses if contribution became needful.... For more than five years Salmon dealt with Meinhard on the assumption that the enterprise was a subsisting one with mutual rights and duties, or so at least the triers of the facts, weighing the circumstantial evidence, might not unreasonably infer. By tacit, if not express approval, he continued and preserved it. We think it is too late now, when charged as a trustee, to come forward with the claim that it had been disrupted and dissolved.

The judgment should be modified by providing that at the option of the defendant Salmon there may be substituted for a trust attaching to the lease a trust attaching to the shares of stock, with the result that one-half of such shares together with one additional share will in that event be allotted to the defendant Salmon and the other shares to the plaintiff, and as so modified the judgment should be affirmed with costs.

ANDREWS, J. (dissenting).

... I am of the opinion that the issue here is simple. Was the transaction in view of all the circumstances surrounding it unfair and inequitable? I reach this conclusion for two reasons. There was no general partnership, merely a joint venture for a limited object, to end at a fixed time. The new lease, covering additional property, containing many new and unusual terms and conditions, with a possible duration of eighty years, was more nearly the purchase of the reversion than the ordinary renewal with which the authorities are concerned.

....

Were this a general partnership between Mr. Salmon and Mr. Meinhard I should have little doubt as to the correctness of this result assuming the new lease to be an offshoot of the old. Such a situation involves questions of trust and confidence to a high degree; it involves questions of good will; many other considerations. As has been said, rarely if ever may one partner without the knowledge of the other acquire for himself the renewal of a lease held by the firm, even if the new lease is to begin after the firm is dissolved. Warning of such an intent, if he is managing partner, may not be sufficient to prevent the application of this rule.

We have here a different situation governed by less drastic principles. I assume that where parties engage in a joint enterprise each owes to the other the duty of the utmost good faith in all that relates to their common venture. Within its scope they stand in a fiduciary relationship. I assume prima facie that even as between joint adventurers one may not secretly obtain a renewal of the lease of property actually used in the joint adventure where the possibility of renewal is expressly or impliedly involved in the enterprise. I assume also that Mr. Meinhard had an equitable interest in the Bristol Hotel lease. Further, that an expectancy of renewal inhered in that lease. Two questions then arise. Under his contract did he share in that expectancy? And if so, did that expectancy mature into a graft of the original lease? To both questions my answer is "no."

... Under the circumstances here presented had the lease run to both the parties I doubt whether the taking by one of a renewal without the knowledge of the other would cause interference by a court of equity. An illustration may clarify my thought. A and B enter into a joint venture to resurface a highway between Albany and Schenectady. They rent a parcel of land for the storage of materials. A, unknown to B, agrees with the lessor to rent that parcel and one adjoining it after the venture is finished, for an iron foundry. Is the act unfair? Would any general statements, scattered here and there through opinions dealing with other circumstance, be thought applicable? In other words, the mere fact that the joint venturers rent property together does not call for the strict rule that applies to general partners. Many things may excuse what is there forbidden. Nor here does any possibility of renewal exist as part of the venture. The nature of the undertaking excludes such an idea....

The judgment of the courts below should be reversed and a new trial ordered, with costs in all courts to abide the event.

Section 10: The Liability of a Partnership for the Activities of a Partner

Revised Uniform Partnership Act § 305: Partnership Liable for Partner's Actionable Conduct

(a) A partnership is liable for loss or injury caused to a person, or for a penalty incurred, as a result of a wrongful act or omission, or other actionable conduct, of a partner acting in the ordinary course of business of the partnership or with authority of the partnership....

Comment

... The scope of the section has been expanded by deleting from UPA Section 13, "not being a partner in the partnership." This is intended to permit a partner to sue the partnership on a tort or other theory during the term of the partnership, rather than being limited to the remedies of dissolution and an accounting....

The section has also been broadened to cover no-fault torts by the addition of the phrase, "or other actionable conduct."

Moren v. Jax Rest.

679 N.W.2d 165 (Minn. 2004)[10]

CRIPPEN, J.

...

Facts

Jax Restaurant, the partnership, operates its business in Foley, Minnesota. One afternoon in October 2000, Nicole Moren, one of the Jax partners, completed her day shift at Jax at 4:00 P.M. and left to pick up her two-year-old son Remington from day care. At about 5:30, Moren returned to the restaurant with Remington after learning that her sister and partner, Amy Benedetti, needed help. Moren called her husband who told her that he would pick Remington up in about 20 minutes.

Because Nicole Moren did not want Remington running around the restaurant, she brought him into the kitchen with her, set him on top of the counter, and began rolling out pizza dough using the dough-pressing machine. As she was making pizzas, Remington reached his hand into the dough press. His hand was crushed, and he sustained permanent injuries.

Through his father, Remington commenced a negligence action against the partnership. The partnership served a third-party complaint on Nicole Moren, arguing that, in the event it was obligated to compensate Remington, the partnership was entitled to indemnity or contribution from Moren for her negligence. The district court's summary judgment was premised on a legal conclusion that Moren has no obligation to indemnify Jax Restaurant so long as the injury occurred while she was engaged in ordinary business conduct. The district court rejected the partnership's argument that its obligation to compensate Remington is diminished in proportion to the predominating negligence of Moren as a mother, although it is responsible for her conduct as a business owner. This appeal followed.

Issue

Does Jax Restaurant have an indemnity right against Nicole Moren in the circumstances of this case?

Analysis

...

Under Minnesota's Uniform Partnership Act of 1994 (UPA), a partnership is an entity distinct from its partners, and as such, a partnership may sue and be sued in the name of the partnership. "A partnership is liable for loss or injury caused to a person ... as a result of a wrongful act or omission, or other actionable conduct, of a partner acting in the ordinary course of business of the partnership or with authority of the partnership." Minn. Stat. § 323A.3-05(a) (2002). Accordingly, a "partnership shall ... indemnify a partner for liabilities incurred by the partner in the ordinary course of the business of the partnership...." Minn. Stat. § 323A.4-01(c) (2002). Stated conversely, an "act of a partner which is not apparently for carrying on in the ordinary course the partnership business or business of the kind carried on by the partnership binds the partnership only if the act was

10. Thanks to Dennis Hynes and Mark Loewenstein for identifying and discussing this case in *Agency, Partnership, and the LLC: The Law of Unincorporated Business Enterprises.*

authorized by the other partners." Minn. Stat. § 323A.3-01(2) (2002). Thus, under the plain language of the UPA, a partner has a right to indemnity from the partnership, but the partnership's claim of indemnity from a partner is not authorized or required.

The district court correctly concluded that Nicole Moren's conduct was in the ordinary course of business of the partnership and, as a result, indemnity by the partner to the partnership was inappropriate. It is undisputed that one of the cooks scheduled to work that evening did not come in, and that Moren's partner asked her to help in the kitchen. It also is undisputed that Moren was making pizzas for the partnership when her son was injured. Because her conduct at the time of the injury was in the ordinary course of business of the partnership, under the UPA, her conduct bound the partnership and it owes indemnity to her for her negligence.

Appellant heavily relies on one foreign case for the proposition that a partnership is entitled to a contribution or indemnity from a partner who is negligent. See Flynn v. Reaves, 135 Ga. App. 651, 218 S.E.2d 661 (Ga. Ct. App. 1975). In Flynn, the Georgia Court of Appeals held that "where a partner is sued individually by a plaintiff injured by the partner's sole negligence, the partner cannot seek contribution from his co-partners even though the negligent act occurred in the course of the partnership business." Id. at 663. But this case is inapplicable because the Georgia court applied common law partnership and agency principles and, like appellant, makes no mention of the UPA, which is the law in Minnesota.

Appellant also claims that because Nicole Moren's action of bringing Remington into the kitchen was partly motivated by personal reasons, her conduct was outside the ordinary course of business. Because it has not been previously addressed, there is no Minnesota authority regarding this issue. But there are two cases from outside of Minnesota that address the issue in a persuasive fashion. Grotelueschen v. Am. Family Ins. Co., 171 Wis. 2d 437, 492 N.W.2d 131, 137 (Wis. 1992) (An "act can further part personal and part business purposes and still occur in the ordinary course of the partnership."); Wolfe v. Harms, 413 S.W.2d 204, 215 (Mo. 1967) ("Even if the predominant motive of the partner was to benefit himself or third persons, such does not prevent the concurrent business purpose from being within the scope of the partnership."). Adopting this rationale, we conclude that the conduct of Nicole Moren was no less in the ordinary course of business because it also served personal purposes. It is undisputed that Moren was acting for the benefit of the partnership by making pizzas when her son was injured, and even though she was simultaneously acting in her role as a mother, her conduct remained in the ordinary course of the partnership business.

The district court determined, and appellant strenuously disputes, that Amy Benedetti authorized Nicole's conduct, or at least that her conduct of bringing Remington into the kitchen was not prohibited by the rules of the partnership. Because under Minnesota law authorization from the other partners is merely an alternative basis for establishing partnership liability, we decline to address the issue of whether Nicole Moren's partner authorized her conduct.[11]

11. As stated earlier, under Minn. Stat. § 323A.3-05 a "partnership is liable for loss or injury caused to a person ... as a result of a wrongful act ... of a partner acting in the ordinary course of business of the partnership or with authority of the partnership." And under Minn. Stat. § 323A.4-01(c) a partnership must indemnify a partner for liabilities incurred by the partner in the ordinary course of the business of the partnership. [Court's footnote. — ed.]

Decision

Because Minnesota law requires a partnership to indemnify its partners for the result of their negligence, the district court properly granted summary judgment to respondent Nicole Moren. In addition, we conclude that the conduct of a partner may be partly motivated by personal reasons and still occur in the ordinary course of business of the partnership.

Affirmed.

Orosco v. Sun-Diamond Corp, 51 Cal. App. 4th 1659 (1997). "Normally, of course, a partnership or joint venture is liable to an injured third party for the torts of a partner or venturer acting in furtherance of the enterprise. (9 Witkin, Summary of Cal. Law (9th ed. 1989) Partnership, § 21, p. 421.) However, a joint venture sued for the negligence of one venturer is entitled to indemnity from the negligent venturer."

Section 11: Individual Partners' Liability for Partnership Obligations

Obligations of a partnership can arise in many ways. As we saw in the previous section, a partnership is liable for torts committed by a partner within the scope of the partnership. As we saw in earlier sections, partners by default have actual and apparent authority to enter into contracts, and the partnership may incur liability (such as for breach of contract) under them.

If the partnership is solvent, it simply has an obligation to pay its bills. Legal questions arise, however, when a partnership is unable to pay its bills. In theory, the law faces a choice here: who bears the risk of a partnership's insolvency—(1) the third parties to whom the partnership owes money or (2) the partners themselves?

In a general partnership, the answer is squarely (2). This conclusion—essentially just a policy choice that characterizes the general-partnership form—is often described by saying that a general partnership does not shield its partners from the liabilities of the firm (although of course these liabilities are often vicarious). As we will see (and evaluate) later in the book, the general partnership is the only business organization in which all the owners and operators are responsible for the obligations of the organization; all the other business entities adopt some version of the countervailing policy choice, favoring the owners over third parties.

Under the UPA, the liability of the partners for partnership obligations was fairly direct. For partnership torts, the individual partners were "jointly and severally" liable for partnership torts and for certain kinds of unjust enrichment, and "jointly" liable for all other partnership obligations. *See* UPA § 15. What this meant, broadly speaking, was that if any partner committed a tort in the course of the partnership, the victim could recover directly against any partner. For contract claims against the partnership, third parties would ordinarily need to sue all the partners individually (this is what "joint" liability means, versus "joint and several") and then could recover against all of them individually. Though procedurally more complicated, the result was very similar to joint and several liability: any solvent partners could be fully responsible for the obligations of the partnership.

RUPA simplifies partner liability, declaring that all such liability is joint and several. But it provides for a somewhat more formal procedural mechanism to ensure that the partnership assets are fully exhausted before a creditor can bring a claim.

Revised Uniform Partnership Act (1997) § 306: Partner's Liability

(a) Except as otherwise provided in [subsection (b)], all partners [of a general partnership] are liable jointly and severally for all obligations of the partnership unless otherwise agreed by the claimant or provided by law.

(b) A person admitted as a partner into an existing partnership is not personally liable for any partnership obligation incurred before the person's admission as a partner.

Revised Uniform Partnership Act (1997) § 307: Actions by and Against Partnership and Partners

...

(b) An action may be brought against the partnership and, to the extent not inconsistent with Section 306, any or all of the partners in the same action or in separate actions.

(c) A judgment against a partnership is not by itself a judgment against a partner. A judgment against a partnership may not be satisfied from a partner's assets unless there is also a judgment against the partner.

(d) A judgment creditor of a partner may not levy execution against the assets of the partner to satisfy a judgment based on a claim against the partnership unless the partner is personally liable for the claim under Section 306 and:

(1) a judgment based on the same claim has been obtained against the partnership and a writ of execution on the judgment has been returned unsatisfied in whole or in part;

(2) the partnership is a debtor in bankruptcy;

(3) the partner has agreed that the creditor need not exhaust partnership assets;

(4) a court grants permission to the judgment creditor to levy execution against the assets of a partner based on a finding that partnership assets subject to execution are clearly insufficient to satisfy the judgment, that exhaustion of partnership assets is excessively burdensome, or that the grant of permission is an appropriate exercise of the court's equitable powers; or

(5) liability is imposed on the partner by law or contract independent of the existence of the partnership.

...

Gildon v. Simon Prop. Group, Inc., 145 P.3d 1196 (Wash. 2006). "Applying well-settled rules of statutory construction and common sense, and considering the RUPA as a whole, a better reading of [§ 307(d)] is that when a plaintiff sues the partnership, he or she cannot enforce the judgment against a partner who is not personally liable without first exhausting partnership assets. But a plaintiff need not sue the partnership as a precondition for proceeding against a partner. This is so because nothing in the statute requires the plaintiff to sue the partnership in addition to an individual partner....

"The initial draft of RUPA § 307(d) provided that '[a] claimant may proceed directly against the assets of a partner' without exhausting partnership assets only if the partnership is bankrupt, the partner is independently liable, or the claimant obtains either the partner's or the court's consent to direct suit. J. Dennis Hynes, *The Revised Uniform Partnership Act: Some Comments on the Latest Draft of RUPA*, 19 Fla. St. U.L.Rev. 727 (1992) (quoting Uniform Partnership Act (Draft for Partial Approval June 7, 1991)). The draft provision was criticized for being unduly burdensome on claimants, particularly tort victims who had no opportunity to contract around an exhaustion requirement. *See, e.g.*, Hynes, *supra*; Larry E. Ribstein, *The Revised Uniform Partnership Act: Not Ready for Prime Time*, 49 Bus. Law. 45 (1993). In revising § 307(d), the drafters substituted 'judgment creditor' for 'claimant,' suggesting that the provision relates to postjudgment execution procedure, not a partner's capacity to be sued. Further, the initial draft of RUPA § 307(c) provided that a judgment creditor may not execute judgment against a partner's personal assets based on 'a claim that *could have been successfully asserted* against the partnership' without first exhausting partnership assets. Hynes, *supra*, (quoting Uniform Partnership Act (Draft for Partial Approval June 7, 1991) § 307(c) (emphasis added)). The drafters substituted the language 'a claim against the partnership' for 'a claim that could have been successfully asserted against the partnership.' The changes clarify that the exhaustion requirement does not diminish the scope of a partner's liability or immunize a partner from suit when a plaintiff cannot or does not join the partnership. Rather, [§ 307(d)] restricts a plaintiff's postjudgment execution remedies."

Section 12: The Partner's Partnership Interest

Another important question in organizational law is the degree to which individual owners—like general partners in a partnership—may sell or otherwise transfer their ownership stakes in the enterprise. Given modern access to personal investments in the stock of public corporations, you have probably encountered the notion that ownership units of companies can sometimes be freely bought and sold. As we will later see, that is a feature of corporations and some other types of organizations, but it is not a feature of partnerships.

By default, partners cannot sell their "share" of a general partnership; they cannot, in other words, sell their right to be a partner (and thus to participate in the control of the business) to someone else. Nor can an individual creditor force a partner to do so. Partners may, however, freely assign their rights to receive income from the partnership, and creditors may seek an order that forces an insolvent partner to do so. This right to receive income is called the partner's "interest" in the partnership.

Revised Uniform Partnership Act (1997) § 401(i)

A person may become a partner only with the consent of all of the partners.

Revised Uniform Partnership Act (1997) § 502: Partner's Transferable Interest in Partnership

The only transferable interest of a partner in the partnership is the partner's share of the profits and losses of the partnership and the partner's right to receive distributions. The interest is personal property.

Revised Uniform Partnership Act (1997) § 503: Transfer of Partner's Transferable Interest

(a) A transfer, in whole or in part, of a partner's transferable interest in the partnership:

(1) is permissible;

(2) does not by itself cause the partner's dissociation or a dissolution and winding up of the partnership business; and

(3) does not, as against the other partners or the partnership, entitle the transferee, during the continuance of the partnership, to participate in the management or conduct of the partnership business, to require access to information concerning partnership transactions, or to inspect or copy the partnership books or records.

(b) A transferee of a partner's transferable interest in the partnership has a right:

(1) to receive, in accordance with the transfer, distributions to which the transferor would otherwise be entitled;

(2) to receive upon the dissolution and winding up of the partnership business, in accordance with the transfer, the net amount otherwise distributable to the transferor; and

(3) to seek under Section 801(6) a judicial determination that it is equitable to wind up the partnership business.

(d) Upon transfer, the transferor retains the rights and duties of a partner other than the interest in distributions transferred.

(e) A partnership need not give effect to a transferee's rights under this section until it has notice of the transfer.

(f) A transfer of a partner's transferable interest in the partnership in violation of a restriction on transfer contained in the partnership agreement is ineffective as to a person having notice of the restriction at the time of transfer.

Bauer v. Blomfield Company/Holden Joint Venture

849 P.2d 1365 (Alaska 1993)

BURKE, Justice.

MATTHEWS, Justice, with whom RABINOWITZ, Chief Justice, joins, dissenting.

William J. Bauer, assignee of a partnership interest, sued the partnership and the individual partners, claiming that partnership profits were wrongfully withheld from him. The superior court granted summary judgment to the partnership and individual partners, and dismissed Bauer's complaint with prejudice. We affirm.

I

In 1986 William Bauer loaned $800,000 to Richard Holden and Judith Holden. To secure the loan, the Holdens assigned to Bauer "all of their right, title and interest" in a partnership known as the Blomfield Company/Holden Joint Venture. The other members of the partnership—Charles Alfred (Chuck) Blomfield, Patricia A. Blomfield, Charles Anthony (Tony) Blomfield and Richard H. Monsarrat—consented to the assignment. According to the consent document, their consent was given "pursuant to AS 32.05.220."[12]

When the Holdens defaulted on the loan, Bauer sent the following notice to the partnership members: "William Bauer hereby gives notice that he is exercising his rights to receive all distributions of income and principal from the Blomfield Company/Holden Joint Venture Partnership." Thereafter, for a time, the partnership income share payable to the Holdens was paid monthly to Bauer.

In January, 1989 the partners stopped making income payments to Bauer. They, instead, agreed to use the income of the partnership to pay an $877,000 "commission" to partner Chuck Blomfield. Bauer was not a party to this agreement; he was notified of the agreement after the fact by means of a letter dated January 10, 1989. Bauer was not asked to consent to the agreement, and he never agreed to forego payment of his assigned partnership income share or to pay part of the "commission" to Blomfield. The amount Bauer would have received, had the "commission" not been paid, was $207,567.

Blomfield's $877,000 commission represented five percent of the increased gross rental income earned by the partnership from lease extensions obtained from the state by Blomfield on partnership properties leased by the state. These and other lease extensions were obtained when a private claim made against the state by Chuck Blomfield and Patricia Blomfield for $1,900,000 was settled. Other lease extensions thus obtained were on properties not owned by the partnership; these properties were owned by the Blomfields and were leased by them to the state. One of the conditions upon which Chuck and Patricia Blomfield based their settlement was the agreement of the partners to pay Chuck Blomfield an $877,000 commission for the lease extensions that he obtained on the partnership's properties.

II

Insisting that his assigned right to the Holdens' share of the partnership's income had been violated, Bauer filed suit in superior court against the partnership and all of the partners except the Holdens. Bauer sought declaratory and injunctive relief, and damages. His various claims were dismissed, with prejudice, when the court concluded that Bauer's assignment from the Holdens did not make him a member of the partnership. Therefore, he was not entitled to complain about a decision made with the consent of all the partners. This appeal followed.

---

12. The court's footnote here quoted the pre-RUPA text of the Alaska statute:

(a) A conveyance by a partner of a partner's interest in the partnership does not by itself dissolve the partnership, nor as against the other partners in the absence of agreement, entitle the assignee, during the continuance of the partnership, to interfere in the management or administration of the partnership business or affairs, or to require any information or account of partnership transactions or to inspect the partnership books, but it entitles the assignee to receive in accordance with the assignee's contract the profits to which the ... assigning partner would otherwise be entitled.
(b) In the case of a dissolution of the partnership, the assignee is entitled to receive the assignor's interest and may require an account from the date only of the last account agreed to by all of the partners.

III

The assignment to Bauer of the Holdens' "right, title and interest" in the partnership, did not, in and of itself, make Bauer a partner in the Blomfield Company/Holden Joint Venture. See AS 32.05.220. We are unpersuaded by Bauer's argument that he should be considered a de facto partner.

As the Holdens' assignee, Bauer was not entitled "to interfere in the management or administration of the partnership business or affairs, or to require any information or account of partnership transactions or to inspect the partnership books." AS 32.05.220(a).[13]

The "interest" that was assigned to Bauer was the Holdens' "share of the [partnership's] profits and surplus." AS 32.05.210.[14] The assignment only entitled Bauer to "receive ... the [partnership profits to which the [Holdens] would otherwise be entitled." AS 32.05.220(a) (emphasis added). Because all of The Blomfield Company/Holden Joint Venture partners agreed that Chuck Blomfield was entitled to receive an $877,000 commission, to be paid out of partnership income, we agree with the superior court's conclusion that there were no partnership profits which the Holdens, and thus Bauer, were entitled to receive until the commission was fully paid.

AFFIRMED.

MATTHEWS, Justice, with whom RABINOWITZ, Chief Justice, joins, dissenting.

It is a well-settled principle of contract law that an assignee steps into the shoes of an assignor as to the rights assigned. Today, the court summarily dismisses this principle in a footnote and leaves the assignee barefoot.

The court's analysis, set out in three cursory paragraphs is this: (1) Bauer was not a partner; (2) Bauer, as an assignee, was not entitled to interfere in the management of the partnership; (3) Bauer's assignment entitled him to receive only the profits the Holdens would have received; and (4) Bauer was due nothing because no profits were distributed. These statements are generally correct as far as they go. However, they do not address the issue in dispute: whether the partners owe Bauer a duty of good faith and fair dealing.

The court is correct to state that Bauer's assignment entitles him to nothing if the partnership decides to forego a distribution. However, this statement leaves unanswered the crucial question that must first be asked: was the partners' decision to pay Blomfield a "commission," thereby depleting profits for distribution, a decision made in good faith? Until this question is answered, we cannot know if Bauer was unjustly deprived of that to which he is entitled.

The court dismisses the main issue in a short footnote, stating "we are unwilling to hold that partners owe a duty of good faith and fair dealing to assignees of a partner's

---

13. We are unwilling to hold that partners owe a duty of good faith and fair dealing to assignees of a partner's interest. To do so would undermine the clear intent of AS 32.05.220(a). Partners should be able to manage their partnership without regard for the concerns of an assignee, who may have little interest in the partnership venture. As commentators have explained:

> The U.P.A. rules concerning assignment of partnership interests and the rights of assignees balance the interests of assignees, assignors, and nonassigning partners in a way that is suited to the very closely held business. Although the assignee's impotence obviously limits the market value of the partners' interest, the partners need to be protected from interference by unwanted strangers.

Alan R. Bromberg and Larry E. Ribstein, Partnership § 3:61 (1988). [Court's footnote.—ed.]

14. AS 32.05.210 provides: "A partner's interest in the partnership is the partner's share of the profits and surplus." [Court's footnote.—ed.]

interest." The court reasons that to find such a duty "would undermine the clear intent of AS 32.05.220(a). Partners should be able to manage their partnership without regard for the concerns of an assignee...." The court is correct in noting that Bauer has no management rights in the partnership. Bauer's attempt to enforce his right to profits under the assignment is not, however, an interference with the management of the partnership. Requiring the partners to make decisions regarding distributions in good faith does not interfere with management, it merely requires that the partners fulfill their existing contractual duties to act in good faith.

I further disagree with the court's interpretation of the intent of the statute. The statute's intent is to assure that an assignee does not interfere in the management of the partnership while receiving "the profits to which the assigning partner would otherwise be entitled." AS 32.05.220(a). As interpreted by the court, the statute now allows partners to deprive an assignee of profits to which he is entitled by law for whatever outrageous motive or reason. The court's opinion essentially leaves the assignee of a partnership interest without remedy to enforce his right.[15]

Upon formation of the Blomfield Company/Holden Joint Venture, a contractual relationship arose among the partners. This court has held that a covenant of good faith and fair dealing is implied in all contracts. We have noted that the basis for imposing this duty "is a hybrid of social policy and an effort to further the expectations of the contracting parties that the promises will be executed in good faith." Alaska Pacific, 794 P.2d at 947. The duty of good faith and fair dealing "requires 'that neither party ... do anything which will injure the right of the other to receive the benefits of the agreement.'" *Klondike Indus. Corp. v. Gibson*, 741 P.2d 1161, 1168 (Alaska 1987) (quoting *Guin*, 591 P.2d at 1291).

One element of the contract between the Holdens and the partnership is the Holdens' right to receive their share of profits when a distribution is made. As an element of the partnership contract, this right is accompanied by the duty of the parties to deal fairly and in good faith. The partnership has a right to decide not to make a distribution, but in making this decision, the partnership must act in good faith.

The Holdens assigned to Bauer that part of the partnership contract that entitled the Holdens to receive distributions. Under the law of assignments, Bauer steps into the shoes of the Holdens as to this distribution right. Accompanying this contract right is the partners' duty to act in good faith. Thus, as the assignee of that element of the contract, the partners owe Bauer a duty of good faith and fair dealing in deciding whether to make a distribution.

Holding that, as a matter of law, the partners owe Bauer a duty of good faith when deciding whether to make a distribution does not resolve the dispute in this case. Whether the decision to pay the "commission" in lieu of making a distribution was made in good faith is a factual question. See 3A Arthur L. Corbin, *Corbin on Contracts* §654B, at 89 (Supp. 1992) ("Good faith always involves questions of fact.... If there is a

15. The court notes that the Uniform Partnership Act balances the rights of assignees, assignors, and nonassigning partners. One of the ways in which the U.P.A. accomplishes this is to provide the assignee with the right to petition a court for dissolution of the partnership. The U.P.A. states that upon application of an assignee, the court must decree a dissolution if the partnership was a partnership at will at the time of assignment. U.P.A. §32(2)(b). Although the Alaska Partnership Act was copied from the U.P.A., due to an error in cross-referencing, it is unclear that an assignee in Alaska has the right to apply for a dissolution. Thus he may be deprived of one of the "balances" that the U.P.A. sets up for his protection. [Court's footnote.—ed.]

dispute as to why someone did what he did, there is a question of fact for the jury."). As the moving party on a motion for summary judgment, the burden is on the partnership to demonstrate that no genuine issue existed as to whether the decision to pay the 5% "commission" was made in good faith. The partnership presented little to no evidence on this issue.[16] This court should thus remand to the superior court for a factual determination of whether or not the decision by the partners to pay Blomfield's "commission" was made in good faith.

The court's decision today effectively leaves an assignee with no remedy to enforce his right to receive partnership profits. Without such a remedy, his assignment becomes worthless. As I believe this result is contrary to basic contract and assignment law, I dissent from the court's opinion.

Revised Uniform Limited Liability Company Act (2006) § 112, cmt. b.

The law of unincorporated business organizations is only beginning to grapple in a modern way with the tension between the rights of an organization's owners to carry on their activities as they see fit (or have agreed) and the rights of transferees of the organization's economic interests. (Such transferees can include the heirs of business founders as well as former owners who are "locked in" as transferees of their own interests.)

If the law categorically favors the owners, there is a serious risk of expropriation and other abuse. On the other hand, if the law grants former owners and other transferees the right to seek judicial protection, that specter can "freeze the deal" as of the moment an owner leaves the enterprise or a third party obtains an economic interest.

Bauer v. Blomfield Co./Holden Joint Venture, 849 P.2d 1365 (Alaska 1993) illustrates this point nicely. The case arose after all the partners had approved a commission arrangement with a third party and the arrangement dried up all the partnership profits. When an assignee of a partnership interest objected, the court majority flatly rejected not only the claim but also the assignee's right to assert the claim. A mere assignee "was not entitled to complain about a decision made with the consent of all the partners." A footnote explained, "We are unwilling to hold that partners owe a duty of good faith and fair dealing to assignees of a partner's interest."

The dissent, invoking the law of contracts, asserted that the majority had turned the statutory protection of the partners' management prerogatives into an instrument for abuse of assignees....

The *Bauer* majority is consistent with the limited but long-standing case law in this area (all of it pertaining to partnerships rather than LLCs). This subsection follows the Bauer majority and other cases by expressly subjecting transferees and dissociated members to operating agreement amendments made after the transfer or dissociation.

---

16. In support of its contention that the decision to pay the "commission" was fair, the partnership argued that the amount paid to Blomfield was the "standard" rate. The only evidence presented by the partnership was the testimony of Blomfield himself that a 5% "commission" was standard. One should view this with some skepticism as Blomfield was dealing with a tenant who was already in the building and did not have to be located or persuaded to move in. Furthermore, the rate Blomfield received is greater than 5% as the rent on which the "commission" is based is a future stream of income, not a present lump sum. After discounting future rental income to its present value, Blomfield's "commission" is greater than 5%. [Court's footnote. —ed.]

The issue of whether, in extreme and sufficiently harsh circumstances, transferees might be able to claim some type of duty or obligation to protect against expropriation is a question for other law.

Section 13: The Dissociation of a Partner

As the materials on the entity and aggregate theories of the partnership made clear, a partnership historically was viewed merely as a collection of the particular partners who had agreed to co-own a for-profit business. When one of those partners left, the partnership—in some metaphysical sense—no longer existed, much as we might say a recipe is not the "same" recipe when an ingredient is removed from it.

Under the UPA, a partnership was said to be *dissolved* by default upon any partner's exit from the partnership. Historically, the *dissolution* of a partnership was closely associated with its impending "winding up" (a process involving the sorting out of its final affairs) and eventual termination, although even the UPA did not mandate that relatively harsh result. Of course, nobody expected a large law partnership to disappear merely because one of the partners retired. For one thing, the UPA's rule that any partner's departure triggered dissolution was only a default rule, and the partners could by agreement—known as a *continuation agreement*—provide for a partnership's effective continuation even after it was dissolved by a partner's departure. There were a variety of other exceptions to this rule, which, after all, could lead to a significant and needless disruption to an otherwise profitable business.

A significant part of RUPA updates and rationalizes the end-of-life issues associated with partnerships. For one thing, it more or less drops the term *dissolution*, because that term is ambiguous between (1) a partner's exit and (2) the triggering of the winding-up process. Instead, RUPA introduces a new concept called *dissociation*, which covers a partner's exit from a partnership.

This section will consider what triggers a dissociation, and it will also consider some of the partners' rights and duties associated with rightful and wrongful dissociation. The remainder of this book's coverage of general partnerships will then discuss the consequences of dissociation. RUPA provides that a dissolution can have either of two broad consequences. First, in some circumstances, the default result of UPA is the desirable one, and in those cases a dissociation will lead to a winding up of the partnership's affairs followed by a termination in the existence of the partnership. Second, a dissociation can lead to a mandatory buy-out of the partner's interest, followed by a continuation of the same partnership entity as existed before the dissociation.

Revised Uniform Partnership Act § 601: Events Causing a Partner's Dissociation

A partner is dissociated from a partnership upon the occurrence of any of the following events:

(1) the partnership's having notice of the partner's express will to withdraw as a partner or on a later date specified by the partner;

(2) an event agreed to in the partnership agreement as causing the partner's dissociation;

(3) the partner's expulsion pursuant to the partnership agreement;

(4) the partner's expulsion by the unanimous vote of the other partners if:

(i) it is unlawful to carry on the partnership business with that partner;

(ii) there has been a transfer of all or substantially all of that partner's transferable interest in the partnership, other than a transfer for security purposes, or a court order charging the partner's interest, which has not been foreclosed;

(iii) within 90 days after the partnership notifies a corporate partner that it will be expelled because it has filed a certificate of dissolution or the equivalent, its charter has been revoked, or its right to conduct business has been suspended by the jurisdiction of its incorporation, there is no revocation of the certificate of dissolution or no reinstatement of its charter or its right to conduct business; or

(iv) a partnership that is a partner has been dissolved and its business is being wound up;

(5) on application by the partnership or another partner, the partner's expulsion by judicial determination because:

(i) the partner engaged in wrongful conduct that adversely and materially affected the partnership business;

(ii) the partner willfully or persistently committed a material breach of the partnership agreement or of a duty owed to the partnership or the other partners under Section 404; or

(iii) the partner engaged in conduct relating to the partnership business which makes it not reasonably practicable to carry on the business in partnership with the partner;

(6) the partner's:

(i) becoming a debtor in bankruptcy;

(ii) executing an assignment for the benefit of creditors;

(iii) seeking, consenting to, or acquiescing in the appointment of a trustee, receiver, or liquidator of that partner or of all or substantially all of that partner's property; or

(iv) failing, within 90 days after the appointment, to have vacated or stayed the appointment of a trustee, receiver, or liquidator of the partner or of all or substantially all of the partner's property obtained without the partner's consent or acquiescence, or failing within 90 days after the expiration of a stay to have the appointment vacated;

(7) in the case of a partner who is an individual:

(i) the partner's death;

(ii) the appointment of a guardian or general conservator for the partner; or

(iii) a judicial determination that the partner has otherwise become incapable of performing the partner's duties under the partnership agreement;

(8) in the case of a partner that is a trust or is acting as a partner by virtue of being a trustee of a trust, distribution of the trust's entire transferable interest in the partnership, but not merely by reason of the substitution of a successor trustee;

(9) in the case of a partner that is an estate or is acting as a partner by virtue of being a personal representative of an estate, distribution of the estate's entire transferable interest in the partnership, but not merely by reason of the substitution of a successor personal representative; or

(10) termination of a partner who is not an individual, partnership, corporation, trust, or estate.

Girard Bank v. Haley

460 Pa. 237 (Pa. 1975)

This suit in equity was brought by appellants' decedent, Anna Reid, who averred in her complaint that she had dissolved a partnership between herself and the defendants, and prayed that the business of the firm be wound-up and its assets distributed.... The principal question for decision is whether the partnership was dissolved during Mrs. Reid's lifetime, as she averred and her personal representatives urge, or upon her death, as the trial court found.

The following facts are not in dispute. On September 28, 1958, Mrs. Reid and the three defendants, appellees here, entered into a written partnership agreement for the purpose of leasing for profit certain real property located in Montgomery County, Pennsylvania. Mrs. Reid was to manage the property, and the defendants were to perform the physical labor necessary to maintain the premises in good condition. The initial partnership assets consisted of real estate valued at $50,000 and $10,000 in cash, both contributed by Mrs. Reid, and an additional sum of $10,000 in cash contributed in equal shares by the three other partners. By letter addressed to her partners, the defendants, Mrs. Reid notified them that she was dissolving the partnership and requested that the partnership assets be liquidated as soon as possible.[17] Meetings between the partners following receipt of this letter failed to produce agreement for a plan for liquidation or as to the respective rights of the parties in the assets of the partnership. This

---

17. The letter was undated, but the record establishes that it was sent on February 10, 1971. The text of the letter was as follows:

"Gentlemen:

I hereby notify you that I am terminating the partnership which the four of us entered into on the 28th day of September 1958, and request that steps be taken to liquidate the assets of the Partnership as soon as possible. I hereby authorize you to deal with my attorney, J. William Wetter, Jr., in the matter of negotiating the steps necessary to bring this matter to a speedy and satisfactory conclusion.

"I trust that our friendship will continue and that you will recognize that terminating this partnership has been necessitated by my need to clarify the status of my various assets at this particular time.

Very truly yours,
Anna Reid" [Court's footnote.—ed.]

suit praying for a winding up of the affairs of the partnership and a liquidation of its assets was then brought.

The chancellor found that the partnership had been dissolved, not by Mrs. Reid's letter, but rather by her death, and concluded that the defendants, as surviving partners, were entitled to exercise their option under the partnership agreement to purchase the interest of the deceased partner. Having determined that the defendants had in fact exercised their option to purchase Mrs. Reid's interest, the chancellor entered a decree nisi ordering the defendants to pay the estate in discharge of the purchase price the sum of $29,165.48 plus seventy per cent of the income of the partnership for the calendar year 1971. Exceptions filed by the executors to the adjudication were dismissed and the decree nisi was adopted as the final decree. This appeal followed.

None of the parties disputes the chancellor's conclusion that the partnership has been dissolved; the dispute, as indicated at the outset, is when that event occurred. Dissolution of a partnership is statutorily defined as "the change in the relation of the partners caused by any partner ceasing to be associated in the carrying on, as distinguished from the winding up, of the business." Uniform Partnership Act § 29 ("the Act"). There is no doubt that dissolution of a partnership will be caused by the death of any partner, § 31(4) of the Act, 59 P.S. § 93 (1964).... If, however, dissolution occurred during the lifetime of Mrs. Reid, [the portions of the partnership agreement] which are concerned solely with the effect of the death of a partner, are not germane. The agreement being otherwise silent as to winding up and liquidation, the provisions of the Act will control.

The chancellor was impressed with the fact that the decedent "was a strong willed person" who dominated the partnership enterprise (Adjudication, R. 421a), that the defendant partners had each contributed many thousands of hours of hard work and planning to the "joint venture", and that neither Mrs. Reid (who testified at the first hearing, but who then, according to the adjudication, "appeared confused and feeble") nor her personal representatives had offered "evidence to justify a termination." (Opinion, R. 437a). In supposing that justification was necessary the learned court below fell into error. Dissolution of a partnership is caused, under § 31 of the Act, 59 P.S. § 93 (1964), "by the express will of any partner." The expression of that will need not be supported by any justification. If no "definite term or particular undertaking [is] specified in the partnership agreement", such an at-will dissolution does not violate the agreement between the partners; indeed, an expression of a will to dissolve is effective as a dissolution even if in contravention of the agreement. We have recognized the generality of a dissolution at will. If the dissolution results in breach of contract, the aggrieved partners may recover damages for the breach and, if they meet certain conditions, may continue the firm business for the duration of the agreed term or until the particular undertaking is completed.

There is no doubt in our minds that Mrs. Reid's letter ... effectively dissolved the partnership between her and her three partners. It was definite and unequivocal: "I am terminating the partnership which the four of us entered into on the 28th day of September, 1958." The effective termination date is therefore February 10, 1971, and Mrs. Reid's subsequent death after this litigation was in progress is an irrelevant factor in determining the rights of the parties.

The remaining question is whether or not the unilateral dissolution made by Mrs. Reid violated the partnership agreement. The agreement contains no provision fixing a definite term, and the sole "undertaking" to which it refers is that of maintaining and leasing real property. This statement is merely one of general purpose, however, and cannot be said to set forth a "particular undertaking" within the meaning of that phrase as it is used in the Act. A "particular undertaking" under the statute must be capable of accomplishment at some time, although the exact time may be unknown and unascertainable at the date of the agreement. Leasing property, like many other trades or businesses, involves entering into a business relationship which may continue indefinitely; there is nothing "particular" about it. We thus conclude, on the record before us, that the dissolution of the partnership was not in contravention of the agreement....

Page v. Page

359 P.2d 41 (Cal. 1961)

TRAYNOR, J.

Plaintiff and defendant are partners in a linen supply business in Santa Maria, California. Plaintiff appeals from a judgment declaring the partnership to be for a term rather than at will.

The partners entered into an oral partnership agreement in 1949. Within the first two years each partner contributed approximately $43,000 for the purchase of land, machinery, and linen needed to begin the business. From 1949 to 1957 the enterprise was unprofitable, losing approximately $62,000. The partnership's major creditor is a corporation, wholly owned by plaintiff, that supplies the linen and machinery necessary for the day-to-day operation of the business. This corporation holds a $47,000 demand note of the partnership. The partnership operations began to improve in 1958. The partnership earned $3,824.41 in that year and $2,282.30 in the first three months of 1959. Despite this improvement plaintiff wishes to terminate the partnership.

The Uniform Partnership Act provides that a partnership may be dissolved "By the express will of any partner when no definite term or particular undertaking is specified." The trial court found that the partnership is for a term, namely, "such reasonable time as is necessary to enable said partnership to repay from partnership profits, indebtedness incurred for the purchase of land, buildings, laundry and delivery equipment and linen for the operation of such business...." Plaintiff correctly contends that this finding is without support in the evidence.

Defendant testified that the terms of the partnership were to be similar to former partnerships of plaintiff and defendant, and that the understanding of these partnerships was that "we went into partnership to start the business and let the business operation pay for itself—put in so much money, and let the business pay itself out." There was also testimony that one of the former partnership agreements provided in writing that the profits were to be retained until all obligations were paid.

Upon cross-examination defendant admitted that the former partnership in which the earnings were to be retained until the obligations were repaid was substantially different from the present partnership. The former partnership was a limited partnership and provided for a definite term of five years and a partnership at will thereafter. Defendant insists, however, that the method of operation of the former partnership showed an understanding that all obligations were to be repaid from profits. He nevertheless concedes that there was no understanding as to the term of the present partnership in the event of losses. He was asked: "[Was] there any discussion with reference to the continuation of the business in the event of losses?" He replied, "Not that I can remember." He was then asked, "Did you have any understanding with Mr. Page, your brother, the plaintiff in this action, as to how the obligations were to be paid if there were losses?" He replied, "Not that I can remember. I can't remember discussing that at all. We never figured on losing, I guess."

Viewing this evidence most favorable for defendant, it proves only that the partners expected to meet current expenses from current income and to recoup their investment if the business were successful.

Defendant contends that such an expectation is sufficient to create a partnership for a term under the rule of *Owen v. Cohen*, 19 Cal.2d 147, 150. In that case we held that when a partner advances a sum of money to a partnership with the understanding that the amount contributed was to be a loan to the partnership and was to be repaid as soon as feasible from the prospective profits of the business, the partnership is for the term reasonably required to repay the loan. It is true that Owen v. Cohen, supra, and other cases hold that partners may impliedly agree to continue in business until a certain sum of money is earned, or one or more partners recoup their investments, or until certain debts are paid, or until certain property could be disposed of on favorable terms. In each of these cases, however, the implied agreement found support in the evidence.

In *Owen v. Cohen, supra*, the partners borrowed substantial amounts of money to launch the enterprise and there was an understanding that the loans would be repaid from partnership profits. In *Vangel v. Vangel*, one partner loaned his copartner money to invest in the partnership with the understanding that the money would be repaid from partnership profits. In *Mervyn Investment Co. v. Biber*, one partner contributed all the capital, the other contributed his services, and it was understood that upon the repayment of the contributed capital from partnership profits the partner who contributed his services would receive a one-third interest in the partnership assets. In each of these cases the court properly held that the partners impliedly promised to continue the partnership for a term reasonably required to allow the partnership to earn sufficient money to accomplish the understood objective. In *Shannon v. Hudson*, the parties entered into a joint venture to build and operate a motel until it could be sold upon favorable and mutually satisfactory terms, and the court held that the joint venture was for a reasonable term sufficient to accomplish the purpose of the joint venture.

In the instant case, however, defendant failed to prove any facts from which an agreement to continue the partnership for a term may be implied. The understanding to which defendant testified was no more than a common hope that the partnership earnings would pay for all the necessary expenses. Such a hope does not establish even by implication a "definite term or particular undertaking" as required by section 15031, subdivision (1) (b), of the Corporations Code. All partnerships are ordinarily entered into with the hope that they will be profitable, but that alone does not make them all partnerships for a term and obligate the partners to continue in the partnerships until all of the losses over a period of many years have been recovered.

Defendant contends that plaintiff is acting in bad faith and is attempting to use his superior financial position to appropriate the now profitable business of the partnership. Defendant has invested $43,000 in the firm, and owing to the long period of losses his interest in the partnership assets is very small. The fact that plaintiff's wholly owned corporation holds a $47,000 demand note of the partnership may make it difficult to sell the business as a going concern. Defendant fears that upon dissolution he will receive very little and that plaintiff, who is the managing partner and knows how to conduct the operations of the partnership, will receive a business that has become very profitable because of the establishment of Vandenberg Air Force Base in its vicinity. Defendant charges that plaintiff has been content to share the losses but now that the business has become profitable he wishes to keep all the gains.

There is no showing in the record of bad faith or that the improved profit situation is more than temporary. In any event these contentions are irrelevant to the issue whether the partnership is for a term or at will. Since, however, this action is for a declaratory judgment and will be the basis for future action by the parties, it is appropriate to point out that defendant is amply protected by the fiduciary duties of copartners.

Even though the Uniform Partnership Act provides that a partnership at will may be dissolved by the express will of any partner, this power, like any other power held by a fiduciary, must be exercised in good faith.

We have often stated that "Partners are trustees for each other, and in all proceedings connected with the conduct of the partnership every partner is bound to act in the highest good faith to his copartner and may not obtain any advantage over him in the partnership affairs by the slightest misrepresentation, concealment, threat or adverse pressure of any kind." Although Civil Code, section 2411, embodying the foregoing language, was repealed upon the adoption of the Uniform Partnership Act, it was not intended by the adoption of that act to diminish the fiduciary duties between partners.

A partner at will is not bound to remain in a partnership, regardless of whether the business is profitable or unprofitable. A partner may not, however, by use of adverse pressure "freeze out" a copartner and appropriate the business to his own use. A partner may not dissolve a partnership to gain the benefits of the business for himself, unless he fully compensates his copartner for his share of the prospective business opportunity. In this regard his fiduciary duties are at least as great as those of a shareholder of a corporation.

In the case of *In re Security Finance Co.*, 49 Cal.2d 370, 376-377, we stated that although shareholders representing 50 per cent of the voting power have a right under Corporations Code, section 4600, to dissolve a corporation, they may not exercise such right in order "to defraud the other shareholders [citation], to 'freeze out' minority shareholders [citation], or to sell the assets of the dissolved corporation at an inadequate price. [Citation.]"

Likewise in the instant case, plaintiff has the power to dissolve the partnership by express notice to defendant. If, however, it is proved that plaintiff acted in bad faith and violated his fiduciary duties by attempting to appropriate to his own use the new prosperity of the partnership without adequate compensation to his copartner, the dissolution would be wrongful and the plaintiff would be liable as provided by subdivision (2) (a) of Corporations Code, section 15038 (rights of partners upon wrongful dissolution) for violation of the implied agreement not to exclude defendant wrongfully from the partnership business opportunity.

The judgment is reversed.

Nicholes v. Hunt, 541 P.2d 820 (Or. 1975). "The partnership in this case is founded upon an oral agreement evidenced by certain exhibits and testimony offered. Generally this is sufficient to establish a partnership relationship. Plaintiff argues that the partnership was not one that could be terminated at will. Plaintiff concedes that there is no express agreement which establishes the duration of the partnership, but contends that a definite term can be implied from the fact that plaintiff was obligated to make seven annual payments on the balance of his capital contribution. Plaintiff relies on *Vangel v. Vangel*, 116 Cal App 2d 615, 254 P2d 919 (1953); *Zeibak v. Nasser*, 12 Cal 2d 1, 82 P2d 375 (1938).

"These cases stand as exceptions to the general rule that a partnership is one at will in the absence of an agreement to the contrary. In both *Vangel* and *Zeibak* the court found that the partners had impliedly agreed to form a partnership of a specific duration, notwithstanding their failure to expressly provide therefor." The court noted many similar cases but observed, "There are an equal number of cases wherein courts have refused to imply a fixed term."

Revised Uniform Partnership Act (1997) § 602: Partner's Power to Dissociate; Wrongful Dissociation

(a) A partner has the power to dissociate at any time, rightfully or wrongfully, by express will pursuant to Section 601(1).

(b) A partner's dissociation is wrongful only if:

(1) it is in breach of an express provision of the partnership agreement; or

(2) in the case of a partnership for a definite term or particular undertaking, before the expiration of the term or the completion of the undertaking:

(i) the partner withdraws by express will, unless the withdrawal follows within 90 days after another partner's dissociation by death or otherwise under Section 601(6) through (10) or wrongful dissociation under this subsection;

(ii) the partner is expelled by judicial determination under Section 601(5);

(iii) the partner is dissociated by becoming a debtor in bankruptcy; or

(iv) in the case of a partner who is not an individual, trust other than a business trust, or estate, the partner is expelled or otherwise dissociated because it willfully dissolved or terminated.

(c) A partner who wrongfully dissociates is liable to the partnership and to the other partners for damages caused by the dissociation. The liability is in addition to any other obligation of the partner to the partnership or to the other partners.

Note on the Consequences of Dissociation

RUPA makes the consequences of dissociation clearer and easier to understand than the analogous situations under the UPA. Put simply, as noted earlier, the dissociation of a partner results either in (1) a payment to the partner based on the value of the part-

Figure 1

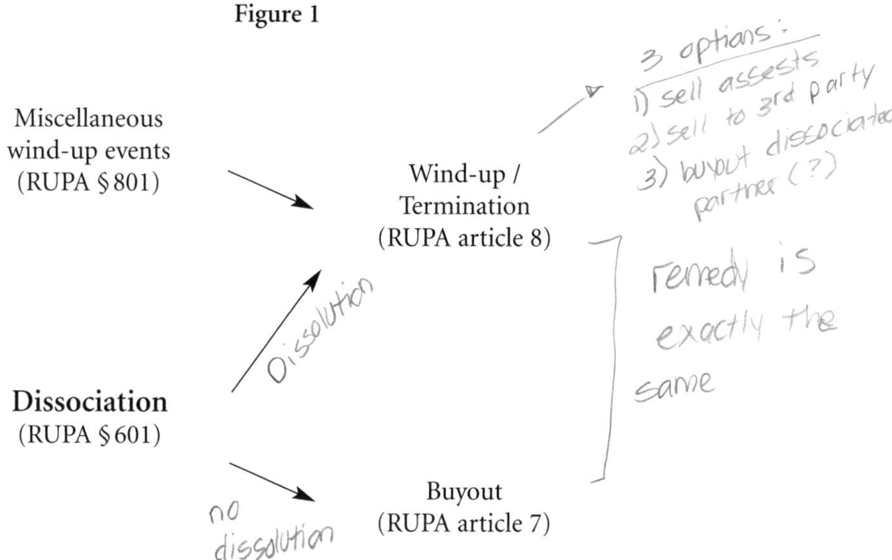

ner's ownership stake in the partnership or (2) a winding up and eventual termination of the partnership. Other events can cause the winding up and termination of a partnership as well, as Figure 1 demonstrates.

RUPA's structure concerning end-of-life partnership issues is somewhat confusing, however. As we have seen, §§ 601–602 describe the way a partner individually dissociates from a partnership. The next section, § 603—sometimes called RUPA's "switching provision"—describes the two possible consequences of dissociation shown in the diagram above, but it does not specify which possibility governs following any particular dissociation. It merely reads: "If a partner's dissociation results in a dissolution and winding up of the partnership business, [Article] 8 applies; otherwise, [Article] 7 applies [and the partner's share is bought out, followed by an indefinite continuation of the partnership]." To determine which of these two possibilities will occur, we need to jump to § 801, which describes *all* of the events—not just those related to dissociation—that lead to the winding up and termination of a partnership.

Note that § 603 and §801 appear to refer to a notion of dissolution, as in the UPA. For example, § 603 refers to a "dissolution and winding up." It may appear that these sections reintroduce a notion of dissolution into RUPA, but the term has no effect. For example, you can read § 801, *infra*, as if it began "A partnership's business must be wound up ..."

Revised Uniform Partnership Act (1997) § 801: Events Causing Dissolution and Winding Up of Partnership Business

A partnership is dissolved, and its business must be wound up, only upon the occurrence of any of the following events:

(1) in a partnership at will, the partnership's having notice from a partner, other than a partner who is dissociated under Section 601(2) through (10), of that partner's express will to withdraw as a partner, or on a later date specified by the partner;

(2) in a partnership for a definite term or particular undertaking:

(i) within 90 days after a partner's dissociation by death or otherwise under Section 601(6) through (10) or wrongful dissociation under Section 602(b), the express will of at least half of the remaining partners to wind up the partnership business, for which purpose a partner's rightful dissociation pursuant to Section 602(b)(2)(i) constitutes the expression of that partner's will to wind up the partnership business;

(ii) the express will of all of the partners to wind up the partnership business; or

(iii) the expiration of the term or the completion of the undertaking;

(3) an event agreed to in the partnership agreement resulting in the winding up of the partnership business;

(4) an event that makes it unlawful for all or substantially all of the business of the partnership to be continued, but a cure of illegality within 90 days after notice to the partnership of the event is effective retroactively to the date of the event for purposes of this section;

(5) on application by a partner, a judicial determination that:

(i) the economic purpose of the partnership is likely to be unreasonably frustrated;

(ii) another partner has engaged in conduct relating to the partnership business which makes it not reasonably practicable to carry on the business in partnership with that partner; or

(iii) it is not otherwise reasonably practicable to carry on the partnership business in conformity with the partnership agreement; or

(6) on application by a transferee of a partner's transferable interest, a judicial determination that it is equitable to wind up the partnership business:

(i) after the expiration of the term or completion of the undertaking, if the partnership was for a definite term or particular undertaking at the time of the transfer or entry of the charging order that gave rise to the transfer; or

(ii) at any time, if the partnership was a partnership at will at the time of the transfer or entry of the charging order that gave rise to the transfer.

Section 14: The Buyout of a Partner's Share After Dissociation

Drashner v. Sorenson

63 N.W.2d 255 (S.D. 1954)

SMITH, P. J.

In January 1951 the plaintiff, C. H. Drashner, and defendants, A. D. Sorenson and Jacob P. Deis, associated themselves as co-owners in the real estate, loan and insurance business at Rapid City. For a consideration of $7500 they purchased the real estate and insurance agency known as J. Schumacher Co. located in an office room on the ground floor of the Alex Johnson Hotel building. The entire purchase price was advanced for the partnership by the defendants, but at the time of trial $3,000 of that sum had been repaid to them by the partnership. Although, as will appear from facts presently to be outlined, their operations were not unsuccessful, differences arose and on June 15, 1951 plaintiff commenced this action in which he sought an accounting, dissolution and winding up of the partnership. The answer and counterclaim of defendants prayed for like relief.

The cause came on for trial September 4, 1951. The court among others made the following findings. "That thereafter the plaintiff violated the terms of said partnership agreement, in that he demanded a larger share of the income of the said partnership than he was entitled to receive under the terms of said partnership agreement; that the plaintiff was arrested for reckless driving and served a term in jail for said offense; that the plaintiff demanded that the defendants permit him to draw money for his own personal use out of the moneys held in escrow by the partnership; that the plaintiff spent a large amount of time during business hours in the Brass Rail Bar in Rapid City, South Dakota, and other bars, and neglected his duties in connection with the business of the said partnership. * * * That the plaintiff, by his actions hereinbefore set forth, has made it impossible to carry on the partnership." The conclusions adopted read as follows: I "That the defendants are entitled to continue the partnership and have the value of the plaintiff's interest in the partnership business determined, upon the filing and approval of a good and sufficient bond, conditioned upon the release of the plaintiff from any liability arising out of the said partnership, and further conditioned upon the payment by the defendants to the plaintiff of the value of plaintiffs' interest in the partnership as determined by the Court." II "That in computing the value of the plaintiff's interest in the said partnership, the value of the good will of the business shall not be considered." III "That the value of the partnership shall be finally determined upon a hearing before this Court, * * *" and IV "That the plaintiff shall be entitled to receive one-third of the value of the partnership property owned by the partnership on the 12th day of September, 1951, not including the good will of the business, after the payment of the liabilities of the partnership and the payment to the defendants of the invested capital in the sum of $4,500.00." Judgment was accordingly entered dissolving the partnership as of September 12, 1951.

After hearing at a later date the court found: I "That the value of the said partnership property on the 12th day of September, 1951, was the sum of Four Thousand Four Hundred Ninety-eight and 90/100 Dollars ($4498.90), and on said date there was due and owing by the partnership for accountant's services the sum of Four Hundred Eighty Dollars ($480.00), and that on said date the sum of Four Thousand Five Hundred Dollars ($4500.00) of the capital invested by the defendants had not been returned to the defendants." and II "That there is not sufficient partnership property to reimburse the defendants for their invested capital." Thereupon the court decreed "that the plaintiff had no interest in the property of the said partnership", and that the defendants were the sole owners thereof.

The assignments of error are predicated upon insufficiency of the evidence to support the findings and conclusions. Of these assignments, only those which question whether the court was warranted in finding that (a) the plaintiff caused the dissolution wrongfully, and (b) the value of the partnership property, exclusive of good will, was $4498.90 on the 12th day of September, 1951, merit discussion. A preliminary statement is necessary to place these issues in their framework.

The agreement of the parties contemplated an association which would continue at least until the $7500 advance of defendants had been repaid from the gross earnings of the business. Hence, it was not a partnership at will. Vangel v. Vangel, 116 Cal. App. 2d 615, 254 P.2d 919; Zeibak v. Nasser, 12 Cal. 2d 1, 82 P.2d 375. In apparent recognition of that fact, both plaintiff and defendants sought dissolution in contravention of the partnership agreement, see SDC 49.0603 (2) under SDC 49.0604(1) (d) on the ground that the adverse party had caused the dissolution wrongfully by willfully and persistently committing a breach of the partnership agreement, and by so conducting himself in matters relating to the partnership business as to render impracticable the carrying on of the business in partnership with him.

By [section 38(2)(c)] of the Uniform Partnership Act it is provided:

> "(2) If the business is continued under paragraph (2) (b) of this section the right as against his copartners and all claiming through them in respect of their interests in the partnership, to have the value of his interest in the partnership, less any any damages caused to his copartners by the dissolution, ascertained and paid to him in cash, or the payment secured by bond approved by the Court, and to be released from all existing liabilities of the partnership; but in ascertaining the value of the partner's interest the value of the good will of the business shall not be considered." ...

From this background we turn to a consideration of the evidence from which the trial court inferred that plaintiff caused the dissolution wrongfully.

The breach between the parties resulted from a continuing controversy over the right of plaintiff to withdraw sufficient money from the partnership to defray his living expenses. Plaintiff was dependent upon his earnings for the support of his family. The defendants had other resources. Plaintiff claimed that he was to be permitted to draw from the earnings of the partnership a sufficient amount to support himself and family. The defendants asserted that there was a definite arrangement for the allocation of the income of the partnership and there was no agreement for withdrawal by plaintiff of more than his allotment under that plan. Defendants' version of the facts was corroborated by a written admission of plaintiff offered in evidence. From evidence thus sharply in conflict, the trial court made a finding, reading as follows: "That the oral partnership agreement between the parties provided that each of the three partners were to draw as compensation one-third of one-half of the commissions earned upon sales made by the partners; that the other one-half of the commissions earned on sales made by the partners and one-half of the commissions earned upon sales made by salesmen employed by the partnership, together with the earnings from the insurance business carried on by the partnership, was to be placed in a fund to be used for the payment of the operating expenses of the partnership, and after the payment of such operating expenses to be used to reimburse the defendants for the capital advanced in the purchase of the Julius Schumacher business and the capital advanced in the sum of Eight Hundred Dollars ($800.00) for the operating expenses of the business."

As an outgrowth of this crucial difference, there was evidence from which a court could reasonably believe that plaintiff neglected the business and spent too much time in a nearby bar during business hours. At a time when plaintiff had overdrawn his partners and was also indebted to one of defendants for personal advances, he requested $100 and his request was refused. In substance he then said, according to the testimony of the defendant Deis, that he would see that he "gets some money to run on", if they "didn't give it to him he was going to dissolve the partnership and see that he got it." Thereafter plaintiff pressed his claims through counsel, and eventually brought this action to dissolve the partnership. The claim so persistently asserted was contrary to the partnership agreement found by the court.

The foregoing picture of the widening breach between the parties is drawn almost entirely from the evidence of defendants. Of course, plaintiff's version of the agreement of the parties, and of the ensuing differences, if believed, would have supported findings of a different order by the trier of the fact. It cannot be said, we think, that the trial court acted unreasonably in believing defendants, and we think it equally clear the court could reasonably conclude that the insistent and continuing demands of the plaintiff and his attendant conduct rendered it reasonably impracticable to carry on the business in partnership with him. It follows, we are of the opinion, the evidence supports the finding that plaintiff caused the dissolution wrongfully.

This brings us to a consideration of the sufficiency of the evidence to support the finding of the court that the property of the partnership was of the value of $4498.90 as of the date of dissolution.

Bitter complaint is made because the trial court refused to consider the good will of this business in arriving at its conclusion. The feeling of plaintiff is understandable. These partners must have placed a very high estimate upon the value of the good will of this agency because they paid Mr. Schumacher $7500 to turn over that office with its very moderate fixtures and its listing of property, together with an agreement that he would not engage in the business in Rapid City for at least two years. No doubt they attached some of this good will value to the location of the business which was under only a month to month letting. Their estimate of value was borne out by the subsequent history of the business. Its real estate commissions, earned but only partly received, grossed $21,528.25 and its insurance commissions grossed $661.21 in the period January 15 to August 31, 1951. In that period the received commissions paid all expenses, including the commissions of salesmen, retired $3,000 of the $7500 purchase price advanced by defendants, and all of $800 of working capital so advanced, allowed the parties to withdraw $1453.02 each, and accumulated a cash balance of $2221.43. In addition the partnership has commissions due which we shall presently discuss. Notwithstanding this indication of the great value of the good will of this business, the statute does not require the court to take it into consideration in valuing the property of the business in these circumstances. The statute provides such a sanction for causing the dissolution of a partnership wrongfully. [UPA § 38(2)(c)(2)] quoted *supra*. The court applied the statute.

With the most valuable asset of the business eliminated, what remained? It is agreed that a group of bills receivable were of the value of $777.47. There was cash in the amount of $2221.43. Subtracting these two amounts from $4498.90, the overall value fixed by the finding, it appears that the court estimated the remaining assets to be of a value of $1500. The evidence dealing with those items must be briefly examined.

The furniture and fixtures were described by Mr. Schumacher. He stated the original cost when he installed them several years before, and also stated that in his own mind he had valued them at $1,000 when selling the business. They were carried on the books as at a value of $452. They included a large desk, two smaller ones, a filing cabinet, a smaller cabinet, a typ[e]writer, a counter, some chairs, neon signs, a partition, and some supplies.

In addition to the bills receivable above mentioned of the agreed value of $777.47, there were items of commission due in the amount of $8100. Most of these had been placed with attorneys for collection. Plaintiff expressed the opinion that they were good, and defendants testified they were worthless. Neither one explained the deals out of which they arose, or the worth of the debtors.

Another asset was the listings of real estate for sale. Respective customers had listed real property with the agency for sale, usually at a fixed price, and had agreed that the agency should receive a 5% commission. Here again the parties took opposing extreme positions. The defendants suggested that this list of property was embraced within the good will of the business, and therefore the court was not required to consider its value. Predicated on the testimony of a witness that particular listings with which he was familiar were of the value of 5% of the sale price named therein, plaintiff asserts that the court was required to place a high estimate of value on these assets. Neither view is persuasive.

Although these listings may have resulted in part at least from the good will of customers toward the agency, we are firm in our conviction that they are not embraced within the concept of the good will described in the Uniform Partnership Act. According to our statutory definition "The good will of a business is the expectation of continued public patronage * * ." SDC 51.0810. Elsewhere it is defined as "* * * that element of value which inheres in the fixed and favorable consideration of customers, arising from an established and well-known and well-conducted business." 38 C.J.S., Good Will, § 1, page 948. Rather than being an element of good will value, these listings take on the aspect of going concern value as that concept is customarily employed in fixing rates for utilities. Until such a list is established a real estate agency is not a going concern. Money, time, energy and skill go into its establishment. Therefore, we think it would be reasonable, in fixing the overall value of a real estate business to attach such a value to its list of property for sale as is comparable to the expense involved in its establishment. The reason it cannot be valued on an exchange basis, is that these listings are not transferable, and are revocable at will. Beck v. Howard, 43 S.D. 179, 178 N.W. 579. In the instant case, we do not understand that the trial court failed to attach any value to this asset. In arriving at the conclusion that these listings should not carry a high estimate of value, the court was undoubtedly influenced by the foregoing considerations and by the further fact that plaintiff had been with the office for several years and had secured many of these listings, and therefore, the probability was not remote that some of them would follow him out of the agency. The trial court was not supplied with any very substantial basis for estimating the value of this asset.

That the $1500 value placed on all of these described assets was conservative we do not question. However, after mature study and reflection we have concluded that the court's finding is not against the clear weight of the evidence appearing in this record. Hence we are not at liberty to disturb it.

The brief of plaintiff includes some discussion of his right to a share in the profits from the date of the dissolution until the final judgment. It does not appear from the record that this claim was presented to the trial court, or that the net profit of the business during that period was evidenced. Because that issue was not presented below, it is not before us.

The judgment of the trial court is affirmed.

All the Judges concur.

Revised Uniform Partnership Act (1997) § 602, cmt. 3

Under UPA Section 38(2)(c)(II), in addition to an offset for damages, the goodwill value of the partnership is excluded in determining the value of a wrongfully dissociating partner's partnership interest. Under RUPA, however, unless the partnership's goodwill is damaged by the wrongful dissociation, the value of the wrongfully dissociating partner's interest will include any goodwill value of the partnership. If the firm's goodwill is damaged, the amount of the damages suffered by the partnership and the remaining partners will be offset against the buyout price.

Note on RUPA's Buyout Provisions

RUPA Article 7, particularly § 701, describes the mechanics of the buyout of a dissociating partner's interest. It applies when "a partner is dissociated from a partnership without resulting in a dissolution and winding up of the partnership business under Section 801." RUPA § 701.

Section 701 is an exceedingly detailed, complex section of the statute. The basic principle behind it, however, is simple: the dissociated partner's interest is the value the partner would have received "if, on the date of dissociation, the assets of the partnership were sold at a price equal to the greater of the liquidation value or the value based on a sale of the entire business as a going concern without the dissociated partner and the partnership were wound up as of that date." The statute adds that "Interest must be paid from the date of dissociation to the date of payment." RUPA § 701(b).

This provision raises several questions about valuation, which we will consider shortly. Article 7 continues, however, with a variety of other, relatively minor provisions. The highlights of these provisions, expressed simply, are as follows:

- Damage owed by a wrongfully dissociating partner—and indeed all other debts from the partner to the partnership—are subtracted from the buyout price, with interest. § 701(c).
- A partnership can choose to defer the buyout of a wrongfully dissociating partner who leaves a partnership for a term before the end of the term, "unless the partner establishes to the satisfaction of the court that earlier payment will not cause undue hardship to the business of the partnership. A deferred payment must be adequately secured and bear interest." § 701(h).
- Various subsections of the statute provide for the timing and ordering of claims between the partnership and the partner; for our purposes, these are simply administrative details. §§ 701(e)–(g), (i).
- The partnership must indemnify the partner for essentially all partnership liabilities, including those that arose prior to dissociation. § 701(d). Of course, this indemnification will not shield the partner from liability to third parties if the partnership ends up insolvent; the provision simply provides an ordering to the way that third-party claims are satisfied. Practically speaking, its major effect is to make clear that the dissociating partner will not face new liability (in indemnity or contribution) to the remaining partners for new third-party claims, even for those that arise out of events that preceded the dissociation.
- Section 702 provides that a dissociating partner may still have RUPA's analogue to apparent authority under § 301—that is, the former partner may bind the partnership even without actual authority if the former partner acts within the ordinary course of the partnership—for two years following the dissociation. This provides a bright-line rule to protect third parties who deal with the former partner and who did not reasonably know of the partner's dissociation. Unambigu-

ously, however, under Article 7 the former partner is liable to the partnership for any loss it incurs through the former partner's post-dissociation actions. (Recall that this is not necessarily true, under §301, for a partner who mistakenly acts without actual authority but who does not violate the "gross negligence" standard of care under RUPA.)

Note on Business Valuation

The valuation of a business is an extensive, complex topic, but at its core it resembles any other sort of valuation problem. Such problems are familiar to most Contracts students. For example, in a breach of a contract to sell goods under UCC Article 2, the UCC provides in many cases for damages measured by the difference between the contract price and the market price. Often the notion of a "market price" is artificial and speculative. For example, if *S* promises to sell *B* a 2003 Mercedes C230K with 105,000 miles and then breaches, *B*'s market-price damages may depend on the information *B* can establish in court concerning recent, sales of similar cars. There is not a thick market in old, used vehicles, but perhaps *B* can find a slightly newer car sold 20 miles away, a slightly older but less-used car sold 100 miles away, etc. A court—or of course the parties if they settle—must determine from this disorganized data the market price of a hypothetical vehicle.

Much the same is true in valuing a business. Like any other asset, it can be difficult to fix a value when there is no ready market for resale. Courts may use a variety of approaches to determine a business's value, including (1) sales of recent businesses, (2) the value of the business's underlying assets, and (3) the value of the expected future profits of the business.

The first of these possibilities is straightforward and matches the example of a car sale under the UCC. The second may be appropriate in cases where the value of a partnership or other business depends largely on a few key assets that the business holds. For example, in the case of a partnership to buy land, build a house on it, and eventually sell the house, the market value of the resulting land and house will likely dictate the value of the partnership.

The third approach, based on expected profits, is more complicated and requires some financial discussion. One reason that the value of a business's assets may not be sufficient to determine the value of the whole business is that an operating business may be worth more than the sum of its parts: it has value because it is an operating organization that can earn money with those parts. Much as a living human is worth far more than the value of the metals in his or her body, an operating business is ordinarily worth more than the property it owns.

To measure this operational value, it is common to compute an expected stream of earnings over the lifetime of the business. If the business is expected to last only a short time, this stream of earnings would be easy to compute. For example, if a business exists only to sell a casebook that is expected to be used for just two years, the earnings from the business will be very close to the sales from the first year plus the sales from the second year. The stream of earnings would be "very close to" this sum, not identical to it, because future earnings need to be *discounted* to present value. This concept, a core notion in finance, simply reflects the common recognition that a fixed sum of money is more valuable today than in the future. If nothing else, it can be invested or spent now, rather than later. Thus, receiving $1,000 next year might be worth only $980 or so this year. The precise value will depend on interest rates, investment possibilities, individual preferences, and possibly other factors.

This same discounting explains why even a business that is expected to last indefinitely can have a finite value today. Suppose a business is expected to earn $10,000 in profits per year forever and that, for each year, the earnings are discounted by 10%. The first year's earnings are worth $10,000; the second year's are worth 90% of $10,000 ($9,000); the third year's are worth 90% of $9,000 ($8730); and so on. It turns out that even an infinite stream of such discounted earnings approaches a particular, finite value—in this case, $310,000, or 31 times the expected annual earnings of the business. (A higher discounting rate would lead to a lower sum, and vice-versa.) Economic conditions and other factors can affect the appropriate discounting rate, but the basic idea is always the same. Similarly, there can be various estimates of the future earnings of a partnership—often, in big cases, established through expert testimony—but the fundamental question is simply a factual one.

To compute a dissociating partner's buyout price, courts ordinarily will begin by computing the value of the whole partnership. Recall that § 701(b) specifies that the business's value is to be computed as "the greater of the liquidation value or the value based on a sale of the entire business as a going concern without the dissociated partner and the partnership were wound up as of that date." In this context, "liquidation" is a term that largely refers to the net value of the partnership's assets. Since this value is ordinarily less than the value of a business as a "going concern," RUPA here merely confirms an ordinary principle of valuation.

After computing the value of the business, the partner's share is calculated. As we will see in discussing the winding up of partnerships in the next section, first the partner's capital account must be reconciled (so that the partner must make up negative balances and will receive positive balances). Then, the partner's share of the business is credited based on the partner's agreed share of profits.

RUPA does not dictate, further than that, the procedure that a court is to use to value a dissociating partner's share. It is meant to allow common-law courts to respond appropriately to the variety of facts that may influence business valuation. As the official comment to § 701 describes:

> "Buyout price" is a new term. It is intended that the term be developed as an independent concept appropriate to the partnership buyout situation, while drawing on valuation principles developed elsewhere.
>
> .... Liquidation value is not intended to mean distress sale value. Under general principles of valuation, the hypothetical selling price in either case should be the price that a willing and informed buyer would pay a willing and informed seller, with neither being under any compulsion to deal.

Dixon v. Crawford, McGilliard, Peterson & Yelish, 262 P.3d 108 (Wash. Ct. App. 2011)."[RUPA] gives the court discretion to determine the buyout price of a dissociated partner's interest, and we will not disturb its decision absent abuse of that discretion."

Warnick v. Warnick

133 P.3d 997, 1004 (Wyo. 2006)

BURKE, Justice.

Wilbur K. Warnick, Dee J. Warnick and Warnick Ranches (collectively, Warnick Ranches) appeal the district court's determination of the amount owed to a withdrawing partner. Warnick Ranches claims the district court should have considered evidence of costs of a hypothetical asset sale to reduce the buyout price. We affirm.

Issue

Warnick Ranches states its issue on appeal as:

> Did the District Court abuse its discretion in excluding evidence offered by [Warnick Ranches] regarding the costs of liquidating partnership assets in determining the buy-out price of a dissociated partner under [RUPA] 701(b)?....

Discussion

In calculating the buyout price for Randall Warnick's interest in the partnership, the district court valued the partnership assets without making any deduction for expenses that Warnick Ranches argued would be incurred if those assets were sold. On appeal, Warnick Ranches claims that the district court should have allowed expert testimony concerning costs associated with the sale of ranch assets and challenges the district court's ruling that costs of sale were too speculative.

Calculation of the Buyout Price

The district court was charged with calculating the amount owed to Randall Warnick pursuant to the applicable provisions of RUPA [§§ 603 and 701]. That amount, or the buyout price, is the amount that would have been paid to the dissociating partner following a settlement of partnership accounts upon the winding up of the partnership, if, on the date of dissociation, the assets of the partnership were sold at a price equal to the greater of the liquidation value or the value based on a sale of the business as a going concern without the dissociating partner. "[P]artnership assets must first be applied to discharge partnership liabilities to creditors, including partners who are creditors." [RUPA] 808(b). The interplay between RUPA § 701(b) and § 808(b) requires that obligations to known creditors must be deducted before a partner distribution can be determined. "[T]hus, the buyout price is the net of all known liabilities." John W. Larson, *Florida's New Partnership Law: The Revised Uniform Partnership Act and Limited Liability Partnerships*, 23 Fla. St. U. L. Rev. 201, 234 (1995). Stated another way, "[i]n computing the buyout price, the amount the dissociating partner receives is reduced by his or her share of partnership liabilities." Donald J. Weidner and John W. Larson, *The Revised Uniform Partnership Act: The Reporters' Overview*, 49 Bus. Law. 1, 12 (1993).

The purpose of [a previous] remand was for the district court to consider liabilities—partner advances, which had previously been omitted from its calculation. Warnick Ranches makes no argument that costs associated with a hypothetical sale of ranch assets should be considered a partnership liability. Its argument focuses solely upon the valuation of the partnership's assets under [RUPA § 701(b)]. Accordingly, our review is similarly limited, and we need not consider costs of sale as a liability, affecting the amount that would have been "distributable" to Randall Warnick under [RUPA § 807] or the settlement of partnership accounts.

At this juncture, Warnick Ranches claims that the district court erred in the first step of its calculation of the buyout price by overvaluing the ranch assets. The asserted error is the district court's failure to deduct estimated sales expenses of $50,000 from the value of the partnership assets. As the basis for its argument, Warnick Ranches states that the appraiser was prepared to testify about the "liquidation value" of the ranch assets. A common understanding of liquidation is "[t]he act or process of converting assets into cash." Black's Law Dictionary 950 (8th ed. 2004). Warnick Ranches appears to assume that the liquidation value of the ranch is the amount of cash that would remain following a sale. This assumption is not supported by the pertinent statutory language and the circumstances of this case.

Critical to our determination in this case is the recognition that the assets of this partnership were not, in fact, liquidated. Instead, the record reflects that the assets were retained by Warnick Ranches. Randall Warnick's dissociation from the partnership did not require the winding up of the partnership. We acknowledge that when a business is not actually dissolving, "valuation may be difficult and will have to be based to some extent on estimates and appraisals." Lieberman v. Wyoming.com LLC, 2004 WY 1, P27, 82 P.3d 274, 284 (Wyo. 2004) (Lehman, J., dissenting, with whom Kite, J., joins). However, the district court held its hearing several years after the date of valuation, and there was no question that the partnership's ranching operations had continued following Randall Warnick's departure. There was no evidence of any actual, intended, or pending sale before the district court at the time of dissociation, and, therefore, asset liquidation was only hypothetical. Accordingly, the deduction urged by Warnick Ranches is for hypothetical costs. See Taffi v. United States (In re Taffi), 68 F.3d 306, 309 (9th Cir. 1995) (costs of sale are hypothetical where the property is not actually being sold). As we will explain, because of the hypothetical nature of the urged $50,000 deduction, we find that the district court's calculation was not erroneous.

If, in applying [RUPA § 701(b)], we were to interpret the term "liquidation value" in isolation, we might envision an amount representing the net proceeds resulting from a distress sale. However, that interpretation is precluded by the language contained in the statute, [which refers to "a price equal to the greater of the liquidation value or the value based on a sale of the entire business as a going concern without the dissociated partner"].

In analyzing this provision, we must consider all of the language contained therein:

> We are guided by the full text of the statute, paying attention to its internal structure and the functional relation between the parts and the whole. Each word of a statute is to be afforded meaning, with none rendered superfluous. Further, the meaning afforded to a word should be that word's standard popular meaning unless another meaning is clearly intended. If the meaning of a word is unclear, it should be afforded the meaning that best accomplishes the statute's purpose.

Rodriguez v. Casey, 2002 WY 111, P10, 50 P.3d 323, 326-27 (Wyo. 2002) (internal citations omitted). When read as a whole and in a manner consistent with its purpose, we find the statute does not support Warnick Ranches' proposed meaning of liquidation value.

Liquidation value is one of two identified methods for valuing the partnership assets. Application of the two methods to the same partnership may yield two distinct values. The Massachusetts Supreme Court compared the two methods, noting:

> The method of valuation of a partnership interest in a going concern necessarily differs from the valuation of the same interest at the point of liquidation.

> The liquidation value looks to the value of the partnership's assets less its liabilities and determines each partner's appropriate share. When valuing a going concern, however, the market value of the partnership interest itself is what is at stake, rather than the percentage of net assets it represents. Depending on circumstances, the market value of the partnership interest may be more or less than the value of the same percentage of net assets.

Anastos v. Sable, 443 Mass. 146, 819 N.E.2d 587, 590-91 (Mass. 2004). By providing two approaches, [RUPA] contemplates variations that could result from differing appraisal techniques and varying business circumstances.

Significantly, the buyout price under [RUPA § 701(b)] involves use of the greater value resulting from the alternate valuation methods. Warnick Ranches' argument seems to assume that the district court's calculation incorporated the liquidation value of the partnership assets. We see room for disagreement based upon the record. The district court did not specify which valuation method was selected, and it was therefore possible that the value used in the buyout price calculation represented the going concern value of the ranch. Warnick Ranches makes no argument that costs of sale should also be deducted from the going concern value because, under its rationale, the $50,000 deduction is required only as part and parcel of liquidation value. Were we to conclude that the district court used a figure which represented the going concern value, our analysis could end here without further discussion of hypothetical costs of sale.

However, even if the district court valued the partnership assets using liquidation value, the deduction for costs associated with a hypothetical sale would not be warranted. Contrary to the interpretation asserted by Warnick Ranches, liquidation value is not the amount of the seller's residual cash following a sale. We find that the meaning of liquidation value in the statute is best understood by comparing it to the other method provided. When contrasted with "going concern value" it is clear that "liquidation value" simply means the sale of the separate assets rather than the value of the business as a whole.

Additionally, under either valuation method, Wyo. Stat. Ann. § 17-21-701(b) directs that the sale price be determined "on the basis of the amount that would be paid by a willing buyer to a willing seller, neither being under any compulsion to buy or sell, and with knowledge of all relevant facts." The legislature chose to supplement the Uniform Laws version of this provision by adding this sentence [from the official comment of RUPA], lending added significance to this language. This "willing buyer" and "willing seller" language does not present a novel legal concept, as it sets forth precisely what has long been the legal definition or test of "fair market value." Black's Law Dictionary 1587 (8th ed. 2004). "Fair market value is generally defined as the amount at which property would change hands between a willing buyer and a willing seller, neither being under any compulsion to buy or sell and both having reasonable knowledge of the relevant facts." Lieberman, P28 n.1 (citing Black's Law Dictionary 597 (6th ed. 1990) and Wyo. Stat. Ann § 39-11-101(a)(vi) (LexisNexis 2001) (defining fair market value as used for taxation purposes)).

Section 15: Winding Up and Termination

Note on Winding Up and Termination

Recall that there are two possible consequences of a dissociation: (1) buyout and (2) winding up and termination. Furthermore, other events, as described in RUPA § 801, may cause a winding up and termination.

Under § 801, there are essentially four events that frequently—by default—cause a winding up of the partnership business. First, a partner intentionally withdraws from a partnership at will (and the partnership agreement does not provide for continuation of the business on such an event). Second, a partnership for a term, or for a definite undertaking, completes its term or undertaking—or all partners in such partnerships agree to wind up the business.[18] Third, the partnership agreement mandates winding up. (For example, a partnership agreement might specify that upon some condition, the partnership will stop operating.) Fourth, a partner (or in some cases the transferee of a partner's interest) applies for a ruling from a court, under § 801(5), basically on the grounds that it is best to wind up the partnership rather than let it continue. There are a variety of other, usually more minor events that can trigger a winding up, so it is worth rereading § 801 in full at this point.

Winding up is ordinarily a process by which the partnership resolves its accounts, ends its affairs, and then finally *terminates*, or ceases to exist. RUPA's official comment to § 801 describes the process as follows:

> In effect, [winding up] means the scope of the partnership business contracts to completing work in process and taking such other actions as may be necessary to wind up the business. Winding up the partnership business entails selling its assets, paying its debts, and distributing the net balance, if any, to the partners in cash according to their interests. The partnership entity continues, and the partners are associated in the winding up of the business until winding up is completed. When the winding up is completed, the partnership entity terminates.

The first, simplest part of winding up involves the continuation of a relatively mundane part of the operational life of the business: it must collect payments that are due, pay its invoices, and provide in most cases for an orderly termination. The winding-up process may continue for quite a while; for example, RUPA § 803 contemplates the possibility that a partnership, while winding up, may need to file and defend against lawsuits, settle remaining disputes with customers and suppliers, and so on.

Winding up is often managed much like any other partnership business is managed. RUPA § 803 gives the partners (except those who have wrongfully dissociated) the right to participate in the winding-up process, except that partners can apply for judicial supervision of winding up. A court may grant this supervision as it sees fit.

Finally, in an ordinary winding up, the partnership sells its remaining assets. Selling its assets does not necessarily imply, however, that the "business" of the partnership will not continue. As we discussed in evaluating methods for business valuation, often a business is far more valuable as a "going concern" than as an inert collection of assets.

---

18. Also, RUPA provides that in a partnership for a term or a definite undertaking, when a partner dies, wrongfully dissociates, enters bankruptcy, or on a variety of other similar kinds of dissociations, half the remaining partners can choose to wind up the partnership business. RUPA § 801(2)(i).

Selling the partnership's assets may in some cases involve what, from the outside, looks like a total sale of "the business." For example, if a partnership operates a restaurant and the partnership is winding up, the partnership might sell the whole restaurant—its lease, equipment, licenses, employment relationships, goodwill, and so on—to a new operator. Winding up the partnership does not mean the restaurant itself must shut down; it may simply continue under new management. To put it differently, it is the partnership *entity* that winds up and eventually terminates, not necessarily the *business* that the partnership was operating.

Indeed, a former partner, a group of them, or some combination of former partners and outsiders might buy the business—if, for example, they bid the most for it at an auction. In practice, then, there needn't always be a sharp practical distinction between winding up and buyout; the distinction is largely a legal, technical difference concerning whether Article 7 or Article 8 under RUPA governs the partnership following a dissociation.

Creel v. Lilly

729 A.2d 385 (Md. 1999)

CHASANOW, J.

The primary issue presented in this appeal is whether Maryland's Uniform Partnership Act (UPA), Maryland Code (1975, 1993 Repl. Vol., 1998 Supp.), Corporations and Associations Article, § 9-101 et seq., permits the estate of a deceased partner to demand liquidation of partnership assets in order to arrive at the true value of the business. Specifically, Petitioner (Anne Creel) maintains that the surviving partners have a duty to liquidate all partnership assets because (1) there is no provision in the partnership agreement providing for the continuation of the partnership upon a partner's death and (2) the estate has not consented to the continuation of the business. Respondents (Arnold Lilly and Roy Altizer) contend that because the surviving partners wound up the partnership in good faith, in that they conducted a full inventory, provided an accurate accounting to the estate for the value of the business as of the date of dissolution, and paid the estate its proportionate share of the surplus proceeds, they are under no duty to liquidate the partnership's assets upon demand of the deceased partner's estate....

At the outset we note there is a partnership agreement in the instant case that, while somewhat unclear, seems to provide for an alternative method of winding up the partnership rather than a liquidation of all assets. The circuit court and intermediate appellate court both found the agreement unclear as to dissolution and winding up of the business upon the death of a partner and correctly turned to UPA as an interpretative aid. In looking specifically at the trial court's order, the trial judge referred to the partnership agreement and UPA but was not explicit as to which one he primarily relied on in holding that a forced sale of all assets was not required in this case. Regardless, the trial judge's interpretation of the partnership agreement and holding are in conformity with UPA.

Due to our uncertainty as to whether the trial court's holding was based primarily on the partnership agreement or UPA, and also because clarification of the liquidation issue implicates other aspects of partnership law, we will examine not only the partnership agreement itself, but also Maryland's UPA and applicable case law, the cases in other jurisdictions that have interpreted the liquidation issue under UPA, and the newly adopted RUPA. For the reasons stated in this opinion, we concur in the finding of the courts below that Respondents are under no duty to "liquidate on demand" by Petitioner, as UPA does not mandate a forced sale of all partnership assets in order to ascertain the true value of the business. Winding up is not always synonymous with liquidation, which can be a harsh, drastic, and often unnecessary course of action. A preferred method in a good faith winding up, which was utilized in this case, is to pay the deceased partner's estate its proportionate share of the value of the partnership, derived from an accurate accounting, without having to resort to a full liquidation of the business. To hold otherwise vests excessive power and control in the deceased partner's estate, to the extreme disadvantage of the surviving partners. Thus, on this issue, we affirm the judgment of the Court of Special Appeals.

In this appeal, Petitioner also asks us to award the estate its share of the partnership profits generated by the Respondents' alleged continued use of the partnership assets for the period of time during which Petitioner claims the Respondents neither liquidated the business nor agreed to pay the estate its proper percentage share of the partnership. We reject Petitioner's request and agree with the courts below that there is no basis for damages because Good Ole Boys Racing (Good Ole Boys) is a successor partnership and not a continuation of Joe's Racing, which was properly wound up and terminated before the new partnership began operations.

I. Background

On approximately June 1, 1993, Joseph Creel began a retail business selling NASCAR racing memorabilia. His business was originally located in a section of his wife Anne's florist shop, but after about a year and a half he decided to raise capital from partners so that he could expand and move into his own space. On September 20, 1994, Mr. Creel entered into a partnership agreement—apparently prepared without the assistance of counsel—with Arnold Lilly and Roy Altizer to form a general partnership called "Joe's Racing." The partnership agreement covered such matters as the partnership's purpose, location, and operations, and stated the following regarding termination of the business:

> "7. TERMINATION
>
> (a) That, at the termination of this partnership a full and accurate inventory shall be prepared, and the assets, liabilities, and income, both in gross and net, shall be ascertained: the remaining debts or profits will be distributed according to the percentages shown above in the 6(e).
>
> ***
>
> (d) Upon the death or illness of a partner, his share will go to his estate. If his estate wishes to sell his interest, they must offer it to the remaining partners first."

The three-man partnership operated a retail store in the St. Charles Towne Center Mall in Waldorf, Maryland. For their initial investment in Joe's Racing, Mr. Lilly and Mr. Altizer each paid $6,666 in capital contributions, with Mr. Creel contributing his inventory and supplies valued at $15,000. Pursuant to the partnership agreement, Mr. Lilly and Mr. Altizer also paid $6,666 to Mr. Creel ($3,333 each) "for the use and rights to the business known as Joe's Racing Collectables." The funds were placed in a partnership bank account with First Virginia Bank-Maryland. All three partners were signatories to this account, but on May 19, 1995, unknown to Mr. Lilly and Mr. Altizer, Mr. Creel altered the account so that only he had the authority to sign checks. It was only after Mr. Creel's death that Mr. Lilly and Mr. Altizer realized they could not access the account funds, which were frozen by the bank upon Mr. Creel's passing. Moreover, on approximately February 20, 1995, Mr. Creel paid a $5,000 retainer to an attorney without his partners' knowledge. He wanted the attorney to prepare documents for the marketing of franchises for retail stores dealing in racing memorabilia.

Joe's Racing had been in existence for almost nine months when Mr. Creel died on June 14, 1995. Mrs. Creel was appointed personal representative of his estate. In this capacity, and acting without the knowledge of the surviving partners, Mrs. Creel and the store's landlord agreed to shorten the lease by one month so that it expired on August 31, 1995. June, July, and August's rent was paid by Mr. Lilly and Mr. Altizer....

II. Discussion and Analysis

A.

....

Over time, the UPA rule requiring automatic dissolution of the partnership upon the death of a partner, in the absence of consent by the estate to continue the business or an agreement providing for continuation, with the possible result of a forced sale of all partnership assets was viewed as outmoded by many jurisdictions including Maryland. The development and adoption of RUPA by the National Conference of Commissioners on Uniform State Laws (NCCUSL) mitigated this harsh UPA provision of automatic dissolution and compelled liquidation.

RUPA's underlying philosophy differs radically from UPA's, thus laying the foundation for many of its innovative measures. RUPA adopts the "entity" theory of partnership as opposed to the "aggregate" theory that the UPA espouses. Under the aggregate theory, a partnership is characterized by the collection of its individual members, with the result being that if one of the partners dies or withdraws, the partnership ceases to exist. On the other hand, RUPA's entity theory allows for the partnership to continue even with the departure of a member because it views the partnership as "an entity distinct from its partners."

This adoption of the entity theory, which permits continuity of the partnership upon changes in partner identity, allows for several significant changes in RUPA. Of particular importance to the instant case is that under RUPA "a partnership no longer automatically dissolves due to a change in its membership, but rather the existing partnership may be continued if the remaining partners elect to buy out the dissociating partner."... This major RUPA innovation therefore delineates two possible paths for a partnership to follow when a partner dies or withdraws: "one leads to the winding up and termination of the partnership and the other to continuation of the partnership and purchase of the departing partner's share." Will the Revised Uniform Partnership Act Ever Be Uniformly Adopted?, 48 Fla. L. Rev. at 583 (footnote omitted). Critically, under RUPA the estate of the deceased partner no longer has to consent in order for the business to be continued nor does the estate have the right to compel liquidation....

Along with 18 other states, Maryland has adopted RUPA, effective July 1, 1998, with a phase-in period during which the two Acts will coexist. As of January 1, 2003, RUPA will govern all Maryland partnerships. In adopting RUPA, the Maryland legislature was clearly seeking to eliminate some of UPA's harsh provisions, such as the automatic dissolution of a viable partnership upon the death of a partner and the subsequent right of the estate of the deceased partner to compel liquidation. In essence, the NCCUSL drafted RUPA to reflect the emerging trends in partnership law. RUPA is intended as a flexible, modern alternative to the more rigid UPA and its provisions are consistent with the reasonable expectations of commercial parties in today's business world.

B.

As discussed earlier, the traditional manner in which UPA allows for the continuation of the partnership upon the death of a partner is to either obtain the consent of the deceased partner's estate or include a continuation clause in the partnership agreement. There have been several cases in other jurisdictions, however, where neither of these conditions was met and the court elected another option under UPA instead of a "fire sale" of all the partnership assets to ensure that the deceased partner's estate received its fair share of the partnership. See Cutler v. Cutler, 165 B.R. 275, 278 (Bankr. D. Ariz. 1994) ("The winding up process does not necessarily mean that the assets of the partnership must be liquidated, although that is one option."). These jurisdictions have recognized the unfairness and harshness of a compelled liquidation and found other judicially acceptable means of winding up a partnership under UPA, such as ordering an in-kind distribution of the assets or allowing the remaining partners to buy out the withdrawing partner's share of the partnership.

While the following cases have not involved the specific situation that we are faced with here—dissolution upon the death of a partner—the options the various courts have adopted to avoid a compelled liquidation of all partnership assets are equally applicable to the instant case. A dissolution is a dissolution and a winding-up process is a winding-up process, no matter what the underlying reason is for its occurrence. The reason for the dissolution is relevant when liabilities are being apportioned among partners, such as in a wrongful dissolution, but such is not the concern in the instant case. Many of these cases also involve a continued partnership, as opposed to a successor partnership like Good Ole Boys, but again the various courts' reasons for not compelling a sale of all assets in order to arrive at the true value of the business are equally applicable to the instant case.

We look to the case law of other jurisdictions because this is a case of first impression in Maryland. The Maryland cases cited by Petitioner and Respondent in their briefs and during arguments are inapposite and offer little assistance in the task before us. We now turn to a discussion of out-of-state cases that have confronted the issue of whether, under UPA, a compelled liquidation in a dissolution situation is always mandated or whether there are other judicially acceptable alternatives.

1. In-Kind Distribution

We first examine the cases where the court elected to order an in-kind distribution rather than a compelled liquidation in order to ascertain the true value of the partnership. An in-kind distribution is the actual division and distribution of the physical assets themselves. See Black's Law Dictionary 475 (6th ed. 1990)(defining "distribution in kind" as "[a] transfer of property as is'"). In Nicholes v. Hunt, the parties orally agreed to form a partnership for the manufacture and sale of shot. 273 Ore. 255, 541 P.2d 820, 822–23 (Or. 1975). The relationship between the two partners quickly soured, with Nicholes alleging that he was being wrongfully excluded from the business by Hunt. Nicholes sought a dissolution decree, requesting that the partnership assets be liquidated at a sale. In holding that the partnership assets could be apportioned without resorting to a sale, the Supreme Court of Oregon stated: "*There is no express provision in [UPA] which establishes liquidation by sale as the exclusive mode of distributing partnership assets after dissolution.* Although the basic rule is that any partner has the right to force liquidation by sale, the rule has been subject to criticism...." Nicholes, 541 P.2d at 827 (emphasis added).

The court went on to quote extensively from a law review article, stating in pertinent part:

"'*The liquidation right will be injurious to the business in many, perhaps in most, cases. One authority has described it as "ruinous."* Whether it really is depends on the relative value of the business sold and the business retained. Such values are partly subjective and partly influenced by specific facts. But, it is rare that a small business, which is the kind most partnerships are, can be sold for as much as the owners think it is worth to themselves. This is true if it is disposed of intact as a going concern, and even more so if it is sold piecemeal. *In short, the likelihood of loss of value is great enough to require every partnership to look to the ways of denying or restricting the liquidation right.*'" (Emphasis added).

Nicholes, 541 P.2d at 827 (quoting Alan R. Bromberg, *Partnership Dissolution—Causes, Consequences, and Cures*, 43 Tex. L. Rev. 631, 647-48 (1965) (footnote omitted))....

2. Buy-Out Option

We turn to the line of cases where the court allowed the remaining partners to buy out the withdrawing partner's interest in the partnership, rather than mandate a forced sale of assets to derive the true value of the business.

In Gregg v. Bernards, 250 Ore. 458, 443 P.2d 166 (Or. 1968), Gregg appealed from a decree that dissolved the partnership and vested in Bernards the title to a race horse, the main partnership asset, upon payment by Bernards to Gregg the value of his partnership interest and also his share of the profit. The Supreme Court of Oregon affirmed the trial court's alternative resolution—a buy-out option—to a forced sale of the race horse.

Goergen v. Nebrich also involved a court refusing to order a public sale of the partnership assets in a dissolution situation and instead mandating a buy-out option. 12 Misc. 2d 1011, 174 N.Y.S.2d 366 (N.Y. Sup. Ct. 1958). Dissolution of the two-person partnership was sought on the basis of one partner's incompetency due to illness. After the decree was entered, the incompetent partner died and his estate wanted a public sale of all partnership assets. The New York court held that the partnership assets must be properly appraised to ascertain the true value of the business, but stated that "this does not mean that there must be a ... sale of the partnership assets." Goergen, 174 N.Y.S.2d at 369. The court held that because the surviving partner wanted to continue the business, "it would be inequitable and unfair to the surviving partner to have a public sale." Goergen, 174 N.Y.S.2d at 369....

C.

In applying the law discussed in Part II.A. and B. to the facts of this case, we want to clarify that while UPA is the governing act, our holding is also consistent with RUPA and its underlying policies. The legislature's recent adoption of RUPA indicates that it views with disfavor the compelled liquidation of businesses and that it has elected to follow the trend in partnership law to allow the continuation of business without disruption, in either the original or successor form, if the surviving partners choose to do so through buying out the deceased partner's share.

In this appeal, however, we would arrive at the same holding regardless of whether UPA or RUPA governs. Although our holding departs from the general UPA rule that the representative of the deceased partner's estate has a right to demand liquidation of the partnership, as we discuss in this subsection, infra, our position of "no forced sale" hardly represents a radical departure from traditional partnership law. The cases discussed in Part II.B., supra, many of which arose early in UPA's existence, illustrate the lengths other courts have gone to in order to avoid a compelled liquidation and adopt an alternative method for ascertaining the true value of a partnership. With that background, we turn to a discussion of the two issues Mrs. Creel raises in this appeal.

1. Compelled Liquidation Issue

The first issue is whether the Creel estate has the right to demand liquidation of Joe's Racing where its partnership agreement does not expressly provide for continuation of the partnership and where the estate does not consent to continuation. Before we move on to our analysis of the compelled liquidation issue, we point out that our finding that Good Ole Boys is a successor partnership, rather than a continuation of Joe's Racing, does not negate the need for a complete discussion of this issue. Unless there is consent to continue the business or an agreement providing for continuation, upon the death of a partner the accurate value of the partnership must be ascertained as of the date of dissolution and the proportionate share paid to the deceased partner's estate, no matter if we are dealing with a subsequent new partnership or a continuation of the original business. If a compelled liquidation of all partnership assets is seen as the only way to arrive at its true value, then property from the original partnership will have to be sold whether the present business is a continuation or a successor business; regardless, the potential harm of such a "fire sale" affects both equally. See Part II.C.2., for a full discussion of our characterization of Good Ole Boys.

a.

Because a partnership is governed by any agreement between or among the partners, we must begin our analysis of the compelled liquidation issue by examining the Joe's Racing partnership agreement. We reiterate that both UPA and RUPA only apply when there is either no partnership agreement governing the partnership's affairs, the agreement is silent on a particular point, or the agreement contains provisions contrary to law. See §§9-401, 9- 608, 9-609, 9-611, 9-613, and 9-614, which contain phrases such as "subject to any agreement between [the partners]," "unless otherwise agreed," "subject to any agreement to the contrary," and "in the absence of any agreement to the contrary." See also §9A-103(a). Thus, when conflicts between partners arise, courts must first look to the partnership agreement to resolve the issue....

The pertinent paragraph and subsections of the Joe's Racing partnership agreement are as follows:

> "7. TERMINATION
>
> (a) That, at the termination of this partnership a full and accurate inventory shall be prepared, and the assets, liabilities, and income, both in gross and net, shall be ascertained: the remaining debts or profits will be distributed according to the percentages shown above in the 6(e).
>
> ***
>
> (d) Upon the death or illness of a partner, his share will go to his estate. If his estate wishes to sell his interest, they must offer it to the remaining partners first."

Even though the partnership agreement uses the word "termination," paragraph 7(a) is really discussing the dissolution of the partnership and the attendant winding-up process that ultimately led to termination. Paragraph 7(a) requires that the assets, liabilities, and income be "ascertained," but it in no way mandates that this must be accomplished by a forced sale of the partnership assets. Indeed, a liquidation or sale of assets is not mentioned anywhere in 7(a).

In this case, the winding-up method outlined in 7(a) was followed exactly by the surviving partners: a full and accurate inventory was prepared on August 31, 1995; this information was given to an accountant, who ascertained the assets, liabilities, and income of the partnership; and finally, the remaining debt or profit was distributed according to the percentages listed in 6(e).[19]

As determined by the trial court, the interest of Joseph Cudmore, who never signed the partnership agreement, reverted to Joseph Creel, who was entitled to a 52 percent share.

Mrs. Creel argues that the partnership agreement does not address the winding-up process and that we should look to UPA's default rules to fill in this gap. Her contention is incorrect. We only turn to UPA and its liquidation rule if there is no other option, and such is clearly not the case here. While this partnership agreement was drafted without the assistance of counsel and is not a sophisticated document that provides for every contingency, if it states the intention of the parties it is controlling. As we stated in Klein v. Weiss:

> "A partnership is, of course, a contractual relation to which the principles of contract law are fully applicable.... One of the essential elements for formation of a contract is a manifestation of agreement or mutual assent by the parties to the terms thereof; in other words, to establish a contract the minds of the parties must be in agreement as to its terms." (Citations omitted).

284 Md. 36, 63, 395 A.2d 126, 141 (1978).

Thus, when we look to the intention of the parties as reflected in 7(a) of the partnership agreement, the trial judge could conclude that the partners did not anticipate that a "fire sale" of the partnership assets would be necessary to ascertain the true value of Joe's Racing. Paragraph 7(a) details the preferred winding-up procedure to be followed, to include an inventory, valuation, and distribution of debt or profit to the partners.

Moreover, paragraph 7(d), which discusses what happens to a partner's share of the business upon his death, also makes no mention of a sale or liquidation as being essential in order to determine the deceased partner's proportionate interest of the partnership. On the contrary, 7(d) appears to be a crude attempt to draft a "continuation clause" in the form of a buy-out option by providing that the deceased partner's share of the partnership goes to his estate, and if the estate wishes to sell this interest it must first be offered to the remaining partners. See § 9A-701, which details the purchase of the dissociated partner's interest. In contrast to consenting to the continuation of the business, Mrs. Creel made it plain that she wanted the business "dissolved and the affairs of the company wound up;" however, this does not mean a liquidation was required. Particularly in light of Maryland's recent adoption of RUPA, paragraph 7(d) of the partnership agreement can be interpreted to mean that because Mrs. Creel did not wish to remain in business with Lilly and Altizer, they had the option to buy out her deceased husband's interest.

In short, when subsections (a) and (d) of paragraph 7 are read in conjunction, it is apparent that the partners did not intend for there to be a liquidation of all partnership assets upon the death of a partner. Paragraph 7(a) delineates the winding-up procedure, which was methodically followed by Lilly and Altizer. Paragraph 7(d) dictates what hap-

---

19. Paragraph 6(e) of the partnership agreement states "that the net profits or net losses be divided as follows:

Joseph Creel 28%
Arnold Lilly 24%
Joseph Cudmore 24%
Roy Altizer 24%" [Court's footnote.—ed.]

pens to the partnership in the event of a partner's death, and it can be interpreted as allowing a buy-out option if the deceased partner's estate no longer wishes to remain in business with the surviving partners, as was clearly the case here. Therefore, the trial judge could have concluded that Lilly and Altizer exercised this 7(d) buy-out option, and subsequently began a new partnership, when they followed the winding-up procedure dictated by 7(a) and presented the Creel estate with its share of Joe's Racing.

Assuming arguendo that the Joe's Racing partnership agreement cannot be interpreted as outlining an alternative to liquidation in winding up the partnership in the event of a dissolution caused by a partner's death, we still find that a sale of all partnership assets is not required under either UPA or RUPA in order to ascertain the true value of the business. Support for this is found in Maryland's recent adoption of RUPA, which encourages businesses to continue in either their original or successor form, and also the holdings of out-of-state cases where other options besides a "fire sale" have been chosen when a partnership is dissolved under UPA. See full discussions in Part II.A. and B., supra....

b.

We find it is sound public policy to permit a partnership to continue either under the same name or as a successor partnership without all of the assets being liquidated. Liquidation can be a harmful and destructive measure, especially to a small business like Joe's Racing, and is often unnecessary to determining the true value of the partnership....

c.

Our goal in this case, and in cases of a similar nature, is to prevent the disruption and loss that are attendant on a forced sale, while at the same time preserving the right of the deceased partner's estate to be paid his or her fair share of the partnership. With our holding, we believe this delicate balance has been achieved. For the reasons stated, we hold that paragraph 7, subsections (a) and (d), of the partnership agreement should be interpreted as outlining an alternative method of winding-up Joe's Racing and arriving at its true value other than a "fire sale" of all its assets. Even if there were no partnership agreement governing this case, however, we hold that Maryland's UPA—particularly in light of the legislature's recent adoption of RUPA—does not grant the estate of a deceased partner the right to demand liquidation of a partnership where the partnership agreement does not expressly provide for continuation of the partnership and where the estate does not consent to continuation. To hold otherwise vests excessive power and control in the estate of the deceased partner, to the extreme disadvantage of the surviving partners. We further hold that where the surviving partners have in good faith wound up the business and the deceased partner's estate is provided with an accurate accounting allowing for payment of a proportionate share of the business, then a forced sale of all partnership assets is unwarranted.

2. Damages Issue

The second issue is whether the Creel estate is entitled to its partnership percentage share of the profits generated by the surviving partners' alleged continued use of the partnership assets. Mrs. Creel argues that because Lilly and Altizer did not liquidate the partnership as she demanded, they continued the partnership with the use of partnership property and inventory. For this reason, and also because she alleges they did not pay her the proper share of Joe's Racing, Mrs. Creel claims she is entitled to damages from this continued use. Her contention can be quickly dispensed with due to the trial judge's implicit finding that Joe's Racing was not continued, but instead was properly wound up on

August 31, 1995. Therefore, as Good Ole Boys is a successor partnership to Joe's Racing and not a continuation business, there are no "continuation" damages at issue.

When the winding-up process is complete, any monies owed to the deceased partner's estate cease as of this date. The courts below correctly found that Joe's Racing was wound up as of August 31, 1995; thus, the Creel estate is not owed anything beyond this date. We agree with the trial court's finding that the surviving partners "sought to close out the partnership and took all reasonable steps to do so." Lilly and Altizer did all that was required per paragraph 7 of the partnership agreement and § 9-609(a) of UPA to efficiently and in good faith wind up the partnership; within two months of Mr. Creel's death, the partnership had been properly wound up and terminated. We concur with the trial court's finding that "the proper method of winding up is outlined generally in Section 9-609(a), which states that persons claiming through a partner in a dissolution situation may have the partnership's property applied to discharge its liabilities and the surplus applied to pay in cash the net amount owing to the respective parties."....

McCormick v. Brevig, 96 P.3d 697 (Mont. 2004). "Clark invites this Court to take a liberal reading of [RUPA Article 8] and cites *Creel v. Lilly* (Md. 1999), 729 A.2d 385, in support of the proposition that judicially acceptable alternatives exist to compelled liquidation in a dissolution situation. At issue in *Creel* was whether the surviving partners of a partnership had a duty to liquidate all partnership assets because there was no provision in the partnership agreement providing for the continuation of the partnership upon a partner's death, and the estate had not consented to the continuation of business. After examining cases in which other courts had elected to order an in-kind distribution rather than a compelled liquidation, or had allowed the remaining partners to purchase the withdrawing partner's interest in the partnership, the court concluded that the UPA did not mandate a forced sale of all partnership assets in order to ascertain the true value of the business, and that "winding up" was not always synonymous with liquidation. The court further noted that it would have reached the same conclusion regardless of whether the UPA or RUPA governed since, under RUPA, the remaining partners could have elected to continue business following the death of one of the partners.

"However, of critical distinction between the facts in *Creel* and the case *subjudice* is the manner in which the partners exited the entity. In *Creel* one of the partners had died. Here, Joan sought a court ordered dissolution of the Partnership. Under RUPA, the death of a partner triggers the provisions of [RUPA Article 7], which allows for the purchase of the dissociated partner's interest in the partnership, much like what was ordered in *Creel*. Conversely, a court ordered dissolution pursuant to [RUPA Article 8], as in this case, results in the dissolution and winding up of the partnership. Thus, *Creel* is both legally and factually distinguishable.

"Furthermore, the cases relied upon by the court in Creel in reaching its conclusion that liquidation of assets was not always mandated upon dissolution, are likewise pre-RUPA holdings, which are inapposite to the facts at issue in this case.

"Accordingly, we conclude that when a partnership's dissolution is court ordered pursuant to [RUPA § 801(5)], the partnership assets necessarily must be reduced to cash in order to satisfy the obligations of the partnership and distribute any net surplus in cash to the remaining partners in accordance with their respective interests. By adopting a judicially created alternative to this statutorily mandated requirement, the District Court erred."

Revised Uniform Partnership Act (1997) § 807: Settlements of Accounts and Contributions Among Partners

(a) In winding up a partnership's business, the assets of the partnership, including the contributions of the partners required by this section, must be applied to discharge its obligations to creditors, including, to the extent permitted by law, partners who are creditors. Any surplus must be applied to pay in cash the net amount distributable to partners in accordance with their right to distributions under subsection (b).

(b) Each partner is entitled to a settlement of all partnership accounts upon winding up the partnership business. In settling accounts among the partners, profits and losses that result from the liquidation of the partnership assets must be credited and charged to the partners' accounts. The partnership shall make a distribution to a partner in an amount equal to any excess of the credits over the charges in the partner's account. A partner shall contribute to the partnership an amount equal to any excess of the charges over the credits in the partner's account but excluding from the calculation charges attributable to an obligation for which the partner is not personally liable under Section 306.

(c) If a partner fails to contribute the full amount required under subsection (b), all of the other partners shall contribute, in the proportions in which those partners share partnership losses, the additional amount necessary to satisfy the partnership obligations for which they are personally liable under Section 306. A partner or partner's legal representative may recover from the other partners any contributions the partner makes to the extent the amount contributed exceeds that partner's share of the partnership obligations for which the partner is personally liable under Section 306.

(d) After the settlement of accounts, each partner shall contribute, in the proportion in which the partner shares partnership losses, the amount necessary to satisfy partnership obligations that were not known at the time of the settlement and for which the partner is personally liable under Section 306.

(e) The estate of a deceased partner is liable for the partner's obligation to contribute to the partnership.

(f) An assignee for the benefit of creditors of a partnership or a partner, or a person appointed by a court to represent creditors of a partnership or a partner, may enforce a partner's obligation to contribute to the partnership.

Note on Capital Accounts and Termination

Once all of its "external" accounts are settled, the partnership then distributes and collects money from the partners, essentially reconciling the partners' capital accounts and then distributing whatever remains as partnership profits (or collecting from the partners, in proportion to their share of losses, if liabilities exceed assets).

The original UPA perhaps made this prioritization clearer than RUPA's more specific language. UPA § 40 provided:

(b) The liabilities of the partnership shall rank in order of payment, as follows:

I. Those owing to creditors other than partners,

II. Those owing to partners other than for capital and profits, [e.g., loans by partners to the partnership]

III. Those owing to partners in respect of capital,

IV. Those owing to partners in respect of profits.

RUPA chooses to eliminate the distinction between category I and II (presumably on the basis that a debt is a debt, regardless of whether it's owed to a partner or to some other party).[20] It otherwise effectively preserves the UPA's prioritization, however. Under RUPA § 807, debt is reconciled first, then capital accounts—and what remains after that is a profit or a loss.

Kovacik v. Reed

315 P.2d 314 (Cal. 1957)

SCHAUER, J.

In this suit for dissolution of a joint venture and for an accounting, defendant appeals from a judgment that plaintiff recover from defendant one half the losses of the venture. We have concluded that inasmuch as the parties agreed that plaintiff was to supply the money and defendant the labor to carry on the venture, defendant is correct in his contention that the trial court erred in holding him liable for one half the monetary losses, and that the judgment should therefore be reversed.

.... From the "condensed statement of the oral proceedings" included in the settled statement, it appears that plaintiff, a licensed building contractor in San Francisco, operated his contracting business as a sole proprietorship under the fictitious name of "Asbestos Siding Company." Defendant had for a number of years worked for various building contractors in that city as a job superintendent and estimator.

Early in November, 1952, "Kovacik [plaintiff] told Reed [defendant] that Kovacik had an opportunity to do kitchen remodeling work for Sears Roebuck Company in San Francisco and asked Reed to become his job superintendent and estimator in this venture. Kovacik said that he had about $10,000.00 to invest in the venture and that, if Reed would superintend and estimate the jobs, Kovacik would share the profits with Reed on a 50-50 basis. Kovacik did not ask Reed to agree to share any loss that might result and Reed did not offer to share any such loss. The subject of a possible loss was not discussed in the inception of this venture. Reed accepted Kovacik's proposal and commenced work for the venture shortly after November 1, 1952.... Reed's only contribution was his own labor. Kovacik provided all of the venture's financing through the credit of Asbestos Siding Company, although at times Reed purchased materials for the jobs in his own name or on his account for which he was reimbursed....

"The venture bid on and was awarded a number of ... remodeling jobs ... in San Francisco. Reed worked on all of the jobs as job superintendent.... During ... August, 195, Kovacik, who at that time had all of the financial records of the venture in his possession, ... informed Reed that the venture had been unprofitable and demanded con-

---

20. On the other hand, because partners are liable for partnership obligations, external debt effectively ends up prioritized anyway. As RUPA explains in its official comment:

> In effect, [§ 807] abolishes the priority rules in UPA Section 40(b) ... which subordinate the payment of inside debt to outside debt.... Ultimately, however, a partner whose "debt" has been repaid by the partnership is personally liable, as a partner, for any outside debt remaining unsatisfied.... Accordingly, the obligation to contribute sufficient funds to satisfy the claims of outside creditors may result in the equitable subordination of inside debt when partnership assets are insufficient to satisfy all obligations to non-partners.

tribution from Reed as to amounts which Kovacik claimed to have advanced in excess of the income received from the venture. Reed at no time promised, represented or agreed that he was liable for any of the venture's losses, and he consistently and without exception refused to contribute to or pay any of the loss resulting from the venture.... The venture was terminated on August 31, 1953."

Kovacik thereafter instituted this proceeding, seeking an accounting of the affairs of the venture and to recover from Reed one half of the losses. Despite the evidence above set forth from the statement of the oral proceedings, showing that at no time had defendant agreed to be liable for any of the losses, the trial court "found"—more accurately, we think, concluded as a matter of law—that "plaintiff and defendant were to share equally all their joint venture profits and losses between them," and that defendant "agreed to share equally in the profits and losses of said joint venture." Following an accounting taken by a referee appointed by the court, judgment was rendered awarding plaintiff recovery against defendant of some $4,340, as one half the monetary losses[21] found by the referee to have been sustained by the joint venture.

It is the general rule that in the absence of an agreement to the contrary the law presumes that partners and joint adventurers intended to participate equally in the profits and losses of the common enterprise, irrespective of any inequality in the amounts each contributed to the capital employed in the venture, with the losses being shared by them in the same proportions as they share the profits.

However, it appears that in the cases in which the above stated general rule has been applied, each of the parties had contributed capital consisting of either money or land or other tangible property, or else was to receive compensation for services rendered to the common undertaking which was to be paid before computation of the profits or losses.

Where, however, as in the present case, one partner or joint adventurer contributes the money capital as against the other's skill and labor, all the cases cited, and which our research has discovered, hold that neither party is liable to the other for contribution for any loss sustained. Thus, upon loss of the money the party who contributed it is not entitled to recover any part of it from the party who contributed only services.

The rationale of this rule is that where one party contributes money and the other contributes services, then in the event of a loss each would lose his own capital—the one his money and the other his labor. Another view would be that in such a situation the parties have, by their agreement to share equally in profits, agreed that the values of their contributions—the money on the one hand and the labor on the other—were likewise equal; it would follow that upon the loss, as here, of both money and labor, the parties have shared equally in the losses. Actually, of course, plaintiff here lost only some $8,680—or somewhat less than the $10,000 which he originally proposed and agreed to invest....

It follows that the conclusion of law upon which the judgment in favor of plaintiff for recovery from defendant of one half the monetary losses depends is untenable, and

21. The record is silent as to the factors taken into account by the referee in determining the "loss" suffered by the venture. However, there is no contention that defendant's services were ascribed any value whatsoever. It may also be noted that the trial court "found" that "neither plaintiff nor defendant was to receive compensation for their services rendered to said joint venture, but plaintiff and defendant were to share equally all their joint venture profits and losses between them." Neither party suggests that plaintiff actually rendered services to the venture in the same sense that defendant did. And, as is clear from the settled statement, plaintiff's proposition to defendant was that plaintiff would provide the money as against defendant's contribution of services as estimator and superintendent. [Court's footnote.—ed.]

that the judgment should be reversed. Consequently, it is unnecessary to dispose of defendant's further contention that plaintiff could not in any event recover, because the joint venture did not hold or apply for a general contractor's license or any other license, and was thus tainted with illegality.

The judgment is reversed.

Revised Uniform Partnership Act § 401, cmt. 2. "The default rules apply, as does UPA Section 18(a), where one or more of the partners contribute no capital, although there is case law to the contrary. See, e.g., Kovacik v. Reed, 49 Cal. 2d 166, 315 P.2d 314 (1957); Becker v. Killarney, 177 Ill. App. 3d 793, 523 N.E.2d 467 (1988). It may seem unfair that the contributor of services, who contributes little or no capital, should be obligated to contribute toward the capital loss of the large contributor who contributed no services. In entering a partnership with such a capital structure, the partners should foresee that application of the default rule may bring about unusual results and take advantage of their power to vary by agreement the allocation of capital losses."

Melvin Aron Eisenberg & James D. Cox, *Corporations and Other Business Organizations* 132 (10th ed.). "The approach taken in *Kovacik* is sound. If a services-only partner has been fully compensated for his services, it is hard to see why he should not be required to contribute toward making up a capital loss. Otherwise, a capital partner would bear all the partnership's loss and the services-only partner would bear none [if the event that a partnership lost the full value of the capital partner's contributions and then dissolved].

"[RUPA's official comment's] attempt at justification does more to show why RUPA ... is wrong than why it is right. The Comment begins by frankly recognizing that the result 'may seem unfair.' It then states that even if the rule is unfair the partners can contract around it. Of course, any rule of partnership law, no matter how foolish, could be 'justified' by the argument that it can be contracted around. The point of partnership law, however, should be to make good rules that the parties probably would have agreed to if they had addressed the issue, not to make bad rules that the partners can contract around. Furthermore, many partners don't know partnership law, and therefore won't realize they need to contract around any given rule. Indeed, because persons can be partners without having an intention to form a partnership, many partners don't even realize that they are partners, let alone realize that they should consider contracting around any given rule of partnership law."

In a note discussing the differences between joint ventures and partnerships, in connection with *Kovacik*, Eisenberg and Cox suggest that courts may sometimes classify a relationship as a joint venture instead of a partnership in order to avoid an undesirable rule in the UPA or RUPA: "The line between a joint venture and a partnership is exceedingly thin.... As a realistic matter, what seems to be involved is this: Some rules of the [statutes] produce unsatisfactory results in certain kinds of cases. Courts that want to avoid these results will sometimes do so, if they plausibly can, by holding that a 'special rule' applies to joint ventures, and that the enterprise in the case at hand is a joint venture and therefore falls within the special rule. In many or most such cases, the desired result could probably be reached, without applying special rules to joint ventures, by finding that the parties had an implied agreement that overrides the relevant rule of the [statutes]."

Problem

Rachel and Evan enter into a partnership under RUPA called Apalachi Cola with the purpose of manufacturing a new soda drink, Mrs. Ginger. Rachel contributes $30,000, and Evan will operate the partnership with no salary as long as it exists. The partners orally agree to split the profits and losses equally.

After a year, the partnership has spent its $30,000 in cash and has no cash or assets left. Because she still believes in the eventual profitability of the Mrs. Ginger soft drink, Rachel makes the partnership a loan of $10,000, and the partnership also borrows $10,000 from a local bank. These new loans do no good, however, and after the partnership has spent through them, Rachel withdraws and seeks a judicial dissolution under RUPA § 801(5).

What are the obligations among the parties?

Revised Uniform Partnership Act (1997) § 802: Partnership Continues After Dissolution

(b) At any time after the dissolution of a partnership and before the winding up of its business is completed, all of the partners, including any dissociating partner other than a wrongfully dissociating partner, may waive the right to have the partnership's business wound up and the partnership terminated. In that event:

(1) the partnership resumes carrying on its business as if dissolution had never occurred, and any liability incurred by the partnership or a partner after the dissolution and before the waiver is determined as if dissolution had never occurred....

Chapter 4

Other Partnership Forms

Section 1: The Limited Liability Partnership

The limited liability partnership (LLP) is a very simple form that is closely related to the general partnership. Indeed, it is governed by the same statute, RUPA, and it operates almost identically to the general partnership. There are two important differences between these organizational forms, however. One is just procedural: a partnership must specifically elect and file a statement with the government to become an LLP, whereas general partnerships can arise naturally out of the course of conduct of the parties. The other difference is substantive: in a limited liability partnership, the individual partners are not liable for partnership obligations.

Revised Uniform Partnership Act (1997) § 1001: Statement of Qualification

(a) A partnership may become a limited liability partnership pursuant to this section.

(b) The terms and conditions on which a partnership becomes a limited liability partnership must be approved by the vote necessary to amend the partnership agreement except, in the case of a partnership agreement that expressly considers obligations to contribute to the partnership, the vote necessary to amend those provisions.

(c) After the approval required by subsection (b), a partnership may become a limited liability partnership by filing a statement of qualification [with the government containing the name, address, and other information about the partnership]....

Comment

.... The unanimous vote default rule reflects the significance of a partnership becoming a limited liability partnership. In general, upon such a filing each partner is released from the personal contribution obligation imposed under this Act in exchange for relinquishing the right to enforce the contribution obligations of other partners under this Act. The wisdom of this bargain will depend on many factors including the relative risks of the partners' duties and the assets of the partnership.

Revised Uniform Partnership Act (1997) § 1002: Name

The name of a limited liability partnership must end with "Registered Limited Liability Partnership," "Limited Liability Partnership," "R.L.L.P.," "L.L.P.," "RLLP," or "LLP."

Revised Uniform Partnership Act (1997) § 306: Partner's Liability

(c) An obligation of a partnership incurred while the partnership is a limited liability partnership, whether arising in contract, tort, or otherwise, is solely the obligation of the partnership. A partner is not personally liable, directly or indirectly, by way of contribution or otherwise, for such an obligation solely by reason of being or so acting as a partner. This subsection applies notwithstanding anything inconsistent in the partnership agreement that existed immediately before the vote required to become a limited liability partnership under Section 1001(b).

Comment

When an obligation is incurred is determined by other law. Under that law, and for the limited purpose of determining when partnership contract obligations are incurred, the reasonable expectations of creditors and the partners are paramount.... For the limited purpose of determining when partnership tort obligations are incurred, a distinction is intended between injury and the conduct causing that injury. The purpose of the distinction is to prevent unjust results. Partnership obligations under or relating to a tort generally are incurred when the tort conduct occurs rather than at the time of the actual injury or harm. This interpretation prevents a culpable partnership from engaging in wrongful conduct and then filing a statement of qualification to sever the vicarious responsibility of its partners for future injury or harm caused by conduct that occurred prior to the filing.

Note on Terminology

As Mel Eisenberg has pointed out, *see* Eisenberg & Cox, *supra*, at 415, the term "limited liability" may be confusing. The term is very commonly used to express the idea that an individual owner or manager of a business does not face vicarious liability for the business's obligations. The phrase arises from the notion that the potential loss that a partner faces is "limited" to the partner's contributions to the partnership. "No vicarious business liability" or "limited loss" would perhaps be clearer phrases, but the use of the phrase "limited liability" in this context is almost universal.

Note that RUPA does not limit the liability of LLP partners for their *personal* torts. For example, suppose that a partner in an LLP negligently drives a truck in the course of partnership business and injures a third-party victim. If the victim sues the driver, the driver is not exempt from personal liability because he or she was acting as a partner in the scope of ordinary partnership business. As RUPA § 306(c) specifies, "A partner is not personally liable ... *solely by reason of being or so acting as a partner*" (emphasis added); a partner may still be liable simply because of his or her own negligence. RUPA's official comment to § 306(c) also makes this clear: "partners remain personally liable for their personal misconduct." Of course, as we have seen, the partner may in some cases seek indemnity from the partnership, but that indemnity does not affect the right of the victim to recover from the negligent partner individually.

Accordingly, the main protections for partners in an LLP are that (1) they will face no personal liability for the torts—such as malpractice—committed by other partners in the ordinary course of the partnership's business (or, of course, the partnership's employees), and (2) they will face no personal liability on the LLP's contracts, unless they are themselves also a party to the contract or make a separate personal guarantee.

Roe v. Ladymon, 318 S.W.3d 502 (Tex. App. 2010). Blane Ladymon had, as a general partner of Metro LLP, signed a contract with Kimberlea Roe under which Metro would remodel Roe's house. Roe, unsatisfied with the work, sought to compel Ladymon to arbitrate the dispute under the form's arbitration clause, alleging that "Ladymon was bound to arbitrate as a representative [of] Metro LLP.

"Roe argues Ladymon consented to arbitrate claims against him individually because he was 'a signatory to the contract' and 'a representative of Metro.' Ladymon did sign the contract as a partner of Metro LLP and initialed each page in the blank for 'Contractor.' However, the contract identifies the parties to the contract as Roe, the owner, and Metro LLP, the contractor; Ladymon individually is not identified as a party. Moreover, Ladymon's signature on the contract does not render him personally a party to the contract because he clearly indicated he was signing on behalf of contractor, Metro LLP, and not on his own behalf. See ... Restatement (Second) of Agency § 320 (1958) ("Unless otherwise agreed, a person making or purporting to make a contract with another as agent for a disclosed principal does not become a party to the contract."). Further, being a partner in a registered limited liability partnership, and thus its 'representative,' does not make the partner personally liable for the obligations of the limited liability partnership. While an agent of a disclosed principal may agree to substitute his own responsibility for that of the principal or to add his responsibility to that of the principal, there is no indication here that Ladymon did so merely by signing the contract as a partner of a limited liability partnership."

Note on Limited Liability Partnerships

Given that most partners probably benefit personally from not being liable for partnership obligations, why are any organizations general partnerships rather than limited liability partnerships? The simplest reason is lack of planning: many entities form general partnerships without any specific knowledge of organizational law, and they may not even intend to be governed by general partnership law. Effectively, the LLP form, with its formal filing requirement, gives a benefit (in the form of reduced liability) to those who are aware of the law and choose to exercise the benefit. To put it differently, it exempts knowledgeable, well-informed partners from vicarious liability for partnership obligations if they so choose. The wisdom and desirability of permitting this exemption depends on the reasons for vicarious liability in the first place—reasons that, as we have discussed, are contentious.

Another reason that LLPs were not always used is that they were not always available. Historically, it was common to see their use restricted, by statute, to professional partnerships (such as law firms or accountancies). Under RUPA, however, LLPs are generally available.

As a descriptive matter, the trend in modern organizational law has been decisively in favor of restricting vicarious business liability. The rise of the LLP, along with the limited liability company (LLC) and some changes in the limited partnership (LP) form—the latter two of which we have yet to cover in detail—make it very easy to avoid such liability. This trend can probably be explained by a conception of the political process known as *public choice theory*, a school of thought in economics and political science that explains that when a policy favors a concentrated group but has costs that are spread widely over society, lobbying and other factors will often cause those policies to be enacted even if they are not advantageous to society overall. Businesspeople often want to cut off their potential vicarious liability for business activities; potential tort victims of business probably do not want this, but they are less organized. To put it simply, it is very common to see chambers of commerce, but there are no chambers of people who might one day be hit by delivery trucks.

Ederer v. Gursky

881 N.E.2d 204 (N.Y. 2007)

READ, J.

This appeal calls upon us to explore the nature and scope of Partnership Law § 26(b). We hold that this provision does not shield a general partner in a registered limited liability partnership from personal liability for breaches of the partnership's or partners' obligations to each other.

I

The relationship that deteriorated into this acrimonious dispute began promisingly enough in 1998 when plaintiff Louis Ederer affiliated with the law firm of Gursky & Associates, PC, which promptly changed its name to Gursky & Ederer, PC ("the PC"). Ederer joined the PC as a salaried, non-equity contract partner, but he had an understanding with defendant Steven R. Gursky, the PC's sole shareholder, that if their practice developed as anticipated, he would become a full equity partner in about two years' time.

Right on schedule, in May 2000 Gursky orally agreed to increase Ederer's annual compensation by about 17% and to make him a 30% shareholder in the PC as of July 1, the beginning of the PC's fiscal year. Ederer committed to purchase his 30% interest for $600,000, to be paid for by Gursky's taking an additional $150,000 from the PC's yearly distributions for each of the following four years. Finally, Gursky agreed that when the PC took on additional partners, his 70% equity interest would be diluted up to 25% before Ederer's 30% interest was reduced.

In February 2001, the PC became a registered limited liability partnership known as Gursky & Ederer, LLP ("the LLP"). Significantly, there was no written partnership agreement. The LLP began billing all new legal services, while the PC billed and collected work-in-process and preexisting accounts receivable, and loaned money to the LLP to fund its start-up. In July 2001, the LLP admitted three new partners, defendants Mitchell B. Stern, Martin Feinberg and Michael A. Levine. They collectively acquired a 15% interest in the LLP, leaving Gursky with a 55% interest while Ederer retained his 30% interest.

Ederer received his 30% share of the PC's profits for the fiscal years ending June 30, 2001 and June 30, 2002, less the $150,000 owed to Gursky each year. In 2002, both Ederer and Gursky loaned the PC a portion of their respective shares of the PC's profits. Sometime prior to June 30, 2003, the LLP assumed these loans in exchange for the furniture, fixtures and equipment that it acquired from the PC.

In July 2002, the LLP increased Ederer's annual compensation by about 28%. Gursky also agreed to forgive the remaining $300,000 owed by Ederer for the purchase of his 30% equity interest. Ederer characterizes this gesture as an acknowledgment of his major contributions to the firm's revenue growth; Gursky, as a concession made solely upon Ederer's assurances that he was committed to remaining with the LLP to assure its long-term success.

In June 2003, Ederer advised Gursky that he was withdrawing as a partner in the LLP and a shareholder in the PC. Ederer chalks up his decision to a severe falling out with Gursky in early 2003 over the representation of a firm client. Gursky retorts that Ederer left because the LLP was cash-strapped and unprofitable, and blames him in no small part for this purported state of affairs.

On June 26, 2003, Ederer entered into a withdrawal agreement with the PC and the LLP, which Gursky signed as president of the PC and a partner in the LLP. Under this agreement, Ederer agreed to remain a partner in the LLP so as to serve as lead counsel for a trial scheduled to commence in Georgia on June 30, 2003, although he was not obligated to delay his withdrawal from the LLP beyond July 8. In exchange, the LLP agreed to "continue to pay [Ederer his] regular draw and other compensation through the date of [his] withdrawal from the [the LLP]"; to have files on which he was working transferred to his new firm upon the client's request; to give him the opportunity to review his client's bills before the LLP asked for payment; and to allow him and/or his representatives (including accountants) access to the LLP's and PC's books and records after his withdrawal from the LLP.

The PC was dissolved on June 30, 2003, although formal dissolution papers were not filed with the Secretary of State until March 2004. Ederer withdrew from the LLP on or about July 4, 2003 after having helped secure a $2 million verdict in the Georgia trial, which generated a $600,000 contingency fee for the LLP. After Ederer's departure, the LLP continued in business under the name Gursky & Partners, LLP until March 1, 2005, when it ceased operations.

In December 2003, Ederer commenced this action against the PC, the LLP, Gursky & Partners, LLP, and Gursky, Stern, Feinberg and Levine, seeking an accounting and asserting breach of the withdrawal agreement. In his amended verified complaint dated November 1, 2005, Ederer sought an accounting of his interest in the PC (the first cause of action) and the LLP (the second cause of action), and asserted causes of action for breach of contract relating to Gursky's May 2000 oral agreement to pay him 30% of the PC's profits (the third cause of action), the June 2003 written agreement to pay him for the two weeks he tried the Georgia case for the LLP (the fourth cause of action), and the unpaid portion of his loan to the PC in 2002 (the fifth cause of action).

In their verified answer dated November 7, 2005, defendants denied the gravamen of Ederer's complaint; and interposed numerous affirmative defenses as well as counterclaims sounding in breach of fiduciary duty, conversion, tortious interference with contractual relations, fraud and deceit and fraudulent inducement, breach of contract, and unjust enrichment. Defendants also counterclaimed for a declaration that the withdrawal agreement was void because entered into under the duress of Ederer's alleged threat not to try the case in Georgia.

On November 7, 2005, defendants moved to dismiss the complaint as to defendants Gursky, Stern, Feinberg and Levine; to dismiss the first and second causes of action for an accounting and the third cause of action for breach of contract (the May 2000 oral agreement), or, in the alternative, for summary judgment in favor of all defendants upon these causes of action; and/or for summary judgment in favor of defendants "providing that goodwill should not be valued in connection with an accounting of the affairs of [the PC] and/or [the LLP]." As relevant to this appeal, defendants argued that Ederer's complaint set forth no cognizable causes of action upon which relief could be granted against the individual defendants because Partnership Law §26(b) shielded them from any personal liability.

On November 30, 2005, Ederer opposed defendants' motion and cross-moved for partial summary judgment on liability on his first and second causes of action for an accounting, and his third, fourth and fifth causes of action for breach of contract. He asked Supreme Court to direct that a trial be held on damages with respect to the accounting; and requested summary judgment dismissing defendants' counterclaims.

Supreme Court determined that Ederer was entitled to an accounting against all defendants because Partnership Law § 26, which places limits on the personal liability of partners in an LLP, applies "to debts of the partnership or the partners to third parties" and "has nothing to do with a partner's fiduciary obligation to account to his partners for the assets of the partnership." The trial court also rejected defendants' argument that "an accounting of Ederer's interest in [the PC] should not be allowed both because [he] was not a shareholder in the P.C., and because the P.C. had effectively transferred all of its remaining assets to the LLP as of the date of [his] withdrawal from the firm, rendering the accounting of the P.C. duplicative." The court determined that, "[b]ecause of confusion of the location of the firm's assets at the time [Ederer] left the firm, in order for the accounting of [his] interest to be complete, it must necessarily include an accounting of the firm's assets taken by Gursky from the P.C., as well as an accounting of [Ederer's] partnership in the LLP."

In sum, Supreme Court denied defendants' motions in all respects; granted so much of Ederer's cross motion as sought to dismiss defendants' counterclaims for fraud, breach of contract, a declaration that the withdrawal agreement was void, and unjust enrichment, but concluded that there were triable issues of fact precluding dismissal of defendants' counterclaims for breach of fiduciary duty, conversion, and tortious interference with contractual relations; declared the withdrawal agreement valid and enforceable; granted so much of the cross motion as sought partial summary judgment for an accounting against all defendants; and referred the issue of the accounting of the PC and the LLP to a special referee to hear and report with recommendations, or, upon stipulation of the parties, for the special referee or another referee designated by the parties to determine the issue. The trial court further ordered the motion to be held in abeyance pending receipt of the special referee's report and recommendations and a motion under CPLR 4403, or receipt of a determination; and directed the remainder of the action to continue. Defendants appealed.

The Appellate Division affirmed Supreme Court's order on December 5, 2006, concluding that "Partnership Law § 26(b), limiting the liability of partners of a limited liability partnership, does not exempt ... partners from their individual obligations to account to a withdrawing partner under the earlier enacted and unamended Partnership Law § 74" and "does not exempt the individual defendants from liability to plaintiff for breaches of firm-related agreements between them". Although individual defendants argued that they had not entered into any agreements with Ederer, "it appears that the assets of the PC, with which [Ederer] entered into three agreements, were transferred to the successor LLP, in which all of the individual defendants were partners. The nature and value of the PC's assets, and [Ederer's] interest therein, will be determined in the accounting, and to the extent any of the defendants are in possession of those assets, they may be obliged to pay them over to [Ederer]" (id. at 167).

Defendants subsequently moved in the Appellate Division for leave to appeal to this Court. On March 20, 2007, the Appellate Division granted defendants' motion and certified the following question to us: "Was the order of Supreme Court, as affirmed by this Court, properly made?" Defendants limited the appeal to this Court to challenging so much of the Appellate Division order as affirmed Supreme Court's denial of the individual defendants' motion for summary judgment. To the extent appealed from, as limited by defendants' brief, we now affirm, answering the certified question in the affirmative.

II

This appeal comes down to a dispute over the effect of the Legislature's 1994 amendments to section 26 of the Partnership Law. As originally adopted by the Legislature in 1919, section 26 was identical to section 15 of the Uniform Partnership Act (UPA), which was drafted by the National Conference of Commissioners on Uniform State Laws and approved by the Conference in 1914. Prior to its amendment in 1994, section 26 provided that

> "[a]ll partners are liable
>
> "1. Jointly and severally for everything chargeable to the partnership under sections twenty-four and twenty-five.
>
> "2. Jointly for all other debts and obligations of the partnership; but any partner may enter into a separate obligation to perform a partnership contract."

Section 24 specifies that "[w]here, by any wrongful act or omission of any partner acting in the ordinary course of the business of the partnership, or with the authority of his copartners, loss or injury is caused to any person, not being a partner in the partnership, or any penalty is incurred, the partnership is liable therefor to the same extent as the partner so acting or omitting to act." Section 25 binds the partnership to "make good the loss"

> "1. Where one partner acting within the scope of his apparent authority receives money or property of a third person and misapplies it; and
>
> "2. Where the partnership in the course of its business receives money or property of a third person and the money or property so received is misapplied by any partner while it is in the custody of the partnership."

Partnership Law § 26, as originally enacted, and its prototype, section 15 of the UPA, have always been understood to mean what they plainly say: general partners are jointly and severally liable to non-partner creditors for all wrongful acts and breaches of trust committed by their partners in carrying out the partnership's business, and jointly liable for all other debts to third parties. This proposition follows naturally from the very nature of a partnership, which is based on the law of principal and agent. Just as a principal is liable for the acts of its agents, each partner is personally responsible for the acts of other partners in the ordinary course of the partnership's business. In addition to this vicarious liability to non-partner creditors, each partner concomitantly has an obligation to share or bear the losses of the partnership through contribution and indemnification in the context of an ongoing partnership (see Partnership Law §§ 40[1],[2] as originally enacted, which is identical to sections 18[a],[b] of the UPA); and contribution upon dissolution and winding up (see Partnership Law § 65 as originally enacted, which is identical to section 34 of the UPA; and Partnership Law § 71[d] as originally enacted, which is identical to section 40[d] of the UPA).

The nationwide initiative to create a new business entity combining the flexibility of a partnership without the onus of this traditional vicarious liability originated with a law adopted

> "in Texas in 1991, following the savings and loan crisis. At that time, a number of legal and accounting firms faced potentially ruinous judgments arising out of their professional services for banks and thrifts which thereafter failed. Because these professional firms were typically organized as general partnerships,

> this liability also threatened the personal assets of their constituent partners. The Texas LLP statute protected such partners (at least prospectively) from this unlimited personal exposure without requiring a reorganization of their business structure"

(Walker, New York Limited Liability Companies and Partnerships: A Guide to Law and Practice § 14:3, at 344-345 [1 West's NY Prac Series 2002]; see also Fortney, "Seeking Shelter in the Minefield of Unintended Consequences—The Traps of Limited Liability Law Firms," 54 Wash & Lee L Rev 717, 724 [1997] [noting that following the failure of a number of Texas financial institutions, regulators sued these institutions' professional advisers, including attorneys, for damages far exceeding their law firms' insurance coverage; and that because "(a)ttorneys could not fathom the possibility of their personal, nonexempt assets being subject to execution for judgment arising from their partners' malpractice," they were "spurred (to seek) legislative changes to limit their vicarious liability"]; Keatinge, et al., "Limited Liability Partnerships: The Next Step in the Evolution of the Unincorporated Business Organization," 51 Bus Law 147, 174 [1995-1996] ["The principal impetus in the enactment of (limited liability partnership) legislation has been the limitation of vicarious liability to third parties"]).

In New York, the Legislature enacted limited liability partnership legislation as a rider to the New York Limited Liability Company Law (see Walker, § 14:2, at 344). This legislation eliminated the vicarious liability of a general partner in a registered limited liability partnership by amending section 26 of the Partnership Law, and making conforming changes to sections 40(1), (2), 65 and 71(d). Specifically, new section 26(b) creates an exception to the vicarious liability otherwise applicable by virtue of section 26(a) (original section 26 [section 15 of the UPA]), by providing that "[e]xcept as provided by subdivisions (c) and (d) of this section, no partner of a partnership which is a registered limited liability partnership is liable or accountable, directly or indirectly (including by way of indemnification, contribution or otherwise), for any debts, obligations or liabilities of, or chargeable to, the registered limited liability partnership or each other, whether arising in tort, contract or otherwise, which are incurred, created or assumed by such partnership while such partnership is a registered limited liability partnership, solely by reason of being such a partner."

Section 26(c) excludes from section 26(b)'s liability shield "any negligent or wrongful act or misconduct committed by [a partner] or by any person under his or her direct supervision and control while rendering professional services on behalf of [the] registered limited liability partnership." Section 26(d) allows partners to opt out from or reduce the reach of section 26(b)'s protection from vicarious liability.

As one commentator has noted, by "expressly provid[ing] that limited liability includes liability by way of indemnification or contribution," section 26(b) precludes the potential for a plaintiff to "attempt an end-run around the liability shield of [section 26(b)] by first asserting a claim against the [limited liability partnership] and then arguing that the general partnership statute requires the [limited liability partnership] partners to make contributions to the [limited liability partnership]" (Johnson, "Limited Liability for Lawyers: General Partners Need Not Apply," 51 Bus Law 85, 110 [1995-1996]). The Legislature further expressed its intention to negate a partner's indemnification or contribution obligations with respect to liabilities for which the partner was not vicariously liable by making sections 40(1), (2), 65 and 71(d) subject to section 26(b).

Defendants point out that section 26(b) eliminates the liability of a partner in a limited liability partnership for "any debts" without distinguishing between debts owed to a third party or to the partnership or each other. As a result, they contend, the Legislature did not "leave open to conjecture whether § 26(b) was intended to cover debts which may be owed by the [limited liability partnership] (or one partner) to other partners." This argument ignores, however, that the phrase "any debts" is part of a provision (section 26) that has always governed only a partner's liability to third parties, and, in fact, is part of article 3 of the Partnership Law ("Relations of Partners to Persons Dealing with the Partnership)," not article 4 ("Relations of Partners to One Another"). The logical inference, therefore, is that "any debts" refers to any debts owed a third party, absent very clear legislative direction to the contrary.

Defendants also note that chapter 576's legislative history illustrates the desire to enact liability protection for partners in limited liability partnerships that is "the same as that accorded to shareholders of a professional corporation organized under the BCL [and] as that accorded to members of a professional LLC" (Senate Introducer Mem in Support, Bill Jacket, L 1994, ch 576). They point out that "the legislative history of the LLP Act plainly indicates that the Legislature intended to provide an even greater shield of individual liability to partners in LLPs than that enacted by other states as of the date of the legislation."

These observations are correct, but do not advance defendants' cause. Chapter 576 does, in fact, afford limited liability partners the same protection from third-party claims as New York law provides shareholders in professional corporations or professional limited liability companies. And unlike New York, most states "have adopted a partial liability shield protecting the partners only from vicarious personal liability for all partnership obligations arising from negligence, wrongful acts or misconduct, whether characterized as tort, contract or otherwise, committed while the partnership is an LLP" (see Prefatory Note Addendum to Uniform Partnership Act [1997], [explaining that RUPA, by contrast, "provid(es) for a corporate-styled shield which protects partners from vicarious personal liability for all partnership obligations incurred while a partnership is a limited liability partnership"]; see also Walker, § 14:5, at 346 ["The type of LLP generally permitted by the states (other than Minnesota and New York) ... offers less insulation against personal liability than many other types of organization"]). Nowhere in the voluminous commentary on limited liability partnerships has anyone suggested that New York (or any other state) has adopted a statute expanding the concept of limited liability in the way asserted by defendants.

Next, defendants make two arguments in their attempt to reconcile their interpretation of section 26(b) with Partnership Law § 74, which gives a partner "[t]he right to an account of his interest ... as against the winding up partners or the surviving partners or the person or partnership continuing the business, at the date of dissolution, in the absence of agreement to the contrary" (see also Partnership Law § 43, which is identical to section 21 of the UPA [see Uniform Partnership Act [1914] § 21, Comment, at 194 (indicating that the words "and hold as trustee for the partnership any profits" were meant to "indicate clearly that the partnership can claim as their own any property or money that can be traced" in a situation where a specific sum of partnership money or property is in the hands of an insolvent partner)]). First, they argue that their fiduciary duty as partners to account to one another "is not the same as the personal liability for the debts disclosed by the accounting." But the remedy of accounting is restitutionary by definition (see Eichengrun, "Remedying the Remedy of Accounting," 60 Ind L J 463, 463 [1984-1985] [In an accounting, "(t)he plaintiff must establish some basis for the obligation to account, the defendant is ordered to account, and the plaintiff then gets an order directing payment of the sum of money found due"]; see also Belsheim, "The Old Action of Account," 45 Harv L Rev 466 [1931-1932]). Second, defendants claim that a partner is only personally liable for debts disclosed in an accounting which are attributable to that partner's own torts or wrongful conduct or supervisory lapses, as excluded by Partnership Law § 26(c) from the protection of section 26(b). If the Legislature had intended to qualify section 74 in this manner, however, it surely would have explicitly made section 74 subject to sections 26(b) and/or 26(c). It did not do so for the same reason that defendants arguments fail generally: section 26(b) only addresses a partner's vicarious liability for partnership obligations.

In closing, we emphasize that the law of partnerships contemplates a written agreement among partners specifying the terms of their relationship. The Partnership Law's provisions are, for the most part, default requirements that come into play in the absence of an agreement. For example, the right to an accounting exists, "absen[t an] agreement to the contrary" (Partnership Law § 74). Partners might agree, as among themselves, to limit the right to contribution or indemnification or to exclude it altogether. In this case, however, there was no written partnership agreement; therefore, the provisions of the Partnership Law govern.

Accordingly, the order of the Appellate Division, insofar as appealed from, should be affirmed, with costs, and the certified question should be answered in the affirmative.

SMITH, J. (dissenting):

The text of Partnership Law § 26 (b) seems clear to me: "no partner of a partnership which is a registered limited liability partnership is liable ... for any debts, obligations or liabilities of ... the registered limited liability partnership ... whether arising in tort, contract or otherwise." The statute contains two specific exceptions, applicable when a partner acts wrongfully or when partners agree to vary the liability scheme (Partnership Law § 26 [c], [d]), but there is no exception for liabilities to former partners claiming a share of the partnership's net assets. We should not create an exception that the Legislature did not. The majority draws a distinction between liability to "third parties" and liabilities to former partners—but a former partner is a third party where the partnership is concerned, and there is no good reason to treat him more favorably than any other third party.

No one suggests that section 26 (b) exempts partners from any of their fiduciary duties; if a partner has diverted partnership funds to himself, or otherwise received more than his fair share, he will not escape liability and his former partners, as well as his existing partners, will be made whole. The issue is whether a former partner claiming his partnership share may reach the personal assets of partners who are no more blameworthy, and have no more been unjustly enriched, than he has.

I can think of two situations in which this issue may be important. First, without any fault by any partner, the business of the partnership may go badly after a partner withdraws from the firm but before he is paid his share, leaving the firm without enough assets to satisfy his claim. (This is apparently what happened here.) Secondly, the partnership's insolvency may result from the fault of a partner who is himself insolvent; in that case, the question is whether the former partner can proceed against the innocent remaining partners.

In the first case, there is no apparent reason why a former partner should be allowed to collect his debt when other third party creditors may not; in fact, the Partnership Law provides in another context that debts to non-partners have a preferred status. In the second case, the rule adopted by the majority can produce even more clearly perverse results. Take an extreme example: Suppose there are three partners, two with a 49% interest each and one with a 2% interest. One of the 49% partners withdraws, and is entitled to 49% of the firm's assets. Before he can be paid, however, it is found that the other 49% partner has stolen all of those assets, lost them at a casino and gone bankrupt. Why should the innocent 2% partner have to make good the former partner's large loss?

If the Gursky & Ederer firm had remained a professional corporation, instead of turning itself into a limited liability partnership, the result in this case would not be in question: the individual shareholders of the corporation would not be liable for its obligation to Ederer. I do not see why the partners of an LLP should have an obligation that the shareholders of a PC do not, and I therefore dissent.

Section 2: The Limited Partnership: Introduction and Limited Liability

Despite the similarity in name, the limited partnership (LP) form reflects a more significant departure from the law of general partnerships than does the LLP. The limited partnership is a distinct entity, structured very differently from the general partnership.

The central characteristic of a limited partnership is that there are two different kinds of partners: (1) general partners, who are responsible for operating the business and who are vicariously liable for the business's obligations, and (2) limited partners, who ordinarily have a limited role (if any) in operating the business and who are not responsible for the business's obligations.

General partners in a limited partnership have a role broadly similar to those in general partnerships. For example, they have authority to bind the partnership into contracts. The law of limited partnerships differs largely in the rights and duties associated with limited partners. Because the archetypal limited partner is a passive investor, for example, it is common—though not the default in the Uniform Limited Partnership Act[1]—for an LP agreement to provide for free transferability of limited partnership "stakes" in an LP, often called "partnership units." Indeed, many publicly traded entities are in fact limited partnerships, although of course most companies traded on the public exchanges (such as the New York Stock Exchange or NASDAQ) are corporations. As another example, a default statutory provision governing limited partners in a modern limited partnership specifies that a limited partner has no authority to bind the LP by virtue of such a position. See ULPA (2001) § 302.

Uniform Limited Partnership Act (2001) § 401: Becoming General Partner

A person becomes a general partner:

(1) as provided in the partnership agreement;

(2) [by a vote of "limited partners owning a majority of the rights to receive distributions as limited partners" to continue the limited partnership and elect one or more general partners] following the dissociation of a limited partnership's last general partner;

. . .

(4) with the consent of all the partners.

---

1. See ULPA (2001) § 301.

Donald J. Weidner, *The Existence of State and Tax Partnerships: A Primer*

11 Fla. St. U. L. Rev. 1 (1983)

Based on the French Societe en Commandite,[2] the limited partnership acts generally authorized the creation of partnerships with two classes of "partners," general and limited. This basic approach is similar to that utilized today. General partners are what we normally think of as partners, persons with full and equal power to run the business who are unlimitedly personally liable to the contract and tort creditors of the business. Limited partners, on the other hand, were passive investors who could lose their protected status as limited partners if they took part in the control of the business. In short, if the limited partners were truly passive investors, and if they followed a statutorily prescribed procedure for publicly recording their status as passive investors, they would be insulated from personal liability to the creditors of the partnership.

Limited partnership statutes spread, and limited partnerships became quite popular. However, by the late nineteenth century, interest in limited partnerships began to fade as the corporate form became more freely available. State legislatures had been passing, and then liberalizing, general incorporation acts. Initially, for example, it was common for state statutes to limit how long a corporate charter could last. Like today's so-called "sunset" legislation, corporate charters were created to expire, for example, after 20 years; only in time would perpetual corporations become acceptable. There were also limits on the amount of capital any particular corporation could have because the fear of unlimited accumulations of wealth lingered. Over time various restrictions were gradually, then rapidly liberalized, as some states actually competed with each other for success in what came to be perceived as the lucrative business of selling corporate charters.

The limited partnership had not completely disappeared from the economic scene by the beginning of the twentieth century. It still had its uses, and that of Andrew Carnegie is one of the more notable. It is not entirely fortuitous that when general incorporation statutes were finally enacted, the corporation, at least at one level, appeared less regal and more "American." Indeed, the corporate structure looked very much like the American government. There were the shareholders, the people, who had the right to vote to elect a board of directors, a Congress, to make basic policy decisions. The board of directors, in turn, appointed management to carry out its basic policy mandates. Andrew Carnegie considered this model of the corporation an unwanted extension of democracy. He was an extraordinarily successful capitalist who felt that any investor participating in the profitability of his enterprise should be grateful for his profits and not meddle in management, by voting or otherwise. Carnegie did not want to be hampered by minority shareholders, so he held Carnegie Steel in a limited partnership. The state statute authorizing the creation of limited partnerships was attractive precisely because it said that limited partners are not to take part in the control of the business. Andrew Carnegie notwithstanding, the limited partnership form lay fairly dormant until the middle of the twentieth century when, for reasons of federal income tax law rather than state law, it exploded into popular usage and came to be a household word in middle and upper class America.

2. The phrase basically means "sponsorship company" in French, the typical "sponsor" (commanditaire) being the financial investor with limited control and liability. This particular organizational form is reportedly uncommon in modern France. [–ed.]

Note on the Uniform Limited Partnership Acts

There have been four significant versions of the uniform statute that governs limited partnerships: (1) the Uniform Limited Partnership Act (ULPA) of 1916, (2) the Revised act (RULPA) of 1976, (3) significant amendments to RULPA passed in 1985; and (4) the new Uniform Limited Partnership act of 2001, commonly referred to as the "Re-Revised Uniform Limited Partnership Act," or Re-RULPA.

Probably the most significant difference among these acts is the degree of liability protection they provide to limited partners. Before the rise of LLPs and LLCs, businesspeople and investors in partnerships faced a tradeoff between (1) the benefits of participating in the ownership and control of a business and (2) the liability that would tend to come along with that control. (They could avoid this tradeoff by setting up a corporation, but that raised a different set of tradeoffs, implicating taxes.) As with the rise of LLPs and LLCs, the trend in the various versions of ULPA has largely been to make it easier for businesspeople and investors to elect to exempt themselves from vicarious liability for the obligations of businesses—that is, to achieve limited liability. As with LLPs, limited partners would always be personally liable for their own personal torts, contractual guarantees, and so on; the question is how much vicarious business liability they could avoid.

Limited liability for limited partners in limited partnerships evolved as follows:

1. The 1916 act, ULPA § 7, specified that a "limited partner shall not become liable as a general partner unless, in addition to the exercise of his rights and powers as a limited partner, he takes part in the control of the business." The phrase "liable as a general partner" referred to the vicarious business liability of a general partner. Though this statutory provision codified an older common-law rule, it remained a largely open-ended, factual question what level of control would make a limited partner vicariously liable for the obligations of a limited partnership.
2. The 1976 act, RULPA § 303, provided as follows:

> (a) Except as provided in subsection (d),[3] a limited partner is not liable for the obligations of a limited partnership unless he [or she] is also a general partner or, in addition to the exercise of his [or her] rights and powers as a limited partner, he [or she] takes part in the control of the business. However, if the limited partner's participation in the control of the business is not substantially the same as the exercise of the powers of a general partner, he [or she] is liable only to persons who transact business with the limited partnership with actual knowledge of his participation in control....

The force of this provision was to narrow liability compared to ULPA § 7. The first sentence of RULPA § 303(a) extends liability to limited partners in situations very similar to those covered by ULPA § 7, but the second sentence restricts that liability in some cases. Particularly, except in cases where a limited partner more or less acts overall as if he or she were a general partner (and the limited-partner status is just effectively a

3. Subsection (d) is a relatively minor subsection that concerns the limited partnership's name. It makes a limited partner who "knowingly permits his [or her] name to be used in the name of the limited partnership" liable to "creditors who extend credit to the limited partnership without actual knowledge that the limited partner is not a general partner," unless the name "(i) ... is also the name of a general partner or the corporate name of a corporate general partner, or (ii) the business of the limited partnership had been carried on under that name before the admission of that limited partner." RULPA § 303(d), 102(2).

sham), the limited partner will be liable only in contract to those third parties who actually know of the limited partner's control.

Moreover, RULPA § 303(b) provided a "safe harbor"—that is, a list of activities that did not count as the sort of control that made a limited partner vicariously liable for the obligations of the partnership:

> (b) A limited partner does not participate in the control of the business within the meaning of subsection (a) solely by doing one or more of the following:
>
> (1) being a contractor for or an agent or employee of the limited partnership or of a general partner;
>
> (2) consulting with and advising a general partner with respect to the business of the limited partnership;
>
> (3) acting as surety for the limited partnership;
>
> (4) approving or disapproving an amendment to the partnership agreement or
>
> (5) voting on one or more of the following matters:
>
> (i) the dissolution and winding up of the limited partnership;
>
> (ii) the sale, exchange, lease, mortgage, pledge, or other transfer of all or substantially all of the assets of the limited partnership other than in the ordinary course of its business;
>
> (iii) the incurrence of indebtedness by the limited partnership other than in the ordinary course of its business;
>
> (iv) a change in the nature of the business;
>
> (v) removal of a general partner.

Just to be safe, subsection (c) added: "The enumeration in subsection (b) does not mean that the possession or exercise of any other powers by a limited partner constitutes participation by him [or her] in the business of the limited partnership."

3. The 1985 amendments to RULPA changed the text of § 303(a) of the 1976 act as follows, with strikeouts indicating removed text and underlines indicating added text:

> (a) Except as provided in subsection (d), a limited partner is not liable for the obligations of a limited partnership unless he [or she] is also a general partner or, in addition to the exercise of his [or her] rights and powers as a limited partner, he [or she] ~~takes part~~ participates in the control of the business. However, if the limited ~~partner's participation~~ partner participates in the control of the business ~~is not substantially the same as the exercise of the powers of a general partner,~~ he [or she] is liable only to persons who transact business with the limited partnership ~~with actual knowledge of his participation in control~~ reasonably believing, based upon the limited partner's conduct, that the limited partner is a general partner.

The 1985 amendments thus removed the part of the statute under which a limited partner could be liable for acting in "substantially the same" way as a general partner; no longer did it matter whether the label of "limited partner" was broadly a sham. Moreover, the third party's belief concerning the limited partner's status now, under the 1985 amendments, had to rest directly "upon the limited partner's conduct," whereas in the 1976 version of RULPA liability could rest merely on the third party's knowledge. And that third party's belief had to be reasonable; essentially, the test focused on what could reasonably be inferred from the limited partner's manifestations, so that the limited partner could more directly control the danger of liability.

The 1985 amendments also expanded the safe harbor to include a variety of new activities, some of which were relatively minor and some of which were potentially very broad. For example, the safe harbor now included both "matters related to the business of the limited partnership not otherwise enumerated in [the safe harbor], which the partnership agreement states in writing may be subject to the approval or disapproval of limited partners" and "exercising any right or power permitted to limited partners under this [act] and not specifically enumerated in this subsection."

4. Continuing the obvious trend, the 2001 act (called ULPA or Re-RULPA), in § 303, eliminates limited-partner liability entirely:

> An obligation of a limited partnership, whether arising in contract, tort, or otherwise, is not the obligation of a limited partner. A limited partner is not personally liable, directly or indirectly, by way of contribution or otherwise, for an obligation of the limited partnership solely by reason of being a limited partner, even if the limited partner participates in the management and control of the limited partnership.

As of 2013, the 2001 act (called ULPA or Re-RULPA) has been adopted by nineteen states, including California, Illinois, Florida, and Washington DC. (The earlier versions of the acts were adopted in nearly every state.)

The 2001 act's removal of the potential for vicarious business liability for limited partners is consistent with the availability of LLPs, LLCs, and another entity known as the limited liability limited partnership (LLLP)—an LP in which even the general partner faces no liability. That is, regardless of the general desirability of the clear trend in favor of limiting the liability of businesspeople and investors, it would be hard to justify a provision in the LP statute that made it easier for a creditor or tort victim to recover against a limited partner in an LP compared to a general partner in an LLP. The comment to the 2001 ULPA states this justification explicitly: "In a world with LLPs, LLCs and, most importantly, LLLPs, the control rule has become an anachronism. This Act therefore takes the next logical step in the evolution of the limited partner's liability shield and renders the control rule extinct." ULPA (2001) § 303 cmt.

ULPA itself permits LLLPs and provides, in a provision analogous to RUPA's for LLPs, that general partners in an LP that elects to become an LLLP are not individually liable for partnership obligations. *See* ULPA (2001) § 404(c).

Holzman v. De Escamilla

195 P.2d 833 (Cal. App. 1948)

MARKS, J.

This is an appeal by James L. Russell and H. W. Andrews from a judgment decreeing they were general partners in Hacienda Farms Limited, a limited partnership, from February 27 to December 1, 1943, and as such were liable as general partners to the creditors of the partnership.

Early in 1943, Hacienda Farms Limited was organized as a limited partnership, with Ricardo de Escamilla as the general partner and James L. Russell and H. W. Andrews as limited partners.

The partnership went into bankruptcy in December, 1943, and Lawrence Holzman was appointed and qualified as trustee of the estate of the bankrupt. On November 13, 1944, he brought this action for the purpose of determining that Russell and Andrews, by taking part in the control of the partnership business, had become liable as general partners to the creditors of the partnership. The trial court found in favor of the plaintiff on this issue and rendered judgment to the effect that the three defendants were liable as general partners.

The findings supporting the judgment are so fully supported by the testimony of certain witnesses, although contradicted by Russell and Andrews, that we need mention but a small part of it. We will not mention conflicting evidence as conflicts in the evidence are settled in the trial court and not here.

De Escamilla was raising beans on farm lands near Escondido at the time the partnership was formed. The partnership continued raising vegetable and truck crops which were marketed principally through a produce concern controlled by Andrews.

The record shows the following testimony of de Escamilla:

> "A. We put in some tomatoes. Q. Did you have a conversation or conversations with Mr. Andrews or Mr. Russell before planting the tomatoes? A. We always conferred and agreed as to what crops we would put in.... Q. Who determined that it was advisable to plant watermelons? A. Mr. Andrews.... Q. Who determined that string beans should be planted? A. All of us. There was never any planting done—except the first crop that was put into the partnership as an asset by myself, there was never any crop that was planted or contemplated in planting that wasn't thoroughly discussed and agreed upon by the three of us; particularly Andrews and myself."

De Escamilla further testified that Russell and Andrews came to the farms about twice a week and consulted about the crops to be planted. He did not want to plant peppers or egg plant because, as he said, "I don't like that country for peppers or egg plant; no, sir," but he was overruled and those crops were planted. The same is true of the watermelons.

Shortly before October 15, 1943, Andrews and Russell requested de Escamilla to resign as manager, which he did, and Harry Miller was appointed in his place.

Hacienda Farms Limited maintained two bank accounts, one in a San Diego bank and another in an Escondido bank. It was provided that checks could be drawn on the signatures of any two of the three partners. It is stated in plaintiff's brief, without any contradiction (the checks are not before us) that money was withdrawn on 20 checks signed by Russell and Andrews and that all other checks except three bore the signatures of de Escamilla, the general partner, and one of the other defendants. The general partner had no power to withdraw money without the signature of one of the limited partners.

Section 2483 of the Civil Code [based on ULPA (1916) §7] provides as follows:

> A limited partner shall not become liable as a general partner unless, in addition to the exercise of his rights and powers as a limited partner, he takes part in the control of the business.

The foregoing illustrations sufficiently show that Russell and Andrews both took "part in the control of the business." The manner of withdrawing money from the bank accounts is particularly illuminating. The two men had absolute power to withdraw all the partnership funds in the banks without the knowledge or consent of the general partner. Either Russell or Andrews could take control of the business from de Escamilla by refusing to sign checks for bills contracted by him and thus limit his activities in the management of the business. They required him to resign as manager and selected his successor. They were active in dictating the crops to be planted, some of them against the wish of de Escamilla. This clearly shows they took part in the control of the business of the partnership and thus became liable as general partners.

Judgment affirmed.

Section 3: The Limited Partnership: Fiduciary Duties

Uniform Limited Partnership Act (2001) §408: General Standards of General Partner's Conduct

(a) The only fiduciary duties that a general partner has to the limited partnership and the other partners are the duties of loyalty and care under subsections (b) and (c).

(b) A general partner's duty of loyalty to the limited partnership and the other partners is limited to the following:

(1) to account to the limited partnership and hold as trustee for it any property, profit, or benefit derived by the general partner in the conduct and winding up of the limited partnership's activities or derived from a use by the general partner of limited partnership property, including the appropriation of a limited partnership opportunity;

(2) to refrain from dealing with the limited partnership in the conduct or winding up of the limited partnership's activities as or on behalf of a party having an interest adverse to the limited partnership; and

(3) to refrain from competing with the limited partnership in the conduct or winding up of the limited partnership's activities.

(c) A general partner's duty of care to the limited partnership and the other partners in the conduct and winding up of the limited partnership's activities is limited to refraining from engaging in grossly negligent or reckless conduct, intentional misconduct, or a knowing violation of law.

(d) A general partner shall discharge the duties to the partnership and the other partners under this [Act] or under the partnership agreement and exercise any rights consistently with the obligation of good faith and fair dealing.

Gotham Partners, L.P. v. Hallwood Realty Partners, L.P.

817 A.2d 160 (Del. 2002)

VEASEY, C.J.

. . .

Facts

Hallwood Realty Partners, L.P. ("the Partnership") is a Delaware limited partnership that owns commercial office buildings and industrial parks in several locations in the

United States and lists its partnership units on the American Stock Exchange. Gotham Partners, L.P. ("Gotham") is a hedge fund, the investments of which include real estate. It is the largest independent limited partner in the Partnership with approximately 14.8 percent of the outstanding partnership units. Hallwood Realty Corporation ("the General Partner") is the sole general partner and is a wholly-owned subsidiary of Hallwood Group Incorporated ("HGI"), which owned 5.1 percent of the outstanding partnership units before the transactions challenged in this case. Anthony Gumbiner and William Guzzetti were members of the board of directors of the General Partner. They were also officers of HGI at the time of the challenged transaction.[4]

In 1994, the Partnership's units were trading at a low price because of the ongoing economic recession in real estate. On October 12, 1994, Guzzetti proposed to the Partnership's board of directors that it approve a reverse split,[5] a unit option plan, and an odd lot tender offer subject to HGI's willingness to finance the transactions by buying any fractional units generated by a reverse split and any units purchased by the Partnership in an odd lot tender offer.[6] At the time, more than half of the Partnership's units were held in odd lots and could be resold to HGI. Guzzetti told the board that HGI was the only source of financing available and that the transactions would, among other things, raise the trading price of the Partnership's units, reduce the Partnership's administrative costs, and give odd lot holders the chance to sell at market price without incurring brokerage fees. The Partnership's board approved the transactions, citing Guzzetti's reasons.

At first, HGI declined to provide funding for the reverse split and odd lot offer. But, by March 1995, HGI was willing to fund the Reverse Split and Option Plan, which were approved by the non-HGI directors on the General Partner's board. HGI purchased 30,000 units, approximately 1.6 percent of the Partnership's equity, through the Reverse Split. The Option Plan resulted in officers and employees of the General Partner purchasing 86,000 units or 4.7 percent of the Partnership's equity. Through these two transactions, HGI increased its ownership of outstanding Partnership units from 5.1 percent to approximately 11.4 percent.

By May 1995, HGI was willing to fund an odd lot tender offer. Guzzetti called a special meeting of the General Partner's board of directors after circulating a memorandum indicating that 55 percent of the Partnership's units were held in odd lots and thus could be tendered in the odd lot offer. The non-HGI directors voted as a "special committee" to approve the Odd Lot Offer. The purchase price of an odd lot was putatively set at the five-day market average referenced in Section 9.01(b) of the Partnership Agreement. No valuation information was shared with the board.

The Odd Lot Offer began on June 5, 1995. The accompanying press release indicated that the Partnership would resell any tendered odd lot units to HGI, affiliates of HGI, or

---

4. Gumbiner, a corporate lawyer, owned 30% of HGI's shares between 1994 and 1995 and was the chairman of the board of directors and chief executive officer of the General Partner at the time of the challenged transactions. Guzzetti, a former lawyer, is an executive vice-president of HGI and was the president of the Partnership and a member of the General Partner's board of directors at the time of the challenged transactions. [Court's footnote. —ed.]

5. A reverse split reduces the number of outstanding units and consequently increases the per unit value of each unit. Reverse splits usually create odd lots. [Court's footnote. —ed.]

6. An odd lot offer is a tender offer by the issuer for blocks of fewer than one hundred outstanding units or shares. Such "odd lots" are considered small and thus create inefficient administrative costs for issuers and may be difficult to sell at an attractive price. Odd lot offers are designed to provide liquidity to small holders and to reduce issuer costs. [Court's footnote. —ed.]

other institutional investors. The Odd Lot Offer and Resale was pitched to the public and the American Stock Exchange as a resale to HGI of existing, listed Partnership units, not as an issuance of new, unlisted units. Consequently, the Partnership never filed a listing application with the American Stock Exchange for the units sold to HGI, and the Partnership's accounting books did not treat the Odd Lot Resale to HGI as an issuance of units.

From June 9 to July 25, 1995, when the Odd Lot Offer closed, the Partnership purchased 293,539 units from odd lot holders and placed them in a holding account. The Partnership then resold the units to HGI at the same price the Partnership paid for them, approximately $4.1 million. The Odd Lot Resale resulted in HGI purchasing approximately 23.4 percent of the Partnership's outstanding units. Thus, HGI increased its stake in the outstanding Partnership units from 11.4 percent to 29.7 percent and solidified its control over the Partnership. The Partnership Agreement requires the written consent or affirmative vote by at least 66 and 1/3 percent of the limited partners to remove a general partner.

Gotham began purchasing Partnership units in 1994 and owned 14.8 percent of the outstanding units as of September 1996. Gotham was aware of the Odd Lot Offer and Resale but did not complain to the Partnership until January 1997 when it requested access to the Partnership's books and records. The Partnership denied the request.

Preliminary Proceedings in the Court of Chancery

.... On June 20, 1997, Gotham filed [an] action in the Court of Chancery alleging derivative claims[7] in connection with the Odd Lot Offer and Resale, the Reverse Split, and the Option Plan. Gotham alleged that these transactions were unfair to the Partnership's unitholders because HGI paid an unfairly low price to acquire control over the Partnership. Gotham's claims included breaches by the General Partner of traditional fiduciary duties and contractually based fiduciary duties. The claims also charged Gumbiner and Guzzetti, the General Partner's HGI-affiliated directors, and HGI itself with aiding and abetting those breaches. Gotham and the Partnership negotiated a settlement of the books and records action but the derivative action continued.

On summary judgment, the Court of Chancery sustained the contractual fiduciary duty claims and dismissed the traditional fiduciary duty claims on the ground that the Partnership Agreement supplanted traditional fiduciary duties and provided for contractual fiduciary duties by which the defendants' conduct would be measured. The Vice Chancellor found that Sections 7.05 and 7.10(a) of the Partnership Agreement operate together as a contractual statement of the entire fairness standard, with Section 7.05 substantively requiring fair price and Section 7.10(a) substantively requiring fair dealing. No appeal has been taken from this ruling....

Decision After Trial

After trial, the Court of Chancery found the defendants liable for their conduct associated with the Odd Lot Resale to HGI, but upheld their conduct connected with the Reverse Split and the Option Plan. The Vice Chancellor found that the Odd Lot Resale,

7. A "derivative claim" is a claim in which a limited partner seeks to act for the LP and cause it to sue someone that the limited partner believes has wronged the LP—often a general partner. Limited partners do not ordinarily have the authority to act for LPs, but the derivative action provides a mechanism by which they can vindicate the LP's rights when general partners (who often are the alleged wrongdoers or have a similar sort of conflict of interest) are unwilling to cause the LP to file a lawsuit. *See* ULPA (2001) § 1002. [—ed.]

unlike the other two transactions, did not involve an issuance of units, but rather a resale of existing units to HGI. As a result, the Vice Chancellor found "inapplicable" the protections of Section 9.01 of the Partnership Agreement, which authorizes the General Partner to issue Partnership Units of any kind to any person without the consent or approval of the Limited Partners. Instead, the Vice Chancellor continued, the Odd Lot Resale was subject to Partnership Agreement Sections 7.05 and 7.10(a), which provide for the contractually created fiduciary duties of entire fairness.

The Vice Chancellor found that the General Partner breached the contractual fiduciary duties of entire fairness because (1) the General Partner never formed the Audit Committee as required by Section 7.10(a) to review and approve the Odd Lot Offer and Resale, and (2) the General Partner failed to perform a market check or obtain any reliable financial analysis indicating that the Odd Lot Resale would be conducted on the same terms obtainable from a third party. The Court of Chancery thus held the General Partner liable for breach of the contractually created fiduciary duties of entire fairness contained in the Partnership Agreement and found HGI, Gumbiner, and Guzzetti jointly and severally liable with the General Partner for aiding and abetting its breach.

Gotham requested rescission, or money damages and sterilization of voting rights. The Court of Chancery awarded money damages plus compound interest instead of rescission, in part because it found that Gotham delayed challenging the transaction "for nearly two years, and then filed suit to rescind only after it was clear that the market price [of the Partnership units] was up substantially and on a sustainable basis." The Vice Chancellor then went on to find that the challenged transactions were not "conceived of as a conscious scheme to entrench the General Partner's control and enrich HGI" improperly. He stated that if he had been convinced otherwise, "I might be inclined to grant rescission despite Gotham's torpid pace."

Gotham then filed a direct appeal in this Court contesting the remedy. The General Partner, HGI, Gumbiner, and Guzzetti filed cross appeals asserting that the Court of Chancery erred by finding Section 9.01(a) of the Partnership Agreement inapplicable to the Odd Lot Offer and Resale or, alternatively, by holding HGI, Gumbiner, and Guzzetti liable for aiding and abetting the General Partner's breach of its contractually created fiduciary duties and by awarding compound interest on a damages award.

Issues on Appeal

On appeal, Gotham argues that the Court of Chancery was required to award rescission as a matter of law and, even if an award of monetary damages were appropriate, the Court of Chancery erred in its calculation of the damages by failing to account for a control premium. Gotham seeks reversal in part of the judgment of the Court of Chancery and a remand to the court with instructions to order rescission of the Odd Lot Resale to HGI. Alternatively, Gotham seeks an award of rescissory damages or sterilization of HGI's voting rights connected to the Odd Lot Resale units, or both.

The General Partner, HGI, Gumbiner, and Guzzetti, contend in their cross appeal that the Court of Chancery erred: (1) by finding the Odd Lot Resale to HGI subject to Sections 7.05 and 7.10(a) of the Partnership Agreement, which provide for contractual fiduciary duties of entire fairness, instead of Section 9.01, which authorizes the General Partner to issue Partnership Units of any kind to any person without the consent or approval of the Limited Partners; (2) by finding HGI, Gumbiner, and Guzzetti jointly and severally liable with the General Partner for aiding and abetting a breach of a contractually created fiduciary duty; and (3) by awarding compound interest on money damages. We will address the cross appeals first.

Whether the Court of Chancery Erred By Ruling That the Odd Lot Resale to HGI Was A Resale of Partnership Units

This Court reviews de novo the Court of Chancery's interpretation of written agreements and Delaware law.

As the Vice Chancellor noted at summary judgment, a general partner owes the traditional fiduciary duties of loyalty and care to the limited partnership and its partners, but DRULPA § 17-1101(d)(2) "expressly authorizes the ... modification, or enhancement of these fiduciary duties in the written agreement governing the limited partnership." Indeed, we have recognized that, by statute, the parties to a Delaware limited partnership have the power and discretion to form and operate a limited partnership "in an environment of private ordering" according to the provisions in the limited partnership agreement. We have noted that DRULPA embodies "the policy of freedom of contract" and "maximum flexibility." DRULPA's "basic approach is to permit partners to have the broadest possible discretion in drafting their partnership agreements and to furnish answers only in situations where the partners have not expressly made provisions in their partnership agreement" or "where the agreement is inconsistent with mandatory statutory provisions." In those situations, a court will "look for guidance from the statutory default rules, traditional notions of fiduciary duties, or other extrinsic evidence." But, if the limited partnership agreement unambiguously provides for fiduciary duties, any claim of a breach of a fiduciary duty must be analyzed generally in terms of the partnership agreement.

The Vice Chancellor found, and the parties do not contest, that Partnership Agreement Sections 7.05 and 7.10(a) set forth fiduciary duties of entire fairness owed by the General Partner to its partners generally in self-dealing transactions, such as the Odd Lot Resale. Section 7.05 expressly permits the Partnership to enter into self-dealing transactions with the General Partner or its affiliate "provided that the terms of any such transaction are substantially equivalent to terms obtainable by the Partnership from a comparable unaffiliated third party." Section 7.10(a) requires the General Partner to form an independent Audit Committee that shall review and approve self-dealing transactions between the Partnership and the General Partner and any of its affiliates. The Vice Chancellor found, and the parties do not contest, that Sections 7.05 and 7.10(a) "operate together as a contractual statement of the traditional entire fairness standard [of fair price and fair dealing], with § 7.05 reflecting the substantive aspect of that standard and § 7.10 reflecting the procedural aspect of that standard."

Because the Partnership Agreement provided for fiduciary duties, the Vice Chancellor properly held that the Partnership Agreement, as a contract, provides the standard for determining whether the General Partner breached its duty to the Partnership through its execution of the Odd Lot Resale. As the Vice Chancellor stated, the Partnership Agreement "leaves no room for the application of common law fiduciary duty principles to measure the General Partner's conduct" because the Partnership Agreement "supplanted fiduciary duty and became the sole source of protection for the public unitholders of the Partnership." Thus, "the General Partner was subject, by contract, to a fairness standard akin to the common law one applicable to self-dealing transactions by fiduciaries."

The General Partner, HGI, Gumbiner, and Guzzetti apparently concede: (1) the General Partner's conduct associated with the Odd Lot Resale did not comply with Sections 7.05 and 7.10(a) of the Partnership Agreement because, as the Vice Chancellor found; (2) the Audit Committee never reviewed or approved the Odd Lot Resale to HGI; and (3) the General Partner never obtained a reliable financial analysis indicating that the

Odd Lot Resale would be conducted on the same terms obtainable from an independent third party. Nonetheless, they argue that they are not liable for failing to comply with Sections 7.05 and 7.10(a) because Section 9.01 alone governed the Odd Lot Resale. They assert that the Odd Lot Resale was an issuance rather than a resale of Partnership units to HGI. The defendants seek the protection of Section 9.01, which gives the General Partner absolute and independent authority to issue additional Partnership units to any person or entity, including affiliates such as HGI.

The Vice Chancellor properly found that the Odd Lot Resale was a resale of Partnership units to HGI and thus Section 9.01 is inapplicable. It is undisputed that the Partnership's accounting books did not treat the sale of odd lots to HGI as an issuance of units. Furthermore, the Partnership units from the Odd Lot Resale were listed on the American Stock Exchange, but the Resale was presented to the Exchange as a resale, not as an issuance. The Vice Chancellor properly found that the Odd Lot Resale was structured as a resale, in part to avoid American Stock Exchange Rule 713, which requires that holders approve additional issuances as a prerequisite to the shares or units' listing on the Exchange. Thus, the General Partner is liable for breaching the contractually created fiduciary duties of entire fairness provided by Sections 7.05 and 7.10(a) of the Partnership Agreement....

Whether the Court of Chancery Erred by Holding HGI, Gumbiner, and Guzzetti Jointly and Severally Liable with the General Partner for Aiding and Abetting

HGI, Gumbiner, and Guzzetti argue that only the General Partner was a party to the Partnership Agreement, and therefore they cannot be held liable for breach of the Agreement. They also assert that there is no cause of action under Delaware law for aiding and abetting a breach of contract. This Court reviews de novo the Court of Chancery's interpretation of Delaware law.

HGI, Gumbiner, and Guzzetti are correct that they cannot be held liable for breach of the Partnership Agreement because they were not parties to it. "It is a general principle of contract law that only a party to a contract may be sued for breach of that contract." But, the Court of Chancery properly held HGI, Gumbiner, and Guzzetti jointly and severally liable with the General Partner for aiding and abetting the General Partner's breach of fiduciary duties created by the Partnership Agreement....

In this case, the General Partner had a fiduciary relationship with the Partnership and its limited partners as defined by the Partnership Agreement. The General Partner breached Sections 7.05 and 7.10(a), which impose the fiduciary duties of entire fairness. HGI, Gumbiner, and Guzzetti knowingly participated in the breach of fiduciary duties, and the limited partners consequently were injured. The Vice Chancellor correctly noted that "where a corporate General Partner fails to comply with a contractual standard [of fiduciary duty] that supplants traditional fiduciary duties and the General Partner's failure is caused by its directors and controlling stockholder, the directors and controlling stockholders remain liable." The Court of Chancery thus properly held HGI, Gumbiner, and Guzzetti jointly and severally liable with the General Partner for the General Partner's breach of the Partnership Agreement's fiduciary duties of entire fairness....

Whether the Court of Chancery Had Discretion Not to Grant Rescission in This Case

Gotham makes three arguments to support its claim that the Court of Chancery erred by refusing to order rescission of the Odd Lot Resale: (1) rescission is required by law; (2) rescission is appropriate because the Odd Lot Resale was the result of a breach of a contractually created fiduciary duty or the aiding and abetting of that breach; and

(3) rescission is appropriate because, without it, the defendants will retain their ill-gotten advantage of control over the Partnership and will be unjustly enriched by their breach of the Partnership Agreement.

Gotham's first contention is incorrect. Rescission "is not given for every serious mistake and it is neither given nor withheld automatically, but is awarded as a matter of judgment."

Gotham's second and third arguments might be persuasive but for the fact that the Court of Chancery found that: (1) Gotham delayed bringing suit for an injunction or rescission until it "tested the waters" and the Partnership's publicly listed units rose in value; and (2) the Odd Lot Resale was not "a conscious scheme to entrench the General Partner's control and enrich HGI through sales of Partnership units on the cheap in deals effected without procedural safeguards or full disclosure." We cannot conclude on this record that these findings of fact are clearly erroneous.

The Court of Chancery has noted: "It is a well-established principle of equity that a plaintiff waives the right to rescission by excessive delay in seeking it." Furthermore, "[i]t is not a matter of laches and there is no requirement that the defendant show prejudice from the delay. [Rather, i]t is the plaintiff's burden to prove promptness, not the defendant's to prove delay." The Court of Chancery thus has the discretion not to grant rescission where delay allows the plaintiff "to sit back and 'test the waters, 'waiting to assert a claim for rescission until after [the] stock price has increased." Gotham never sought an injunction despite its knowledge as early as June 5, 1995 that the Odd Lot Offer units would be resold to HGI. Rather, Gotham waited until nearly two years had passed before seeking rescission. Gotham attempts to persuade this Court that any delay on its side was the result of Gotham complying with this Court's instruction that prospective plaintiffs request access to books and records before filing suit. 60 But Gotham did not request access to the Partnership's books and records until almost a year and a half after the Odd Lot Resale.

The Vice Chancellor thus properly found that Gotham failed to meet its burden to prove promptness because it substantially and unjustifiably delayed seeking rescission. As the Vice Chancellor stated, Gotham's delay enabled it "to see what the market price for Partnership units would do, and to sue only if the Odd Lot Offer resales turned out to be favorable to HGI." Indeed, "Gotham sat back and let HGI take the risk of its purchases for nearly two years, and then filed suit to rescind only after it was clear that the market was up substantially on a sustainable basis."

The Vice Chancellor properly did not view Gotham's delay alone as the determinative factor. As he noted, rescission nonetheless might be a possible remedy if the Odd Lot Resale had been "a conscious scheme to entrench the General Partner's control and enrich HGI through sales of Partnership units on the cheap in deals effected without procedural safeguards or full disclosure." Because Gotham unjustifiably delayed challenging the Odd Lot Resale and the defendants did not intend to entrench the General Partner or improperly enrich HGI, we find that the Vice Chancellor was within his discretion in refusing to grant rescission in this case, even though the result of the challenged transaction was to secure control by the defendants. Given the result of control and the defendants' conduct, however, an adequate, rationally-articulated substitute remedy must be awarded.

Whether the Court of Chancery Abused Its Discretion by Failing to Account for a Control Premium

The Court of Chancery awarded money damages of approximately $3.4 million based on a per unit value of $25.84 for each Partnership unit resold to HGI. The court gave equal weight to four factors: book value, Gotham's comparables for minority stakes in other limited partnerships, the per unit price of an unrelated Spring 1996 repurchase of Partnership units, and the average price paid by the Partnership during the Odd Lot Offer. Gotham notes that none of the four factors "takes account of the lock on control that HGI obtained in the Resale." Gotham emphasizes that, at trial, Gumbiner valued control of the Partnership at $50 to $55 million and that only a mere $3.4 million was awarded as monetary damages. Gotham argues that this Court should reverse on this issue and remand to the Court of Chancery for a new remedy calculation that accounts for the value of control of the Partnership. This Court reviews the Court of Chancery's fashioning of remedies for abuse of discretion.

The Partnership Agreement provides for contractual fiduciary duties of entire fairness. Although the contract could have limited the damage remedy for breach of these duties to contract damages, it did not do so. The Court of Chancery is not precluded from awarding equitable relief as provided by the entire fairness standard where, as here, the general partner breached its contractually created fiduciary duty to meet the entire fairness standard and the partnership agreement is silent regarding damages. The Court of Chancery in this case may award equitable relief as provided by the entire fairness standard and is not limited to contract damages for two reasons: (1) this case involves a breach of the duty of loyalty and such a breach permits broad, discretionary, and equitable remedies; and (2) courts will not construe a contract as taking away other forms of appropriate relief, including equitable relief, unless the contract explicitly provides for an exclusive remedy.

In this case, as the Vice Chancellor properly found, the fiduciary duties provided for by the Partnership Agreement supplanted common law fiduciary duty principles, but "some of the agreement's provisions were 'in some sense ... an explicit acceptance of the default duty of loyalty and fair dealing.'" The General Partner breached its duty of loyalty by failing to comply with the contractually created entire fairness standard during the Odd Lot Resale, which resulted in the General Partner and its corporate parent solidifying their control over the Partnership. Where there is "a breach of the duty of loyalty, as here, 'potentially harsher rules come into play' and 'the scope of recovery for a breach of the duty of loyalty is not to be determined narrowly [because] the strict imposition of penalties under Delaware law are designed to discourage disloyalty.'" Therefore, the Court of Chancery's "powers are complete to fashion any form of equitable and monetary relief as may be appropriate."

In addition, courts will not construe a contract "as taking away a common law remedy unless that result is imperatively required." For example, this Court has held that, even if a contract specifies a remedy for breach of that contract, "a contractual remedy cannot be read as exclusive of all other remedies [if] it lacks the requisite expression of exclusivity." The Maryland Court of Appeals also has held that "mere inclusion" of a money damages clause as the specified remedy for a breach will not "negate the possibility of injunctive [or other equitable or legal] relief in a proper case." Therefore, even where a partnership agreement specifies a remedy for breach of that contract, the Court of Chancery is not prohibited from awarding other equitable or legal remedies, at least unless the partnership agreement explicitly states that the specified remedy is the exclusive remedy. In addition, where the partnership agreement is silent regarding remedies, the Court of Chancery has the discretion to award any form of legal and/or equitable relief and is not limited to awarding contract damages for breach of the agreement. The Vice Chancellor thus had the discretion to apply any equitable and/or legal remedy applicable in corporate cases where the controlling entity fails the test of entire fairness.

The question is whether he abused that discretion by not ordering adequate damages or equitable remedies to account for the control premium.

In this case, Gotham requested rescission, or rescissory damages and sterilization of the voting rights attached to the Odd Lot Resale units. The Vice Chancellor, as discussed above, had the discretion not to grant rescission because Gotham unjustifiably delayed contesting the Odd Lot Resale and the defendants did not intend to entrench the General Partner or unfairly enrich HGI through the challenged transaction. Although the Vice Chancellor found that the defendants did not intend for the General Partner to become entrenched or HGI to be unjustly enriched, the Odd Lot Resale had that effect. The Court of Chancery was thus required to remedy that effect by compensating the limited partners for a control premium. As the Vice Chancellor recognized, the Audit Committee—whose contractually-mandated functions were not implemented—conceivably would have "taken into account the fact that the Odd Lot resales were of particular advantage to HGI and demanded value for that advantage in exchange" because "the Odd Lot resales solidified HGI's control." Consequently, we find that the Vice Chancellor abused his discretion in fashioning the remedy in this case by failing (1) to address and decide the applicability of rescissory damages, and (2) to include in the damages calculation a premium for the control acquired by HGI through the Odd Lot Resale.

The Partnership is entitled to receive, at a minimum, what the Partnership units sold to HGI would have been worth at the time of the Odd Lot Resale if the General Partner had complied with the Partnership Agreement. We thus reverse the judgment of the Court of Chancery regarding the remedy in this case, and we remand for procedures, such as expansion of the record, as may be necessary and appropriate to accomplish two objectives. First, the Court of Chancery should seek to quantify how the challenged transaction would have been consummated had the defendants adhered to the Partnership Agreement's contractual entire fairness provisions. Specifically, the court should determine and consider what price the Audit Committee would have approved for the Odd Lot Offer resales to HGI if the Audit Committee had been aware that the transaction would result in HGI solidifying control over the Partnership. Second, the Court of Chancery should reconsider and award some form or combination of the various equitable remedies available to the limited partnership, including rescissory damages, sterilization of voting rights, and other appropriate methods of accounting for a control premium. We note that the Court of Chancery has the discretion to consider afresh in light of the above analysis whether or not to order rescission.

Conclusion

We affirm the judgment of the Court of Chancery that (1) the contractual fiduciary duties of entire fairness contained in the Partnership Agreement applied to the disputed transaction in this case; (2) defendants HGI, Gumbiner, and Guzzetti are jointly and severally liable with the General Partner because they aided and abetted the General Partner's breach of the contractually created fiduciary duties of entire fairness; (3) the Court of Chancery has the discretion not to grant rescission where the plaintiff unjustifiably delays seeking that remedy, provided that the court articulates and orders a reasonable alternative remedy; and (4) the court has discretion to award compound interest on the resulting damage remedy.

We reverse the judgment of the Court of Chancery regarding the calculation of damages. We remand, as discussed above, for the court to fashion a remedy according to its discretion that accounts for a control premium.

Jurisdiction is not retained.

Chapter 5

Closely Held Corporations

In the United States, corporations are ordinarily studied in depth in a specialized course. They are the most significant form for large American businesses. This book's coverage of corporations is not meant as a substitute for a Corporations course. Instead, our coverage of corporations is meant to shed light on three basic questions that concern "closely held" corporations—that is, those with few owners, whose structure and function are ordinarily not that different, in substantive terms, from that of a partnership. The three questions are as follows:

1. How are corporations *different*, structurally speaking, from partnerships?
2. What are the *restrictions* on the structure of corporations? That is, in what ways is their structure rigid, unchangeable even by the parties' agreement?
3. What fiduciary duties, and similar protections, are there for noncontrolling participants in a corporation?

These questions will help us understand several important features of organizational law. First, they will clarify some features of partnership law, corporate law, and eventually the law of LLCs (which draws its principles largely from partnership law and corporate law). Second, the study of corporate law's rigidities will highlight the benefits of LLCs in particular; the best way to understand the role of the LLC—which has emerged as the leading organizational choice for small American businesses—is to recognize the restrictions in corporate law that the LLC form *removes*.

Section 1: Background on Corporation Law

Like limited partnerships, corporations are always creatures of statute; they cannot be formed casually like general partnerships. Corporation-law statutes differ from state to state in many details, but they have a central feature in common: they authorize the creation of a particular sort of quasi-democratic organization in which there are two groups: (1) shareholders, who own shares of the corporation, and (2) a board of directors, which governs or at least oversees the corporation as to all ordinary business and has the power to appoint corporate agents. The shareholders ordinarily elect the board, and the shareholders are ordinarily necessary to approve various significant changes to the corporation (such as a voluntary dissolution). Ordinarily, the shareholders do not directly govern the corporation; as in a republic or representative democracy, they elect those who do. Or, more accurately in many cases, they elect a board of directors that then appoints agents who do—typically the "officers" of a corporation, such as the chief executive officer (CEO).

Corporations are always entities; indeed, historically, the view of partnerships as entities ordinarily had, at least implicitly, the corporate model in mind. Thus, corporations can own property in their own names, sue, be sued, enter into contracts, and so on.

A characteristic feature of American corporations, by default, is limited liability. Though most statutes provide ways for corporations to waive this protection if they do not want it, ordinarily neither the shareholders nor the directors are liable for corporate obligations. Historically, however, corporations were associated with particular formalities (and perhaps expenses), as well as an unfavorable tax status; accordingly, parties needed to choose between the favorable tax status of partnerships and the liability protections that corporations offered. The need for that choice has largely gone away under modern law, because limited liability is so easy to achieve (as we have seen in our study of limited partnerships and will see further in our study of LLCs).

This book's coverage of corporate statutes uses the Model Business Corporation Act (MBCA) as a central example. The MBCA was issued by a committee of the American Bar Association, and it has been adopted in about half the American states. We will also look at individual state statutes occasionally.[1]

Section 2: Corporate Structure: The Board of Directors

To create a corporation, incorporators usually file a document called the *articles of incorporation* or *certificate of incorporation* with the state. This document, subject to the statutes, is the governing document of the corporation. Like a partnership agreement, it can direct details of the governance of the organization. For example, if the statutes permit it to do so, it might require a supermajority vote of the directors or shareholders as to certain business decisions.

It may be helpful to arrange the various sources of governance law for a corporation into the following hierarchy: (1) the statutes ultimately govern (subject, of course, to the state and federal constitutions); (2) unless the statutes direct otherwise, the articles of incorporation can specify authoritative procedures for governing the corporation; (3) a document called the *bylaws* may record governing principles subordinate to the articles; (4) following the articles and the bylaws, the shareholders elect the board of directors; (5) the board appoints authorized officers and agents.

Model Business Corporation Act § 8.01(b): Requirement for and Functions of Board of Directors

All corporate powers shall be exercised by or under the authority of the board of directors of the corporation, and the business and affairs of the corporation shall be managed

1. Often, Corporations courses focus on Delaware law, because for historical and other reasons, many businesses decide to incorporate in Delaware. Delaware is crucially important in understanding widely held, "public" corporations, but is less central for our purposes. Nonetheless, because of its influence on corporate law generally, we will look more closely at Delaware law than the law of most other individual states.

by or under the direction, and subject to the oversight, of its board of directors, subject to any limitation set forth in the articles of incorporation or in an [authorized] agreement....

Charlestown Boot & Shoe Co. v. Dunsmore

60 N.H. 85 (1880)

Demurrer to the declaration in which the following facts were alleged:—The plaintiffs are a manufacturing corporation having for its object a dividend of profits, and commenced business in 1871. Dunsmore was elected director in 1871 and Willard in 1873, and entered upon the discharge of their duties, and have continued so to act by virtue of successive elections until the present time. December 10, 1874, the corporation voted to choose a committee to act with the directors to close up its affairs, and chose one Osgood for such committee. Osgood tendered his services, but the defendants refused to act with him, and contracted new debts to a larger extent than allowed by law. By their negligence, debts due to the corporation to the amount of $2,161.23 have been wholly lost. By their negligence in disposing of the goods of the corporation, a loss has accrued of $3,300.40. By their neglect to sell the buildings and machinery of the corporation when they might and ought, and were urged by Osgood to sell, the same depreciated in value to the extent of $20,000.

Also for that the plaintiffs owned and possessed a certain shop of the value of $10,000, and a large amount of machinery and fixtures of the value of $10,000; "and whereas it was the duty of said defendants, directors as aforesaid, to procure sufficient and proper insurance against fire to be made on said property, and keep the same so sufficiently insured, of all which the said defendants had notice, yet they did not and would not keep the said property so insured, and afterwards, to wit, on the 28th day of April, 1878, while the said property was so remaining without insurance, the same was wholly consumed by fire and wholly lost to the plaintiff, whereby the plaintiff suffered great loss and damage, to wit, $20,000."

SMITH, J.

The provision of the statute is, that the business of a dividend paying corporation shall be managed by the directors. The statute reads, "The business of every such corporation shall be managed by the directors thereof, subject to the by-laws and votes of the corporation, and under their direction by such officers and agents as shall be duly appointed by the directors or by the corporation." G. L., c. 148, s. 3; Gen. Stats., c. 134, s. 3. The only limitation upon the judgment or discretion of the directors is such as the corporation by its by-laws and votes shall impose. It may define its business, its nature and extent, prescribe rules and regulations for the government of its officers and members, and determine whether its business shall be wound up or continued; but when it has thus acted, the business as thus defined and limited is to be managed by its directors, and by such officers and agents under their direction as the directors or the corporation shall appoint. The statute does not authorize a corporation to join another officer with the directors, nor compel the directors to act with one who is not a director. They are bound to use ordinary care and diligence in the care and management of the business of the corporation, and are answerable for ordinary negligence. There is no difference in this respect between the agents of corporations and those of natural persons, unless expressly made by the charter or by-laws. It would be unreasonable to hold them responsible for the management of the affairs of the corporation if compelled to act with one who to a greater or less extent could control their acts. The statute not only entrusts the management of the business of the corporation to the directors, but places its other officers and agents under their direction. When a statute provides that powers granted to a corporation shall be exercised by any set of officers or any particular agents, such powers can be exercised only by such officers or agents, although they are required to be chosen by the whole corporation; and if the whole corporation attempts to exercise powers which by the charter are lodged elsewhere, its action upon the subject is void. The vote choosing Osgood a committee to act with the directors in closing up the affairs of the plaintiff corporation was inoperative and void.

The declaration also alleges that it was the duty of the defendants, as directors, to keep the property of the corporation insured. There is no statute that makes it the duty of the directors of a corporation to keep its property insured, and there are no facts alleged from which we can say, as matter of law, that it was the duty of the defendants to insure the property of the corporation.

Demurrer sustained.

Section 3: Electing the Board

By default, there is a single class of "common" shares that elect the board of directors in a modern corporation. Voting is per share, so that the owner of 60% of the shares of a corporation could, by default, appoint the entire board of directors.

Many corporate statutes, including the MBCA, allow a corporation's articles to choose particular alternatives to the default structure. It is common to permit the following modifications:

1. **Cumulative voting.** By default, election of directors is by "plurality." *See, e.g.*, MBCA § 7.28. Suppose there are two shareholders, *A* and *B*. *A* owns 80% of the shares of the corporation and *B* owns 20% of the shares. By default, *A* will elect the entire board. This will be true, similarly, if *A* owns 40% of the shares and there is no organized group in opposition.

However, a provision in the corporation's articles allowing for cumulative voting will permit *B* to elect some part of the board roughly proportional to the portion of the corporation's shares that she owns. Thus, for example, in a five-person board, *B* could be able to elect one director.

Because the board of directors operates by plurality voting itself (by default), electing one director won't give *B*'s representative control of the company. But directors have certain rights to access information, to attempt to influence board policy through deliberation, and to influence the corporation in other ways. As a result, cumulative voting may provide a useful advantage to minority shareholders.

2. **Staggered boards.** Ordinarily, all directors are periodically elected at once, much like the United States House of Representatives. Often, statutes provide for the opportunity for a corporation's articles to elect "staggered" boards, much like the United States Senate. The statutes often prescribe particular limits for staggering boards. For example, MBCA § 8.06 provides as follows:

> The articles of incorporation may provide for staggering the terms of directors by dividing the total number of directors into two or three groups, with each group containing one-half or one-third of the total, as near as may be. In that event, the terms of directors in the first group expire at the first annual shareholders' meeting after their election, the terms of the second group expire at the second annual shareholders' meeting after their election, and the terms of the third group, if any, expire at the third annual shareholders' meeting after their election. At each annual shareholders' meeting held thereafter, directors shall be chosen for a term of two years or three years, as the case may be, to succeed those whose terms expire.

Much as in the Senate, the primary effect of staggered boards is to slow a potential change in control of the corporation. For example, staggered boards might prevent someone who has purchased a large percentage of the shares of the corporation from electing the board for several years—which in turn may discourage people from acquiring shares in the first place with an intent to change the board. In large corporations, staggered boards are often used to prevent "hostile takeovers"—attempts by shareholders to gain control of the company by electing new directors.

3. Classified shares. The articles (and often, pursuant to the articles, the board) can create different *classes* of shares, some of which have different voting rights from others. This is a common modern technique for limiting the power of certain kinds of shareholders in a corporation. For example, a corporation could issue economic "shares" to employees but prevent them from controlling the board. MBCA § 8.04 provides as follows: "If the articles of incorporation authorize dividing the shares into classes, the articles may also authorize the election of all or a specified number of directors by the holders of one or more authorized classes of shares." *See also* MBCA § 6.02 (permitting the board to classify unissued shares "without shareholder approval").

Using these various techniques, a corporation's articles can have significant flexibility under modern law to determine which sort of shareholders can direct the board's election and the schedule on which they do so. For example, the articles of incorporation can effectively give one shareholder, or at least one type of shareholder, perpetual control of the board.

Model Business Corporation Act § 8.08: Removal of Directors by Shareholders

(a) The shareholders may remove one or more directors with or without cause unless the articles of incorporation provide that directors may be removed only for cause.

(b) If a director is elected by a voting group of shareholders, only the shareholders of that voting group may participate in the vote to remove him.

(c) If cumulative voting is authorized, a director may not be removed if the number of votes sufficient to elect him under cumulative voting is voted against his removal. If cumulative voting is not authorized, a director may be removed only if the number of votes cast to remove him exceeds the number of votes cast not to remove him.

(d) A director may be removed by the shareholders only at a meeting called for the purpose of removing him and the meeting notice must state that the purpose, or one of the purposes, of the meeting is removal of the director.

Model Business Corporation Act § 8.09: Removal of Directors by Judicial Proceeding

(a) The [court] may remove a director of the corporation from office in a proceeding commenced by or in the right of the corporation if the court finds that (1) the director engaged in fraudulent conduct with respect to the corporation or its shareholders, grossly abused the position of director, or intentionally inflicted harm on the corporation; and (2) considering the director's course of conduct and the inadequacy of other available remedies, removal would be in the best interest of the corporation....

(d) Nothing in this section limits the equitable powers of the court to order other relief.

Model Business Corporation Act § 8.10: Vacancy on Board

(a) Unless the articles of incorporation provide otherwise, if a vacancy occurs on a board of directors, including a vacancy resulting from an increase in the number of directors:

(1) the shareholders may fill the vacancy;

(2) the board of directors may fill the vacancy; or

(3) if the directors remaining in office constitute fewer than a quorum of the board, they may fill the vacancy by the affirmative vote of a majority of all the directors remaining in office.

(b) If the vacant office was held by a director elected by a voting group of shareholders, only the holders of shares of that voting group are entitled to vote to fill the vacancy if it is filled by the shareholders, and only the directors elected by that voting group are entitled to fill the vacancy if it is filled by the directors....

Schnell v. Chris-Craft Industries, Inc.

285 A.2d 437 (Del. 1971)

HERRMAN, J.

This is an appeal from the denial by the Court of Chancery of the petition of dissident stockholders for injunctive relief to prevent management [i.e., "managing directors"] from advancing the date of the annual stockholders' meeting from January 11, 1972, as previously set by the by-laws, to December 8, 1971.

The opinion below is reported at 285 A.2d 430. This opinion is confined to the frame of reference of the opinion below for the sake of brevity and because of the strictures of time imposed by the circumstances of the case.

It will be seen that the Chancery Court considered all of the reasons stated by management as business reasons for changing the date of the meeting; but that those reasons were rejected by the Court below in making the following findings:

"I am satisfied, however, in a situation in which present management has disingenuously resisted the production of a list of its stockholders to plaintiffs or their confederates and has otherwise turned a deaf ear to plaintiffs' demands about a change in management designed to lift defendant from its present business doldrums, management has seized on a relatively new section of the Delaware Corporation Law for the purpose of cutting down on the amount of time which would otherwise have been available to plaintiffs and others for the waging of a proxy battle. Management thus enlarged the scope of its scheduled October 18 directors' meeting to include the by-law amendment in controversy after the stockholders committee had filed with the S.E.C. its intention to wage a proxy fight on October 16.

"Thus plaintiffs reasonably contend that because of the tactics employed by management (which involve the hiring of two established proxy solicitors as well as a refusal to produce a list of its stockholders, coupled with its use of an amendment to the Delaware Corporation Law to limit the time for contest), they are given little chance, because of the exigencies of time, including that required to clear material at the S.E.C., to wage a successful proxy fight between now and December 8. * * *."

In our view, those conclusions amount to a finding that management has attempted to utilize the corporate machinery and the Delaware Law for the purpose of perpetuating itself in office; and, to that end, for the purpose of obstructing the legitimate efforts of dissident stockholders in the exercise of their rights to undertake a proxy contest against management. These are inequitable purposes, contrary to established principles of corporate democracy. The advancement by directors of the by-law date of a stockholders' meeting, for such purposes, may not be permitted to stand.

When the by-laws of a corporation designate the date of the annual meeting of stockholders, it is to be expected that those who intend to contest the reelection of incumbent management will gear their campaign to the by-law date. It is not to be expected that management will attempt to advance that date in order to obtain an inequitable advantage in the contest.

Management contends that it has complied strictly with the provisions of the new Delaware Corporation Law in changing the by-law date. The answer to that contention, of course, is that inequitable action does not become permissible simply because it is legally possible.

Management relies upon American Hardware Corp. v. Savage Arms Corp., 37 Del.Ch. 10, 135 A.2d 725, aff'd 37 Del.Ch. 59, 136 A.2d 690 (1957). That case is inapposite for two reasons: it involved an effort by stockholders, engaged in a proxy contest, to have the stockholders' meeting adjourned and the period for the proxy contest enlarged; and there was no finding there of inequitable action on the part of management. We agree with the rule of American Hardware that, in the absence of fraud or inequitable conduct, the date for a stockholders' meeting and notice thereof, duly established under the by-laws, will not be enlarged by judicial interference at the request of dissident stockholders solely because of the circumstance of a proxy contest. That, of course, is not the case before us.

We are unable to agree with the conclusion of the Chancery Court that the stockholders' application for injunctive relief here was tardy and came too late. The stockholders learned of the action of management unofficially on Wednesday, October 27, 1971; they filed this action on Monday, November 1, 1971. Until management changed the date of the meeting, the stockholders had no need of judicial assistance in that connection. There is no indication of any prior warning of management's intent to take such action; indeed, it appears that an attempt was made by management to conceal its action as long as possible. Moreover, stockholders may not be charged with the duty of anticipating inequitable action by management, and of seeking anticipatory injunctive relief to foreclose such action, simply because the new Delaware Corporation Law makes such inequitable action legally possible.

Accordingly, the judgment below must be reversed and the cause remanded, with instructions to nullify the December 8 date as a meeting date for stockholders; to reinstate January 11, 1972 as the sole date of the next annual meeting of the stockholders of the corporation; and to take such other proceedings and action as may be consistent herewith regarding the stock record closing date and any other related matters.

WOLCOTT, C.J. (dissenting):

I do not agree with the majority of the Court in its disposition of this appeal. The plaintiff stockholders concerned in this litigation have, for a considerable period of time, sought to obtain control of the defendant corporation. These attempts took various forms.

In view of the length of time leading up to the immediate events which caused the filing of this action, I agree with the Vice Chancellor that the application for injunctive relief came too late.

Ringling Bros.–Barnum & Bailey Combined Shows, Inc. v. Ringling

53 A.2d 441 (Del. 1947)

PEARSON, J., delivering the opinion of the court:

The Court of Chancery was called upon to review an attempted election of directors at the 1946 annual stockholders meeting of the corporate defendant. The pivotal questions concern an agreement between two of the three present stockholders, and particularly the effect of this agreement with relation to the exercise of voting rights by these two stockholders. At the time of the meeting, the corporation had outstanding 1000 shares of capital stock held as follows: 315 by petitioner Edith Conway Ringling; 315 by defendant Aubrey B. Ringling Haley (individually or as executrix and legatee of a deceased husband); and 370 by defendant John Ringling North. The purpose of the meeting was to elect the entire board of seven directors. The shares could be voted cumulatively. Mrs. Ringling asserts that by virtue of the operation of an agreement between her and Mrs. Haley, the latter was bound to vote her shares for an adjournment of the meeting, or in the alternative, for a certain slate of directors. Mrs. Haley contends that she was not so bound for reason that the agreement was invalid, or at least revocable.

The two ladies entered into the agreement in 1941. It makes like provisions concerning stock of the corporate defendant and of another corporation, but in this case, we are concerned solely with the agreement as it affects the voting of stock of the corporate defendant. The agreement recites that each party was the owner "subject only to possible claims of creditors of the estates of Charles Ringling and Richard Ringling, respectively" (deceased husbands of the parties), of 300 shares of the capital stock of the defendant corporation; that in 1938 these shares had been deposited under a voting trust agreement which would terminate in 1947, or earlier, upon the elimination of certain liability of the corporation; that each party also owned 15 shares individually; that the parties had "entered into an agreement in April 1934 providing for joint action by them in matters affecting their ownership of stock and interest in" the corporate defendant; that the parties desired "to continue to act jointly in all matters relating to their stock ownership or interest in" the corporate defendant (and the other corporation). The agreement then provides as follows:

"Now, Therefore, in consideration of the mutual covenants and agreements hereinafter contained the parties hereto agree as follows:

"1. Neither party will sell any shares of stock or any voting trust certificates in either of said corporations to any other person whosoever, without first making a written offer to the other party hereto of all of the shares or voting trust certificates proposed to be sold, for the same price and upon the same terms and conditions as in such proposed sale, and allowing such other party a time of not less than 180 days from the date of such written offer within which to accept same.

"2. In exercising any voting rights to which either party may be entitled by virtue of ownership of stock or voting trust certificates held by them in either of said corporation, each party will consult and confer with the other and the parties will act jointly in exercising such voting rights in accordance with such agreement as they may reach with respect to any matter calling for the exercise of such voting rights.

"3. In the event the parties fail to agree with respect to any matter covered by paragraph 2 above, the question in disagreement shall be submitted for arbitration to Karl D. Loos, of Washington, D. C. as arbitrator and his decision thereon shall be binding upon the parties hereto. Such arbitration shall be exercised to the end of assuring for the respective corporations good management and such participating therein by the members of the Ringling family as the experience, capacity and ability of each may warrant. The parties may at any time by written agreement designate any other individual to act as arbitrator in lieu of said Loos.

"4. Each of the parties hereto will enter into and execute such voting trust agreement or agreements and such other instruments as, from time to time they may deem advisable and as they may be advised by counsel are appropriate to effectuate the purposes and objects of this agreement.

"5. This agreement shall be in effect from the date hereof and shall continue in effect for a period of ten years unless sooner terminated by mutual agreement in writing by the parties hereto.

"6 The agreement of April 1934 is hereby terminated.

"7. This agreement shall be binding upon and inure to the benefit of the heirs, executors, administrators and assigns of the parties hereto respectively."

The Mr. Loos mentioned in the agreement is an attorney and has represented both parties since 1937, and, before and after the voting trust was terminated in late 1942, advised them with respect to the exercise of their voting rights. At the annual meetings in 1943 and the two following years, the parties voted their shares in accordance with mutual understandings arrived at as a result of discussions. In each of these years, they elected five of the seven directors. Mrs. Ringling and Mrs. Haley each had sufficient votes, independently of the other, to elect two of the seven directors. By both voting for an additional candidate, they could be sure of his election regardless of how Mr. North, the remaining stockholder, might vote.[2]

---

2. Each lady was entitled to cast 2205 votes (since each had the cumulative voting rights of 315 shares, and there were 7 vacancies in the directorate). The sum of the votes of both is 4410, which is sufficient to allow 882 votes for each of 5 persons. Mr. North, holding 370 shares, was entitled to cast

Some weeks before the 1946 meeting, they discussed with Mr. Loos the matter of voting for directors. They were in accord that Mrs. Ringling should cast sufficient votes to elect herself and her son; and that Mrs. Haley should elect herself and her husband; but they did not agree upon a fifth director. The day before the meeting, the discussions were continued, Mrs. Haley being represented by her husband since she could not be present because of illness. In a conversation with Mr. Loos, Mr. Haley indicated that he would make a motion for an adjournment of the meeting for sixty days, in order to give the ladies additional time to come to an agreement about their voting. On the morning of the meeting, however, he stated that because of something Mrs. Ringling had done, he would not consent to a postponement. Mrs. Ringling then made a demand upon Mr. Loos to act under the third paragraph of the agreement "to arbitrate the disagreement" between her and Mrs. Haley in connection with the manner in which the stock of the two ladies should be voted. At the opening of the meeting, Mr. Loos read the written demand and stated that he determined and directed that the stock of both ladies be voted for an adjournment of sixty days. Mrs. Ringling then made a motion for adjournment and voted for it. Mr. Haley, as proxy for his wife, and Mr. North voted against the motion. Mrs. Ringling (herself or through her attorney, it is immaterial which,) objected to the voting of Mrs. Haley's stock in any manner other than in accordance with Mr. Loos' direction. The chairman ruled that the stock could not be voted contrary to such direction, and declared the motion for adjournment had carried. Nevertheless, the meeting proceeded to the election of directors. Mrs. Ringling stated that she would continue in the meeting "but without prejudice to her position with respect to the voting of the stock and the fact that adjournment had not been taken." Mr. Loos directed Mrs. Ringling to cast her votes

882 for Mrs. Ringling,

882 for her son, Robert, and

441 for a Mr. Dunn,

who had been a member of the board for several years. She complied. Mr. Loos directed that Mrs. Haley's votes be cast

882 for Mrs. Haley,

882 for Mr. Haley, and

441 for Mr. Dunn.

Instead of complying, Mr. Haley attempted to vote his wife's shares

1103 for Mrs. Haley, and

1102 for Mr. Haley.

Mr. North voted his shares

864 for a Mr. Woods,

863 for a Mr. Griffin, and

863 for Mr. North.

2590 votes, which obviously cannot be divided so as to give to more than two candidates as many as 882 votes each. It will be observed that in order for Mrs. Ringling and Mrs. Haley to be sure to elect five directors (regardless of how Mr. North might vote) they must act together in the sense that their combined votes must be divided among five different candidates and at least one of the five must be voted for by both Mrs. Ringling and Mrs. Haley. [Court's footnote.—ed.]

The chairman ruled that the five candidates proposed by Mr. Loos, together with Messrs. Woods and North, were elected. The Haley-North group disputed this ruling insofar as it declared the election of Mr. Dunn; and insisted that Mr. Griffin, instead, had been elected. A directors' meeting followed in which Mrs. Ringling participated after stating that she would do so "without prejudice to her position that the stockholders' meeting had been adjourned and that the directors' meeting was not properly held." Mr. Dunn and Mr. Griffin, although each was challenged by an opposing faction, attempted to join in voting as directors for different slates of officers. Soon after the meeting, Mrs. Ringling instituted this proceeding.

The Vice-Chancellor determined that the agreement to vote in accordance with the direction of Mr. Loos was valid as a "stock pooling agreement" with lawful objects and purposes, and that it was not in violation of any public policy of this state. He held that where the arbitrator acts under the agreement and one party refuses to comply with his direction, "the Agreement constitutes the willing party * * * an implied agent possessing the irrevocable proxy of the recalcitrant party for the purpose of casting the particular vote." It was ordered that a new election be held before a master, with the direction that the master should recognize and give effect to the agreement if its terms were properly invoked.

Before taking up defendants' objections to the agreement, let us analyze particularly what it attempts to provide with respect to voting, including what functions and powers it attempts to repose in Mr. Loos, the "arbitrator". The agreement recites that the parties desired "to continue to act jointly in all matters relating to their stock ownership or interest in" the corporation. The parties agreed to consult and confer with each other in exercising their voting rights and to act jointly—that is, concertedly; unitedly; towards unified courses of action—in accordance with such agreement as they might reach. Thus, so long as the parties agree for whom or for what their shares shall be voted, the agreement provides no function for the arbitrator. His role is limited to situations where the parties fail to agree upon a course of action. In such cases, the agreement directs that "the question in disagreement shall be submitted for arbitration" to Mr. Loos "as arbitrator and his decision thereon shall be binding upon the parties." These provisions are designed to operate in aid of what appears to be a primary purpose of the parties, "to act jointly" in exercising their voting rights, by providing a means for fixing a course of action whenever they themselves might reach a stalemate.

Should the agreement be interpreted as attempting to empower the arbitrator to carry his directions into effect? Certainly there is no express delegation or grant of power to do so, either by authorizing him to vote the shares or to compel either party to vote them in accordance with his directions. The agreement expresses no other function of the arbitrator than that of deciding questions in disagreement which prevent the effectuation of the purpose "to act jointly." The power to enforce a decision does not seem a necessary or usual incident of such a function. Mr. Loos is not a party to the agreement. It does not contemplate the transfer of any shares or interest in shares to him, or that he should undertake any duties which the parties might compel him to perform. They provided that they might designate any other individual to act instead of Mr. Loos. The agreement does not attempt to make the arbitrator a trustee of an express trust. What the arbitrator is to do is for the benefit of the parties, not for his own benefit. Whether the parties accept or reject his decision is no concern of his, so far as the agreement or the surrounding circumstances reveal. We think the parties sought to bind each other, but to be bound only to each other, and not to empower the arbitrator to enforce decisions he might make.

From this conclusion, it follows necessarily that no decision of the arbitrator could ever be enforced if both parties to the agreement were unwilling that it be enforced, for the obvious reason that there would be no one to enforce it. Under the agreement, something more is required after the arbitrator has given his decision in order that it should become compulsory; at least one of the parties must determine that such decision shall be carried into effect. Thus, any "control" of the voting of the shares, which is reposed in the arbitrator, is substantially limited in action under the agreement in that it is subject to the overriding power of the parties themselves.

The agreement does not describe the undertaking of each party with respect to a decision of the arbitrator other than to provide that it "shall be binding upon the parties". It seems to us that this language, considered with relation to its context and the situations to which it is applicable, means that each party promised the other to exercise her own voting rights in accordance with the arbitrator's decision. The agreement is silent about any exercise of the voting rights of one party by the other. The language with reference to situations where the parties arrive at an understanding as to voting plainly suggests "action" by each, and "exercising" voting rights by each, rather than by one for the other. There is no intimation that this method should be different where the arbitrator's decision is to be carried into effect. Assuming that a power in each party to exercise the voting rights of the other might be a relatively more effective or convenient means of enforcing a decision of the arbitrator than would be available without the power, this would not justify implying a delegation of the power in the absence of some indication that the parties bargained for that means. The method of voting actually employed by the parties tends to show that they did not construe the agreement as creating powers to vote each other's shares; for at meetings prior to 1946 each party apparently exercised her own voting rights, and at the 1946 meeting, Mrs. Ringling, who wished to enforce the agreement, did not attempt to cast a ballot in exercise of any voting rights of Mrs. Haley. We do not find enough in the agreement or in the circumstances to justify a construction that either party was empowered to exercise voting rights of the other.

Having examined what the parties sought to provide by the agreement, we come now to defendants' contention that the voting provisions are illegal and revocable. They say that the courts of this state have definitely established the doctrine "that there can be no agreement, or any device whatsoever, by which the voting power of stock of a Delaware corporation may be irrevocably separated from the ownership of the stock, except by an agreement which complies with Section 18" of the Corporation Law, Rev. Code 1935, § 2050, and except by a proxy coupled with an interest. They rely on Perry v. Missouri-Kansas P. L. Co., 22 Del. Ch. 33, 191 A. 823; In re Public Industrials Corporation, 19 Del. Ch. 398, 168 A. 82, reported as In re Chilson, 19 Del. Ch. 398, 168 A. 82; Aldridge v. Franco Wyoming Oil Co., 24 Del. Ch. 126, 7 A. 2d 753; affirmed in 24 Del. Ch. 349, 14 A. 2d 380; Belle Isle Corporation v. Corcoran, ante p. 318, 29 Del. Ch. 554, 49 A. 2d 1; and contend that the doctrine is derived from Section 18 itself, Rev. Code of Del. 1935, § 2050. The statute reads, in part, as follows:

"Sec. 18. Fiduciary Stockholders; Voting Power of; Voting Trusts:—Persons holding stock in a fiduciary capacity shall be entitled to vote the shares so held, and persons whose stock is pledged shall be entitled to vote, unless in the transfer by the pledgor on the books of the corporation he shall have expressly empowered the pledgee to vote thereon, in which case only the pledgee, or his proxy may represent said stock and vote thereon.

"One or more stockholders may by agreement in writing deposit capital stock of an original issue with or transfer capital stock to any person or persons, or corporation or corporations authorized to act as trustee, for the purpose of vesting in said person or persons, corporation or corporations, who may be designated Voting Trustee or Voting Trustees, the right to vote thereon for any period of time determined by such agreement, not exceeding ten years, upon the terms and conditions stated in such agreement. Such agreement may contain any other lawful provisions not inconsistent with said purpose. * * * Said Voting Trustees may vote upon the stock so issued or transferred during the period in such agreement specified; stock standing in the names of such Voting Trustees may be voted either in person or by proxy, and in voting said stock, such Voting Trustees shall incur no responsibility as stockholder, trustee or otherwise, except for their own individual malfeasance."[3]

In our view, neither the cases nor the statute sustain the rule for which the defendants contend. Their sweeping formulation would impugn well-recognized means by which a shareholder may effectively confer his voting rights upon others while retaining various other rights. For example, defendants' rule would apparently not permit holders of voting stock to confer upon stockholders of another class, by the device of an amendment of the certificate of incorporation, the exclusive right to vote during periods when dividends are not paid on stock of the latter class. The broad prohibitory meaning which defendants find in Section 18 seems inconsistent with their concession that proxies coupled with an interest may be irrevocable, for the statute contains nothing about such proxies. The statute authorizes, among other things, the deposit or transfer of stock in trust for a specified purpose, namely, "vesting" in the transferee "the right to vote thereon" for a limited period; and prescribes numerous requirements in this connection. Accordingly, it seems reasonable to infer that to establish the relationship and accomplish the purpose which the statute authorizes, its requirements must be complied with. But the statute does not purport to deal with agreements whereby shareholders attempt to bind each other as to how they shall vote their shares. Various forms of such pooling agreements, as they are sometimes called, have been held valid and have been distinguished from voting trusts. We think the particular agreement before us does not violate Section 18 or constitute an attempted evasion of its requirements, and is not illegal for any other reason. Generally speaking, a shareholder may exercise wide liberality of judgment in the matter of voting, and it is not objectionable that his motives may be for personal profit, or determined by whims or caprice, so long as he violates no duty owed his fellow shareholders. The ownership of voting stock imposes no legal duty to vote at all. A group of shareholders may, without impropriety, vote their respective shares so as to obtain advantages of concerted action. They may lawfully contract with each other to vote in the future in such way as they, or a majority of their group, from time to time determine. (See authorities listed above.) Reasonable provisions for cases of failure of the group to reach a determination because of an even division in their ranks seem unobjectionable. The provision here for submission to the arbitrator is plainly designed as a deadlock-breaking measure, and the arbitrator's decision cannot be enforced unless at least one of the parties (entitled to cast one-half of their combined votes) is willing that it be enforced. We find the provision reasonable. It does not appear that the agreement enables the parties to take any unlawful advantage of the outside

3. Omitted portions of the section provide requirements for the filing of a copy of the agreement in the principal Delaware office of the corporation for the issuance of certificates of stock to the voting trustees, for the voting of stock where there are more than one voting trustee, and for the extension of the agreement for additional periods, not exceeding ten years each. [Court's footnote.—ed.]

shareholder, or of any other person. It offends no rule of law or public policy of this state of which we are aware.

Legal consideration for the promises of each party is supplied by the mutual promises of the other party. The undertaking to vote in accordance with the arbitrator's decision is a valid contract. The good faith of the arbitrator's action has not been challenged and, indeed, the record indicates that no such challenge could be supported. Accordingly, the failure of Mrs. Haley to exercise her voting rights in accordance with his decision was a breach of her contract. It is no extenuation of the breach that her votes were cast for two of the three candidates directed by the arbitrator. His directions to her were part of a single plan or course of action for the voting of the shares of both parties to the agreement, calculated to utilize an advantage of joint action by them which would bring about the election of an additional director. The actual voting of Mrs. Haley's shares frustrates that plan to such an extent that it should not be treated as a partial performance of her contract.

Throughout their argument, defendants make much of the fact that all votes cast at the meeting were by the registered shareholders. The Court of Chancery may, in a review of an election, reject votes of a registered shareholder where his voting of them is found to be in violation of rights of another person. It seems to us that upon the application of Mrs. Ringling, the injured party, the votes representing Mrs. Haley's shares should not be counted. Since no infirmity in Mr. North's voting has been demonstrated, his right to recognition of what he did at the meeting should be considered in granting any relief to Mrs. Ringling; for her rights arose under a contract to which Mr. North was not a party. With this in mind, we have concluded that the election should not be declared invalid, but that effect should be given to a rejection of the votes representing Mrs. Haley's shares. No other relief seems appropriate in this proceeding. Mr. North's vote against the motion for adjournment was sufficient to defeat it. With respect to the election of directors, the return of the inspectors should be corrected to show a rejection of Mrs. Haley's votes, and to declare the election of the six persons for whom Mr. North and Mrs. Ringling voted.

This leaves one vacancy in the directorate. The question of what to do about such a vacancy was not considered by the court below and has not been argued here. For this reason, and because an election of directors at the 1947 annual meeting (which presumably will be held in the near future) may make a determination of the question unimportant, we shall not decide it on this appeal. If a decision of the point appears important to the parties, any of them may apply to raise it in the Court of Chancery, after the mandate of this court is received there.

An order should be entered directing a modification of the order of the Court of Chancery in accordance with this opinion.

Model Business Corporation Act § 7.30: Voting Trusts

(a) One or more shareholders may create a voting trust, conferring on a trustee the right to vote or otherwise act for them, by signing an agreement setting out the provisions of the trust (which may include anything consistent with its purpose) and transferring their shares to the trustee. When a voting trust agreement is signed, the trustee shall prepare a list of the names and addresses of all owners of beneficial interests in the trust, together with the number and class of shares each transferred to the trust, and deliver copies of the list and agreement to the corporation's principal office.

(b) A voting trust becomes effective on the date the first shares subject to the trust are registered in the trustee's name. A voting trust is valid for not more than 10 years after its effective date unless extended under subsection (c).

(c) All or some of the parties to a voting trust may extend it for additional terms of not more than 10 years each by signing an extension agreement and obtaining the voting trustee's written consent to the extension. An extension is valid for 10 years from the date the first shareholder signs the extension agreement. The voting trustee must deliver copies of the extension agreement and list of beneficial owners to the corporation's principal office. An extension agreement binds only those parties signing it.

Model Business Corporation Act § 7.31: Voting Agreements

(a) Two or more shareholders may provide for the manner in which they will vote their shares by signing an agreement for that purpose. A voting agreement created under this section is not subject to the provisions of section 7.30.

(b) A voting agreement created under this section is specifically enforceable.

Melvin Aron Eisenberg & James D. Cox, *Corporations and Other Business Organizations* 464–65 (10th ed.). "A number of older cases held shareholder voting agreements either invalid or revocable at will, but the modern rule is that shareholder voting agreements are normally valid. However, a voting agreement is invalid if it is based on a 'private benefit'—that is, a side payment—given by one party to the other in exchange for his vote. [This rule] is an application of the broader principle, well-established in corporate law, that a shareholder may not sell his vote. See, e.g., Chew v. Inverness Management Corp., 352 A.2d 426 (Del. Ch. 1967)....

Because the courts are sometimes reluctant to specifically enforce voting agreements [and, at least in the past, inclined to give damages instead], the parties to such an agreement may expressly or impliedly substitute a self-executing remedy, such as giving each other proxies to vote each other's stock....

Even if a proxy is expressly conferred in connection with a voting agreement, a further problem remains. Classically a proxy has been treated as an agency relationship, in which the shareholder is the principal and the proxyholder is the agent. It is a rule of agency law, however, that a principal can terminate an agent's authority at will, even if the termination is in breach of contract.... There is an exception to this rule in cases where the agent holds a 'power coupled with an interest'.... Accordingly, the safest way to insure that a proxy will be irrevocable is to confer it upon a proxyholder who has an 'interest' in the shares to which the proxy relates. Relatively clear examples are cases where the proxyholder is a pledgee of the shares or has agreed to purchase the shares."

Model Business Corporation Act § 7.32: Shareholder Agreements

(a) An agreement among the shareholders of a corporation that complies with this section is effective among the shareholders and the corporation even though it is inconsistent with one or more other provisions of this Act in that it:

(1) eliminates the board of directors or restricts the discretion or powers of the board of directors;
(2) governs the authorization or making of distributions whether or not in proportion to ownership of shares, subject the limitations in section 6.40;
(3) establishes who shall be directors or officers of the corporation, or their terms of office or manner of selection or removal;
(4) governs, in general or in regard to specific matters, the exercise or division of voting power by or between the shareholders and directors or by or among any of them, including use of weighted voting rights or director proxies;
(5) establishes the terms and conditions of any agreement for the transfer or use of property or the provision of services between the corporation and any shareholder, director, officer or employee of the corporation or among any of them;
(6) transfers to one or more shareholders or other persons all or part of the authority to exercise the corporate powers or to manage the business and affairs of the corporation, including the resolution of any issue about which there exists a deadlock among directors or shareholders;
(7) requires dissolution of the corporation at the request of one or more of the shareholders or upon the occurrence of a specified event or contingency; or
(8) otherwise governs the exercise of the corporate powers or the management of the business and affairs of the corporation or the relationship among the shareholders, the directors and the corporation, or among any of them, and is not contrary to public policy.

(b) An agreement authorized by this section shall be:
(1) set forth (A) in the articles of incorporation or bylaws and approved by all persons who are shareholders at the time of the agreement or (B) in a written agreement that is signed by all persons who are shareholders at the time of the agreement and is made known to the corporation;
(2) subject to amendment only by all persons who are shareholders at the time of the amendment, unless the agreement provides otherwise; and
(3) valid for 10 years, unless the agreement provides otherwise.

(c) The existence of an agreement authorized by this section shall be noted conspicuously on the front or back of each certificate for outstanding shares or on the information statement required by section 6.26(b). If at the time of the agreement the corporation has shares outstanding represented by certificates, the corporation shall recall the outstanding certificates and issue substitute certificates that comply with this subsection. The failure to note the existence of the agreement on the certificate or information statement shall not affect the validity of the agreement or any action taken pursuant to it. Any purchaser of shares who, at the time of purchase, did not have knowledge of the existence of the agreement shall be entitled to rescission of the purchase. A purchaser shall be deemed to have knowledge of the existence of the agreement if its existence is noted on the certificate or information statement for the shares in compliance with this subsection and, if the shares are not represented by a certificate, the information statement is delivered to the purchaser at or prior to the time of purchase of the shares. An action to enforce the right of rescission authorized by this subsection must be commenced within the earlier of 90 days after discovery of the existence of the agreement or two years after the time of purchase of the shares.

(d) An agreement authorized by this section shall cease to be effective when shares of the corporation are listed on a national securities exchange or regularly traded in a market maintained by one or more members of a national or affiliated securities association. If the agreement ceases to be effective for any reason, the board of directors may, if the agreement is contained or referred to in the corporation's articles of incorporation or bylaws, adopt an amendment to the articles of incorporation or bylaws, without shareholder action, to delete the agreement and any references to it.

(e) An agreement authorized by this section that limits the discretion or powers of the board of directors shall relieve the directors of, and impose upon the person or persons in whom such discretion or powers are vested, liability for acts or omissions imposed by law on directors to the extent that the discretion or powers of the directors are limited by the agreement.

(f) The existence or performance of an agreement authorized by this section shall not be a ground for imposing personal liability on any shareholder for the acts or debts of the corporation even if the agreement or its performance treats the corporation as if it were a partnership or results in failure to observe the corporate formalities otherwise applicable to the matters governed by the agreement.

(g) Incorporators or subscribers for shares may act as shareholders with respect to an agreement authorized by this section if no shares have been issued when the agreement is made.

Section 4: Corporate Purpose and the Practical Power of the Board

Because the corporate form entails, by default, a representative structure in which those who have an economic interest in the entity (that is, the shareholders) do not control it directly, questions concerning the scope of the board and management of a corporation—and thus the *purposes* of a corporation—have arisen more frequently than they have under partnership law.

For example, except in bad faith, a partner ordinarily can vote, for personal reasons, not to expand a business; there is no fiduciary duty for a partner to pursue all opportunities from which other partners can profit. In a for-profit corporation, however, what happens when an elected board decides that the corporation should not seek profit?

This question has historically interacted with a related question: what are the legal *powers* of a corporation? In the past, the state often chartered corporations for very limited purposes, such as to build a bridge or conduct a particular kind of overseas trade. As the role of corporations in American business rose, corporations' powers expanded; today, nearly every corporation is authorized to conduct any lawful business properly entered into by its agents. Thus, for example, under MBCA § 3.02, "[u]nless its articles of incorporation provide otherwise, every corporation has ... the same powers as an individual to do all things necessary or convenient to carry out its business and affairs." Under § 3.01, "Every corporation incorporated under this Act has the purpose of engaging in any lawful business unless a more limited purpose is set forth in the articles of incorporation."

Acts outside the powers of the corporation—a concept that no longer arises frequently—were called *ultra vires*, a Latin phrase that simply means "beyond the powers," and courts could void them.

Dodge v. Ford Motor Co.

170 N.W. 668 (Mich. 1919)

OSTRANDER, J.

[Plaintiffs, the Dodge brothers, challenged retention of money by the Ford Motor Company and its proposed plan to use that money in a particular business expansion.]

There is little, if anything, in the bill of complaint which suggests the contention that the smelting of iron ore as a part of the process of manufacturing motors is, or will be, an activity ultra vires the defendant corporation. On the contrary, the bill charges that the erection of smelters and such other buildings, machinery and appliances as are intended to go along with the business of smelting ore is part of a general plan of expansion of the business of defendant corporation which is in itself unwise and which is put into operation for the purpose of absorbing profits which ought to be distributed to shareholders. Restraint is asked, not because the smelting business is ultra vires the corporation, but because the whole plan of expansion is inimical to shareholders' rights and was formulated and will be carried out in defiance of those rights.

The gray iron parts of a Ford car weigh, in the rough, 268.90 pounds, and when finished 215.71 pounds. This iron, as now made by defendants, costs, per car, at the prices of iron when the cause was tried, $11.184. The malleable iron parts weigh, finished, per car, 69.63 pounds and would cost $6.757. The total cost per car of gray and malleable iron parts is less than $18.

The smelter proposition involves, of course, much more than the initial expenditure for a plant. It involves the use of a large amount of capital to secure the finished product for the cars. Quantities of iron ore must be purchased and carried in stock, coal for the coke ovens must be purchased, the plant must be maintained. If the plant produces the necessary iron and 800,000 cars are made in a year, something more than 270,000,000 pounds of iron will be produced, and if, as is claimed by Mr. Ford, the cost is reduced to the company by one-half and better iron made, a saving of nine or ten dollars on the cost of each car will be the result. Presumably, this saving will also be reflected in the profits made from sales of parts. Ultimately, the result will be either a considerable additional profit upon each car sold or it will permit a reduction in the selling price of cars and parts. The process proposed to be used has not been used, commercially.

The contention that the project is ultra vires the defendant corporation appears to have been made upon the application for a preliminary restraining order, and at the hearing on the merits, as a reason for denying the right to invest instead of distributing the money which the proposed plant will cost, with no claim of surprise upon the part of defendants.

Strictly, upon the pleadings, the question of ultra vires is not for decision, and this is not seriously denied. Assuming, however, in view of the course taken at the hearing, it is proper to express an opinion upon the point, it must be said that to make castings from iron ore rather than to make them from pig iron, as defendant is now doing, eliminating one usual process, is not beyond the power of the corporation. In its relation to the finished product, iron ore, an article of commerce, is not very different from lumber. It is admitted that the defendant company may not undertake to smelt ore except for its own uses. Defendant corporation is organized to manufacture motors and automobiles and their parts. To manufacture implies the use of means of manufacturing as well as the material. No good reason is perceived for saying that as matter of power it may not manufacture all of an automobile. In doing so, it need not rely upon the statute grant of incidental powers. Extreme cases may be put, as, for example, if it may make castings from iron ore, may it invest in mines which produce the ore and in means for transporting the ore from mine to factory? Or, if it may make the rubber tires for cars, may it own and exploit a rubber plantation in Brazil, or elsewhere? No such case is presented, and until presented need not be considered.

As we regard the testimony as failing to prove any violation of anti-trust laws or that the alleged policy of the company, if successfully carried out, will involve a monopoly other than such as accrues to a concern which makes what the public demands and sells it at a price which the public regards as cheap or reasonable, the case for plaintiffs must rest upon the claim, and the proof in support of it, that the proposed expansion of the business of the corporation, involving the further use of profits as capital, ought to be enjoined because inimical to the best interests of the company and its shareholders, and upon the further claim that in any event the withholding of the special dividend asked for by plaintiffs is arbitrary action of the directors requiring judicial interference.

The rule which will govern courts in deciding these questions is not in dispute. It is, of course, differently phrased by judges and by authors, and, as the phrasing in a particular instance may seem to lean for or against the exercise of the right of judicial interference with the actions of corporate directors, the context, or the facts before the court, must be considered. This court, in Hunter v. Roberts, Throp & Co., 83 Mich. 63, 71, recognized the rule in the following language:

"It is a well-recognized principle of law that the directors of a corporation, and they alone, have the power to declare a dividend of the earnings of the corporation, and to determine its amount. Courts of equity will not interfere in the management of the directors unless it is clearly made to appear that they are guilty of fraud or misappropriation of the corporate funds, or refuse to declare a dividend when the corporation has a surplus of net profits which it can, without detriment to its business, divide among its stockholders, and when a refusal to do so would amount to such an abuse of discretion as would constitute a fraud, or breach of that good faith which they are bound to exercise towards the stockholders."....

To develop the points now discussed, and to a considerable extent they may be developed together as a single point, it is necessary to refer with some particularity to the facts.

When plaintiffs made their complaint and demand for further dividends the Ford Motor Company had concluded its most prosperous year of business. The demand for its cars at the price of the preceding year continued. It could make and could market in the year beginning August 1, 1916, more than 500,000 cars. Sales of parts and repairs would necessarily increase. The cost of materials was likely to advance, and perhaps the price of labor, but it reasonably might have expected a profit for the year of upwards of $60,000,000. It had assets of more than $132,000,000, a surplus of almost $112,000,000, and its cash on hand and municipal bonds were nearly $54,000,000. Its total liabilities, including capital stock, were a little over $20,000,000. It had declared no special dividend during the business year except the October, 1915, dividend. It had been the practice, under similar circumstances, to declare larger dividends. Considering only these facts, a refusal to declare and pay further dividends appears to be not an exercise of discretion on the part of the directors, but an arbitrary refusal to do what the circumstances required to be done. These facts and others call upon the directors to justify their action, or failure or refusal to act. In justification, the defendants have offered testimony tending to prove, and which does prove, the following facts. It had been the policy of the corporation for a considerable time to annually reduce the selling price of cars, while keeping up, or improving, their quality. As early as in June, 1915, a general plan for the expansion of the productive capacity of the concern by a practical duplication of its plant had been talked over by the executive officers and directors and agreed upon, not all of the details having been settled and no formal action of directors having been taken. The erection of a smelter was considered, and engineering and other data in connection therewith secured. In consequence, it was determined not to reduce the selling price of cars for the year beginning August 1, 1915, but to maintain the price and to accumulate a large surplus to pay for the proposed expansion of plant and equipment, and perhaps to build a plant for smelting ore. It is hoped, by Mr. Ford, that eventually 1,000,000 cars will be annually produced. The contemplated changes will permit the increased output.

The plan, as affecting the profits of the business for the year beginning August 1, 1916, and thereafter, calls for a reduction in the selling price of the cars. It is true that this price might be at any time increased, but the plan called for the reduction in price of $80 a car. The capacity of the plant, without the additions thereto voted to be made (without a part of them at least), would produce more than 600,000 cars annually. This number, and more, could have been sold for $440 instead of $360, a difference in the return for capital, labor and materials employed of at least $48,000,000. In short, the plan does not call for and is not intended to produce immediately a more profitable business but a less profitable one; not only less profitable than formerly but less profitable than it is admitted it might be made. The apparent immediate effect will be to diminish the value of shares and the returns to shareholders.

It is the contention of plaintiffs that the apparent effect of the plan is intended to be the continued and continuing effect of it and that it is deliberately proposed, not of record and not by official corporate declaration, but nevertheless proposed, to continue the corporation henceforth as a semi-eleemosynary institution and not as a business institution. In support of this contention they point to the attitude and to the expressions of Mr. Henry Ford.

Mr. Henry Ford is the dominant force in the business of the Ford Motor Company. No plan of operations could be adopted unless he consented, and no board of directors can be elected whom he does not favor. One of the directors of the company has no stock. One share was assigned to him to qualify him for the position, but it is not claimed that he owns it. A business, one of the largest in the world, and one of the most profitable, has been built up. It employs many men, at good pay.

"My ambition," said Mr. Ford, "is to employ still more men, to spread the benefits of this industrial system to the greatest possible number, to help them build up their lives and their homes. To do this we are putting the greatest share of our profits back in the business."

"With regard to dividends, the company paid sixty per cent. on its capitalization of two million dollars, or $1,200,000, leaving $58,000,000 to reinvest for the growth of the company. This is Mr. Ford's policy at present, and it is understood that the other stockholders cheerfully accede to this plan."

He had made up his mind in the summer of 1916 that no dividends other than the regular dividends should be paid, "for the present."

"Q. For how long? Had you fixed in your mind any time in the future, when you were going to pay—

"A. No.

"Q. That was indefinite in the future?

"A. That was indefinite, yes, sir."

The record, and especially the testimony of Mr. Ford, convinces that he has to some extent the attitude towards shareholders of one who has dispensed and distributed to them large gains and that they should be content to take what he chooses to give. His testimony creates the impression, also, that he thinks the Ford Motor Company has made too much money, has had too large profits, and that although large profits might be still earned, a sharing of them with the public, by reducing the price of the output of the company, ought to be undertaken. We have no doubt that certain sentiments, philanthropic and altruistic, creditable to Mr. Ford, had large influence in determining the policy to be pursued by the Ford Motor Company—the policy which has been herein referred to.

It is said by his counsel that—

"Although a manufacturing corporation cannot engage in humanitarian works as its principal business, the fact that it is organized for profit does not prevent the existence of implied powers to carry on with humanitarian motives such charitable works as are incidental to the main business of the corporation."

And again:

"As the expenditures complained of are being made in an expansion of the business which the company is organized to carry on, and for purposes within the powers of the corporation as hereinbefore shown, the question is as to whether such expenditures are rendered illegal because influenced to some extent by humanitarian motives and purposes on the part of the members of the board of directors."

In discussing this proposition, counsel have referred to decisions such as Hawes v. Oakland, 104 U.S. 450; Taunton v. Royal Ins. Co., 2 Hem. & Miller, 135; Henderson v. Bank of Australasia, L.R. 40 Ch. Div. 170; Steinway v. Steinway & Sons, 40 N.Y. Supp. 718; People, ex rel. Metropolitan Life Ins. Co., v. Hotchkiss, 136 App. Div. 150 (120 N.Y. Supp. 649). These cases, after all, like all others in which the subject is treated, turn finally upon the point, the question, whether it appears that the directors were not acting for the best interests of the corporation. We do not draw in question, nor do counsel for the plaintiffs do so, the validity of the general propositions stated by counsel nor the soundness of the opinions delivered in the cases cited. The case presented here is not like any of them. The difference between an incidental humanitarian expenditure of corporate funds for the benefit of the employees, like the building of a hospital for their use and the employment of agencies for the betterment of their condition, and a general purpose and plan to benefit mankind at the expense of others, is obvious. There should be no confusion (of which there is evidence) of the duties which Mr. Ford conceives that he and the stockholders owe to the general public and the duties which in law he and his codirectors owe to protesting, minority stockholders. A business corporation is organized and carried on primarily for the profit of the stockholders. The powers of the directors are to be employed for that end. The discretion of directors is to be exercised in the choice of means to attain that end and does not extend to a change in the end itself, to the reduction of profits or to the nondistribution of profits among stockholders in order to devote them to other purposes.

There is committed to the discretion of directors, a discretion to be exercised in good faith, the infinite details of business, including the wages which shall be paid to employees, the number of hours they shall work, the conditions under which labor shall be carried on, and the prices for which products shall be offered to the public. It is said by appellants that the motives of the board members are not material and will not be inquired into by the court so long as their acts are within their lawful powers. As we have pointed out, and the proposition does not require argument to sustain it, it is not within the lawful powers of a board of directors to shape and conduct the affairs of a corporation for the merely incidental benefit of shareholders and for the primary purpose of benefiting others, and no one will contend that if the avowed purpose of the defendant directors was to sacrifice the interests of shareholders it would not be the duty of the courts to interfere.

We are not, however, persuaded that we should interfere with the proposed expansion of the business of the Ford Motor Company. In view of the fact that the selling price of products may be increased at any time, the ultimate results of the larger business cannot be certainly estimated. The judges are not business experts. It is recognized that plans must often be made for a long future, for expected competition, for a continuing as well as an immediately profitable venture. The experience of the Ford Motor Company is evidence of capable management of its affairs. It may be noticed, incidentally, that it took from the public the money required for the execution of its plan and that the very considerable salaries paid to Mr. Ford and to certain executive officers and employees were not diminished. We are not satisfied that the alleged motives of the directors, in so far as they are reflected in the conduct of the business, menace the interests of shareholders. It is enough to say, perhaps, that the court of equity is at all times open to complaining shareholders having a just grievance.

Assuming the general plan and policy of expansion and the details of it to have been sufficiently, formally, approved at the October and November, 1917, meetings of directors, and assuming further that the plan and policy and the details agreed upon were for the best ultimate interest of the company and therefore of its shareholders, what does it amount to in justification of a refusal to declare and pay a special dividend, or dividends? The Ford Motor Company was able to estimate with nicety its income and profit. It could sell more cars than it could make. Having ascertained what it would cost to produce a car and to sell it, the profit upon each car depended upon the selling price. That being fixed, the yearly income and profit was determinable, and, within slight variations, was certain.

There was appropriated—voted—for the smelter $11,325,000. As to the remainder voted there is no available way for determining how much had been paid before the action of directors was taken and how much was paid thereafter, but assuming that the plans required an expenditure sooner or later of $9,895,000 for duplication of the plant, and for land and other expenditures $3,000,000, the total is $24,220,000. The company was continuing business, at a profit—a cash business. If the total cost of proposed expenditures had been immediately withdrawn in cash from the cash surplus (money and bonds) on hand August 1, 1916, there would have remained nearly $30,000,000.

Defendants say, and it is true, that a considerable cash balance must be at all times carried by such a concern. But, as has been stated, there was a large daily, weekly, monthly, receipt of cash. The output was practically continuous and was continuously, and within a few days, turned into cash. Moreover, the contemplated expenditures were not to be immediately made. The large sum appropriated for the smelter plant was payable over a considerable period of time. So that, without going further, it would appear that, accepting and approving the plan of the directors, it was their duty to distribute on or near the first of August, 1916, a very large sum of money to stockholders.

In reaching this conclusion, we do not ignore, but recognize, the validity of the proposition that plaintiffs have from the beginning profited by, if they have not lately, officially, participated in, the general policy of expansion pursued by this corporation. We do not lose sight of the fact that it had been, upon an occasion, agreeable to the plaintiffs to increase the capital stock to \$100,000,000 by a stock dividend of \$98,000,000. These things go only to answer other contentions now made by plaintiffs and do not and cannot operate to estop them to demand proper dividends upon the stock they own. It is obvious that an annual dividend of sixty per cent. upon \$2,000,000, or \$1,–\$200,000, is the equivalent of a very small dividend upon \$100,000,000, or more.

The decree of the court below fixing and determining the specific amount to be distributed to stockholders is affirmed. In other respects, except as to the allowance of costs, the said decree is reversed. Plaintiffs will recover interest at five per cent. per annum upon their proportional share of said dividend from the date of the decree of the lower court. Appellants will tax the costs of their appeal, and two-thirds of the amount thereof will be paid by plaintiffs. No other costs are allowed.

Note on Dodge v. Ford and the Power of Controllers

A well-advised Henry Ford would likely not have lost *Dodge v. Ford* today, in part because of the broad powers that modern statutes and courts give directors and managers. In particular, though the directors and managers of a corporation ordinarily have a duty to act reasonably (just as people ordinarily do under tort law), this *duty of care* is limited by a principle known as the *business-judgment rule*—a rule that courts will not judge the business decisions of informed directors and managers except in extreme cases. The statutory materials that follow show the standards of *conduct*, and then of *liability*, for corporate directors under the MBCA; they then show various further sorts of flexibilities that the MBCA and state statutes provide.

Model Business Corporation Act § 8.30(b): Standards of Conduct for Directors

The members of the board of directors or a committee of the board, when becoming informed in connection with their decision-making function or devoting attention to their oversight function, shall discharge their duties with the care that a person in a like position would reasonably believe appropriate under similar circumstances.

Model Business Corporation Act § 8.31: Standards of Liability for Directors

(a) A director shall not be liable to the corporation or its shareholders for any decision to take or not to take action, or any failure to take any action, as a director, unless the party asserting liability in a proceeding establishes that

(1) [various defenses, permitted in the articles of incorporation or available under the statute, are unavailable]

(2) the challenged conduct consisted or was the result of:

(i) action not in good faith; or

(ii) a decision

(A) which the director did not reasonably believe to be in the best interests of the corporation, or

(B) as to which the director was not informed to an extent the director reasonably believed appropriate in the circumstances; or

(iii) a lack of objectivity due to the director's familial, financial or business relationship with, or a lack of independence due to the director's domination or control by, another person having a material interest in the challenged conduct

(A) which relationship or which domination or control could reasonably be expected to have affected the director's judgment respecting the challenged conduct in a manner adverse to the corporation, and

(B) after a reasonable expectation to such effect has been established, the director shall not have established that the challenged conduct was reasonably believed by the director to be in the best interests of the corporation; or

(iv) a sustained failure of the director to devote attention to ongoing oversight of the business and affairs of the corporation, or a failure to devote timely attention, by making (or causing to be made) appropriate inquiry, when particular facts and circumstances of significant concern materialize that would alert a reasonably attentive director to the need therefore; or

(v) receipt of a financial benefit to which the director was not entitled or any other breach of the director's duties to deal fairly with the corporation and its shareholders that is actionable under applicable law.

Model Business Corporation Act § 3.02

[By default, corporations have powers ...]

(13) to make donations for the public welfare or for charitable, scientific, or educational purposes;

(14) to transact any lawful business that will aid governmental policy;

(15) to make payments or donations, or do any other act, not inconsistent with law, that furthers the business and affairs of the corporation

---

New York Business Corporation Law § 717: Duty of Directors

(b) In taking action, including, without limitation, action which may involve or relate to a change or potential change in the control of the corporation, a director shall be entitled to consider, without limitation, (1) both the long-term and the short-term interests of the corporation and its shareholders and (2) the effects that the corporation's actions may have in the short-term or in the long-term upon any of the following:

(i) the prospects for potential growth, development, productivity and profitability of the corporation;

(ii) the corporation's current employees;

(iii) the corporation's retired employees and other beneficiaries receiving or entitled to receive retirement, welfare or similar benefits from or pursuant to any plan sponsored, or agreement entered into, by the corporation;

(iv) the corporation's customers and creditors; and

(v) the ability of the corporation to provide, as a going concern, goods, services, employment opportunities and employment benefits and otherwise to contribute to the communities in which it does business.

Nothing in this paragraph shall create any duties owed by any director to any person or entity to consider or afford any particular weight to any of the foregoing or abrogate any duty of the directors, either statutory or recognized by common law or court decisions.

---

eBay Domestic Holdings, Inc. v. Newmark, 16 A.3d 1 (Del. Ch. 2010). CHANDLER, C. "Jim and Craig did prove that they personally believe craigslist should not be about the business of stockholder wealth maximization, now or in the future. As an abstract matter, there is nothing inappropriate about an organization seeking to aid local, national, and global communities by providing a website for online classifieds that is largely devoid of monetized elements. Indeed, I personally appreciate and admire Jim's and Craig's desire to be of service to communities. The corporate form in which craigslist operates, however, is not an appropriate vehicle for purely philanthropic ends, at least not when there are other stockholders interested in realizing a return on their investment. Jim and Craig opted to form craigslist, Inc. as a for-profit Delaware corporation and voluntarily accepted millions of dollars from eBay as part of a transaction whereby eBay became a stockholder. Having chosen a for-profit corporate form, the craigslist directors are bound by the fiduciary duties and standards that accompany that form. Those standards include acting to promote the value of the corporation for the benefit of its stockholders. The 'Inc.' after the company name has to mean at least that. Thus, I cannot accept as valid for the purposes of implementing the [challenged action] a corporate policy that specifically, clearly, and admittedly seeks not to maximize the economic value of a for-profit Delaware corporation for the benefit of its stockholders—no matter whether those stockholders are individuals of modest means or a corporate titan of online commerce. If Jim and Craig were the only stockholders affected by their decisions, then there would be no one to object. eBay, however, holds a significant stake in craigslist, and Jim and Craig's actions affect others besides themselves."

Lynn Stout, *Why We Should Stop Teaching Dodge v. Ford*

3 VA. L. & BUS. REV. 163 (2008)

Perhaps many people do share the Michigan Supreme Court's view that it is desirable for corporations to pursue only profits for shareholders. But why do they believe this is desirable?

At least until fairly recently, many corporate experts found the answer to this question in economic theory. Not too long ago, it was conventional economic wisdom that the shareholders in a corporation are the sole residual claimants in the firm, meaning shareholders are entitled to all the "residual" profits left over after the firm has met its fixed contractual obligations to employees, customers, and creditors. This assumption suggests that corporations are run best when they are run for shareholders' benefit alone, because if other corporate stakeholders' interests are fixed by their contracts, maximizing the shareholders' residual claim means maximizing the total social value of the firm.

Time has been unkind to this perspective. Advances in economic theory have made clear that shareholders generally are not, and probably cannot be, the sole residual claimants in firms. For example, modern options theory teaches that business risk that increases the expected value of the equity interest in a corporation must simultaneously reduce the supposedly "fixed" value of creditors' interests. Another branch of the economic literature focuses on the contracting problems that surround specific investment in "team production," suggesting how a legal rule requiring corporate directors to maximize shareholder wealth ex post might well have the perverse effect of reducing shareholder wealth over time by discouraging non-shareholder groups from making specific investments in corporations ex ante. Yet a third economic concept that undermines the wisdom of shareholder wealth maximization is the idea of externalities: when the pursuit of shareholder profits imposes greater costs on third parties (for instance, customers, employees, or the environment) that are not fully constrained by law, shareholder wealth maximization becomes undesirable, at least from a social perspective.

Finally, it is becoming increasingly well-understood that when a firm has more than one shareholder, the very idea of "shareholder wealth" becomes incoherent. Different shareholders have different investment time frames, different tax concerns, different attitudes toward firm-level risk due to different levels of diversification, different interests in other investments that might be affected by corporate activities, and different views about the extent to which they are willing to sacrifice corporate profits to promote broader social interests, such as a clean environment or good wages for workers. These and other schisms ensure that there is no single, uniform measure of shareholder "wealth" to be "maximized."

Accordingly, most contemporary experts understand that economic theory alone does not permit us to safely assume that corporations are run best when they are run according to the principle of shareholder wealth maximization. Not only is *Dodge v. Ford* bad law from a positive perspective, but it is also bad law from a normative perspective.

Section 5: Special Protections for Minority Shareholders in Closely Held Corporations

As we saw in the last section, the corporate board has duties of care, loyalty, and good faith. The contours of these general duties form a significant part of the law of corporations; they are covered in most law schools' Corporations classes and are one significant limitation on the power of managers in public corporations.

There are more specific duties and relationships in the context of closely held corporations, however. These duties are important to us partly because they affect small corporations and partly because they provide a foundation for our later study of limited liability companies (LLCs).

Donahue v. Rodd Electrotype Co.

328 N.E.2d 505 (Mass. 1975)

TAURO, J.

The plaintiff, Euphemia Donahue, a minority stockholder in the Rodd Electrotype Company of New England, Inc. (Rodd Electrotype), a Massachusetts corporation, brings this suit against the directors of Rodd Electrotype, Charles H. Rodd, Frederick I. Rodd and Mr. Harold E. Magnuson, against Harry C. Rodd, a former director, officer, and controlling stockholder of Rodd Electrotype and against Rodd Electrotype (hereinafter called defendants). The plaintiff seeks to rescind Rodd Electrotype's purchase of Harry Rodd's shares in Rodd Electrotype and to compel Harry Rodd "to repay to the corporation the purchase price of said shares, $36,000, together with interest from the date of purchase." The plaintiff alleges that the defendants caused the corporation to purchase the shares in violation of their fiduciary duty to her, a minority stockholder of Rodd Electrotype.

The trial judge, after hearing oral testimony, dismissed the plaintiff's bill on the merits. He found that the purchase was without prejudice to the plaintiff and implicitly found that the transaction had been carried out in good faith and with inherent fairness. The Appeals Court affirmed with costs. The case is before us on the plaintiff's application for further appellate review....

The evidence may be summarized as follows: In 1935, the defendant, Harry C. Rodd, began his employment with Rodd Electrotype, then styled the Royal Electrotype Company of New England, Inc. (Royal of New England). At that time, the company was a wholly-owned subsidiary of a Pennsylvania corporation, the Royal Electrotype Company (Royal Electrotype). Mr. Rodd's advancement within the company was rapid. The following year he was elected a director, and, in 1946, he succeeded to the position of general manager and treasurer.

In 1936, the plaintiff's husband, Joseph Donahue (now deceased), was hired by Royal of New England as a "finisher" of electrotype plates. His duties were confined to operational matters within the plant. Although he ultimately achieved the positions of plant superintendent (1946) and corporate vice president (1955), Donahue never participated in the "management" aspect of the business.

In the years preceding 1955, the parent company, Royal Electrotype, made available to Harry Rodd and Joseph Donahue shares of the common stock in its subsidiary, Royal of New England. Harry Rodd took advantage of the opportunities offered to him and acquired 200 shares for $20 a share. Joseph Donahue, at the suggestion of Harry Rodd, who hoped to interest Donahue in the business, eventually obtained fifty shares in two twenty-five share lots priced at $20 a share. The parent company at all times retained 725 of the 1,000 outstanding shares. One Lawrence W. Kelley owned the remaining twenty-five shares.

In June of 1955, Royal of New England purchased all 725 of its shares owned by its parent company. The total price amounted to $135,000. Royal of New England remitted $75,000 of this total in cash and executed five promissory notes of $12,000 each, due in each of the succeeding five years. Lawrence W. Kelley's twenty-five shares were also purchased at this time for $1,000. A substantial portion of Royal of New England's cash expenditures was loaned to the company by Harry Rodd, who mortgaged his house to obtain some of the necessary funds.

The stock purchases left Harry Rodd in control of Royal of New England. Early in 1955, before the purchases, he had assumed the presidency of the company. His 200 shares gave him a dominant eighty per cent interest. Joseph Donahue, at this time, was the only minority stockholder.

Subsequent events reflected Harry Rodd's dominant influence. In June, 1960, more than a year after the last obligation to Royal Electrotype had been discharged, the company was renamed the Rodd Electrotype Company of New England, Inc. In 1962, Charles H. Rodd, Harry Rodd's son (a defendant here), who had long been a company employee working in the plant, became corporate vice president. In 1963, he joined his father on the board of directors. In 1964, another son, Frederick I. Rodd (also a defendant), replaced Joseph Donahue as plant superintendent. By 1965, Harry Rodd had evidently decided to reduce his participation in corporate management. That year, Charles Rodd succeeded him as president and general manager of Rodd Electrotype.

From 1959 to 1967, Harry Rodd pursued what may fairly be termed a gift program by which he distributed the majority of his shares equally among his two sons and his daughter, Phyllis E. Mason. Each child received thirty-nine shares. Two shares were returned to the corporate treasury in 1966.

We come now to the events of 1970 which form the grounds for the plaintiff's complaint. In May of 1970, Harry Rodd was seventy-seven years old. The record indicates that for some time he had not enjoyed the best of health and that he had undergone a number of operations. His sons wished him to retire. Mr. Rodd was not averse to this suggestion. However, he insisted that some financial arrangements be made with respect to his remaining eighty-one shares of stock. A number of conferences ensued. Harry Rodd and Charles Rodd (representing the company) negotiated terms of purchase for forty-five shares which, Charles Rodd testified, would reflect the book value and liquidating value of the shares.

A special board meeting convened on July 13, 1970. As the first order of business, Harry Rodd resigned his directorship of Rodd Electrotype. The remaining incumbent directors, Charles Rodd and Mr. Harold E. Magnuson (clerk of the company and a defendant and defense attorney in the instant suit), elected Frederick Rodd to replace his father. The three directors then authorized Rodd Electrotype's president (Charles Rodd) to execute an agreement between Harry Rodd and the company in which the company would purchase forty-five shares for $800 a share ($36,000).

The stock purchase agreement was formalized between the parties on July 13, 1970. Two days later, a sale pursuant to the July 13 agreement was consummated. At approximately the same time, Harry Rodd resigned his last corporate office, that of treasurer.

Harry Rodd completed divestiture of his Rodd Electrotype stock in the following year. As was true of his previous gifts, his later divestments gave equal representation to his children. Two shares were sold to each child on July 15, 1970, for $800 a share. Each was given ten shares in March, 1971. Thus, in March, 1971, the shareholdings in Rodd Electrotype were apportioned as follows: Charles Rodd, Frederick Rodd and Phyllis Mason each held fifty-one shares; the Donahues held fifty shares.

A special meeting of the stockholders of the company was held on March 30, 1971. At the meeting, Charles Rodd, company president and general manager, reported the tentative results of an audit conducted by the company auditors and reported generally on the company events of the year. For the first time, the Donahues learned that the corporation had purchased Harry Rodd's shares. According to the minutes of the meeting, following Charles Rodd's report, the Donahues raised questions about the purchase. They then voted against a resolution, ultimately adopted by the remaining stockholders, to approve Charles Rodd's report. Although the minutes of the meeting show that the stockholders unanimously voted to accept a second resolution ratifying all acts of the company president (he executed the stock purchase agreement) in the preceding year, the trial judge found, and there was evidence to support his finding, that the Donahues did not ratify the purchase of Harry Rodd's shares.

A few weeks after the meeting, the Donahues, acting through their attorney, offered their shares to the corporation on the same terms given to Harry Rodd. Mr. Harold E. Magnuson replied by letter that the corporation would not purchase the shares and was not in a financial position to do so. This suit followed.

In her argument before this court, the plaintiff has characterized the corporate purchase of Harry Rodd's shares as an unlawful distribution of corporate assets to controlling stockholders. She urges that the distribution constitutes a breach of the fiduciary duty owed by the Rodds, as controlling stockholders, to her, a minority stockholder in the enterprise, because the Rodds failed to accord her an equal opportunity to sell her shares to the corporation. The defendants reply that the stock purchase was within the powers of the corporation and met the requirements of good faith and inherent fairness imposed on a fiduciary in his dealings with the corporation. They assert that there is no right to equal opportunity in corporate stock purchases for the corporate treasury. For the reasons hereinafter noted, we agree with the plaintiff and reverse the decree of the Superior Court. However, we limit the applicability of our holding to "close corporations," as hereinafter defined. Whether the holding should apply to other corporations is left for decision in another case, on a proper record.

A. Close Corporations. In previous opinions, we have alluded to the distinctive nature of the close corporation, but have never defined precisely what is meant by a close corporation. There is no single, generally accepted definition. Some commentators emphasize an "integration of ownership and management" (Note, Statutory Assistance for Closely Held Corporations, 71 Harv. L. Rev. 1498 [1958]), in which the stockholders occupy most management positions. Others focus on the number of stockholders and the nature of the market for the stock. In this view, close corporations have few stockholders; there is little market for corporate stock. The Supreme Court of Illinois adopted this latter view in Galler v. Galler, 32 Ill. 2d 16 (1965): "For our purposes, a close corporation is one in which the stock is held in a few hands, or in a few families, and wherein it is not at all, or only rarely, dealt in by buying or selling." Id. at 27. We accept aspects of both definitions. We deem a close corporation to be typified by: (1) a small number of stockholders; (2) no ready market for the corporate stock; and (3) substantial majority stockholder participation in the management, direction and operations of the corporation.

As thus defined, the close corporation bears striking resemblance to a partnership. Commentators and courts have noted that the close corporation is often little more than an "incorporated" or "chartered" partnership. The stockholders "clothe" their partnership "with the benefits peculiar to a corporation, limited liability, perpetuity and the like." In the Matter of Surchin v. Approved Bus. Mach. Co. Inc. 55 Misc. 2d (N. Y.) 888, 889 (Sup. Ct. 1967). In essence, though, the enterprise remains one in which ownership is limited to the original parties or transferees of their stock to whom the other stockholders have agreed, in which ownership and management are in the same hands, and in which the owners are quite dependent on one another for the success of the enterprise. Many close corporations are "really partnerships between two or three people who contribute their capital, skills, experience and labor." Kruger v. Gerth, 16 N. Y. 2d 802, 805 (1965) (Desmond, C.J., dissenting). Just as in a partnership, the relationship among the stockholders must be one of trust, confidence and absolute loyalty if the enterprise is to succeed. Close corporations with substantial assets and with more numerous stockholders are no different from smaller close corporations in this regard. All participants rely on the fidelity and abilities of those stockholders who hold office. Disloyalty and self-seeking conduct on the part of any stockholder will engender bickering, corporate stalemates, and, perhaps, efforts to achieve dissolution.

In Helms v. Duckworth, 249 F. 2d 482 (D. C. Cir. 1957), the United States Court of Appeals for the District of Columbia Circuit had before it a stockholders' agreement providing for the purchase of the shares of a deceased stockholder by the surviving stockholder in a small "two-man" close corporation. The court held the surviving stockholder to a duty "to deal fairly, honestly, and openly with ... [his] fellow stockholders." Id. at 487. Judge Burger, now Chief Justice Burger, writing for the court, emphasized the resemblance of the two-man close corporation to a partnership: "In an intimate business venture such as this, stockholders of a close corporation occupy a position similar to that of joint adventurers and partners. While courts have sometimes declared stockholders 'do not bear toward each other that same relation of trust and confidence which prevails in partnerships,' this view ignores the practical realities of the organization and functioning of a small 'two-man' corporation organized to carry on a small business enterprise in which the stockholders, directors, and managers are the same persons" (footnotes omitted). Id. at 486.

Although the corporate form provides the above-mentioned advantages for the stockholders (limited liability, perpetuity, and so forth), it also supplies an opportunity for the majority stockholders to oppress or disadvantage minority stockholders. The minority is vulnerable to a variety of oppressive devices, termed "freeze-outs," which the majority may employ. See, generally, Note, Freezing Out Minority Shareholders, 74 Harv. L. Rev. 1630 (1961). An authoritative study of such "freeze-outs" enumerates some of the possibilities: "The squeezers [those who employ the freeze-out techniques] may refuse to declare dividends; they may drain off the corporation's earnings in the form of exorbitant salaries and bonuses to the majority shareholder-officers and perhaps to their relatives, or in the form of high rent by the corporation for property leased from majority shareholders ... ; they may deprive minority shareholders of corporate offices and of employment by the company; they may cause the corporation to sell its assets at an inadequate price to the majority shareholders...." F. H. O'Neal and J. Derwin, Expulsion or Oppression of Business Associates, 42 (1961). In particular, the power of the board of directors, controlled by the majority, to declare or withhold dividends and to deny the minority employment is easily converted to a device to disadvantage minority stockholders.

The minority can, of course, initiate suit against the majority and their directors. Self-serving conduct by directors is proscribed by the director's fiduciary obligation to the corporation. However, in practice, the plaintiff will find difficulty in challenging dividend or employment policies. Such policies are considered to be within the judgment of the directors. This court has said: "The courts prefer not to interfere ... with the sound financial management of the corporation by its directors, but declare as a general rule that the declaration of dividends rests within the sound discretion of the directors, refusing to interfere with their determination unless a plain abuse of discretion is made to appear." Crocker v. Waltham Watch Co. 315 Mass. 397, 402 (1944). Judicial reluctance to interfere combines with the difficulty of proof ... to limit the possibilities for relief. Although contractual provisions in an "agreement of association and articles of organization" or in by-laws have justified decrees in this jurisdiction ordering dividend declarations, generally, plaintiffs who seek judicial assistance against corporate dividend or employment policies do not prevail.... But see Dodge v. Ford Motor Co. 204 Mich. 459 (1919); Patton v. Nicholas, 154 Texas 385 (1955).

Thus, when these types of "freeze-outs" are attempted by the majority stockholders, the minority stockholders, cut off from all corporation-related revenues, must either suffer their losses or seek a buyer for their shares. Many minority stockholders will be unwilling or unable to wait for an alteration in majority policy. Typically, the minority stockholder in a close corporation has a substantial percentage of his personal assets invested in the corporation. Galler v. Galler, 32 Ill. 2d 16, 27 (1965). The stockholder may have anticipated that his salary from his position with the corporation would be his livelihood. Thus, he cannot afford to wait passively. He must liquidate his investment in the close corporation in order to reinvest the funds in income-producing enterprises.

At this point, the true plight of the minority stockholder in a close corporation becomes manifest. He cannot easily reclaim his capital. In a large public corporation, the oppressed or dissident minority stockholder could sell his stock in order to extricate some of his invested capital. By definition, this market is not available for shares in the close corporation. In a partnership, a partner who feels abused by his fellow partners may cause dissolution by his "express will ... at any time" (G. L. c. 108A, § 31 [1] [b] and [2]) and recover his share of partnership assets and accumulated profits. If dissolution results in a breach of the partnership articles, the culpable partner will be liable in damages. G. L. c. 108A, § 38 (2) (a) II. By contrast, the stockholder in the close corporation or "incorporated partnership" may achieve dissolution and recovery of his share of the enterprise assets only by compliance with the rigorous terms of the applicable chapter of the General Laws. "The dissolution of a corporation which is a creature of the Legislature is primarily a legislative function, and the only authority courts have to deal with this subject is the power conferred upon them by the Legislature." Leventhal v. Atlantic Fin. Corp. 316 Mass. 194, 205 (1944). To secure dissolution of the ordinary close corporation subject to G. L. c. 156B, the stockholder, in the absence of corporate deadlock, must own at least fifty per cent of the shares (G. L. c. 156B, § 99 [a]) or have the advantage of a favorable provision in the articles of organization (G. L. c. 156B, § 100 [a] [2]). The minority stockholder, by definition lacking fifty per cent of the corporate shares, can never "authorize" the corporation to file a petition for dissolution under G. L. c. 156B, § 99 (a), by his own vote. He will seldom have at his disposal the requisite favorable provision in the articles of organization.

Thus, in a close corporation, the minority stockholders may be trapped in a disadvantageous situation. No outsider would knowingly assume the position of the disadvantaged minority. The outsider would have the same difficulties. To cut losses, the minority stockholder may be compelled to deal with the majority. This is the capstone of the majority plan. Majority "freeze-out" schemes which withhold dividends are designed to compel the minority to relinquish stock at inadequate prices. When the minority stockholder agrees to sell out at less than fair value, the majority has won.

Because of the fundamental resemblance of the close corporation to the partnership, the trust and confidence which are essential to this scale and manner of enterprise, and the inherent danger to minority interests in the close corporation, we hold that stockholders in the close corporation owe one another substantially the same fiduciary duty in the operation of the enterprise that partners owe to one another. In our previous decisions, we have defined the standard of duty owed by partners to one another as the "utmost good faith and loyalty." Stockholders in close corporations must discharge their management and stockholder responsibilities in conformity with this strict good faith standard. They may not act out of avarice, expediency or self-interest in derogation of their duty of loyalty to the other stockholders and to the corporation.

We contrast this strict good faith standard with the somewhat less stringent standard of fiduciary duty to which directors and stockholders of all corporations must adhere in the discharge of their corporate responsibilities. Corporate directors are held to a good faith and inherent fairness standard of conduct and are not "permitted to serve two masters whose interests are antagonistic." Spiegel v. Beacon Participations, Inc. 297 Mass. 398, 411 (1937). "Their paramount duty is to the corporation, and their personal pecuniary interests are subordinate to that duty." Durfee v. Durfee & Canning, Inc. 323 Mass. 187, 196 (1948).

The more rigorous duty of partners and participants in a joint adventure, here extended to stockholders in a close corporation, was described by then Chief Judge Cardozo of the New York Court of Appeals in Meinhard v. Salmon, 249 N. Y. 458 (1928): "Joint adventurers, like copartners, owe to one another, while the enterprise continues, the duty of the finest loyalty. Many forms of conduct permissible in a workaday world for those acting at arm's length, are forbidden to those bound by fiduciary duties.... Not honesty alone, but the punctilio of an honor the most sensitive, is then the standard of behavior." Id. at 463-464. 22

Application of this strict standard of duty to stockholders in close corporations is a natural outgrowth of the prior case law. In a number of cases involving close corporations, we have held stockholders participating in management to a standard of fiduciary duty more exacting than the traditional good faith and inherent fairness standard because of the trust and confidence reposed in them by the other stockholders. In Silversmith v. Sydeman, 305 Mass. 65 (1940), the plaintiff brought suit for an accounting of the liquidation of a close corporation which he and the defendant had owned. In assessing their relative rights in the discount of a note, we had occasion to consider the defendant's fiduciary duty with respect to the financial affairs of the company. We implied that, in addition to the fiduciary duty owed by an officer to the corporation, a more rigorous standard of fiduciary duty applied to the defendant by virtue of the relationship between the stockholders: " ... it could be found that the plaintiff and the defendant were acting as partners in the conduct of the company's business and in the liquidation of its property even though they had adopted a corporate form as the instrumentality by which they should associate in furtherance of their joint venture." Id. at 68.

In Samia v. Central Oil Co. of Worcester, 339 Mass. 101 (1959), sisters alleged that their brothers had systematically excluded them from management, income and partial ownership of a close corporation formed from a family partnership. In rejecting arguments that the plaintiffs' suit was barred by the statute of limitations or laches, we stressed the familial relationship among the parties, which should have given rise to a particularly scrupulous fidelity in serving the interests of all of the stockholders: "All three brothers ... were directors of Central, a small family corporation, not a large publicly owned organization, and as such were in a special position of family trust." Id. at 112.

In Wilson v. Jennings, 344 Mass. 608 (1962), the plaintiffs, stockholders in a close corporation, brought suit on their own behalf and on behalf of the corporation against a number of defendants, including the third stockholder who was generally in charge of corporate operations. The corporation had been organized to exploit a "plastic top" for containers invented by the plaintiffs and another. The defendants appealed from a final decree which, inter alia, cancelled shares of stock issued to the operating stockholder after the original issue, voided an employment contract between the operating stockholder and the corporation, and ordered transfer to the corporation of stock in and dividends from a corporation the operating stockholder had established to manufacture the container tops. Although we modified the decree, we sustained the judge's finding that the operating stockholder had violated his duty to the other stockholders in causing other shares to be issued to himself. Justice Cutter wrote for the court: "[I]t was open to the judge on the evidence to find that Wilson, Malick, and Jennings, on an informal and somewhat ambiguous basis..., had entered into what was essentially a joint venture in corporate form to exploit the plastic top invention; that Jennings was obligated in order 'to get his third [share of the stock] ... to do the financing' and to 'be ... [g]eneral [m]anager of the business, and operate it on behalf of the stockholders'; and that there was a 'mutual understanding that ... [Wilson and Malick] would know what was going on' on the east coast and that they in turn would keep Jennings informed of their own activities. There was evidence that the three way equal division of stock was to be 'permanent.'

"If the parties arranged for a permanent equal participation in Polytop's operations, and undertook the obligation of disclosure to one another of relevant information, a fiduciary relationship arose, in addition to that ... between Jennings, as a director, and Polytop. The evidence justified the conclusion that the relationship was to be one of trust and confidence." Id. at 614-615.

In these and other cases, we have imposed a duty of loyalty more exacting than that duty owed by a director to his corporation or by a majority stockholder to the minority in a public corporation because of facts particular to the close corporation in the cases. In the instant case, we extend this strict duty of loyalty to all stockholders in close corporations. The circumstances which justified findings of relationships of trust and confidence in these particular cases exist universally in modified form in all close corporations. Statements in other cases which suggest that stockholders of a corporation do not stand in a relationship of trust and confidence to one another will not be followed in the close corporation context.

B. Equal Opportunity in a Close Corporation. Under settled Massachusetts law, a domestic corporation, unless forbidden by statute, has the power to purchase its own shares. An agreement to reacquire stock "is enforceable, subject, at least, to the limitations that the purchase must be made in good faith and without prejudice to creditors and stockholders." When the corporation reacquiring its own stock is a close corporation, the purchase is subject to the additional requirement, in the light of our holding in this opinion, that the stockholders, who, as directors or controlling stockholders, caused the corporation to enter into the stock purchase agreement, must have acted with the utmost good faith and loyalty to the other stockholders.

To meet this test, if the stockholder whose shares were purchased was a member of the controlling group, the controlling stockholders must cause the corporation to offer each stockholder an equal opportunity to sell a ratable number of his shares to the corporation at an identical price. Purchase by the corporation confers substantial benefits on the members of the controlling group whose shares were purchased. These benefits are not available to the minority stockholders if the corporation does not also offer them an opportunity to sell their shares. The controlling group may not, consistent with its strict duty to the minority, utilize its control of the corporation to obtain special advantages and disproportionate benefit from its share ownership.

The benefits conferred by the purchase are twofold: (1) provision of a market for shares; (2) access to corporate assets for personal use. By definition, there is no ready market for shares of a close corporation. The purchase creates a market for shares which previously had been unmarketable. It transforms a previously illiquid investment into a liquid one. If the close corporation purchases shares only from a member of the controlling group, the controlling stockholder can convert his shares into cash at a time when none of the other stockholders can. Consistent with its strict fiduciary duty, the controlling group may not utilize its control of the corporation to establish an exclusive market in previously unmarketable shares from which the minority stockholders are excluded.

The purchase also distributes corporate assets to the stockholder whose shares were purchased. Unless an equal opportunity is given to all stockholders, the purchase of shares from a member of the controlling group operates as a preferential distribution of assets. In exchange for his shares, he receives a percentage of the contributed capital and accumulated profits of the enterprise. The funds he so receives are available for his personal use. The other stockholders benefit from no such access to corporate property and cannot withdraw their shares of the corporate profits and capital in this manner unless the controlling group acquiesces. Although the purchase price for the controlling stockholder's shares may seem fair to the corporation and other stockholders under the tests established in the prior case law, the controlling stockholder whose stock has been purchased has still received a relative advantage over his fellow stockholders, inconsistent with his strict fiduciary duty—an opportunity to turn corporate funds to personal use.

The rule of equal opportunity in stock purchases by close corporations provides equal access to these benefits for all stockholders. We hold that, in any case in which the controlling stockholders have exercised their power over the corporation to deny the minority such equal opportunity, the minority shall be entitled to appropriate relief....

C. Application of the Law to this Case. We turn now to the application of the learning set forth above to the facts of the instant case.

The strict standard of duty is plainly applicable to the stockholders in Rodd Electrotype. Rodd Electrotype is a close corporation. Members of the Rodd and Donahue families are the sole owners of the corporation's stock. In actual numbers, the corporation, immediately prior to the corporate purchase of Harry Rodd's shares, had six stockholders. The shares have not been traded, and no market for them seems to exist. Harry Rodd, Charles Rodd, Frederick Rodd, William G. Mason (Phyllis Mason's husband), and the plaintiff's husband all worked for the corporation. The Rodds have retained the paramount management positions.

Through their control of these management positions and of the majority of the Rodd Electrotype stock, the Rodds effectively controlled the corporation. In testing the stock purchase from Harry Rodd against the applicable strict fiduciary standard, we treat the Rodd family as a single controlling group. We reject the defendants' contention that the Rodd family cannot be treated as a unit for this purpose. From the evidence, it is clear that the Rodd family was a close-knit one with strong community of interest. Harry Rodd had hired his sons to work in the family business, Rodd Electrotype. As he aged, he transferred portions of his stock holdings to his children. Charles Rodd and Frederick Rodd were given positions of responsibility in the business as he withdrew from active management. In these circumstances, it is realistic to assume that appreciation, gratitude, and filial devotion would prevent the younger Rodds from opposing a plan which would provide funds for their father's retirement.

Moreover, a strong motive of interest requires that the Rodds be considered a controlling group. When Charles Rodd and Frederick Rodd were called on to represent the corporation in its dealings with their father, they must have known that further advancement within the corporation and benefits would follow their father's retirement and the purchase of his stock. The corporate purchase would take only forty-five of Harry Rodd's eighty-one shares. The remaining thirty-six shares were to be divided among Harry Rodd's children in equal amounts by gift and sale. Receipt of their portion of the thirty-six shares and purchase by the corporation of forty-five shares would effectively transfer full control of the corporation to Frederick Rodd and Charles Rodd, if they chose to act in concert with each other or if one of them chose to ally with his sister. Moreover, Frederick Rodd was the obvious successor to his father as director and corporate treasurer when those posts became vacant after his father's retirement. Failure to complete the corporate purchase (in other words, impeding their father's retirement plan) would have delayed, and perhaps have suspended indefinitely, the transfer of these benefits to the younger Rodds. They could not be expected to oppose their father's wishes in this matter. Although the defendants are correct when they assert that no express agreement involving a quid pro quo—subsequent stock gifts for votes from the directors—was proved, no express agreement is necessary to demonstrate the identity of interest which disciplines a controlling group acting in unison.

On its face, then, the purchase of Harry Rodd's shares by the corporation is a breach of the duty which the controlling stockholders, the Rodds, owed to the minority stockholders, the plaintiff and her son. The purchase distributed a portion of the corporate assets to Harry Rodd, a member of the controlling group, in exchange for his shares. The plaintiff and her son were not offered an equal opportunity to sell their shares to the corporation. In fact, their efforts to obtain an equal opportunity were rebuffed by the corporate representative. As the trial judge found, they did not, in any manner, ratify the transaction with Harry Rodd.

Because of the foregoing, we hold that the plaintiff is entitled to relief. Two forms of suitable relief are set out hereinafter. The judge below is to enter an appropriate judgment. The judgment may require Harry Rodd to remit $36,000 with interest at the legal rate from July 15, 1970, to Rodd Electrotype in exchange for forty-five shares of Rodd Electrotype treasury stock. This, in substance, is the specific relief requested in the plaintiff's bill of complaint. Interest is manifestly appropriate. A stockholder, who, in violation of his fiduciary duty to the other stockholders, has obtained assets from his corporation and has had those assets available for his own use, must pay for that use. In the alternative, the judgment may require Rodd Electrotype to purchase all of the plaintiff's shares for $36,000 without interest. In the circumstances of this case, we view this as the equal opportunity which the plaintiff should have received. Harry Rodd's retention of thirty-six shares, which were to be sold and given to his children within a year of the Rodd Electrotype purchase, cannot disguise the fact that the corporation acquired one hundred per cent of that portion of his holdings (forty-five shares) which he did not intend his children to own. The plaintiff is entitled to have one hundred per cent of her forty-five shares similarly purchased.

The final decree, in so far as it dismissed the bill as to Harry C. Rodd, Frederick I. Rodd, Charles H. Rodd, Mr. Harold E. Magnuson and Rodd Electrotype Company of New England, Inc., and awarded costs, is reversed. The case is remanded to the Superior Court for entry of judgment in conformity with this opinion.

WILKINS, J. (concurring).

I agree with much of what the Chief Justice says in support of granting relief to the plaintiff. However, I do not join in any implication ... that the rule concerning a close corporation's purchase of a controlling stockholder's shares applies to all operations of the corporation as they affect minority stockholders. That broader issue, which is apt to arise in connection with salaries and dividend policy, is not involved in this case. The analogy to partnerships may not be a complete one.

Model Business Corporation Act § 14.30: Grounds for Judicial Dissolution

(a) The [court] may dissolve a corporation:

...

(2) in a proceeding by a shareholder if it is established that:

(i) the directors are deadlocked in the management of the corporate affairs, the shareholders are unable to break the deadlock, and irreparable injury to the corporation is threatened or being suffered, or the business and affairs of the corporation can no longer be conducted to the advantage of the shareholders generally, because of the deadlock;

(ii) the directors or those in control of the corporation have acted, are acting, or will act in a manner that is illegal, oppressive, or fraudulent;

(iii) the shareholders are deadlocked in voting power and have failed, for a period that includes at least two consecutive annual meeting dates, to elect successors to directors whose terms have expired; or

(iv) the corporate assets are being misapplied or wasted;

...

(b) Section 14.30(a)(2) shall not apply in the case of a corporation that, on the date of the filing of the proceeding, has shares that are:

(i) listed on the New York Stock Exchange, the American Stock Exchange or on any exchange owned or operated by the NASDAQ Stock Market LLC, or listed or quoted on a system owned or operated by the National Association of Securities Dealers, Inc.; or

(ii) not so listed or quoted, but are held by at least 300 shareholders and the shares outstanding have a market value of at least $20 million (exclusive of the value of such shares held by the corporation's subsidiaries, senior executives, directors and beneficial shareholders owning more than 10 percent of such shares).

Model Business Corporation Act § 13.02: Right to Appraisal

(a) A shareholder is entitled to appraisal rights, and to obtain payment of the fair value of that shareholder's shares, in the event of any of the following corporate actions:

(1) consummation of a merger to which the corporation is a party (i) if shareholder approval is required for the merger by section 11.04 and the shareholder is entitled to vote on the merger, except that appraisal rights shall not be available to any shareholder of the corporation with respect to shares of any class or series that remain outstanding after consummation of the merger, or (ii) if the corporation is a subsidiary and the merger is governed by section 11.05;

(2) consummation of a share exchange to which the corporation is a party as the corporation whose shares will be acquired if the shareholder is entitled to vote on the exchange, except that appraisal rights shall not be available to any shareholder of the corporation with respect to any class or series of shares of the corporation that is not exchanged;

(3) consummation of a disposition of assets pursuant to section 12.02 if the shareholder is entitled to vote on the disposition;

(4) an amendment of the articles of incorporation with respect to a class or series of shares that reduces the number of shares of a class or series owned by the shareholder to a fraction of a share if the corporation has the obligation or right to repurchase the fractional share so created;

(5) any other amendment to the articles of incorporation, merger, share exchange or disposition of assets to the extent provided by the articles of incorporation, bylaws or a resolution of the board of directors;

(6) consummation of a domestication if the shareholder does not receive shares in the foreign corporation resulting from the domestication that have terms as favorable to the shareholder in all material respects, and represent at least the same percentage interest of the total voting rights of the outstanding shares of the corporation, as the shares held by the shareholder before the domestication;

(7) consummation of a conversion of the corporation to nonprofit status pursuant to subchapter 9C; or

(8) consummation of a conversion of the corporation to an unincorporated entity pursuant to subchapter 9E.

(b) Notwithstanding subsection (a), the availability of appraisal rights under subsections (a)(1), (2), (3), (4), (6) and (8) shall be limited in accordance with the following provisions:

(1) Appraisal rights shall not be available for the holders of shares of any class or series of shares which is:

(i) a covered security under Section 18(b)(1)(A) or (B) of the Securities Act of 1933, as amended; or

(ii) traded in an organized market and has at least 2,000 shareholders and a market value of at least $20 million (exclusive of the value of such shares held by the corporation's subsidiaries, senior executives, directors and beneficial shareholders owning more than 10 percent of such shares); or

(iii) issued by an open end management investment company registered with the Securities and Exchange Commission under the Investment Company Act of 1940 and may be redeemed at the option of the holder at net asset value.

(2) The applicability of subsection (b)(1) shall be determined as of:

(i) the record date fixed to determine the shareholders entitled to receive notice of, and to vote at, the meeting of shareholders to act upon the corporate action requiring appraisal rights; or

(ii) the day before the effective date of such corporate action if there is no meeting of shareholders.

(3) Subsection (b)(1) shall not be applicable and appraisal rights shall be available pursuant to subsection (a) for the holders of any class or series of shares who are required by the terms of the corporate action requiring appraisal rights to accept for such shares anything other than cash or shares of any class or any series of shares of any corporation, or any other proprietary interest of any other entity, that satisfies the standards set forth in subsection (b)(1) at the time the corporate action becomes effective.

(4) Subsection (b)(1) shall not be applicable and appraisal rights shall be available pursuant to subsection (a) for the holders of any class or series of shares where the corporate action is an interested transaction.

Meiselman v. Meiselman

307 S.E.2d 551 (N.C. 1983)

FRYE, J.

In this appeal, we must determine whether Michael Meiselman, a minority shareholder with a substantial percentage of the outstanding stock in a group of family-owned close corporations, is entitled to relief under N.C.G.S. §55-125(a)(4) and N.C.G.S. §55-125.1, the statutes granting trial courts the authority to order dissolution or another more appropriate remedy when "reasonably necessary" for the protection of the "rights or interests" of the complaining shareholder. In so doing, we will articulate for the first time the analysis a trial court is to apply in resolving suits brought under these two statutes.... After outlining in detail the pertinent facts in this case and the development of the law in the area of corporate dissolution, we will address first the question of whether the trial court erred in denying Michael's claim for relief under N.C.G.S. §55-125(a)(4) and N.C.G.S. §55-125.1.

I

Michael Meiselman, the plaintiff and complaining minority shareholder in this action, and Ira Meiselman, one of the defendants in this action, are brothers. Michael, the older of the two, was born in 1932 and has never married. Ira was born ten years later. He is married and has two children. The two men are the only surviving children of Mr. H. B. Meiselman, who immigrated to the United States from Austria in 1913. Over the years, Mr. Meiselman accumulated substantial wealth through his development of several family business enterprises. Specifically, Mr. Meiselman invested in and developed movie theaters and real estate. Several of the enterprises were merged into Eastern Federal Corporation [hereinafter referred to as Eastern Federal], a close corporation, most of the stock of which is owned by Ira and Michael. In addition, there are seven other corporations which, together with Eastern Federal, comprise the Meiselman family business and are the corporate defendants in this case.

Beginning in 1951, Mr. Meiselman started a series of inter vivos transfers of corporate stock in the various corporations which, generally speaking, he divided equally between his two sons. However, in March 1971 Mr. Meiselman transferred 83,072 shares of stock in Eastern Federal to Ira, while Michael received only 1,966 shares in the corporation. The next month Michael transferred the control of his stock in the family corporations to his father in trust, a trust Michael could revoke without his father's consent only if he married a Jewish woman.

The effect, then, of these transfers of stock from Mr. Meiselman to his two sons was to give Ira, the younger son, majority shareholder status in Eastern Federal while relegating Michael, the older son, to the position of minority shareholder. In addition, Ira owns a controlling interest in all of the other family corporations except General Shopping Centers, Inc., the corporation in which he and Michael hold an equal number of shares.

Michael owns 29.82 percent of the total shares in the family corporations, although he contends that once the shares attributed to intercorporate ownership (shares the various corporations own in each other) are distributed between himself and Ira, his ownership would amount to about 43 percent of the family business. The book value of all of the corporations was $11,168,778 as of 31 December 1978. The book value of Michael's shares in all of the corporations, using the 29.82 percent figure, was $3,330,303 as of that date.

As is true of many close corporations, the two shareholders—Michael and Ira—were employed by the family corporations. Michael began working for the family business in 1956 and Ira began nine years later in 1965. The extent of Michael's participation in the family corporations from 1961 until 1973 is not clear. Michael contends that he has worked continuously for the family business except for an interim of about one and one-half years. Ira would characterize Michael's participation differently. At any rate, both sides agree that from 1973 until 1979 Michael was employed by the family business. It is also clear that Ira fired Michael in September 1979, less than one month after Michael filed suit against Ira in connection with Ira's sole ownership of the stock in a corporation which held a management contract with Eastern Federal.

In the certified letter Ira sent to Michael informing Michael that he was being fired, Ira also notified his brother that his car insurance, his hospital insurance and his life insurance policies were all being terminated. In addition, Ira asked his brother in that same letter to return his "Air Travel credit card" and "any other corporate cards you might have as any further use of them is not authorized." Ira then sent his brother a second certified letter demanding payment within ten days to Eastern Federal of Michael's note of $61,500 plus interest of $2,028.66 and the balance of Michael's open account, $19,000. Furthermore, Lawrence A. Poston, Vice President and Treasurer of Eastern Federal stated that the effect of the letter terminating Michael's employment "also was to terminate Michael's participation in the profit-sharing trust."

In his deposition, Ira essentially admitted that he fired his brother in response to the lawsuit Michael had brought challenging Ira's sole ownership of Republic Management Corporation [hereinafter referred to as Republic], the corporation with which Eastern Federal had contracted to provide management services. However, Ira indicated that Michael's loss of employment was only an incidental effect of his termination of the employment contract between the two corporations, a corporate decision he felt was justified in light of the threat of continuing litigation on this matter. Ira stated that "[t]he purpose and the effect of the letter [terminating Michael's employment] were principally to advise [Michael] that we were terminating the arrangement between Eastern Federal and Republic and, correspondingly, that it would alter, affect, or eliminate his source of compensation as applied to Republic."

Republic was formed in 1973. As Ira stated, Republic was a "successor to two, or possibly three, previous companies of the same genre that had operated within the family framework back to 1951." Ira also stated that he did not own all of the stock in those predecessor corporations, that "there were some that I remember in the early years that Michael might have owned 100% of that I didn't." The record indicates that Michael was one of the initial shareholders in 1951 of Fran-Mack Management, Inc., one of those predecessor corporations and that Ira did not become a shareholder in that particular corporation until 31 December 1963.

According to Ira, the function of Republic "was to provide a means whereby, primarily now, administrative and primarily home office expenses utilized on behalf of all the companies, or all the individual operating units, were apportioned back to those individual operating units or operating companies." In short, Republic was "nothing more than a tool" through which the administrative costs incurred in operating the various Meiselman business units—including over 30 theaters—were apportioned.

As noted above, Republic agreed to perform these management services as a result of a contract entered into between it and Eastern Federal. Specifically, Republic agreed to perform the management services in exchange for 5.5 percent of Eastern Federal's theater admissions and concession sales. Although Republic paid Michael an annual salary from 1973 until he was fired in 1979, Michael did not own any of the stock in the management corporation; Ira owned all of it. Although Republic earned profits some years while losing money in others, the net result was that it had retained earnings of over $65,000, earnings which only Ira as sole shareholder in Republic would enjoy and in which Michael claims he is entitled to share. It is this ownership to which Michael objects and upon which he bases his shareholder's derivative claim that Ira has breached the fiduciary duty he owes to the corporate defendants.

We turn now to an examination of the tenor of the relationship existing between Michael and Ira. In his brief, Ira contends "[t]he Record on Appeal reflects no bitterness and hostility between Michael and Ira, other than that which Michael generated after Mr. Meiselman's death in an effort to secure a redistribution of his father's patrimony."

Further, he contends that "Michael was never denied participation in the management of the corporate defendants," that, on the contrary, Michael "voluntarily limited his participation in their affairs."

On the other hand, Michael vehemently denies Ira's characterization of their relationship and of his participation in the management of the corporations. In his deposition, Michael stated that his job has been "out in the field," and that when he had a recommendation to make he was, for the most part, to report it to his brother. Michael indicated that he was allowed to participate in the management of Eastern Federal in this manner apparently until the corporation entered into the management contract with Republic at issue here. Michael characterized this alleged change in his participation of the management of Eastern Federal as follows:

> My brother had the majority of stock in Eastern Federal Corporation before this management contract. As to whether he had the final say in the control of Eastern Federal Corporation, that is the point. He might have been the final say, but when Republic Management started, I lost all say-so because he wouldn't listen to anybody.

In addition, Michael contends that, among other things, he has not been "allowed to even come up to the office and have [sic] been discouraged in getting the full details as to what they [the companies] borrow"; that Ira "will not let me walk in the office where the film buyer is and talk to him, not even [to] help"; that "theaters are being sold without my knowledge and theaters are being built without my knowledge"; and that "my brother solely and without my consent, not only develops but closes, sells, does anything he wants with all of the properties." Finally, Michael claims that although he previously worked 60 to 70 hours a week, he has been "discouraged systematically over a number of years to where I cannot exert the time and effort that I want to."

In examining the record, we are struck by the tone of Ira's comments when referring to his dealings with his brother. Indeed, many of his statements indicate that although Michael may not have been actively prevented from entering the corporate offices, his participation in the decision-making carried on within those offices was less than welcome. For example, in testifying that Michael has never been barred from the home offices of the company, Ira stated that Michael "has exercised the privilege of going there on frequent occasions, *unannounced*, whenever he felt like it." (Emphasis added.) He also stated that "[w]e have never failed, *when he is entitled to notice*, to give him adequate notice of stockholders' meetings." (Emphasis added.) Furthermore, in a letter to Michael's lawyer concerning, among other things, the possibility of Michael's serving on the boards of directors of the family enterprises, Ira's lawyer stated that, "[w]e have no desire to see the productive efforts of the boards be affected by possibly allowing them to function as a forum for airing personal hurts and slights; and we all recognize that the course of business activity for the companies is not going to be altered by Michael's representation."

Apparently in an attempt to further support his contention that Michael has never been excluded from participating in the management of the corporations, Ira testified that two corporate decisions were made or changed on the basis of objections Michael had lodged. In describing the abandonment of a proposed merger to which Michael had objected, Ira testified as follows:

> I don't mean to belittle him. In one of those instances, as a sign we were not completely ignoring him, we made some changes. Specifically, I know of one single complaint and that was a proposed merger of some of these defendants

> [in] 1976, regarding a real estate company similar to our previous merger with Eastern Federal. Unfortunately, my timing was very poor because he was taking his first what he called his pre-test, I'm not sure, I guess it's preparation for the bar exam. He did very poorly with it and it came at the same time, and he just raised cain with me.

The second corporate action to which Michael objected was Ira's sole ownership of the stock in Republic. Ira contends that he terminated the management contract between Republic and Eastern Federal (and in so doing fired Michael) in response to Michael's objections to Ira's sole ownership of Republic. We note, however, that in responding to Michael's objections, Ira terminated the employment contract between the two corporations, and, thus, Michael's employment, even though it was Ira's sole ownership of the stock in Republic and not the contract between Republic and Eastern Federal which was the source of their disagreement.

Perhaps most indicative of the tenor of the relationship between the two brothers is Ira's comment that "[y]es, it is my position in this case that my brother, Michael, suffers as stated there [in defendant's brief] from crippling mental disorders and that was a reason that my father put me in control of the family corporations." Apparently in support of his allegations that his brother suffers from "crippling mental disorders," Ira presented evidence of an argument Michael had with his father which took place about 20 years ago during which Mr. Meiselman castigated Michael for having a non-Jewish woman at a family function. In addition, Ira testified to another fight which occurred between himself and Michael after he had failed to invite Michael to a football game to which all of the males in the family traditionally had been invited.

Finally, it appears the history of this litigation itself indicates a breakdown of the personal relationship between Michael and Ira. In June 1978, about two months after their father's death, Michael and Ira began negotiations in an effort to work out their differences. Over one year later, in August 1979, Michael filed suit. He was fired the next month. In short, this litigation and the tensions inherent in such activity have been going on for over four years now.

We turn now to the history of this litigation as it developed in the courts. In his amended complaint, Michael asked that the trial court "dissolve the Corporate Defendants under the provisions of G.S. 55-125(a) or, in the alternative, order such other relief under the provisions of G.S. 55-125.1 as the Court may deem just and equitable" because such relief is "reasonably necessary" for the protection of Michael's "rights and interests." Before this Court, Michael is requesting relief specifically under N.C.G.S. §55-125.1(a)(4), a buy-out at fair value of Michael's interest in the corporate defendants. He is not seeking dissolution.

With respect to the derivative claim he brought asserting that Ira had breached the fiduciary duty he owes to the corporate defendants through his sole ownership of the stock in Republic, Michael asked that the "profits wrongfully diverted from the Corporate Defendants into Republic Management Corporation" be recovered.

The trial court denied both of Michael's claims. Michael then appealed to the Court of Appeals. In its well-written majority opinion, the Court of Appeals interpreted N.C.G.S. §55-125(a)(4) as authorizing liquidation in cases where the complaining shareholder has shown that "basic 'fairness' compels dissolution." Meiselman v. Meiselman, supra, 58 N.C. App. at 766, 295 S.E. 2d at 254-55. The Court of Appeals concluded that the complaining shareholder is not required to show "bad faith, mismanagement or wrongful conduct, but only real harm." Id. In finding "a plethora of evidence to suggest that Ira's actions have irreparably harmed Michael," the Court of Appeals further concluded that the trial court "misapplied the applicable law and abused its discretion by concluding that relief, other than dissolution, under G.S. 55-125.1 was not reasonably necessary for Michael's protection." Id. at 772, 295 S.E. 2d at 258 (emphasis in original). In so doing, it reversed the trial court judgment and remanded the case to the trial court "for the determination of an appropriate remedy under G.S. 55-125.1 that is reasonably necessary to protect Michael's rights and interests." Id. at 775-776, 295 S.E. 2d at 260.

In addition, the Court of Appeals also determined that the trial court erred in concluding that Ira had not breached the fiduciary duty he owes to the corporate defendants through his sole ownership of Republic. It reversed the judgment of the trial court on this derivative claim and remanded the case to the trial court "for entry of judgment on behalf of the defendant corporation against Ira, as sole owner of Republic, in the total amount of the profits accumulated to date in Republic plus interest and cost of this action." Id.

Judge Hill dissented in this case on both issues. Therefore, defendants appeal to this Court as a matter of right under N.C.G.S. § 7A-30(2).

II

We note at the outset that the enterprises with which we are dealing are close corporations, not publicly held corporations. This distinction is crucial because the two types of corporations are functionally quite different. Indeed, the commentators all appear to agree that "[c]lose corporations are often little more than incorporated partnerships."

...

Professor O'Neal, perhaps the foremost authority on close corporations, points out that many close corporations are companies based on personal relationships that give rise to certain "reasonable expectations" on the part of those acquiring an interest in the close corporation. Those "reasonable expectations" include, for example, the parties' expectation that they will participate in the management of the business or be employed by the company. O'Neal, Close Corporations: Existing Legislation and Recommended Reform, 33 Bus. Law 873, 885 (1978). Other commentators have also noted that those investing in close corporations have some of these same "reasonable expectations." Afterman, Statutory Protection for Oppressed Minority Shareholders: A Model for Reform, 55 Va. L. Rev. 1043, 1064 (1969); Comment, Oppression, supra, at 141; Comment, Deadlock and Dissolution, supra, at 795; Comment, Dissolution Under the California Corporations Code: A Remedy for Minority Shareholders, 22 U.C.L.A. L. Rev. 595, 616 (1975) [hereinafter cited as Comment, Dissolution Under the California Corporations Code].

Thus, when personal relations among the participants in a close corporation break down, the "reasonable expectations" the participants had, for example, an expectation that their employment would be secure, or that they would enjoy meaningful participation in the management of the business—become difficult if not impossible to fulfill. In other words, when the personal relationships among the participants break down, the majority shareholder, because of his greater voting power, is in a position to terminate the minority shareholder's employment and to exclude him from participation in management decisions.

Some may argue that the minority shareholder should have bargained for greater protection before agreeing to accept his minority shareholder position in a close corporation. However, the practical realities of this particular business situation oftentimes do not allow for such negotiations. In his article, Special Characteristics, Problems, and Needs of the Close Corporation, 1969 U. Ill. L.F. 1 (1969), Professor Hetherington, another recognized authority in this field, explains the situation as follows:

> ... the circumstances under which a party takes a minority stock position in a close corporation vary widely. Many involve situations where the minority party, because of lack of awareness of the risks, or because of the weakness of his bargaining position, fails to negotiate for protection. Probably a common instance of this kind occurs where an employee or an outsider is given an opportunity to buy stock in a close corporation wholly or substantially owned by a single stockholder or a small group of associates, often a family. Typically, the controlling individual or group retains a substantial majority position. The opportunity to buy into the business is highly valued by the recipient; his enthusiasm and weak bargaining position make it unlikely almost to a certainty that he will ask for—let alone insist upon—protection for his position as a minority stockholder. Purchases of stock in such situations are likely to be arranged without either party consulting a lawyer. The result is the assumption of a minority stock position without, or with only limited, appreciation of the risks involved.

Id. at 17–18 (footnote omitted).

In short, then, the "minority shareholder who acquired his shares to secure his position with the firm may have lacked sufficient bargaining power to force the majority to agree to terms which would enable him to protect his interests." Comment, Dissolution Under the California Corporations Code, supra, at 603-04. Indeed, as one commentator notes, "close corporations are often formed by friends or family members who simply may not believe that disagreements could ever arise." Id. Furthermore, when a minority shareholder receives his shares in a close corporation from another in the form of a gift or inheritance, as did plaintiff here, the minority shareholder never had the opportunity to negotiate for any sort of protection with respect to the "reasonable expectations" he had or hoped to enjoy in the close corporation.

Unfortunately, when dissension develops in such a situation, as Professor O'Neal notes, "American courts traditionally have been reluctant to interfere in the internal affairs of corporations...." F. O'Neal, Oppression of Minority Shareholders § 9.04, at 582 (1975). This reluctance, as applied to a minority shareholder holding an interest in a close corporation, places the minority shareholder in a remediless situation. As Professor O'Neal points out, when the personal relationship among the participants in a close corporation breaks down, the minority shareholder has neither the power to dissolve the business unit at will, as does a partner in a partnership, nor does he have the "way out" which is open to a shareholder in a publicly held corporation, the opportunity to sell his shares on the open market. 2 F. O'Neal, Close Corporations § 9.02. Thus, the illiquidity of a minority shareholder's interest in a close corporation renders him vulnerable to exploitation by the majority shareholders. E.g., Hetherington and Dooley, supra, at 3-6. Professor Hetherington succinctly outlines in one of his articles the uniquely vulnerable position a minority shareholder occupies in a close corporation:

> The right of the majority to control the enterprise achieves a meaning and has an impact in close corporations that it has in no other major form of business organization under our law. Only in the close corporation does the power to manage carry with it the de facto power to allocate the benefits of ownership

> arbitrarily among the shareholders and to discriminate against a minority whose investment is imprisoned in the enterprise. The essential basis of this power in the close corporation is the inability of those so excluded from the benefits of proprietorship to withdraw their investment at will. The power to withdraw one's capital from a publicly held corporation or from a partnership is unqualified in the sense that the participant's right is not dependent upon misconduct by the management or upon the occurrence of any other event. The shareholder or partner can withdraw his capital for any or no reason.

Hetherington, supra, at 21.

According to Professor O'Neal, the "two principal conceptualistic barriers to the courts' granting relief to aggrieved shareholders" in such a situation are: "(1) the principle of majority rule in corporate management and (2) the business judgment rule." F. O'Neal, Oppression of Minority Shareholders § 9.04 at 582. In explaining the inapplicability of the legal construct firmly established in corporate law that when outvoted the minority must submit to the will of the majority, he writes as follows:

> Apparently without close examination, courts accord the principle of majority rule the same sanctity in corporate enterprises, including small businesses, that it enjoys in the political world. The principle of majority rule is in traditional legal thought a firmly established attribute of the corporate form. Yet not uncommonly a person, unsophisticated in business and financial matters, invests all his assets in a closely held enterprise with an expectation, often reasonable under the circumstances even in the absence of express contract, that he will be a key employee in the company and will have a voice in business decisions. Thus, when courts apply the principle of majority rule in close corporations, they often disappoint the reasonable expectations of the participants.

Id. at 582–83.

In short, then, when the courts fail to provide a remedy for a minority shareholder whose "reasonable expectations" have been disappointed in the close corporation situation, the court, in effect, "compels a continuation of the association by legal constraint—what was once called 'togetherness by injunction'—a prospect which scarcely seems a desirable policy goal." Hetherington, supra, at 29. In other words, an "insistence that the antagonistic parties resolve their differences within the corporate framework" would seem "inconsistent with the traditional hesitance of courts of equity to enforce unwelcome personal relationships." Note, Corporations—Dissolution, supra, at 1463.

Apparently in response to these commentators' uniform calls for reform in this area of corporate law, many state legislatures have enacted statutes giving the tribunals in their states the power to grant relief to minority shareholders under more liberal circumstances. For example, at least seven states have given their courts the authority to grant dissolution of a corporation when the acts of the directors or those in control of the corporation are "oppressive" to the shareholders.

In interpreting the term "oppressive" as used in its dissolution statute, a New York Trial Court recently held in a case of first impression that where two controlling shareholders discharged the minority shareholder as an employee and officer of the two corporations in which he had an interest, thus severely damaging the minority shareholder's "reasonable expectations," their actions were deemed to be "oppressive" under New York Law....

In helping to establish this growing trend toward enactment of more liberal grounds under which dissolution will be granted to a complaining shareholder, the legislature in this State enacted in 1955 N.C.G.S. § 55-125(a)(4), the statute granting superior court judges the "power to liquidate the assets and business of a corporation in an action by a shareholder when it is established" that "[l]iquidation is reasonably necessary for the protection of the rights or interests of the complaining shareholder."....

In short, then, it appears that these new statutory schemes which permit involuntary dissolution of corporations pursuant to actions brought by minority shareholders—and which "virtually every state has"—"represent a concerted effort and recognition by the states that the perpetual existence of the corporate structure at common law is ill-suited to the functional realities of the closely held corporation." However, it is important to recognize that the statutes in question apply to all corporations, not just "close" corporations. Of course, "the rights or interests of the complaining shareholder" will vary according to the circumstances, including the circumstance of the nature of the corporation, whether public or a close corporation. Likewise, whether liquidation (or some alternate form of relief) "is reasonably necessary for the protection of" those "rights or interests" will also depend, to a great extent, on whether the corporation is a public corporation or a close corporation.

III

With this background in mind, we turn now to the primary issue in this case: whether the trial court misapplied the applicable law by concluding that relief under N.C.G.S. § 55-125(a)(4) and N.C.G.S. § 55-125.1 was not "reasonably necessary" for the protection of Michael's "rights or interests" in the defendant corporations....

The basic question at issue is what standard we should adopt to determine whether a minority shareholder is entitled to dissolution or other relief. The statutes require a standard in which all of the circumstances surrounding the parties are considered in deciding whether relief should be granted and, if so, the nature and method of such relief....

In short, ... the "rights or interests" of a shareholder in any given case will not necessarily be the same "rights or interests" of any other shareholder. An articulation of those "rights or interests" will necessarily require a case-by-case determination based on an examination of the entire history of the participants' relationship—an examination not only of the "expectations generated by the participants' original business bargain," but also of the "history of the participants' relationship as expectations alter and new expectations develop over the course of the participants' cooperative efforts in operating the business." O'Neal, supra, at 888. In so holding, we recognize the rule that Professor O'Neal suggests should be applied in a corporation based on a "personal relationship":

> [A] court should give relief, dissolution or some other remedy to a minority shareholder whenever corporate managers or controlling shareholders act in a way that disappoints the minority shareholder's reasonable expectations, even though the acts of the managers or controlling shareholders fall within the literal scope of powers or rights granted them by the corporation act or the corporation's charter or bylaws.
>
> The reasonable expectations of the shareholders, as they exist at the inception of the enterprise, and as they develop thereafter through a course of dealing concurred in by all of them, is perhaps the most reliable guide to a just solution of a dispute among shareholders, at least a dispute among shareholders

> in the typical close corporation. In a close corporation, the corporation's charter and bylaws almost never reflect the full business bargain of the participants.

O'Neal, supra, at 886....

IV

We will now review the "rights or interests" each party contends Michael has in the family corporations. Michael suggests in his brief that the "rights or interests" he has as a shareholder in these close corporations include "rights or interests" in secure employment, fringe benefits which flow from his association with the corporations, and meaningful participation in the management of the family business. As noted above, several commentators have suggested that the "reasonable expectations" of shareholders in close corporations often include some of these same "rights or interests." Afterman, supra, at 1064; O'Neal, supra, at 885; Comment, Deadlock and Dissolution, supra, at 795; Comment, Dissolution Under the California Corporations Code, supra, at 616; Comment, Oppression, supra, at 141. Further, Michael indicates that these "rights or interests" are in need of protection: Michael was fired from his job after suing his brother; his fringe benefits were terminated at that time as well; he has been "systematically" excluded from any meaningful participation in management decisions apparently since the inception of the management contract between Eastern Federal and Republic.

Defendants argue, however, that Michael, as a shareholder, is only entitled to relief if his traditional shareholder rights have been infringed. They contend that those traditional shareholder rights include the right to notice of stockholders' meetings, the right to vote cumulatively, the right of access to the corporate offices and to corporate financial information, and the right to compel the payment of dividends. Because these rights have not been violated, they argue, Michael is not entitled to relief. Indeed, defendants contend that the dividends distributed to Michael have been generous.

While it may be true that a shareholder in, for example, a publicly held corporation may have "rights or interests" defined as defendants argue, a shareholder's rights in a closely held corporation may not necessarily be so narrowly defined. In short, we hold that the shareholder in this case—one who owns stock worth well over $3,000,000 and which accounts for a 30 to 40 percent ownership in these closely held, family-run corporations worth well over $11,000,000 and who also has been employed by the corporations, provided with fringe benefits, and, to some extent, allowed to participate in management decisions—has "rights or interests" more broadly defined than defendants contend. Put another way, Michael's "reasonable expectations" are not as limited as defendants contend....

Because the trial court's findings of fact failed to address the "rights or interests" Michael has in these family corporations, we must remand the case to the trial court for an evidentiary hearing to resolve this issue. On remand, after hearing the evidence, the trial court is to: (1) articulate specifically Michael's "rights or interests"—his "reasonable expectations"—in the corporate defendants; and (2) determine if these "rights or interests" are in need of protection, and, thus, that relief of some sort should be granted. In addition, the trial court is to prescribe the form of relief which the evidence indicates is most appropriate, should it find that relief is warranted. In remanding this case for an evidentiary hearing and new findings, we need not address the issue of whether the trial court abused its discretion in refusing to grant relief to Michael....

Melvin Aron Eisenberg & James D. Cox, *Corporations and Other Business Organizations* 597 (10th ed.). "[T]he 'reasonable expectations' analysis that is made explicit in cases like *Meiselman v. Meiselman*, that is implicit in cases like *Donahue v. Rodd*, and that in part underlies the concept of dissolution for oppression, fills a major gap in corporate law for closely held corporations. It would be a mistake, however, to believe that analysis based on reasonable expectations can be separated from the concept of fairness. One way in which a court determines whether reasonable expectations of minority shareholders have been defeated by majority shareholders is by asking itself what similarly situated shareholders would have probably expected. Often the only way to answer that question is to ask what similarly situation shareholders would have regarded as fair."

Nixon v. Blackwell, 626 A.2d 1366 (Del. 1993). A corporation had two classes of shares: 25% of the company was owned by employees as Class A stock, and 75% of the company was owned by others as Class B stock. The managers of the corporation had provided some benefits (particularly liquidity) in favor of Class A shareholders.

"The record is sufficient to conclude that plaintiffs' claim that the defendant directors have maintained a discriminatory policy of favoring Class A employee stockholders over Class B non-employee stockholders is without merit. The directors have followed a consistent policy originally established by Mr. Barton, the founder of the Corporation, whose intent from the formation of the Corporation was to use the Class A stock as the vehicle for the Corporation's continuity through employee management and ownership.

"Mr. Barton established the Corporation in 1928 by creating two classes of stock, not one, and by holding 100 percent of the Class A stock and 82 percent of the Class B stock. Mr. Barton himself established [a particular practice at issue here] to retain in the employ of the Corporation valuable employees by assuring them that, following their retirement or death, the Corporation will have liquid assets which could be used to repurchase the shares acquired by the employee, which shares may otherwise constitute an illiquid and unsalable asset of his or her estate. Another rational purpose is to prevent the stock from passing out of the control of the employees of the Corporation into the hands of family or descendants of the employee.

"The directors' actions following Mr. Barton's death are consistent with Mr. Barton's plan. An [Employee Stock Ownership Plan, or ESOP, set up by Mr. Barton,] for example, is normally established for employees. Accordingly, there is no inequity in limiting ESOP benefits to the employee stockholders. Indeed, it makes no sense to include non-employees in ESOP benefits. The fact that the Class B stock represented 75 percent of the Corporation's total equity is irrelevant to the issue of fair dealing. The Class B stock was given no voting rights because those stockholders were not intended to have a direct voice in the management and operation of the Corporation. They were simply passive investors—entitled to be treated fairly but not necessarily to be treated equally. The fortunes of the Corporation rested with the Class A employee stockholders and the Class B stockholders benefited from the multiple increases in value of their Class B stock. Moreover, the Board made continuing efforts to buy back the Class B stock."

Model Business Corporation Act § 14.34: Election to Purchase in Lieu of Dissolution

(a) In a proceeding under section 14.30(2) to dissolve a corporation, the corporation may elect or, if it fails to elect, one or more shareholders may elect to purchase all shares owned by the petitioning shareholder at the fair value of the shares. An election pursuant to this section shall be irrevocable unless the court determines that it is equitable to set aside or modify the election....

(e) Upon determining the fair value of the shares, the court shall enter an order directing the purchase upon such terms and conditions as the court deems appropriate, which may include payment of the purchase price in installments, where necessary in the interests of equity, provision for security to assure payment of the purchase price and any additional costs, fees, and expenses as may have been awarded, and, if the shares are to be purchased by shareholders, the allocation of shares among them. In allocating petitioner's shares among holders of different classes of shares, the court should attempt to preserve the existing distribution of voting rights among holders of different classes insofar as practicable and may direct that holders of a specific class or classes shall not participate in the purchase. Interest may be allowed at the rate and from the date determined by the court to be equitable, but if the court finds that the refusal of the petitioning shareholder to accept an offer of payment was arbitrary or otherwise not in good faith, no interest shall be allowed. If the court finds that the petitioning shareholder had probable grounds for relief under paragraphs (ii) or (iv) of section 14.30(2), it may award to the petitioning shareholder reasonable fees and expenses of counsel and of any experts employed by him.

Chapter 6

Limited Liability Companies

Limited liability companies (LLCs) reflect the culmination of several trends in the history of closely held organizations. As we have seen, it has become easier to avoid vicarious business liability in more circumstances over time; as their name suggests, LLCs give such "limited liability" to everyone who opts for it. Like modern corporations as compared with classical corporations, LLCs allow for significant organizational flexibility; there is no need for a board of directors, for example. Indeed, LLCs are flexible enough to accommodate sole proprietorships, entities structured like general partnerships, and entities with separation of control and ownership like most large corporations. They can even be nonprofit entities. And as icing on the cake, the federal government gives LLCs significant flexibility in the way their income is taxed.

In short, while in the past the decision as to which entity a new business should use was a difficult question that involved significant tradeoffs, under modern law the answer to the question "Which entity should our new business use?" is almost always an LLC. The most significant reasons for using another form today are (1) to opt into a state's significant case law concerning some other form of entity, like the corporation or the limited partnership, and (2) to satisfy an industry's or locality's convention. (For example, in Silicon Valley, new technology startups are ordinarily organized as corporations, while certain types of venture funds are still typically organized as limited partnerships. This pattern appears to be motivated largely by convention.) Otherwise, LLCs have become the vehicle of choice—so much so that some say lawyers should advise clients to use LLCs for the simple (and cynical) reason that it is such a normal thing to advise that no malpractice liability will result.

LLCs are creatures of statute; creating an LLC involves opting into a state's relatively new LLC statute. The first LLC statute dates to 1977 in Wyoming, but their rise wasn't complete until the mid-1990s, and there still is relatively little case law on LLCs compared to partnerships and corporations. Moreover, states' LLC statutes have significant differences from one another. As a result, learning the law of LLCs presents a challenge. There is a Uniform Limited Liability Company Act (ULLCA), developed by NCCUSL in 1995 and revised in 2006.[1] (The revised 2006 version is often called Re-ULLCA or RULCCA.) The 1995 version of the act was adopted in only five states, and the 2006 act has been adopted in only seven states (plus Washington DC). Because of significant disparities among states, it is currently difficult to characterize LLC law clearly without oversimplifying. However, there are a few features generally common to LLC statutes in the United States.

---

1. For an interesting summary by the Uniform Law Commission on the changes between the ULLCA and the Re-ULLCA, see Uniform Law Commission, *Why States Should Adopt RULLCA*,

First, LLCs have "members," not unlike partners in partnerships. (The Re-ULLCA's defaults are similar to RUPA's: LLC membership itself ordinarily requires unanimous consent of the existing members, but a member's financial "interest" is freely transferable.) As with limited partnerships, it is ordinarily easy to structure an LLC agreement so that "units," which act much like corporate shares, can trade conveniently. Members are thus, in practice, often treated as a hybrid between partners and shareholders. The LLC statutes do not require the creation of a board, ordinarily do not mandate the same sort of regular meetings as corporations, and generally allow for flexible structure, specified in an operating agreement or similar document. The norm among LLC statutes appears to be that members, by default, control the LLC by majority vote for ordinary business matters and have actual and apparent authority to bind the LLC in such matters. However, statutes often either vary from this default or provide a separate path into which LLCs—in their organizational documents—can opt; this path allows for the creation of "manager-managed LLCs," in which a separate class of managers (who might not be members) both control and have exclusive default authority to bind the LLC.

Second, LLCs, as their name suggests, provide limited liability—that is, they shield their members (and managers, if applicable) from vicarious business liability. There is an exception to this shield in the form of a doctrine called "veil piercing" that, in relatively unusual circumstances, takes away the vicarious-business-liability shield from corporations, LLCs, and other limited-liability entities. Veil piercing is historically a corporate-law concept, preventing corporate managers and shareholders from either (1) using corporations as a vehicle for fraud or (2) intentionally putting too little money in (or draining money out of) a corporation that faces potentially large tort liability. The corporate legal doctrine has largely been imported into LLC law in this area. *See, e.g.*, Kaycee Land and Livestock v. Flahive, 46 P.3d 323 (Wyo. 2002) ("We can discern no reason, in either law or policy, to treat LLCs differently than we treat corporations."). That said, the law on veil piercing is unclear—both in general and as specifically applied to LLCs. For example, one feature of corporate veil-piercing doctrine is that those who do not follow the corporate "formalities"—such as holding the required meetings of shareholders and directors—risk the loss of the corporation's limited-liability protections. LLC statutes, however, generally require no (or at least greatly reduced) formalities, so presumably that criterion of veil piercing does not apply to LLCs.

LLCs often appear to provide a further, additional benefit regarding liability. As the comments to the Re-ULLCA note, unlike partnership statutes, "[v]ery few current LLC statutes contain rules for attributing to an LLC the wrongful acts of the LLC's members or managers." It is unclear, given the limited case law, if this omission reflects a significant new limitation on vicarious liability.

Third, LLCs are entities, like corporations and RUPA partnerships. They retain slightly more ties to their individual members, however, than corporations do—particularly under federal law. For example, because of the tax flexibility mentioned earlier, LLCs can choose "pass-through" federal taxation (under which the members of an LLC will pay tax on the LLC's income personally, rather than paying tax via the LLC), which is unavailable to most corporations. Similarly, because the federal statute concerning diversity jurisdiction refers specifically to "corporations" but not LLCs, the general federal rule is that an LLC is a citizen of *all* of the states in which it has individual members—which makes it more difficult for an LLC, as defendant, to remove a state-law case to a

---

http://www.uniformlaws.org/Narrative.aspx?title=Why States Should Adopt RULLCA (last accessed June 1, 2013).

federal court. *See, e.g.*, Harvey v. Grey Wolf Drilling Co., 542 F.3d 1077 (5th Cir. 2008). LLCs have many other features of corporations; for example, they typically have perpetual duration by default, and they can ordinarily be organized for any legal purposes.

An LLC can be formed with a single individual member, although the benefits of doing this are often misunderstood. For example, a sole proprietor who often drives a truck to make deliveries might decide to form an LLC on the erroneous belief that doing so will protect her from personal liability as a truck driver. If she drives her truck negligently and injures someone, it is true that a claim against the LLC for the damage will probably not endanger her personal assets; that is specifically what "limited liability" means. But the victim, of course, is not required to sue the LLC; the victim could, instead or additionally, sue the driver for her own negligence in operating the vehicle. "I was operating the vehicle for my business" is clearly not a defense, ordinarily, to a tort suit, even if the business is set up in a form that shields the owners from *vicarious* business liability.

LLCs do, however, have some other benefits for individual members. For example, they might well limit contractual, rather than tort, liability for contracts in which the LLC is a party but the individual owner is not. If a single member causes his LLC to receive a loan from a bank, and the bank is (for whatever reason) satisfied to lend to the LLC without requiring an individual guarantee from the single owner, then ordinarily the owner will not be personally obligated to pay back the loan.

The cases and statutory excerpts in this chapter elaborate some of the principles discussed above and highlight recurring problems in LLCs—particularly concerning authority, fiduciary duties, and dissolution.

Section 1: Management and Authority

Revised Uniform Limited Liability Company Act (2006) § 407: Management of Limited Liability Company

(a) A limited liability company is a member-managed limited liability company unless the operating agreement:

  (1) expressly provides that:

    (A) the company is or will be "manager-managed";

    (B) the company is or will be "managed by managers"; or

    (C) management of the company is or will be "vested in managers"; or

  (2) includes words of similar import.

(b) In a member-managed limited liability company, the following rules apply:

  (1) The management and conduct of the company are vested in the members.

  (2) Each member has equal rights in the management and conduct of the company's activities.

  (3) A difference arising among members as to a matter in the ordinary course of the activities of the company may be decided by a majority of the members.

  (4) An act outside the ordinary course of the activities of the company may be undertaken only with the consent of all members.

  (5) The operating agreement may be amended only with the consent of all members.

(c) In a manager-managed limited liability company, the following rules apply:

(1) Except as otherwise expressly provided in this [act], any matter relating to the activities of the company is decided exclusively by the managers.

(2) Each manager has equal rights in the management and conduct of the activities of the company.

(3) A difference arising among managers as to a matter in the ordinary course of the activities of the company may be decided by a majority of the managers.

(4) The consent of all members is required to:

(A) sell, lease, exchange, or otherwise dispose of all, or substantially all, of the company's property, with or without the good will, outside the ordinary course of the company's activities;

(B) approve a merger, conversion, or domestication under [Article] 10;

(C) undertake any other act outside the ordinary course of the company's activities; and

(D) amend the operating agreement.

(5) A manager may be chosen at any time by the consent of a majority of the members and remains a manager until a successor has been chosen, unless the manager at an earlier time resigns, is removed, or dies, or, in the case of a manager that is not an individual, terminates. A manager may be removed at any time by the consent of a majority of the members without notice or cause.

(6) A person need not be a member to be a manager, but the dissociation of a member that is also a manager removes the person as a manager. If a person that is both a manager and a member ceases to be a manager, that cessation does not by itself dissociate the person as a member.

(7) A person's ceasing to be a manager does not discharge any debt, obligation, or other liability to the limited liability company or members which the person incurred while a manager.

(d) An action requiring the consent of members under this [act] may be taken without a meeting, and a member may appoint a proxy or other agent to consent or otherwise act for the member by signing an appointing record, personally or by the member's agent.

(e) The dissolution of a limited liability company does not affect the applicability of this section. However, a person that wrongfully causes dissolution of the company loses the right to participate in management as a member and a manager.

(f) This [act] does not entitle a member to remuneration for services performed for a member-managed limited liability company, except for reasonable compensation for services rendered in winding up the activities of the company.

Comment

...

Subsection (c)—Like subsection (b), this subsection states default rules that, under Section 110, are subject to the operating agreement. For example, a limited liability company's operating agreement might state "This company is manager-managed," Section 102(10)(i), while providing that managers must submit specified ordinary matters for review by the members.

The actual authority of an LLC's manager or managers is a question of agency law and depends fundamentally on the contents of the operating agreement and any separate management contract between the LLC and its manager or managers. These agreements are the primary source of the manifestations of the LLC (as principal) from which a manager (as agent) will form the reasonable beliefs that delimit the scope of the manager's actual authority. RESTATEMENT (THIRD) OF AGENCY § 3.01 (2006). See also RESTATEMENT (SECOND) OF AGENCY §§ 15, 26.

Other information may be relevant as well, such as the course of dealing within the LLC, unless the operating agreement effectively precludes consideration of that information. See Section 110(a)(4) (stating that the operating agreement governs "the means and conditions for amending the operating agreement") and the comment to that subparagraph, which states that:

> [Although this] Act does not specially authorize the operating agreement to limit the sources in which terms of the operating agreement might be found or limit amendments to specified modes ... Paragraph (a)(4) could be read to encompass such authorization. Also, under Section 107 the parol evidence rule will apply to a written operating agreement containing an appropriate merger provision.

If the operating agreement and a management contract conflict, the reasonable manager will know that the operating agreement controls the extent of the manager's rightful authority to act for the LLC—despite any contract claims the manager might have. See Section 111(a)(2) (stating that the operating agreement governs "the rights and duties under this [act] of a person in the capacity of manager") and the comment to that paragraph, which states:

> Because the term "[o]perating agreement.... includes the agreement as amended or restated," Section 102(13), this paragraph gives the members the ongoing power to define the role of an LLC's managers. Power is not the same as right, however, and exercising the power provided by this paragraph might constitute a breach of a separate contract between the LLC and the manager.

See also RESTATEMENT (THIRD) OF AGENCY § 8.13, cmt. b (2006) and RESTATEMENT (SECOND) OF AGENCY, § 432, cmt. b (stating that, when a principal's instructions to an agent contravene a contract between the principal and agent, the agent may have a breach of contract claim but has no right to act contrary to the principal's instructions).

If (i) an LLC's operating agreement merely states that the LLC is manager-managed and does not further specify the managerial responsibilities, and (ii) the LLC has only one manager, the actual authority analysis is simple. In that situation, this subsection:

- serves as "gap filler" to the operating agreement; and thereby
- constitutes the LLC's manifestation to the manager as to the scope of the manager's authority; and thereby
- delimits the manager's actual authority, subject to whatever subsequent manifestations the LLC may make to the manager (e.g., by a vote of the members, or an amendment of the operating agreement).

If the operating agreement states only that the LLC is manager-managed and the LLC has more than one manager, the question of actual authority has an additional aspect. It is necessary to determine what actual authority any one manager has to act alone.

Paragraphs (c)(2), (3), and (4) combine to provide the answer. A single manager of a multi-manager LLC:

- has no actual authority to commit the LLC to any matter "outside the ordinary course of the activities of the company," paragraph (c)(4)(C), or any matter encompassed in paragraph (c)(4); and
- has the actual authority to commit the LLC to any matter "in the ordinary course of the activities of the company," paragraph (c)(3), unless the manager has reason to know that other managers might disagree or the manager has some other reason to know that consultation with fellow managers is appropriate.

The first point follows self-evidently from the language of paragraphs (c)(3) and (c)(4). In light of that language, no manager could reasonably believe to the contrary (unless the operating agreement provided otherwise).

The second point follows because:

- Subsection (c) serves as the gap-filler manifestation from the LLC to its managers, and subsection (c) does <u>not</u> require managers of a multi-manager LLC to act <u>only</u> in concert or after consultation.
- To the contrary, subject to the operating agreement:
  - paragraph (c)(2) expressly provides that "each manager has equal rights in the management and conduct of the activities of the company," and
  - paragraph (c)(3) suggests that several (as well as joint) activity is appropriate on ordinary matters, so long as the manager acting in the matter has no reason to believe that the matter will be controversial among the managers and therefore requires a decision under paragraph (c)(3).

While the individual members of a corporate board of directors lack actual authority to bind the corporation, subsection (c) does not describe "board" management. Instead, subsection (c) provides management rules derived from those that govern the members of a general partnership and multiple general partners of a limited partnership. RUPA, § 401 and ULPA (2001), § 406.

The common law of agency will also determine the apparent authority of an LLC's manager or managers, and in that analysis what the particular third party knows or has reason to know about the management structure and business practices of the particular LLC will always be relevant. RESTATEMENT (THIRD) OF AGENCY § 3.03 cmt. d (2006) ("The nature of an organization's business or activity is relevant to whether a third party could reasonably believe that a [manager] is authorized to commit the organization to a particular transaction.").

As a general matter, however—i.e., as to the apparent authority of the position of LLC manager under this Act—courts may view the position as clothing its occupants with the apparent authority to take actions that reasonably appear within the ordinary course of the company's business. The actual authority analysis stated above supports that proposition; absent a reason to believe to the contrary, a third party could reasonably believe a manager to possess the authority contemplated by the gap-fillers of the statute. But see Section 102(9), cmt. (stating that "confusion around the term 'manager' is common to almost all LLC statutes").

Manitaras v. Beusman, 868 N.Y.S.2d 121 (N.Y. App. 2008). "The plaintiff owns either 49.74% or 49.89% (the parties differ as to the precise figure) of the defendant

Kisco Radio Circle Associates, LLC (hereinafter Kisco Radio). The plaintiff objects to the proposed sale of Kisco Radio's sole asset. The defendants ... approved the sale.

"The defendants made a prima facie showing of entitlement to judgment as a matter of law. Under Kisco Radio's operating agreement, its management is vested in its managing members; only they may bind the company. However, the defendants demonstrated that the operating agreement of Kisco Radio is silent on the issue of the sale of the company's sole asset. Therefore, the default provisions of the Limited Liability Company Law apply. In relevant part, Limited Liability Company Law § 402 (d)(2) provides that the vote of at least the majority in interest of the members entitled to vote is required to approve the sale of all the assets of a limited liability company. That requirement was met here."

Fielbon Dev. Co. v. Colony Bank, 660 S.E.2d 801 (Ga. Ct. App. 2008). Bond, a member/manager of Fielbon (an LLC), received a loan from a bank in the LLC's name but used the proceeds personally.

"In defense to the note, Fielbon ... asserted that an issue of fact existed as to whether the note is enforceable against Fielbon because Colony Bank admitted in the pretrial order and at trial that it became aware, after the fact, that Bond had obtained loan funds in October and November 2003 for his own personal use, and not for legitimate business purposes. They also assert that no Fielbon employee ever filed a written approval or request for a draw. Additionally, they contend that Fielbon should not be liable under the note because under OCGA § 14-11-301 (c), a limited liability corporation is not liable for acts of a member that are 'not apparently for the carrying on in the usual way the business or affairs' of the corporation, and Bond made personal use of some of the loan proceeds. And they argue that had Colony Bank conducted proper inspections, the funds would not have been disbursed at all.

"But there is no dispute that Bond had the authority to sign the promissory note, and to make draws under the loan. Fielbon made such loans in the usual course of its business, and in fact, had a number of such loans at Colony Bank. The evidence shows that the draws were either deposited directly into Fielbon's checking account at the bank or issued to Fielbon in the form of a certified check. Fielbon granted Bond the authority to disburse funds from the checking account and to draw $80,000 in funds for his own living expenses. Thus, Bond had the authority to bind Fielbon under the note, to disburse the loan proceeds and to withdraw Fielbon funds for his own personal use. Nothing in Bond's actions in connection with the loan was so dissimilar from the acts the corporation had authorized him to perform as to make them 'not apparently for the carrying on in the usual way the business or affairs' of the corporation. OCGA § 14-11-301 (c), therefore, does not relieve Fielbon of liability under the note."

Revised Uniform Limited Liability Company Act (2006) § 301: No Agency Power of Member as Member

(a) A member is not an agent of a limited liability company solely by reason of being a member.

(b) A person's status as a member does not prevent or restrict law other than this [act] from imposing liability on a limited liability company because of the person's conduct.

Comment

Subsection (a)—Most LLC statutes, including the original ULLCA, provide for what might be termed "statutory apparent authority" for members in a member-managed limited liability company and managers in a manager-managed limited liability company. This approach codifies the common law notion of apparent authority by position and dates back at least to the original, 1914 Uniform Partnership Act. UPA, § 9 provided that "the act of every partner ... for apparently carrying on in the usual way the business of the partnership ... binds the partnership," and that formulation has been essentially followed by RUPA, § 301, ULLCA, § 301, ULPA (2001), § 402, and myriad state LLC statutes.

This Act rejects the statutory apparent authority approach, for reasons summarized in a "Progress Report on the Revised Uniform Limited Liability Company Act," published in the March 2006 issue of the newsletter of the ABA Committee on Partnerships and Unincorporated Business Organizations:

> The concept [of statutory apparent authority] still makes sense both for general and limited partnerships. A third party dealing with either type of partnership can know by the formal name of the entity and by a person's status as general or limited partner whether the person has the power to bind the entity.
>
> Most LLC statutes have attempted to use the same approach but with a fundamentally important (and problematic) distinction. An LLC's status as member-managed or manager-managed determines whether members or managers have the statutory power to bind. But an LLC's status as member- or manager-managed is not apparent from the LLC's name. A third party must check the public record, which may reveal that the LLC is manager-managed, which in turn means a member as member has no power to bind the LLC. As a result, a provision that originated in 1914 as a protection for third parties can, in the LLC context, easily function as a trap for the unwary. The problem is exacerbated by the almost infinite variety of management structures permissible in and used by LLCs.
>
> The new Act cuts through this problem by simply eliminating statutory apparent authority.

PUBOGRAM, Vol. XXIII, no. 2 at 9-10.

Codifying power to bind according to position makes sense only for organizations that have well-defined, well-known, and almost paradigmatic management structures. Because:

- flexibility of management structure is a hallmark of the limited liability company; and
- an LLC's name gives no signal as to the organization's structure,

it makes no sense to:

- require each LLC to publicly select between two statutorily preordained structures (i.e., manager-managed/member-managed); and then
- link a "statutory power to bind" to each of those two structures.

Under this Act, other law—most especially the law of agency—will handle power-to-bind questions. See the Comment to subsection (b).

Section 2: Fiduciary Duties

Revised Uniform Limited Liability Company Act (2006) § 409: Standards of Conduct for Members and Managers

(a) A member of a member-managed limited liability company owes to the company and, subject to Section 901(b), the other members the fiduciary duties of loyalty and care stated in subsections (b) and (c).

(b) The duty of loyalty of a member in a member-managed limited liability company includes the duties:

(1) to account to the company and to hold as trustee for it any property, profit, or benefit derived by the member:

(A) in the conduct or winding up of the company's activities;

(B) from a use by the member of the company's property; or

(C) from the appropriation of a limited liability company opportunity;

(2) to refrain from dealing with the company in the conduct or winding up of the company's activities as or on behalf of a person having an interest adverse to the company; and

(3) to refrain from competing with the company in the conduct of the company's activities before the dissolution of the company.

(c) Subject to the business judgment rule, the duty of care of a member of a member-managed limited liability company in the conduct and winding up of the company's activities is to act with the care that a person in a like position would reasonably exercise under similar circumstances and in a manner the member reasonably believes to be in the best interests of the company. In discharging this duty, a member may rely in good faith upon opinions, reports, statements, or other information provided by another person that the member reasonably believes is a competent and reliable source for the information.

(d) A member in a member-managed limited liability company or a manager-managed limited liability company shall discharge the duties under this [act] or under the operating agreement and exercise any rights consistently with the contractual obligation of good faith and fair dealing.

(e) It is a defense to a claim under subsection (b)(2) and any comparable claim in equity or at common law that the transaction was fair to the limited liability company.

(f) All of the members of a member-managed limited liability company or a manager-managed limited liability company may authorize or ratify, after full disclosure of all material facts, a specific act or transaction that otherwise would violate the duty of loyalty.

(g) In a manager-managed limited liability company, the following rules apply:

(1) Subsections (a), (b), (c), and (e) apply to the manager or managers and not the members.

(2) The duty stated under subsection (b)(3) continues until winding up is completed.

(3) Subsection (d) applies to the members and managers.

(4) Subsection (f) applies only to the members.

(5) A member does not have any fiduciary duty to the company or to any other member solely by reason of being a member.

Comment

This section follows the structure of many LLC acts, first stating the duties of members in a member-managed limited liability company and then using that statement and a "switching" mechanism, subsection (g), to allocate duties in a manager-managed company. The duties stated in this section are subject to the operating agreement, but Section 110 contains important limitations on the power of the operating agreement to affect fiduciary duties and the obligation of good faith.

This section contains several noteworthy developments in the law of unincorporated business organizations:

- fiduciary duty is "uncabined"—see the Comment to subsections (a) and (b);
- the duty of care is not set at gross negligence—see the Comment to subsection (c); and
- the statutory endorsement of self-interest is omitted—see the Comment to section (e)

The standards, duties, and obligations of this Section are subject to delineation, restriction, and, to some extent, elimination by the operating agreement. See Section 110.

Subsections (a) and (b)—Until the promulgation of RUPA, it was almost axiomatic that: (i) fiduciary duties reflect judge-made law; and (ii) statutory formulations can express some of that law but do not exhaustively codify it. The original UPA was a prime example of this approach.

In an effort to respect freedom of contract, bolster predictability, and protect partnership agreements from second-guessing, the Conference decided that RUPA should fence or "cabin in" all fiduciary duties within a statutory formulation. That decision was followed without re-consideration in ULLCA and ULPA (2001).

This Act takes a different approach. After lengthy discussion in the drafting committee and on the floor of the 2006 Annual Meeting, the Conference decided that: (i) the "corral" created by RUPA does not fit in the very complex and variegated world of LLCs; and (ii) it is impracticable to cabin all LLC-related fiduciary duties within a statutory formulation.

As a result, this Act: (i) eschews "only" and "limited to"—the words RUPA used in an effort to exhaustively codify fiduciary duty; (ii) codifies the core of the fiduciary duty of loyalty; but (iii) does not purport to discern every possible category of overreaching. One important consequence is to allow courts to continue to use fiduciary duty concepts to police disclosure obligations in member-to-member and member-LLC transactions.

Subsection (c)—Although ULLCA, § 409(c) followed RUPA, § 404(c) and provided a gross negligence standard of care, at least a plurality of LLC statutes use an ordinary care standard. Sandra K. Miller, *The Role of the Court in Balancing Contractual Freedom With the Need For Mandatory Constraints on Opportunistic and Abusive Conduct in the LLC*, 152 U. Pa. L. Rev[.] 1609, 1658 (May 2004) (containing two tables characterizing the standard of care under LLC statutes: 21 states with "good faith prudent person" language and 19 states using "gross negligence or willful misconduct" language); Elizabeth

S. Miller and Thomas E. Rutledge, *The Duty of Finest Loyalty and Reasonable Decisions: The Business Judgment Rule in Unincorporated Business Organizations*, 30 Del. J. Corp. L. 343, 366- 368 (2005) (stating that "[a]pproximately eighteen state LLC statutes parallel language formerly used in the MBCA and require managers and managing members to act in good faith and exercise the care of an ordinarily prudent person in a like position under similar circumstances"). See also William J. Callison, *"The Law Does Not Perfectly Comprehend....": The Inadequacy of the Gross Negligence Duty of Care Standard in Unincorporated Business Organizations*, 94 Ky. L.J. 451, 452 (2005-2006) ("examin[ing] the gross negligence standard and find[ing] it wanting, particularly as it has intruded, largely unexamined and by drafting osmosis, into subsequent uniform acts governing limited partnerships and limited liability companies").

In some circumstances, an unadorned standard of ordinary care is appropriate for those in charge of a business organization or similar, non-business enterprise. In others, the proper application of the duty of care must take into account the difficulties inherent in establishing an enterprise's most fundamental policies, supervising the enterprise's overall activities, or making complex business judgments. Corporate law subdivides circumstances somewhat according to the formal role exercised by the person whose conduct is later challenged (e.g., distinguishing the duties of directors from the duties of officers). LLC law cannot follow that approach, because a hallmark of the LLC entity is its structural flexibility.

This subsection, therefore, seeks "the best of both worlds"—stating a standard of ordinary care but subjecting that standard to the business judgment rule to the extent circumstances warrant. The content and force of the business judgment rule vary across jurisdictions, and therefore the meaning of this subsection may vary from jurisdiction to jurisdiction.

That result is intended. In any jurisdiction, the business judgment rule's application will vary depending on the nature of the challenged conduct. There is, for example, very little (if any) judgment involved when a person with managerial power acts (or fails to act) on an essentially ministerial matter. Moreover, under the law of many jurisdictions, the business judgment rule applies similarly across the range of business organizations. That is, the doctrine is sufficiently broad and conceptual so that the formality of organizational choice is less important in shaping the application of the rule than are the nature of the challenged conduct and the responsibilities and authority of the person whose conduct is being challenged.

This Act seeks therefore to invoke rather than unsettle whatever may be each jurisdiction's approach to the business judgment rule.

Subsection (d)—This subsection refers to the "*contractual* obligation of good faith and fair dealing" to emphasize that the obligation is not an invitation to re-write agreements among the members. As explained in the Comment to ULPA (2001), § 305(b):

> The obligation of good faith and fair dealing is not a fiduciary duty, does not command altruism or self-abnegation, and does not prevent a partner from acting in the partner's own self-interest. Courts should not use the obligation to change ex post facto the parties' or this Act's allocation of risk and power. To the contrary, in light of the nature of a limited partnership, the obligation should be used only to protect agreed-upon arrangements from conduct that is manifestly beyond what a reasonable person could have contemplated when the arrangements were made.... In sum, the purpose of the obligation of good faith and fair

> dealing is to protect the arrangement the partners have chosen for themselves, not to restructure that arrangement under the guise of safeguarding it.

At first glance, it may seem strange to apply a contractual obligation to statutory duties and rights—i.e., duties and rights "under this [act]." However, for the most part those duties and rights apply to relationships *inter se* the members and the LLC and function only to the extent not displaced by the operating agreement. In the contract-based organization that is an LLC, those statutory default rules are intended to function like a contract. Therefore, applying the contractual notion of good faith makes sense.

As to whether the obligation stated in this subsection applies to transferees, see the Comment to Section 112(b).

Subsection (e)—Section 409 omits a noteworthy provision, which, beginning with RUPA, has been standard in the uniform business entity acts. RUPA, ULLCA, ULPA (2001) each placed the following language in the subsection following the formulation of the obligation of good faith:

> A member ... does not violate a duty or obligation under this [act] or under the operating agreement merely because the member's conduct furthers the member's own interest.

This language is inappropriate in the complex and variegated world of LLCs. As a proposition of contract law, the language is axiomatic and therefore unnecessary. In the context of fiduciary duty, the language is at best incomplete, at worst wrong, and in any event confusing.

This Act's subsection (e) takes a very different approach, stating a well-established principle of judge-made law. Despite Section 107, the statement is not surplusage. Given this Act's very detailed treatment of fiduciary duties and especially the Act's very detailed treatment of the power of the operating agreement to modify fiduciary duties, the statement is important because its absence might be confusing. (An *ex post* fairness justification is not the same as an *ex ante* agreement to modify, but the topics are sufficiently close for a danger of the affirmative pregnant.)

This Act also omits, as anachronistic and potentially confusing, any provision resembling ULLCA, §409(f) ("A member of a member-managed company may lend money to and transact other business with the company. As to each loan or transaction, the rights and obligations of the member are the same as those of a person who is not a member, subject to other applicable law.") See also ULPA (2001), §112 ("A partner may lend money to and transact other business with the limited partnership and has the same rights and obligations with respect to the loan or other transaction as a person that is not a partner.")

Those provisions originated to combat the notion that debts to partners were categorically inferior to debts to non-partner creditors. That notion has never been part of LLC law, and so a modern uniform LLC act need not include language combating the notion. Moreover, to the uninitiated the language can be confusing, because the words might: (i) seem to undercut the duty of loyalty, which they do not; and (ii) deflect attention from bankruptcy law and the law of fraudulent transfer, which assuredly can look askance at transactions between an entity and an "insider."

[...]

Subsection (g)(5)—This paragraph merely negates a claim of fiduciary duty that is exclusively status-based and does not immunize misconduct.

EXAMPLE: Although a limited liability company is manager-managed, one member who is not a manager owns a controlling interest and effectively, albeit indirectly, controls the company's activities. A member owning a minority interest brings an action for dissolution under Section 701(a)(5)(B) (oppression by "the managers or those members in control of the company"). The court wishes to understand a claim as one alleging a breach of fiduciary duty by the controlling member. Subsection (g)(5) does not preclude that approach.

Revised Uniform Limited Liability Company Act (2006) § 110: Operating Agreement; Scope, Function, and Limitations

(a) Except as otherwise provided in subsections (b) and (c), the operating agreement governs:

(1) relations among the members as members and between the members and the limited liability company;

(2) the rights and duties under this [act] of a person in the capacity of manager;

(3) the activities of the company and the conduct of those activities; and

(4) the means and conditions for amending the operating agreement.

(b) To the extent the operating agreement does not otherwise provide for a matter described in subsection (a), this [act] governs the matter.

(c) An operating agreement may not:

...

(4) subject to subsections (d) through (g), eliminate the duty of loyalty, the duty of care, or any other fiduciary duty;

(5) subject to subsections (d) through (g), eliminate the contractual obligation of good faith and fair dealing under Section 409(d);

(d) If not manifestly unreasonable, the operating agreement may:

(1) restrict or eliminate the duty:

(A) as required in Section 409(b)(1) and (g), to account to the limited liability company and to hold as trustee for it any property, profit, or benefit derived by the member in the conduct or winding up of the company's business, from a use by the member of the company's property, or from the appropriation of a limited liability company opportunity;

(B) as required in Section 409(b)(2) and (g), to refrain from dealing with the company in the conduct or winding up of the company's business as or on behalf of a party having an interest adverse to the company; and

(C) as required by Section 409(b)(3) and (g), to refrain from competing with the company in the conduct of the company's business before the dissolution of the company;

(2) identify specific types or categories of activities that do not violate the duty of loyalty;

(3) alter the duty of care, except to authorize intentional misconduct or knowing violation of law;

(4) alter any other fiduciary duty, including eliminating particular aspects of that duty; and

(5) prescribe the standards by which to measure the performance of the contractual obligation of good faith and fair dealing under Section 409(d).

(e) The operating agreement may specify the method by which a specific act or transaction that would otherwise violate the duty of loyalty may be authorized or ratified by one or more disinterested and independent persons after full disclosure of all material facts.

(f) To the extent the operating agreement of a member-managed limited liability company expressly relieves a member of a responsibility that the member would otherwise have under this [act] and imposes the responsibility on one or more other members, the operating agreement may, to the benefit of the member that the operating agreement relieves of the responsibility, also eliminate or limit any fiduciary duty that would have pertained to the responsibility.

(g) The operating agreement may alter or eliminate the indemnification for a member or manager provided by Section 408(a) and may eliminate or limit a member or manager's liability to the limited liability company and members for money damages, except for:

(1) breach of the duty of loyalty;

(2) a financial benefit received by the member or manager to which the member or manager is not entitled;

...

(4) intentional infliction of harm on the company or a member; or

(5) an intentional violation of criminal law.

---

6 Del. C. § 18-1101 (2013): Construction and application of chapter and limited liability company agreement

(a) The rule that statutes in derogation of the common law are to be strictly construed shall have no application to this chapter.

(b) It is the policy of this chapter to give the maximum effect to the principle of freedom of contract and to the enforceability of limited liability company agreements.

(c) To the extent that, at law or in equity, a member or manager or other person has duties (including fiduciary duties) to a limited liability company or to another member or manager or to another person that is a party to or is otherwise bound by a limited liability company agreement, the member's or manager's or other person's duties may be expanded or restricted or eliminated by provisions in the limited liability company agreement; provided, that the limited liability company agreement may not eliminate the implied contractual covenant of good faith and fair dealing.

(d) Unless otherwise provided in a limited liability company agreement, a member or manager or other person shall not be liable to a limited liability company or to another member or manager or to another person that is a party to or is otherwise bound by a limited liability company agreement for breach of fiduciary duty for the member's or manager's or other person's good faith reliance on the provisions of the limited liability company agreement.

(e) A limited liability company agreement may provide for the limitation or elimination of any and all liabilities for breach of contract and breach of duties (including fiduciary duties) of a member, manager or other person to a limited liability company or to another member or manager or to another person that is a party to or is otherwise bound by a limited liability company agreement; provided, that a limited liability company agreement may not limit or eliminate liability for any act or omission that constitutes a bad faith violation of the implied contractual covenant of good faith and fair dealing.

[...]

(i) A limited liability company agreement that provides for the application of Delaware law shall be governed by and construed under the laws of the State of Delaware in accordance with its terms.

Salm v. Feldstein, 799 N.Y.S.2d 104 (N.Y. App. 2005). "On June 2, 2003, the defendant purchased the plaintiff's membership interest in the company under a redemption and settlement agreement (hereinafter the contract) providing for a payment to the plaintiff in the sum of $3,750,000, and a consulting contract with the plaintiff which would pay him a five-year aggregate sum of $1,350,000. On June 4, 2003, the defendant sold the dealership to a nonparty for the sum of $16 million....

"As the managing member of the company and as a co-member with the plaintiff, the defendant owed the plaintiff a fiduciary duty to make full disclosure of all material facts (see Birnbaum v Birnbaum, 73 NY2d 461, 465, 539 NE2d 574, 541 NYS2d 746 [1989] citing Meinhard v Salmon, 249 NY 458, 468, 164 NE 545 [1928]. Moreover, because the defendant had a fiduciary relationship with the plaintiff, the disclaimers contained in the contract, upon which the defendant relies, did not relieve him of the obligation of full disclosure."

Pappas v Tzolis

982 N.E.2d 576 (N.Y. 2012)

PIGOTT, J.

Plaintiffs Steve Pappas and Constantine Ifantopoulos along with defendant Steve Tzolis formed and managed a limited liability company, for the purpose of entering into a long-term lease on a building in Lower Manhattan. Pappas and Tzolis each contributed $50,000 and Ifantopoulos $25,000, in exchange for proportionate shares in the company. Pursuant to a January 2006 Operating Agreement, Tzolis agreed to post and maintain in effect a security deposit of $1,192,500, and was permitted to sublet the property. The Agreement further provided that any of the three members of the LLC could "engage in business ventures and investments of any nature whatsoever, whether or not in competition with the LLC, without obligation of any kind to the LLC or to the other Members."

Numerous business disputes among the parties ensued. In June 2006, Tzolis took sole possession of the property, which was subleased by the LLC to a company he owned, for approximately $20,000 per month in addition to rent payable by the LLC under the lease. According to plaintiffs, they "reluctantly agreed to do this, because they were looking to lease the building and Tzolis was obstructing this from happening." Pappas, who wanted to sublease the building to others, alleges that Tzolis "not only blocked [his] efforts, he also did not cooperate in listing the Property for sale or lease with any New York real estate brokers." Moreover, Pappas claims that Tzolis "had not made, and was not diligently preparing to make, the improvements ... required to be made under the Lease. Tzolis was also refusing to cooperate in [Pappas's] efforts to develop the Property." Further, Tzolis's company did not pay the rent due.

On January 18, 2007, Tzolis bought plaintiffs' membership interests in the LLC for $1,000,000 and $500,000, respectively. At closing, in addition to an Agreement of Assignment and Assumption, the parties executed a Certificate in which plaintiffs represented that, as sellers, they had "performed [their] own due diligence in connection with [the] assignments.... engaged [their] own legal counsel, and [were] not relying on any representation by Steve Tzolis, or any of his agents or representatives, except as set forth in the assignments & other documents delivered to the undersigned Sellers today," and that "Steve Tzolis has no fiduciary duty to the undersigned Sellers in connection with [the] assignments." Tzolis made reciprocal representations as the buyer.

In August 2007, the LLC, now owned entirely by Tzolis, assigned the lease to a subsidiary of Extell Development Company for $17,500,000. In 2009, plaintiffs came to believe that Tzolis had surreptitiously negotiated the sale with the development company before he bought their interests in the LLC.

Plaintiffs commenced this action against Tzolis in April 2009, claiming that, by failing to disclose the negotiations with Extell, Tzolis breached his fiduciary duty to them. They alleged, in all, eleven causes of action.

Tzolis moved to dismiss plaintiffs' complaint. Supreme Court dismissed the complaint in its entirety, citing the Operating Agreement and Certificate. A divided Appellate Division modified Supreme Court's order, allowing four of plaintiffs' claims to proceed—breach of fiduciary duty, conversion, unjust enrichment, and fraud and misrepresentation—while upholding the dismissal of the rest of the complaint. The dissenting Justices would have dismissed all the causes of action, relying on our recent decision in Centro Empresarial Cempresa S.A. v América Móvil, S.A.B. de C.V. (17 NY3d 269, 952 N.E.2d 995, 929 N.Y.S.2d 3 [2011]).

The Appellate Division granted Tzolis leave to appeal, certifying the question whether its order was properly made. We now answer the certified question in the negative, and reverse.

In their first cause of action, plaintiffs claim that Tzolis was a fiduciary with respect to them and breached his duty of disclosure. Tzolis counters that plaintiffs' claim fails to state a cause of action because, by executing the Certificate, they expressly released him from all claims based on fiduciary duty.

In Centro Empresarial Cempresa S.A. v América Móvil, S.A.B. de C.V., we held that "[a] sophisticated principal is able to release its fiduciary from claims—at least where ... the fiduciary relationship is no longer one of unquestioning trust—so long as the principal understands that the fiduciary is acting in its own interest and the release is knowingly entered into". Where a principal and fiduciary are sophisticated entities and their relationship is not one of trust, the principal cannot reasonably rely on the fiduciary without making additional inquiry. For instance, in Centro, plaintiffs—seasoned and counseled parties negotiating the termination of their relationship—knew that defendants had not supplied them with the financial information to which they were entitled, triggering "a heightened degree of diligence" (id. at 279). In this context, "the principal cannot blindly trust the fiduciary's assertions" (id.). The test, in essence, is whether, given the nature of the parties' relationship at the time of the release, the principal is aware of information about the fiduciary that would make reliance on the fiduciary unreasonable.

Here, plaintiffs were sophisticated businessmen represented by counsel. Moreover, plaintiffs' own allegations make it clear that at the time of the buyout, the relationship between the parties was not one of trust, and reliance on Tzolis's representations as a fiduciary would not have been reasonable. According to plaintiffs, there had been numerous business disputes, between Tzolis and them, concerning the sublease. Both the complaint and Pappas's affidavit opposing the motion to dismiss portray Tzolis as uncooperative and intransigent in the face of plaintiffs' preferences concerning the sublease. The relationship between plaintiffs and Tzolis had become antagonistic, to the extent that plaintiffs could no longer reasonably regard Tzolis as trustworthy. Therefore, crediting plaintiffs' allegations, the release contained in the Certificate is valid, and plaintiffs cannot prevail on their cause of action alleging breach of fiduciary duty.

Practically speaking, it is clear that plaintiffs were in a position to make a reasoned judgment about whether to agree to the sale of their interests to Tzolis. The need to use care to reach an independent assessment of the value of the lease should have been obvious to plaintiffs, given that Tzolis offered to buy their interests for 20 times what they had paid for them just a year earlier.

Plaintiffs' cause of action alleging fraud and misrepresentation must be dismissed for similar reasons. Plaintiffs principally allege that Tzolis represented to them that he was aware of no reasonable prospects of selling the lease for an amount in excess of $2,500,000. However, in the Certificate, plaintiffs "in the plainest language announced and stipulated that [they were] not relying on any representations as to the very matter as to which [they] now claim [they were] defrauded". Moreover, while it is true that a party that releases a fraud claim may later challenge that release as fraudulently induced if it alleges a fraud separate from any contemplated by the release, plaintiffs do not allege that the release was itself induced by any action separate from the alleged fraud consisting of Tzolis's failure to disclose his negotiations to sell the lease.

Plaintiffs' conversion claim is that Tzolis appropriated to himself, without authority, plaintiffs' membership interests in the LLC. "Two key elements of conversion are (1) plaintiff's possessory right or interest in the property and (2) defendant's dominion over the property or interference with it, in derogation of plaintiff's rights". Here, since Tzolis had purchased plaintiffs' interests in the LLC, there could be no interference with their property rights. Therefore, the conversion claim must be dismissed.

Finally, we reject plaintiffs' claim that Tzolis unjustly enriched himself at their expense. The doctrine of unjust enrichment invokes an "obligation imposed by equity to prevent injustice, in the absence of an actual agreement between the parties concerned" (IDT Corp. v Morgan Stanley Dean Witter & Co., 12 NY3d 132, 142, 907 N.E.2d 268, 879 N.Y.S.2d 355 [2009] [emphasis added]). "[A] party may not recover in ... unjust enrichment where the parties have entered into a contract that governs the subject matter" (Cox v NAP Constr. Co., Inc., 10 NY3d 592, 607, 891 N.E.2d 271, 861 N.Y.S.2d 238 [2008]). Because the sale of interests in the LLC was controlled by contracts—the Operating Agreement, the Agreement of Assignment and Assumption, and the Certificate—the unjust enrichment claim fails as a matter of law.

Accordingly, the order of the Appellate Division, insofar as appealed from, should be reversed, with costs, plaintiffs' complaint dismissed in its entirety, and the certified question answered in the negative.

Solar Cells, Inc. v. True N. Partners LLC

2002 Del. Ch. LEXIS 38 (Del. Ch. 2002)

CHANDLER, C.

This action concerns the proposed merger of defendant First Solar, LLC ("First Solar" or the "Company") with and into First Solar Operating, LLC ("FSO"), the wholly-owned operating subsidiary of First Solar Ventures, LLC ("FSV"). The plaintiff, Solar Cells, Inc. ("Solar Cells"), alleges that the individual defendant managers of First Solar, acting at the direction of defendant True North Partners, LLC ("True North" and, collectively, "the defendants"), acted in bad faith in approving the proposed merger and that the defendants will be unable to prove the entire fairness of that merger.

On March 13, 2002, Solar Cells filed a motion for a temporary restraining order requesting that this Court enjoin the proposed merger, which was scheduled to close two days later. The defendants agreed to postpone consummation of the merger in order to permit the parties to conduct the limited discovery necessary to present their positions at a preliminary injunction hearing. Solar Cells' motion for a preliminary injunction was fully briefed and then argued on April 17, 2002. Because I find that Solar Cells has met its burden of establishing a reasonable likelihood that it will be successful on the merits of its claim of a breach of fiduciary duty and that it is threatened by irreparable harm if the merger is consummated, I will enter an Order preliminarily enjoining the merger.

I. BACKGROUND FACTS

Solar Cells, an Ohio corporation, was founded in 1987 by Harold A. McMaster ("McMaster") to develop, design, and manufacture products and processes for photovoltaic electricity generation—technology commonly referred to as "solar power." McMaster designed technologies and processes for manufacturing photovoltaic cells making use of heretofore-unknown techniques that were predicted to revolutionize the solar power industry. These inventions purportedly would permit cost-effective manufacture of photovoltaic cells that produce energy at rates competitive with, or even less than, the present cost of electrical generation using fossil fuels. In order to exploit the potential of these inventions, True North, an Arizona limited liability company, was brought in to provide needed financing. Solar Cells and True North formed First Solar as a Delaware limited liability company in February 1999 to commercialize McMaster's solar technology.

First Solar is managed pursuant to the Operating Agreement of First Solar, LLC ("Operating Agreement"). The Operating Agreement required Solar Cells to contribute patented and proprietary technology—valued in the Operating Agreement at $35 million—to First Solar. True North was to contribute $35 million in capital to First Solar and, also pursuant to the Operating Agreement, was required to, and did, loan First Solar an additional $8 million. In return for their contributions, Solar Cells and First Solar each received 4,500 of First Solar's Class A membership units. Solar Cells also received 100% of First Solar's Class B membership units. [Court's footnote: According to the Operating Agreement, Class A Units had voting rights, and Class B Units had no voting rights.] The business and affairs of First Solar is conducted by five Managers. The Operating Agreement permits True North to elect three of those Managers (the "True North Managers") and Solar Cells to elect the remaining two Managers (the "Solar Cells Managers"). It is undisputed that, since its inception, First Solar has been managed by True North.

First Solar's continuing development and manufacturing expenditures, as well as its inability to produce a marketable product, eventually depleted the Company's initial funding. By early 2001 it became apparent that continued operations would require additional funding. To this end, in March 2001, First Solar retained investment banker Adams, Harkness & Hill, Inc. ("AHH") to find a strategic investor for the Company. In order for the Company to continue operating while AHH searched for a strategic investor, True North agreed to make an additional $15 million loan to First Solar.

The Loan Agreement between First Solar and True North bundled True North's original $8 million loan and the new $15 million loan and represented a funding commitment by True North of up to a total of $23 million through December 31, 2001. Upon either the receipt of outside investment or at the end of its funding commitment, the Loan Agreement gave True North the option of converting some or all of the loan amount into Class A Units of First Solar or to retain the investment as a loan with liquidation preferences. For reasons disputed by the parties (but not relevant to this motion), no outside investors were brought into First Solar.

From December 2001 through March 2002, the parties engaged in unsuccessful negotiations regarding different alternatives for financing and restructuring First Solar. On March 5, 2002, True North purported to convert $250,000 of its outstanding loans to First Solar into Class A Units at a conversion ratio based on a January 8, 2002 AHH valuation of First Solar at $32,000,000. On March 7, 2002, the True North Managers executed a written consent approving the challenged merger of First Solar into FSO, a Delaware limited liability company wholly owned by True North. On March 11, 2002, Solar Cells received notice of the proposed merger, which was scheduled to close on March 15, 2002, and the terms of that merger. In connection with the merger, True North would convert its remaining outstanding loans into equity at the same ratio as the March 5, 2002 conversion. The merger would occur based on a total valuation of First Solar at $32 million with First Solar ownership units being exchanged for ownership units of the surviving company. The end result of the merger-related transactions would be that Solar Cells would go from owning 50% of the Class A Units of First Solar to owning 5% of the membership units of the surviving company. On March 13, 2002, Solar Cells filed a complaint and request for temporary restraining order enjoining consummation of the proposed merger. True North agreed not to cause its Managers to close the merger before this Court's decision on Solar Cells' motion for a preliminary injunction filed in response to that agreement.

II. PRELIMINARY INJUNCTION STANDARD

The standard on a motion for preliminary injunction is well-settled. In order to prevail, a plaintiff must establish: (1) a reasonable likelihood of success on the merits of at least one claim; (2) that irreparable harm will be suffered by the plaintiff if the injunction is denied; and (3) that the harm that the plaintiff will suffer if the injunction is not granted outweighs the harm that the defendant will suffer if the injunction is granted.

III. CONTENTIONS

Solar Cells argues that the manner in which the proposed merger was approved demonstrates that the True North Managers acted in bad faith and breached their fiduciary duties to Solar Cells as a member of First Solar. Because of the defendants' bad faith, Solar Cells contends that the defendants will be required to prove that the proposed merger is entirely fair. Solar Cells argues that it is likely to be successful on the merits because the defendants will be unable to demonstrate that the proposed merger was the result of fair dealing and based on a fair price.

Solar Cells lists three effects of the proposed merger that will irreparably harm it should the merger close. First, because of the purportedly improper conversion ratio used by True North to convert its outstanding First Solar loans to equity, Solar Cells' 50% voting and equity interest in First Solar will be diluted to only a 5% interest in the surviving company. Second, Solar Cells bargained for the right to elect two Managers when negotiating with True North over the creation of First Solar. As a result of the proposed merger, it will lose this bargained-for right. Instead, True North will—through its control of 95% of the voting units of the surviving company—elect all three of the Managers of the surviving LLC. Third, and finally, it is contemplated that outside investors will be brought into the surviving company. Should that happen and this Court later determines that use of an improper conversion caused the equity positions of the parties to be incorrectly established, the interests of third parties would make the resolution of that problem extremely difficult. Solar Cells argues the harm is incalculable and far outweigh any harm that might be suffered by First Solar as a result of enjoining an unfair transaction.

The defendants counter that, as evidenced by the Operating Agreement, the parties unambiguously agreed that the True North Members could control decisions regarding the business and affairs of First Solar. Action by written consent is permitted by the Operating Agreement. A merger need only be approved by a majority of the Managers and True North has veto power over any mergers it does not agree with. The merger was approved by the three True North Managers in the good faith belief that, in light of failed restructuring negotiations between the parties, this was the only option available to save First Solar from a forced sale or liquidation when it runs out of operating money at the end of April 2002. Furthermore, the Operating Agreement acknowledges that there will be conflicts of interest between the True North Managers (two of which are True North principals) and eliminates liability for any conflict of interest transactions that they may engage in. The only requirement is that the True North Managers act in the good faith belief that their actions are in the best interest of First Solar. Because every action taken by the True North Managers with regard to the proposed merger was authorized by the Operating Agreement and made in the good faith belief that it was in the best interest of First Solar, True North insists that this Court should deny Solar Cells' motion.

Although True North disputes the need to establish entire fairness, it contends that both the process and the price of the merger are entirely fair. The process undertaken was clearly authorized by the Operating Agreement and the price was arrived at from a valuation by AHH based on accurate revenue statements and is further supported by an outside valuation.

True North argues that Solar Cells will not be irreparably harmed by the merger. Any dilution suffered by Solar Cells is the result of a valid conversion of True North loans to equity. Solar Cells will be permitted to make further investments in the surviving company on the same basis as True North. There is a reset provision that will reverse part of Solar Cells' dilution if a strategic investor is found during 2002. Although the defendants acknowledge that Solar Cells will not have the right to elect managers of the surviving company, they contend that True North had the right to elect a majority of First Solar Managers and, therefore, was guaranteed control over the business and affairs of the Company. True North merely continues to have the power to control the business and affairs of the surviving company. Since Solar Cells could not control First Solar, it has not lost any power over the company by not being able to elect managers of the surviving company. Having suffered no irreparable harm, defendants contend that the equities clearly balance in their favor and against the motion. They assert that if the injunction is granted, the Company will run out of money by April 30, 2002. Since True North is unwilling to continue funding the Company, it will have to terminate its employees, shut down, and be sold at a bargain in a forced liquidation.

IV. ANALYSIS

A. Likelihood of Success on the Merits

The defendants argue that all of the actions taken in connection with the proposed merger were clearly authorized by the Operating Agreement. They further argue that the Operating Agreement limited any fiduciary duties owed by True North Managers. Section 4.18(a) of the Operating Agreement provides, in relevant part:

> Solar Cells and [First Solar] acknowledge that the True North Managers have fiduciary obligations to both [First Solar] and to True North, which fiduciary obligations may, because of the ability of the True North Managers to control [First Solar] and its business, create a conflict of interest or a potential conflict of interest for the true North Managers. Both [First Solar] and Solar Cells hereby waive any such conflict of interest or potential conflict of interest and agree that neither True North nor any True North Manager shall have any liability to [First Solar] or to Solar Cells with respect to any such conflict of interest or potential conflict of interest, provided that the True North managers have acted in a manner which they believe in good faith to be in the best interest of [First Solar].

I note that this clause purports to limit *liability* stemming from any conflict of interest. Solar Cells has not requested that this Court impose liability on the individual defendants. It is currently only seeking to *enjoin* the proposed merger. Therefore, exculpation for personal liability has no bearing on the likelihood that Solar Cells would be successful on the merits of its contention that the proposed merger is inequitable and should be enjoined. Even if waiver of liability for engaging in conflicting interest transactions is contracted for, that does not mean that there is a waiver of all fiduciary duties to Solar Cells. Indeed, §4.18(a) expressly states that the True North Managers must act in "good faith." It is undisputed that First Solar was, and is, in financial distress. Months of unsuccessful negotiations have been ongoing in an attempt to come to an agreement as to how to remedy that situation. On March 6, 2002, the full Board of Managers met and the True North Managers made no mention of the planned merger. The very next day, March 7, 2002, the three True North Managers met and by written consent approved the proposed merger. No effort was made to inform the Solar Cells Managers that this action was contemplated, or imminent, when those facts were surely known at the time of the March 6 meeting. [Court's footnote: The plaintiff contends that documents produced during discovery reveal that the defendants had been planning the proposed merger since at least February 27, 2002.] At the earliest, Solar Cells was given notice of the fact, and terms, of the proposed merger (which were presented as a fait accompli) via facsimile on March 8, 2002—a week before consummation of a merger that will apparently reduce Solar Cells' interest from 50% to 5%. These actions do not appear to be those of fiduciaries acting in good faith. As the Supreme Court and this Court have made clear, it is not an unassailable defense to say that what was done was in technical compliance with the law. The facts before me make it likely, in my opinion, that the defendants would be required to show the entire fairness of the proposed merger.

The party with the burden of establishing entire fairness must establish that the challenged transaction was the result of fair dealing and offered a fair price. Fair dealing pertains to the process by which the transaction was approved and looks at the terms, structure, and timing of the transaction. Fair price includes all relevant factors "relating to the economic and financial considerations of the proposed merger."

The defendants argue that there is nothing inherently unfair about the structure of the merger—a holding company with a wholly-owned operating subsidiary. Solar Cells points out, however, that there was no independent bargaining mechanism set up to protect its interests. In fact, there was no negotiation at all. All of the decisions regarding the terms of the merger and its approval were made unilaterally by True North through its representative Managers. No advance notice of this merger was given to Solar Cells. The fact that the Operating Agreement permits action by written consent of a majority of the Managers and permits interested transactions free from personal liability does not give a fiduciary free [rein] to approve any transaction he sees fit regardless of the impact on those to whom he owes a fiduciary duty.

The defendants contend that the timing of the merger was dictated by the Company's financial emergency, an emergency they say had been exacerbated by Solar Cells' refusal to negotiate, in good faith, a suitable plan for restructuring the Company. Solar Cells counters that the timing was driven by True North's desire to increase its proportionate ownership while simultaneously squeezing out Solar Cells at an unfair price. Solar Cells argues that the effect of the merger is essentially the same as the terms of a restructuring plan Solar Cells had refused to agree to in February 2002. They contend, in the face of Solar Cells' refusal to accept an unfair restructuring offer voluntarily, that the defendants immediately sought to impose similar terms by way of the proposed merger.

I am unconvinced by defendants' argument that the merger was fair to Solar Cells because Solar Cells retains voting rights in the surviving company. On matters where the unit-holders can vote, Solar Cells is diluted from an equal (50%) voice, to only 5%. Also arguably illusory is the so-called market-reset provision that would raise Solar Cells' initial equity interest in the new entity in the event that the new entity secures third-party financing in 2002. True North has complete control over the managing board and any other decision requiring the vote of unit-holders. Certainly, then, it would be within the power of True North to delay consummation of any proposed third-party investment until after 2002. Such action would seem to be in the self-interest of both True North and any potential third-party investor, as any increase in Solar Cells' equity interest necessarily decreases the equity interest of others. Finally, the ability of Solar Cells to invest new money into the surviving corporation on the same terms as True North hardly remedies the harm suffered by Solar Cells by the initial dilution of its interest as a result of the proposed merger. In my opinion, the facts before me establish a reasonable likelihood that defendants will not be able to establish that the proposed merger was the result of fair dealing.

Application of the entire fairness standard requires a demonstration of both fair dealing and fair price. Having considered the fair dealing component of the standard, I turn now to the fair price analysis.

Solar Cells contends that True North manipulated the valuation of First Solar in order to advantage itself. That is, according to Solar Cells, when True North decided it would become a buyer of First Solar it unilaterally caused AHH to create a fundamentally flawed valuation that is less than one-third of the value calculated by AHH only five months earlier. On the other hand, True North insists that AHH's January 2002 $32 million valuation of First Solar, a calculation that forms the basis of the proposed merger terms, is a more credible calculation of First Solar's value than earlier calculations by AHH. True North contends that the earlier calculations were overly optimistic and were based on outdated financial projections as well as changed market conditions.

For purposes of the present motion only, I am satisfied that there is a reasonable probability that the Court will not find the January 2002 valuation to be entirely fair. First, the author of AHH's January 2002 valuation materials described those materials as a "quick and dirty" analysis of First Solar's value on that date. This contrasts with the earlier valuations in August and November of 2001, valuations that were based on multiple methodologies to arrive at a value for First Solar that ranged from $103 million in August 2001 to $72 million in November 2001, or almost two to three times the January 2002 valuation. Second, AHH's January 2002 valuation employed only a discounted cash flow analysis. Although the lower valuation in January 2002 was the basis upon which True North would acquire a 95% interest in First Solar and Solar Cells would fall to a 5% interest, the significantly lower valuation failed to employ any other method of valuation as a "crosscheck" to the discounted cash flow analysis. Because earlier valuations relied on multiple valuation methodologies, it is a reasonable inference that AHH's "quick and dirty" analysis is less reliable and authoritative. Third, the January 2002 formula used a much lower exit multiple (a 6.9 x free cash flow terminal year multiple) than did earlier valuation formulas (which used an 11 x free cash flow terminal year multiple), with no apparent rationale for that lower multiple. Fourth, AHH's lower valuation resulted from the use of a much higher discount rate (35%) than the valuations it performed only five months earlier (30%), even though the outlook for the solar cell industry was improving in that period and even though interest rates were generally falling.

Judicial determinations of fair price in an entire fairness analysis are difficult even after a full trial on the merits. On the abbreviated record now before the Court in this preliminary injunction context, a fair price analysis is even more problematic. For that reason, I have not found it useful to rely heavily on the deposition and affidavit testimony of the parties' litigation experts. Instead, I conclude that it is reasonably likely this Court will find the January 2002 $32 million valuation of First Solar not to be a fair price because it is irreconcilable with the earlier valuations only a few months before True North decided to go forward with the proposed merger. Because Solar Cells has demonstrated a reasonable likelihood of success on the merits of its entire fairness claim, I turn next to the irreparable harm and balance of the equities component of the preliminary injunction standard.

B. Irreparable Harm

In order to show irreparable harm, the injury must be one for which money damages will not be an adequate remedy. Additionally, the threatened harm must be "imminent, unspeculative, and genuine."

Solar Cells argues that it will be harmed irreparably by the dilution of its equity position and voting power as unit-holders. It also alleges that the loss of its bargained-for participation in company management is an irreparable harm. Finally, it contends that it will be irreparably harmed by the fact that, should a third-party investor be brought into the surviving company, those third-party interests will have to be taken into account by the Court. If it is then later determined that the dilution of Solar Cells' interest was improper it will be difficult, if not impossible, to craft an appropriate remedy for the wrong suffered by Solar Cells. Solar Cells is in imminent, unspeculative, and genuine danger of suffering this harm. The defendants do not argue that these results will not follow from the proposed merger, only whether they constitute harm at all, and if they are, whether they are irreparable harm.

The defendants do not dispute that Solar Cells' equity position and voting power as unit-holders will be diluted. They cite Rovner v. Health-Chem Corp. for the proposition that dilution alone cannot be viewed as irreparable harm. The plaintiff in Rovner could be compensated for any improper dilution of its shares. The plaintiff stockholder in Rovner, moreover, held less than 3% of the eight million shares issued by a publicly-traded company. There was no contention that any dilution would have drastically affected voting power or that the value of the purportedly diluted shares of a public corporation could not be readily valued. Here, not only is dilution not the sole claim of irreparable harm, but the harm alleged is the power inherent in voting 50% of Class A Units compared to voting only 5%. Moreover, accurately valuing this two-member limited liability company may not be possible, as evidenced by the vastly different valuations the parties ascribe to First Solar. Therefore, these are not the types of harm that can be remedied with money damages.

The defendants do not deny that Solar Cells will not have the right to appoint managers of the managing board of the surviving corporation. They argue that since True North had the right to nominate a majority of First Solar's Managers, True North could control the business and affairs of the Company. That reality is unaltered with the surviving company. The defendants reason, therefore, that Solar Cells has suffered no harm by losing its right to appoint managers. That argument carries no weight whatsoever. To accept that assertion would be to believe that every time the ability to elect a manager or director of a corporation is negotiated, there is no benefit derived therefrom if there is not a right to elect a majority of the managers or directors. Such a notion would certainly come as a surprise to all those who have given valuable consideration in negotiating such valueless rights. The right to participate in a management group is a valuable right whether or not that participation includes control of the group. In this case, it is undisputed that Solar Cells will lose that right if the proposed merger closes, thereby suffering an irreparable harm.

Finally, if a third-party investor were brought into the surviving company, the Court would have to consider the interests of that party in formulating relief, if any, later found owing to Solar Cells. The possibility of such investment is not merely speculative, as the defendants claim one of the purposes behind the proposed merger is to make the surviving company more attractive to outside investors. Based on the facts before me, I conclude that Solar Cells is at risk of suffering immediate, irreparable harm if the proposed merger is consummated.

C. Balance of the Equities

The harm suffered by Solar Cells is the irreparable harm discussed above. The harm the defendants allege they will suffer if the injunction is granted is that the Company will run out of money in a matter of days and will be forced to close down and terminate its employees and liquidate assets in the undesirable setting of a forced sale. It does not appear to be a certainty, despite defendants' assertions to the contrary, that True North would let the Company close rather than protecting its investment for the short period of time necessary to reach a final judgment in this matter. Actually, Solar Cells has noted that, under the right terms, McMaster would be willing to make financing available to First Solar. A determination of the likelihood that one of the parties will extend additional financing is not necessary to my decision, however. I am required to balance the harm to the plaintiff if I do not grant the injunction with the harm to the defendants if I do grant the injunction. I note that even if the circumstance the defendants present does occur, that is not a harm that would fall solely on the defendants. Such a forced sale would adversely affect Solar Cells as well. In actuality, this predicted result might have an even greater detrimental effect on Solar Cells. As the defendants have pointed out, True North is entitled to priority repayment of its original $35,000,000 capital contribution before Solar Cells would be able to make a claim to any of the proceeds of a liquidation. As a result, I find that the balance of the equities favors granting Solar Cells' motion for a preliminary injunction against the proposed merger.

V. CONCLUSION

For the reasons stated, I grant plaintiff's motion for preliminary injunction. An Order has been entered in accordance with this decision.

VGS, Inc. v. Castiel

2000 Del. Ch. LEXIS 122 (Del. Ch. 2000), *aff'd* 781 A.2d 696 (Del. 2001), *later proceedings* at 270 F. Supp. 2d 444 (S.D.N.Y. 2003), 864 A.2d 929 (Del. 2004).

STEELE, V.C.

One entity controlled by a single individual forms a one "member" limited liability company. Shortly thereafter, two other entities, one of which is controlled by the owner of the original member, become members of the LLC. The LLC Agreement creates a three-member Board of Managers with sweeping authority to govern the LLC. The individual owning the original member has the authority to name and remove two of the three managers. He also acts as CEO. The unaffiliated third member becomes disenchanted with the original member's leadership. Ultimately the third member's owner, also the third manager, convinces the original member's owner's appointed manager to join him in a clandestine strategic move to merge the LLC into a Delaware corporation. The appointed manager and the disaffected third member do not give the original member's owner, still a member of the LLC's board of managers, notice of their strategic move. After the merger, the original member finds himself relegated to a minority position in the surviving corporation. While a majority of the board acted by written consent, as all involved surely knew, had the original member's manager received notice beforehand that his appointed manager contemplated action against his interests he would have promptly attempted to remove him. Because the two managers acted without notice to the third manager under circumstances where they knew that with notice that he could have acted to protect his majority interest, they breached their duty of loyalty to the original member and their fellow manager by failing to act in good faith. The purported merger must therefore be declared invalid.

The parties tried this case from June 15, 2000 through June 23, 2000. In further detail below, I describe the case's relevant facts and explain the rationale for my ruling.

I. Facts

David Castiel formed Virtual Geosatellite LLC (the "LLC") on January 6, 1999 in order to pursue a Federal Communications Commission ("FCC") license to build and operate a satellite system which its proponents claim could dramatically increase the "real estate" in outer space capable of transmitting high speed internet traffic and other communications. When originally formed, it had only one Member—Virtual Geosatellite Holdings, Inc. ("Holdings"). On January 8, 1999, Ellipso, Inc. ("Ellipso") joined the LLC as its second Member. Several weeks later, on January 29, 1999, Sahagen Satellite Technology Group LLC ("Sahagen Satellite") became the third Member of the LLC.

David Castiel controls both Holdings and Ellipso. Peter Sahagen, an aggressive and apparently successful venture capitalist, controls Sahagen Satellite.

Pursuant to the LLC Agreement, Holdings received 660 units (representing 63.46% of the total equity in the LLC), Sahagen Satellite received 260 units (representing 25%), and Ellipso received 120 units (representing 11.54%). The founders vested management of the LLC in a Board of Managers. As the majority unitholder, Castiel had the power to appoint, remove, and replace two of the three members of the Board of Managers. Castiel, therefore, had the power to prevent any Board decision with which he disagreed. Castiel named himself and Tom Quinn to the Board of Managers. Sahagen named himself as the third member of the Board.

Not long after the formation of the LLC, Castiel and Sahagen were at odds. Castiel contends that Sahagen wanted to control the LLC ever since he became involved, and that Sahagen repeatedly offered, unsuccessfully, to buy control of the LLC. Sahagen maintains that Castiel ran the LLC so poorly that its mission had become untracked, additional necessary capital could not be raised, and competent managers could not be attracted to join the enterprise. Further, Sahagen claims that Castiel directed LLC assets to Ellipso in order to prop up a failing, cash-strapped Ellipso. At trial, these issues and other similar accusations from both sides were explored in great detail. For our purposes here, all that need be concluded is the unarguable fact that Castiel and Sahagen had very different ideas about how the LLC should be managed and operated.

Sahagen ultimately convinced Quinn that Castiel must be ousted from leadership in order for the LLC to prosper. As a result, Quinn (Castiel's nominee) covertly "defected" to Sahagen's camp, and he and Sahagen decided to wrest control of the LLC from Castiel. Many LLC employees and even some of Castiel's lieutenants testified that they believed it to be in the LLC's best interest to take control from Castiel.

On April 14, 2000, without notice to Castiel, Quinn and Sahagen acted by written consent to merge the LLC under Delaware law into VGS, Inc. ("VGS"), a Delaware corporation. Accordingly, the LLC ceased to exist, its assets and liabilities passed to VGS, and VGS became the LLC's legal successor-in-interest. VGS's Board of Directors is comprised of Sahagen, Quinn, and Neel Howard. Of course, the incorporators did not name Castiel to VGS's Board.

On the day of the merger, Sahagen executed a promissory note to VGS in the amount of $10 million plus interest. In return, he received two million shares of VGS Series A Preferred Stock. VGS also issued 1,269,200 shares of common stock to Holdings, 230,800 shares of common stock to Ellipso, and 500,000 shares of common stock to Sahagen Satellite. Once one does the math, it is apparent that Holdings and Ellipso went from having a 75% controlling combined ownership interest in the LLC to having only a 37.5% interest in VGS. On the other hand, Sahagen and Sahagen Satellite went from owning 25% of the LLC to owning 62.5% of VGS.

There can be no doubt why Sahagen and Quinn, acting as a majority of the LLC's board of managers did not notify Castiel of the merger plan. Notice to Castiel would have immediately resulted in Quinn's removal from the board and a newly constituted majority which would thwart the effort to strip Castiel of control. Had he known in advance, Castiel surely would have attempted to replace Quinn with someone loyal to Castiel who would agree with his views. Clandestine machinations were, therefore, essential to the success of Quinn and Sahagen's plan.

II. Analysis

A. The Board of Managers did have authority to act by majority vote.

The LLC Agreement does not expressly state whether the Board of Managers must act unanimously or by majority vote. Sahagen and Quinn contend that because a number of provisions would be rendered meaningless if a unanimous vote was required, a majority vote is implied. Castiel, however, maintains that a unanimous vote must be implied when the majority owner has blocking power.

Section 8.01(b)(i) of the LLC Agreement states that, "the Board of Managers shall initially be composed of three (3) Managers." Sahagen Satellite has the right to designate one member of the initial board, and if the Board of Managers increased in number, Sahagen Satellite could "designate a number of representatives on the Board of Managers that is less than Sahagen's then current Percentage Interest." If unanimity were required, the number of managers would be irrelevant—Sahagen, and his minority interest, would have veto power in any event. The existence of language in the LLC Agreement discussing expansion of the Board is therefore quite telling.

Also persuasive is the fact that Section 8.01(c) of the LLC Agreement, entitled "Matters Requiring Consent of Sahagen," provides that Sahagen's approval is needed for a merger, consolidation, or reorganization of the LLC. If a unanimity requirement indeed existed, there would have been no need to expressly list matters on which Sahagen's minority interest had veto power.

Section 12.01(a)(i) of the LLC Agreement also supports Sahagen's argument. This section provides that the LLC may be dissolved by written consent by either the Board of Managers or by Members holding two-thirds of the Common Units. The effect of this Section is to allow any combination of Holdings and Sahagen Satellite, or Holdings and Ellipso, as Members, to dissolve the LLC. It seems unlikely that the Members designed the LLC Agreement to permit Members holding two-thirds of the Common Units to dissolve the LLC but denied their appointed Managers the power to reach the same result unless the minority manager agreed.

Castiel takes the position that while the Members can act by majority vote, the Board of Managers can act only by unanimous vote. He maintains that if the Board fails to agree unanimously on an issue the issue should be put to an LLC Members' vote with the majority controlling. The practical effect of Castiel's interpretation would be that whenever Castiel and Sahagen disagreed, Castiel would prevail because the issue would be submitted to the Members where Castiel's controlling interest would carry the vote. If that were the case, both Sahagen's Board position and Quinn's Board position would be superfluous. I am confident that the parties never intended that result, or if they had so intended, that they would have included plain and simple language in the agreement spelling it out clearly.

B. By failing to give notice of their proposed action, Sahagen and Quinn failed to discharge their duty of Loyalty to Castiel in good faith

Section 18-404(d) of the LLC Act states in pertinent part:

> Unless otherwise provided in a limited liability company agreement, on any matter that is to be voted on by managers, the managers may take such action without a meeting, without prior notice and without a vote if a consent or consents in writing, setting forth the action so taken, shall be signed by the managers having not less than the minimum number of votes that would be necessary to authorize such action at a meeting (emphasis added).

Therefore, the LLC Act, read literally, does not require notice to Castiel before Sahagen and Quinn could act by written consent. The LLC Agreement does not purport to modify the statute in this regard.

Those observations can not complete the analysis of Sahagen and Quinn's actions, however. Sahagen and Quinn knew what would happen if they notified Castiel of their intention to act by written consent to merge the LLC into VGS, Inc. Castiel would have attempted to remove Quinn, and block the planned action. Regardless of his motivation in doing so, removal of Quinn in that circumstance would have been within Castiel's rights as the LLC's controlling owner under the Agreement.

Section 18-404(d) has yet to be interpreted by this Court or the Supreme Court. Nonetheless, it seems clear that the purpose of permitting action by written consent without notice is to enable LLC managers to take quick, efficient action in situations where a minority of managers could not block or adversely affect the course set by the majority even if they were notified of the proposed action and objected to it. The General Assembly never intended, I am quite confident, to enable two managers to deprive, clandestinely and surreptitiously, a third manager representing the majority interest in the LLC of an opportunity to protect that interest by taking an action that the third manager's member would surely have opposed if he had knowledge of it. My reading of Section 18-404(d) is grounded in a classic maxim of equity—"Equity looks to the intent rather than to the form." In this hopefully unique situation, this application of the maxim requires construction of the statute to allow action without notice only by a constant or fixed majority. It can not apply to an illusory, will-of-the wisp majority which would implode should notice be given. Nothing in the statute suggests that this court of equity should blind its eyes to a shallow, too clever by half, manipulative attempt to restructure an enterprise through an action taken by a "majority" that existed only so long as it could act in secrecy.

Sahagen and Quinn each owed a duty of loyalty to the LLC, its investors and Castiel, their fellow manager. Castiel or his entities owned a majority interest in the LLC and he sat as a member of the board representing entities and interests empowered by the Agreement to control the majority membership of the board. The majority investor protected his equity interest in the LLC through the mechanism of appointment to the board rather than by the statutorily sanctioned mechanism of approval by members owning a majority of the LLC's equity interests. It may seem somewhat incongruous, but this Agreement allows the action to merge, dissolve or change to corporate status to be taken by a simple majority vote of the board of managers rather than rely upon the default position of the statute which requires a majority vote of the equity interest. Instead the drafters made the critical assumption, known to all the players here, that the holder of the majority equity interest has the right to appoint and remove two managers, ostensibly guaranteeing control over a three member board. When Sahagen and Quinn, fully recognizing that this was Castiel's protection against actions adverse to his majority interest, acted in secret, without notice, they failed to discharge their duty of loyalty to him in good faith. They owed Castiel a duty to give him prior notice even if he would have interfered with a plan that they conscientiously believed to be in the best interest of the LLC. [Court's footnote: I make no ruling here as to whether I believe the merger and the resulting recapitalization of the LLC was in the LLC's best interests, nor do I rule here regarding the wisdom of Castiel's actions had he in fact been able to remove Quinn before the merger.] Instead, they launched a preemptive strike that furtively converted Castiel's controlling interest in the LLC to a minority interest in VGS without affording Castiel a level playing field on which to defend his interest. "[Another] traditional maxim of equity holds that equity regards and treats that as done which in good conscience ought to be done." In good conscience, under these circumstances, Sahagen and Quinn should have given Castiel prior notice.

Many hours were spent at trial focusing on contentions that Castiel has proved to be an ineffective leader in whom employees and investors have lost confidence. I listened to testimony regarding delayed FCC licensing, a suggested new management team for the LLC, and the alleged unlocked value of the LLC. A substantial record exists fully flushing out the rancorous relationships of the members and their wildly disparate views on the existing state of affairs as well as the LLC's prospects for the future. But the issue of who is best suited to run the LLC should not be resolved here but in board meetings where all managers are present and all members appropriately represented, and/or in future litigation, if it unfortunately becomes necessary.

Likewise, the parties spent much time and effort arguing over the standard to be applied to the actions taken by Sahagen and Quinn. Specifically, the parties debated whether the standard should be entire fairness or the business judgment rule. It should be clear that the actions of Sahagen and Quinn, in their capacity as managers constituted a breach of their duty of loyalty and that those actions do not, therefore, entitle them to the benefit or protection of the business judgment rule. They intentionally used a flawed process to merge the LLC into VGS, Inc., in an attempt to prevent the member with majority equity interest in the LLC from protecting his interests in the manner contemplated by the very LLC Agreement under which they purported to act. Analysis beyond a look at the process is clearly unnecessary. Perhaps, had notice been given and an attempt then made to block Castiel's anticipated action to replace Quinn, the allegedly disinterested and independent member that Castiel himself had appointed, the analysis might be different. However, this, as all cases must be reviewed as it is presented, not as it might have been.

III. Conclusion

For the reasons stated above, I find that a majority vote of the LLC's Board of Managers could properly effect a merger. But, I also find that Sahagen and Quinn failed to discharge their duty of loyalty to Castiel in good faith by failing to give him advance notice of their merger plans under the unique circumstances of this case and the structure of this LLC Agreement. Accordingly, I declare that the acts taken to merge the LLC into VGS, Inc. to be invalid and the merger is ordered rescinded. An order consistent with this opinion, resolving the current claims of the parties is attached.

Racing Inv. Fund 2000, LLC v. Clay Ward Agency, Inc., 320 S.W.3d 654 (Ky. 2010). An LLC's operating agreement included a provision obliging the members "to contribute to the capital of the Company, on a prorata basis in accordance with their respective Percentage Interests, such amounts as may be reasonably deemed advisable by the Manager from time to time in order to pay operating, administrative, or other business expenses of the Company which have been incurred, or which the Manager reasonably anticipates will be incurred, by the Company."

A plaintiff against the insolvent LLC argued that this provision made individual members liable for the LLC's debts. Held, it did not: The provision was "designed to assure members will contribute additional capital, as deemed necessary by the Manager, to advance [the LLC's] racing venture. While [the plaintiff's] insurance premiums were indeed a legitimate business expense for which the Manager could have made a capital call, that premise alone does not lead a fortiori to the relief ordered by the trial court.

Simply put, [the LLC agreement has] a not-uncommon, on-going capital infusion provision, not a debt-collection mechanism by which a court can order a capital call and, by doing so, impose personal liability on the LLC's members for the entity's outstanding debt. [The plaintiff] insists that its quest to be paid is not about individual member liability, but there is no other way to construe what occurs when a court orders a capital call be made to pay for a particular LLC debt. From any viewpoint, the shield of limited liability has been lifted and the LLC's members have been held individually liable for its debt."

Section 3: Dissolution

Revised Uniform Limited Liability Company Act (2006) § 701: Events Causing Dissolution

(a) A limited liability company is dissolved, and its activities must be wound up, upon the occurrence of any of the following:

(1) an event or circumstance that the operating agreement states causes dissolution;

(2) the consent of all the members;

(3) the passage of 90 consecutive days during which the company has no members;

(4) on application by a member, the entry by [appropriate court] of an order dissolving the company on the grounds that:

(A) the conduct of all or substantially all of the company's activities is unlawful; or

(B) it is not reasonably practicable to carry on the company's activities in conformity with the certificate of organization and the operating agreement; or

(5) on application by a member, the entry by [appropriate court] of an order dissolving the company on the grounds that the managers or those members in control of the company:

(A) have acted, are acting, or will act in a manner that is illegal or fraudulent; or

(B) have acted or are acting in a manner that is oppressive and was, is, or will be directly harmful to the applicant.

(b) In a proceeding brought under subsection (a)(5), the court may order a remedy other than dissolution.

Comment

Subsection(a)(4)—The standard stated here is conventional, and this subsection (a)(4) is non-waivable. Section 110(c)(7).

Subsection (a)(5)—ULLCA § 801(4)(v)[2] contains a comparable provision, although that provision also gives standing to dissociated members. Even in non-ULLCA states, courts have begun to apply close corporation "oppression" doctrine to LLCs.

2. The comment here refers to a provision in the original ULLCA that permits dissolution where "the managers or members in control of the company have acted, are acting, or will act in a manner that is illegal, oppressive, fraudulent, or unfairly prejudicial to the petitioner." [—ed.]

This provision's reference to "those members in control of the company" implies that such members have a duty to avoid acting oppressively toward fellow members.

Subsection (a)(5) is non-waivable. See Section 110(c)(7).

Subsection (b)—In the close corporation context, many courts have reached this position without express statutory authority, most often with regard to court-ordered buyouts of oppressed shareholders. This subsection saves courts and litigants the trouble of re-inventing that wheel in the LLC context. However, unlike, subsection (a)(4) and (5), subsection (b) can be overridden by the operating agreement. Thus, the members may agree to a restrict or eliminate a court's power to craft a lesser remedy, even to the extent of confining the court (and themselves) to the all-or-nothing remedy of dissolution.

3.1: Dissolution for Deadlock

Fisk Ventures, LLC v. Segal 2009

Del. Ch. LEXIS 7 (Del. Ch. Jan. 13, 2009), *aff'd* 2 A.3d 75 (Del. 2010), *further proceedings at* 2009 Del. Ch. LEXIS 86.

CHANDLER, C.

This case presents the narrow question of whether it is "reasonably practicable," under 6 Del. C. § 18-802, for a Delaware limited liability company to continue to operate. When such a company has no office, no employees, no operating revenue, no prospects of equity or debt infusion, and when the company's Board has a long history of deadlock as a result of its governance structure, more than ample reason and sufficient evidence exists to order dissolution. Accordingly, I will grant petitioner's motion for judgment on the pleadings and order that dissolution of the limited liability company occur as contemplated in the company's charter.

I. BACKGROUND

Genitrix, LLC ("Genitrix" or the "Company"), originally a Maryland limited liability company, was formed by Dr. Andrew Segal in 1996 to commercialize his biotechnology concepts of directing the human immune system to attack cancer and infectious diseases. Although initially promising, the Company's financial condition has deteriorated to the point where currently Genitrix is in critical financial straits.

The LLC Agreement provides that Genitrix's business purpose is:

> (a) to engage in research and development, and/or generate through the manufacture and sale and licensing of biomedical technology, including that related to the use of opsonin molecules, in combination with other organic molecules, to produce immunizing and therapeutic drugs for human and animal diseases, and (b) to engage in all action necessary, convenient or incidental to the foregoing. Without the express approval of the Board, the Company shall not engage in any other business activity.

As this Court stated in a previous opinion, "[t]he Company has no office, no capital funds, no grant funds, and generates no revenue." Genitrix, as it currently stands, is unable to operate in furtherance of its business purposes.

In forming Genitrix, Segal obtained a patent rights license from the Whitehead Institute of Biomedical Research ("Whitehead") concerning the Company's core technology. In 1997, Genitrix entered into a Patent License Agreement (the "Whitehead Agreement") with Whitehead and Massachusetts Institute of Technology.

The Whitehead Agreement was entered into among Genitrix, Whitehead, and M.I.T. It provides for the exclusive license to Genitrix of certain patent rights, owned by Whitehead. Genitrix paid for the prosecution and issuance of the patents owned by Whitehead. As set forth in Article 2 of the Whitehead Agreement, the license gives Genitrix the worldwide right to develop, sell and commercialize Licensed Products and Licensed Services derived from the patent rights. Article 11 of the Whitehead Agreement provides that the license is not assignable, except in limited circumstances including "in connection with the sale or transfer of all or substantially all of Genitrix's equity and assets."

In September 1997, H. Fisk Johnson, head of Fisk Ventures, LLC, became an investor in Genitrix. As a condition to Johnson's investment, Genitrix was redomiciled in Delaware. In the initial investment round, Johnson contributed $842,000 in cash in exchange for Class B interests in Genitrix. Investments by other Class C investors brought the total cash investment in Genitrix to $1.1 million. Segal received a $500,000 Class A investment credit in exchange for his contribution of patent rights that he obtained from Whitehead. To continue operating, Genitrix has relied on equity and debt investments and grants from institutions to provide capital. In recent years, both Segal and Fisk Ventures have paid for certain Company expenses.

As a Class B member of Genitrix, Fisk Ventures negotiated a "Put Right" with respect to the Class B membership interests, found in § 11.5 of the LLC Agreement. Section 11.5(a) allows "the holders of the Class B Interests ... to sell any or all of such Member's Class B Interests to the Company on such terms as are set forth herein," at any time after "the fourth anniversary of the date of this Agreement." After exercising the Put Right, the LLC Agreement requires an adjustment of the book value of all Company assets based upon an independent valuation of Genitrix conducted by "a nationally recognized, reputable investment banker."

Under § 11.5(c), the put price for the Class B interests is deemed to "equal the amount of such Class B Interest holder's Capital Account balance after such balance has been adjusted as required by Section 11.5(b)." If that put price "exceeds 50% of the tangible assets of the Company," Genitrix must issue notes to the pertinent Class B holders that are payable one-third within thirty days of receipt of the valuation; one-third on the first anniversary of the exercise date of the Put Right; and the balance on the second anniversary of such exercise. In the event of a default by the Company, the Class B Interest holders may replace one of Segal's representatives with an additional Class B representative.

Fisk Ventures has been free to exercise the Put Right ever since September 11, 2001—the fourth anniversary date of the LLC Agreement. The Put Right permits Fisk Ventures, at their sole discretion, to exit their investment in Genitrix—for fair market value—for any reason or for no reason.

Soon after formation, a four-person Board was organized to manage the affairs of Genitrix, with Segal and Johnson each appointing two representatives. The Genitrix Board now consists of five representatives. Under § 7.5 of the LLC Agreement, the Genitrix Board can only act pursuant to approval of 75% of its members, whether by vote or by written consent.

Segal was originally appointed as both President and Chief Executive Officer of Genitrix. Segal ceased to be CEO of the Company in March 2006, but continues to serve as President.

Only a handful of Board meetings have been held over the entire course of Genitrix's existence. Segal maintains that § 7.5 of the LLC Agreement contemplates that Genitrix's Board can operate by written consent without a meeting, provided that the requisite 75% of the representatives approve such action. Segal and his appointees declined to attend Board meetings from about September 2006 until July 2008, requesting instead that the Board conduct business by e-mail. Segal and the Class B representatives held a two-hour board meeting by telephone on August 5, 2008.

II. ANALYSIS

1. Standard of Review

Judgment on the pleadings is appropriate when accepting as true the nonmoving party's well pleaded facts, "'there is no material fact in dispute and the moving party is entitled to judgment under the law.'" The Court will draw all reasonable inferences in favor of the nonmoving party and "[t]he nonmoving party must therefore be accorded the same benefits as a plaintiff defending a motion under [Court of Chancery] Rule 12(b)(6)."

2. Freedom of Contract and Limited Liability Companies

"Limited Liability Companies are creatures of contract, 'designed to afford the maximum amount of freedom of contract, private ordering and flexibility to the parties involved.'" Delaware's LLC Act thus allows LLC members to "'arrange a manager/investor governance relationship;' the LLC Act provides defaults that can be modified by contract" as deemed appropriate by the LLC's managing members. The LLC Act explicitly states that "[i]t is the policy of this chapter to give the maximum effect to the principle of freedom of contract and to the enforceability of limited liability company agreements."

Genitrix's LLC Agreement provides that the Company "shall be dissolved and its affairs wound up only on the first to occur of the following: (a) the written consent of Members holding at least 75% of the Membership Interests, voting as provided in § 3.5; and (b) the entry of a decree of judicial dissolution of the Company under Section 18-802 of the Act." Segal, as the controlling member of Genitrix's Class A membership interest, opposes dissolution. Since the managing members are hopelessly deadlocked to the extent that 75% of the membership interest in Genitrix will not be voted in favor of dissolution, the only other opportunity for members seeking dissolution would be through a decree of judicial dissolution in accordance with the LLC agreement.

3. Standard for Dissolution of a Limited Liability Company

The Court of Chancery may decree judicial dissolution of a Delaware limited liability company "whenever it is not reasonably practicable to carry on the business in conformity with a limited liability company agreement." Section 18-802 has the "obvious purpose of providing an avenue of relief when an LLC cannot continue to function in accordance with its chartering agreement."

In interpreting § 18-802, this Court has by analogy often looked to the dissolution statute for limited partnerships, 6 Del. C. § 17-802. In so doing, the Court has found that "the test of § 17-802 is whether it is 'reasonably practicable' to carry on the business of a limited partnership, and not whether it is impossible." To decide whether to dissolve a partnership pursuant to § 17-802, the courts have historically looked to the "business of the partnership and the general partner's ability to achieve that purpose in conformity with the partnership agreement." For example, in PC Tower, this Court found that the relevant partnership agreement stated that the partnership's business purpose was to acquire land in the hope of making a future profit. The Court held that the partnership was unable to carry on its business in a reasonably practicable manner because there was (1) a depressed real estate market, (2) property debt was in excess of value, and (3) uncontradicted evidence of a heavily leveraged property where the rent payments were supposed to be forthcoming from a declared insolvent entity. Thus, because it was no longer reasonably practicable to use the partnership's property "for profit and for an investment," the Court ordered dissolution of the partnership.

Applying the same logic in the limited liability company context, there is no need to show that the purpose of the limited liability company has been "completely frustrated." The standard is whether it is reasonably practicable for Genitrix to continue to operate its business in conformity with its LLC Agreement.

The text of § 18-802 does not specify what a court must consider in evaluating the "reasonably practicable" standard, but several convincing factual circumstances have pervaded the case law: (1) the members' vote is deadlocked at the Board level; (2) the operating agreement gives no means of navigating around the deadlock; and (3) due to the financial condition of the company, there is effectively no business to operate.

These factual circumstances are not individually dispositive; nor must they all exist for a court to find it no longer reasonably practicable for a business to continue operating. In fact, the Court in Haley v. Talcott found that although the limited liability company was "technically functioning" and "financially stable," meaning that it received rent checks and paid a mortgage, it should be dissolved because the company's activity was "purely a residual, inertial status quo that just happens to exclusively benefit one of the 50% members." If a board deadlock prevents the limited liability company from operating or from furthering its stated business purpose, it is not reasonably practicable for the company to carry on its business.

4. Judicial Dissolution of a Limited Liability Company

More than sufficient undisputed evidence exists in this case to demonstrate the futility of Genitrix's deadlocked board, the LLC Agreement's failure to prescribe a solution to a potentially deadlocked board, and Genitrix's dire financial straits. For these reasons, and as explained further below, I conclude that it is not reasonably practicable to carry on the business operations of Genitrix in conformity with the LLC Agreement.

a. Genitrix's Board is Deadlocked

Under the LLC Agreement, Genitrix's Board has the exclusive power to manage the business and affairs of the company. The Board is unable to act unless both the Class B and the Class A shareholders agree on a course of action. The LLC Agreement imposes a 75% voting requirement for business issues: "Approval of at least 75% of the Representatives shall be required to authorize any of the actions ... specified in this Agreement as requiring the authorization of the Board." The LLC Agreement requires the cooperation of the Board's managing members in order to accomplish or overcome any issue facing Genitrix. This type of charter provision, unless a "tie-breaking" clause exists, is almost always a recipe for disaster. In this case, unfortunately, the parties are behaving true to form.

Although Genitrix's Board is charged to run the Company, the Board is unable to act and is hopelessly deadlocked. Fisk Ventures and Segal have a long history of disagreement and discord over a wide range of issues concerning the direction and operation of

Genitrix. On one of the most important issues facing the Company, the raising and use of operating capital, the Board is unable to negotiate acceptable terms to all involved parties. Additionally, the Board has even been considerably deadlocked over whether to have Board meetings. The parties have a history of discord and disagreement on almost every issue facing the Company. There exists almost a five-year track record of perpetual deadlock. Indeed, concerning the current issue, dissolution, the Board is equally deadlocked.

Given the Board's history of discord and disagreement, I do not believe that these parties will ever be able to harmoniously resolve their differences. Consequently, I conclude that Genitrix's Board is deadlocked and unable to resolve any issue, including the current issue of dissolution, facing Genitrix.

b. Navigating the Deadlock in The LLC Agreement

In examining the four corners of Genitrix's LLC Agreement I conclude that no provision exists that would allow the Board to circumvent the deadlocked stalemate. The document was negotiated by sophisticated parties engaged in an arm's length negotiation. The product of that negotiation, the LLC Agreement, was carefully drafted in such a way that solved one problem but lead directly to the deadlock now gripping the Company. The provision requiring a 75% vote for Board action was agreed upon by the parties to specifically prohibit board domination by one party over another. The provision has certainly accomplished its intended purpose. Unfortunately, it has also led to a stalemate, and the LLC Agreement on its face provides no means of remedying the situation.

Segal argues that since Fisk Ventures owns a Put Right, provided for in § 11.5 of the LLC Agreement, which allows Fisk Ventures to exit its investment by forcing Genitrix to buy out Fisk Ventures for the fair value of its investment, the LLC Agreement contains a provision that will resolve the Board's deadlock. Segal points to Fisk Ventures' Put Right as a proper "exit mechanism" and as an alternative to judicial dissolution. Under § 11.5, the amount to be paid to the Class B investors is to be determined by an independent valuation. If the price exceeds 50% of the value of Genitrix's tangible assets, they will gain creditor status, giving their holder greater security and a higher priority than they currently have as purely equity members.

Segal ignores the fact, however, that the Put Right contemplated in the LLC Agreement grants its owner an option, to be freely exercised at the will and pleasure of its holder. Nowhere in § 11.5 or in the entire LLC Agreement does the Company have the right to force a buyout if it considers one of its members belligerent or uncooperative. Fisk Ventures holds the option, not Genitrix. Fisk Ventures negotiated for and obtained the Put Right as consideration for its original investment in Genitrix and it would be inequitable for this Court to force a party to exercise its option when that party deems it in its best interests not to do so. I am not permitted to second guess a party's business decision in choosing whether or not to exercise its previously negotiated option rights.

c. Not Reasonably Practicable to Carry on the Business

As noted previously, Genitrix is in dire financial condition. "The Company has no office, no capital funds, no grant funds, and generates no revenue." Genitrix has survived up to this point on equity and debt investments, and on grants from institutions such as the National Institute of Health. The Company does not have any further source of funding, and no realistic expectation of additional grants or infusions of capital.

Segal argues that one of the major sources of Board contention and deadlock has been Fisk Ventures' unwillingness to allow further capital infusion without significant anti-dilution protections. For this reason alone, Segal argues, Genitrix has been unable to raise additional funds. Segal further contends that if Fisk Ventures is forced to exercise its Put Right then Genitrix will be free to raise funds to effect the buy-back. But again, Segal fails to realize that Fisk Ventures has the right to protect itself against what it perceives as Company actions that would diminish the value of its stake in Genitrix. This Court will not substitute its business judgment for that of Fisk Ventures simply because Segal believes that will be in his best interest.

Additionally, Segal believes that dissolution should be denied because it would destroy any value the Company has preserved in its Whitehead Patent License. As stated above, the Whitehead Agreement is the legal vehicle for the grant of significant patent rights now licensed to Genitrix. Under Article 11 of the Whitehead Agreement, the license is not assignable except "in connection with the sale or transfer of all or substantially all of Genitrix's equity and assets." Segal argues that the Company's members will then lose all of the considerable value of that asset, and Genitrix's own patents, which are subordinate to Whitehead's patent, because a purchaser will not be free to operate without a license from Whitehead. This argument is unconvincing.

First, it appears equally likely that a purchaser could enter into a separate licensing agreement with Whitehead for use of its patent. Alternatively, the terms of the Whitehead Agreement could be renegotiated or altered in the sale negotiations. Second, it is ultimately futile to enter into an operating agreement that on its face is doomed to conflict and deadlock, to become mired in a deadlock for years on issues of financing and operations, and then to demand that the Court force the opposing party in the deadlock to capitulate in order to preserve a fleeting hope that additional financing might become available to help preserve some future potential value in a licensing agreement. That argument leads to the same deadlock that now exists on every issue of this company. The value of the Whitehead Agreement is hotly contested and I am unconvinced that any potential value it theoretically might have could not be accessed through a fair and proper sale of the asset. One thing is certain, however. These parties will never be able to reach agreement on how to dispose of this asset, whatever its potential value.

Finally, Segal's argument that Fisk Ventures cannot seek judicial dissolution because it comes to the Court with unclean hands is without merit. The LLC Agreement is a negotiated contract and Fisk Ventures has the right to attempt to maximize its position in accordance with the LLC Agreement's terms. If Fisk Ventures chooses to exercise its leverage under the LLC Agreement to benefit itself, it is perfectly within its right to do so. Additionally, Segal offers no facts to support his contentions that Fisk Ventures seeks dissolution simply to buy Genitrix's assets at fire sale prices. A party cannot simply allege a conclusory inequitable action as a last ditch effort to persuade the Court to deny a motion for judgment on the pleadings and to allow that party an opportunity to take discovery.

Ultimately, even if the financial progress of Genitrix is impeded by the deadlock in the boardroom, if that deadlock cannot be remedied through a legal mechanism set forth within the four corners of the operating agreement, dissolution becomes the only remedy available as a matter of law. The Court is in no position to redraft the LLC Agreement for these sophisticated and well-represented parties.

III. CONCLUSION

This case involves a long-lived corporate dispute that resulted in devastating deadlock to Genitrix's Board and the loss of significant value to all involved. Genitrix's Board is hopelessly deadlocked, and the LLC Agreement fails to anticipate that risk by prescribing a solution to the Board conflict. Further, Genitrix has no office, no operating revenue, and no prospects of equity or debt infusion. Because Genitrix's dire financial straits leave the Company with no reasonably practical means to operate its business, I conclude judicial dissolution in accordance with the LLC Agreement is the best and only option for these parties. For the foregoing reasons, I grant the motion seeking judgment in favor of petitioner on the petition for dissolution.

Matter of 1545 Ocean Ave., LLC

893 N.Y.S.2d 590 (N.Y. App. Div. 2010)

AUSTIN, J.

On this appeal, we are asked to determine whether the Supreme Court properly granted the petition of Crown Royal Ventures, LLC (hereinafter Crown Royal), to dissolve 1545 Ocean Avenue, LLC (hereinafter 1545 LLC). For the following reasons, we answer in the negative and reverse the order of the Supreme Court.

I

1545 LLC was formed in November 2006 when its articles of organization were filed with the Department of State. On November 15, 2006 two membership certificates for 50 units each were issued respectively to Crown Royal and the appellant, Ocean Suffolk Properties, LLC (hereinafter Ocean Suffolk).

On the same date that the membership certificates were issued, an operating agreement was executed by Ocean Suffolk and Crown Royal. The operating agreement provided for two managers: Walter T. Van Houten (hereinafter Van Houten), who was a member of Ocean Suffolk, and John J. King, who was a member of Crown Royal. Each member of 1545 LLC contributed 50% of the capital which was used to purchase premises known as 1545 Ocean Avenue in Bohemia (hereinafter the property) on January 5, 2007. 1545 LLC was formed to purchase the property, rehabilitate an existing building, and build a second building for commercial rental (hereinafter buildings A and B, respectively).

It was agreed by Van Houten and King that they would solicit bids from third parties to perform the necessary demolition and construction work to complete the project. Van Houten, who owns his own construction company, Van Houten Construction (hereinafter VHC), was permitted to submit bids for the project, subject to the approval of the managers.

Ocean Suffolk alleges that when there were no bona fide bidders, the managers agreed to allow VHC to perform the work, while Crown Royal maintains that VHC began demolition and reconstruction on building A without King's consent. In rehabilitating the existing building, Van Houten claims that he discovered and remediated various structural flaws with the claimed knowledge and approval of King or another member of Crown Royal.

King wanted architect Gary Bruno to review the blueprints upon which VHC began demolition since it had been started without the necessary building permits. In addition, King claimed that VHC did not have the proper equipment to efficiently do the excavation and demolition work, causing the billing to be greater than necessary. VHC billed 1545 LLC the sum of $97,322.27 for this work. King claims that he agreed 1545 LLC would pay VHC's invoice on the condition that it would no longer unilaterally do work on the site. Notwithstanding King's demand, VHC continued working on the site. Despite his earlier protests, King did nothing to stop it.

Thereafter, Bruno applied to the Town of Islip for the necessary building permits. The Suffolk County Department of Health required an environmental review whereby a so-called "hot spot" was detected by an environmental engineering firm which proposed to remediate it for $6,500. F&E, the company recommended by Crown Royal to do the remediation work, estimated that the cost for the environmental remediation work would be about $6,675. King claims that Van Houten objected to F&E and had another firm do a separate evaluation without King's approval, while Van Houten asserts that although F&E eventually charged $8,229.63 for its work, payment to F&E by 1545 LLC was made with his approval. Moreover, Van Houten claimed that the separate evaluation was paid for by Ocean Suffolk out of its own account.

Following this incident, King contended that tensions between King and Van Houten escalated. King asserted that things could not continue as they were or else the project would not be finished in an economical or timely manner. King claimed that Van Houten refused to meet on a regular basis; that he proclaimed himself to be a "cowboy"; and that Van Houten stated he would "just get it done." Nevertheless, King acknowledged that the construction work undertaken by VHC was "awesome."

By April 2007, King announced that he wanted to withdraw his investment from 1545 LLC. He proposed to have all vendors so notified telling them that Van Houten was taking over the management of 1545 LLC. As a result, Van Houten viewed King as having resigned as a manager of 1545 LLC.

Ultimately, King sought to have Ocean Suffolk buy out Crown Royal's membership in 1545 LLC or, alternatively, to have Crown Royal buy out Ocean Suffolk. In the interim, King had his attorney send a "stop work" request to Van Houten.

There ensued discussions regarding competing proposals for the buyout of the interest of each member by the other. No satisfactory resolution was realized. Nevertheless, despite disagreement among the members during this difficult period, VHC continued to work unilaterally on the site so that the project was within weeks of completion when this proceeding was commenced whereby further work by Van Houten was enjoined.

II

Article 4.1 of the operating agreement provides that "[a]t any time when there is more than one Manager, any one Manager may take any action permitted under the Agreement, unless the approval of more than one of the Managers is expressly required pursuant to the [operating agreement] or the [Limited Liability Company Law]."

Article 4.12 of the operating agreement entitled, "Regular Meetings," does not require meetings of the managers with any particular regularity. Meetings may be called without notice as the managers may "from time to time determine."

Article 7.4 of the operating agreement provides, "any matter not specifically covered by a provision of the [operating agreement], including without limitation, dissolution of the Company, shall be governed by the applicable provisions of the Limited Liability Company Law." Accordingly, dissolution of 1545 LLC is governed by Limited Liability Company Law article VII.

III

This proceeding was commenced by order to show cause and verified petition seeking the dissolution of 1545 LLC and related relief. The sole ground for dissolution cited by Crown Royal is deadlock between the managing members arising from Van Houten's alleged violations of various provisions of article 4 of the operating agreement. There was no allegation of fraud or frustration of the purpose of 1545 LLC on the part of Ocean Suffolk, Van Houten, and VHC.

Answering the petition, Van Houten, on behalf of his company and Ocean Suffolk, denied the allegations in the petition and set forth their claim that they did business in accordance with the operating agreement. Van Houten alleged that the only significant dissension among the members arose from the inability of the parties to agree on a buyout of each other's interest in 1545 LLC. Significantly, Van Houten alleged, without dispute, that the renovation of building A was within three to four weeks of completion when this proceeding was commenced.

Van Houten also contended that, as a result of King's resignation as a managing member, Crown Royal could not reasonably claim that a deadlock existed. Moreover, there is no evidence that King complied with article 4.8 of the operating agreement by submitting a written resignation. Nevertheless, by May 10, 2007, in anticipation of a buyout of the Crown Royal interest in the venture, the parties were operating as if Van Houten was the sole managing member of 1545 LLC. Indeed, throughout the negotiations for the buyout, the renovation work on building A continued.

IV

[New York] Limited Liability Company Law § 702 provides for judicial dissolution as follows:

> "On application by or for a member, the supreme court in the judicial district in which the office of the limited liability company is located may decree dissolution of a limited liability company whenever it is not reasonably practicable to carry on the business in conformity with the articles of organization or operating agreement" (emphasis added).

The Limited Liability Company Law came into being in 1994. Many of its provisions were amended in 1999 (L 1999, ch 420) to track changes in federal tax code treatment of such entities. Such amendments included changes in how the withdrawal of a member was to be treated (Limited Liability Company Law § 606) and events of dissolution which relate back to the operating agreement (Limited Liability Company Law § 701).

Although various provisions of the Limited Liability Company Law were amended, Limited Liability Company Law § 702 was neither modified nor amended in 1999. In declining to amend Limited Liability Company Law § 702, the Legislature can only have intended the dissolution standard therein provided to remain the sole basis for judicial dissolution of a limited liability company. Phrased differently, since the Legislature, in determining the criteria for dissolution of various business entities in New York, did not cross-reference such grounds from one type of entity to another, it would be inappropriate for this Court to import dissolution grounds from the Business Corporation Law or Partnership Law to the Limited Liability Company Law.

Despite the standard for dissolution enunciated in Limited Liability Company Law § 702, there is no definition of "not reasonably practicable" in the context of the dissolution of a limited liability company. Most New York decisions involving limited liability company dissolution issues have avoided discussion of this standard altogether.

Such standard, however, is not to be confused with the standard for the judicial dissolution of corporations or partnerships.... Limited liability companies ... fall within the ambit of neither the Business Corporation Law nor the Partnership Law.

The language of Limited Liability Company Law § 702 appears to be borrowed from Revised Partnership Law § 121-802 (dissolution is authorized when it is "not reasonably practicable to carry on the business in conformity with the partnership agreement") and Partnership Law § 63 (1) (d), in which dissolution is permitted, inter alia, where a partner's conduct of the partnership business makes it "not reasonably practicable to carry on the business in partnership with him." While there are no New York cases which interpret and apply this standard in the context of limited partnerships, it has been held to mean that, without more, disagreements between the partners with regard to the accounting of the entity are insufficient to warrant dissolution.

The Limited Liability Company Law also clarifies its scope by defining "limited liability company" as "an unincorporated organization of one or more persons having limited liability ... other than a partnership or trust" (Limited Liability Company Law § 102 [m]). Thus, the existence and character of these various entities are statutorily dissimilar as are the laws relating to their dissolution. Indeed, it was found to be improper to apply partnership dissolution standards to a cause for dissolution of a limited liability company.

In the absence of applying Business Corporation Law or Partnership Law dissolution factors to the analysis of what is "not reasonably practicable," the standard for dissolution under Limited Liability Company Law § 702 remains unresolved in New York. However, Limited Liability Company Limited Liability Company Law § 702 is clear that unlike the judicial dissolution standards in the Business Corporation Law and the Partnership Law, the court must first examine the limited liability company's operating agreement to determine, in light of the circumstances presented, whether it is or is not "reasonably practicable" for the limited liability company to continue to carry on its business in conformity with the operating agreement. Thus, the dissolution of a limited liability company under Limited Liability Company Law § 702 is initially a contract-based analysis.

Section 102 (u) of the Limited Liability Company Law defines "operating agreement" as "any written agreement of the members concerning the business of a limited liability company and the conduct of its affairs." Limited Liability Company Law § 417 (a) mandates that the operating agreement contain "provisions not inconsistent with law ... relating to (i) the business of the limited liability company, (ii) the conduct of its affairs and (iii) the rights, powers, preferences, limitations or responsibilities of its members [and] managers." Where an operating agreement, such as that of 1545 LLC, does not address certain topics, a limited liability company is bound by the default requirements set forth in the Limited Liability Company Law.

The operating agreement of 1545 LLC does not contain any specific provisions relating to dissolution. It provides only in article 1.5 that "[t]he Company's term is perpetual from the date of filing of the Articles of Organization ... unless the Company is dissolved."

Crown Royal argues for dissolution based on the parties' failure to hold regular meetings, failure to achieve quorums, and deadlock. The operating agreement, however, does not require regular meetings or quorums (see 1545 LLC operating agreement arts 4.2, 4.13). It only provides, in article 4.12, for meetings to be held at such times as the managers may "from time to time determine." The record demonstrates that the managers, King and Van Houten, communicated with each other on a regular basis without the formality of a noticed meeting which appears to conform with the spirit and letter of the operating agreement and the continued ability of 1545 LLC to function in that context.

King and Van Houten did not always agree as to the construction work to be performed on the 1545 LLC property. King claims that this forced the parties into a "deadlock." "Deadlock" is a basis, in and of itself, for judicial dissolution under Business Corporation Law § 1104. However, no such independent ground for dissolution is available under Limited Liability Company Law § 702. Instead, the court must consider the managers' disagreement in light of the operating agreement and the continued ability of 1545 LLC to function in that context.

It has been suggested that judicial dissolution is only available when the petitioning member can show that the limited liability company is unable to function as intended or that it is failing financially. Neither circumstance is demonstrated by the petitioner here. On the contrary, the purpose of 1545 LLC was feasibly and reasonably being met.

The "not reasonably practicable" standard for dissolution of limited liability companies and partnerships has been examined in other jurisdictions. In Delaware, the Chancery Court has observed, "Given its extreme nature, judicial dissolution is a limited remedy that this court grants sparingly" (Matter of Arrow Inv. Advisors, LLC, 2009 Del Ch LEXIS 66, *8, 2009 WL 1101682, *2 [2009]). In Virginia, dissolution is only available when the business cannot continue "in accord with its ... operating agreement" (Dunbar Group, LLC v Tignor, 267 Va 361, 367, 593 SE2d 216, 218 [2004] [serious differences of opinion among the members and the managers and the comingling of funds was insufficient to warrant a finding that it was not reasonably practicable for the company to continue]). However, where the economic purpose of the limited liability company is not met, dissolution is appropriate (see Kirksey v Grohmann, 2008 SD 76, 754 NW2d 825 [SD 2008]). Several courts take the view that the "not reasonably practicable" standard should be read as "capable of being done logically and in a reasonable, feasible manner" (Taki v Hami, 2001 Mich App LEXIS 777, *8, 2001 WL 672399, *6 [2001] [dissolution granted where the two partners had not spoken in years and there were allegations of violence and expulsion]), or as "one of reasonable practicability, not impossibility" (PC Tower Ctr., Inc. v Tower Ctr. Dev. Assoc. L.P., 1989 Del Ch LEXIS 72, *16, 1989 WL 63901, *6 [1989]).

Here, a single manager's unilateral action in furtherance of the business of 1545 LLC is specifically contemplated and permitted. Article 4.1 of the 1545 LLC operating agreement states: "At any time when there is more than one Manager, any one manager may take any action permitted under the Agreement, unless the approval of more than one of the Managers is expressly required pursuant to the Agreement or the Act" (emphasis added). This provision does not require that the managers conduct the business of 1545 LLC by majority vote. It empowers each manager to act autonomously and to unilaterally bind the entity in furtherance of the business of the entity. The 1545 LLC operating agreement, however, is silent as to the issue of manager conflicts. Thus, the only basis for dissolution can be if 1545 LLC cannot effectively operate under the operating agreement to meet and achieve the purpose for which it was created. In this case, that is the development of the property which purpose, despite the disagreements between the managing members, was being met. As the Delaware Chancery Court noted in Matter of Arrow Inv. Advisors, LLC,

> "The court will not dissolve an LLC merely because the LLC has not experienced a smooth glide to profitability or because events have not turned out exactly as the LLC's owners originally envisioned; such events are, of course, common in the risk-laden process of birthing new entities in the hope that they will become mature, profitable ventures. In part because a hair-trigger dissolution standard would ignore this market reality and thwart the expectations

> of reasonable investors that entities will not be judicially terminated simply because of some market turbulence, dissolution is reserved for situations in which the LLC's management has become so dysfunctional or its business purpose so thwarted that it is no longer practicable to operate the business, such as in the case of a voting deadlock or where the defined purpose of the entity has become impossible to fulfill ...
>
> Dissolution of an entity chartered for a broad business purpose remains possible upon a strong showing that a confluence of situationally specific adverse financial, market, product, managerial, or corporate governance circumstances make it nihilistic for the entity to continue" (2009 Del Ch LEXIS 66, *9-14, 2009 WL 1101682, *2-3 [2009]).

Here, the operating agreement avoids the possibility of "deadlock" by permitting each managing member to operate unilaterally in furtherance of 1545 LLC's purpose.

V

After careful examination of the various factors considered in applying the "not reasonably practicable" standard, we hold that for dissolution of a limited liability company pursuant to Limited Liability Company Law § 702, the petitioning member must establish, in the context of the terms of the operating agreement or articles of incorporation, that (1) the management of the entity is unable or unwilling to reasonably permit or promote the stated purpose of the entity to be realized or achieved, or (2) continuing the entity is financially unfeasible.

VI

Dissolution is a drastic remedy. Although the petitioner has failed to meet the standard for dissolution enunciated here, there are numerous other factors which support the conclusion that dissolution of 1545 LLC is inappropriate under the circumstances of this case.

First, the dispute between King and Van Houten was not shown to be inimicable to achieving the purpose of 1545 LLC. Indeed, the test is "whether it is 'reasonably practicable' to carry on the business of the [LLC], and not whether it is 'impossible'" (Fisk Ventures, LLC v Segal, 2009 Del Ch LEXIS 7, *9-10, 2009 WL 73957, *3 [2009], affd 984 A2d 124 [Del Supr Ct 2009]).

King never objected to the quality of Van Houten's construction work, but only to its expense. The work on building A was all but complete when this proceeding was commenced. King approved and praised it. Further, the parties were operating in conformity with the operating agreement.

Second, there is a remedy available in the Limited Liability Company Law to regulate Van Houten's conduct. Limited Liability Company Limited Liability Company Law § 411 permits a limited liability company to avoid contracts entered into between it and an interested manager, or another limited liability company in which a manager has a substantial financial interest, unless the manager can prove the contract was fair and reasonable. Crown Royal took no action under Limited Liability Company Law § 411 here. Beyond complaining about the cost of VHC's work and seeking to withdraw from 1545 LLC, the record is clear that Crown Royal ratified, albeit grudgingly at times, Van Houten's unilateral efforts.

The notion that 1545 LLC could void the contract with VHC in its entirety may serve as a check on Van Houten's unilaterally hiring his own company for future construction work on the property, and may result in Van Houten being made to disgorge excess moneys paid in derogation of 1545 LLC's best interest at the time of the accounting of the members. In any event, a fair reading of Limited Liability Company Law § 702 demonstrates that an application to dissolve 1545 LLC does not flow from a claim under Limited Liability Company Law § 411.

Finally, if Crown Royal is truly aggrieved by Van Houten's actions as manager, the Court of Appeals has found that a derivative claim is available. Nevertheless, such remedy cannot serve as the basis for dissolution unless the wrongful acts of a managing member which give rise to the derivative claim are contrary to the contemplated functioning and purpose of the limited liability company.

VII

"The appropriateness of an order for dissolution of [the] limited liability company is vested in the sound discretion of the court hearing the petition" (Matter of Extreme Wireless, 299 A.D.2d 549, 550, 750 NYS2d 520 [2002], citing Limited Liability Company Law § 702). However, in applying the standard for dissolution of a limited liability company, upon a review of the evidence submitted, we conclude that the Supreme Court did not providently exercise its discretion in granting the petition for dissolution. Thus, the order of the Supreme Court should be reversed, the petition denied, and the proceeding dismissed.

FISHER, J. (concurring in part and dissenting in part)

A limited liability company may be judicially dissolved when the court, in the exercise of its discretion, finds that it is no longer reasonably practicable for the company to carry on its business in conformity with its articles of organization or operating agreement (see Matter of Extreme Wireless, 299 AD2d at 550; Limited Liability Company Law § 702). I have no serious quarrel with the standard the majority adopts based on its analysis of the authorities it cites. In my view, those authorities and the plain language of the statute suggest that, pursuant to Limited Liability Company Law § 702, it is "not reasonably practicable" for a limited liability company to carry on its business in conformity with its articles of organization or operating agreement when disagreement or conflict among the members regarding the means, methods, or finances of the company's operations is so fundamental and intractable as to make it unfeasible for the company to carry on its business as originally intended.

Here, 1545 Ocean Avenue, LLC (hereinafter 1545 LLC), was formed to purchase a certain piece of property, to rehabilitate a building that stood on it, and to build a second building on the property for commercial rental. The majority recounts the growing disputes between the managers of 1545 LLC, John King and Walter Van Houten, which ultimately led to King's withdrawal from management of 1545 LLC, amid claims, inter alia, that Van Houten had turned the project "into a construction job for [his] own company," that he did work at excessive cost without King's consent, that he violated the parties' agreement that all construction work was to be procured through a competitive bidding process, that he submitted invoices billing 1545 LLC on a time-and- materials basis which King believed was unacceptable for a commercial project, and that Van Houten had refused to fulfill his responsibility to pay real estate taxes and vendors. Many of those allegations were disputed by Van Houten, but the Supreme Court made no findings of fact.

In my view, without a factual finding, we cannot meaningfully decide whether the Supreme Court providently exercised its discretion in finding that the actions of the parties rendered it not reasonably practicable for 1545 LLC to carry on its business in conformity with its articles of organization or operating agreement. Accordingly, I would remit the matter to the Supreme Court, Suffolk County, for a fact-finding hearing and thereafter for a new determination on the petition (cf. Business Corporation Law § 1109; Sobol v Les Pieds Nickels, 262 AD2d 194, 196, 692 NYS2d 336 [1999]; Matter of Giordano v Stark, 229 AD2d 493, 494-495, 645 NYS2d 517 [1996]).

3.2: Dissolution for Oppression

As Re-ULLCA § 701, *supra*, makes clear, the new uniform LLC act specifically provides both (1) a right against oppression for minority members in an LLC and (2) flexible remedies for violations of that right. A major question in modern LLC law, however, is whether courts will expand similar corporate protections to LLCs where the state's LLC statute does not explicitly provide such a remedy. Courts appear to be heading in that direction, but there have to date been very few cases on the matter.

Revised Uniform Limited Liability Company Act (2006) § 404: Sharing of a Right to Distributions Before Dissolution

[...]

(b) A person has a right to a distribution before the dissolution and winding up of a limited liability company only if the company decides to make an interim distribution.

A person's dissociation does not entitle the person to a distribution....

Revised Uniform Limited Liability Company Act (2006) § 603: Effect of Person's Dissociation as Member, cmt.

Subsection (a)(3)—This paragraph accords with Section 404(b)—dissociation does not entitle a person to any distribution. Like most inter se rules in this Act, this one is subject to the operating agreement. For example, the operating agreement has the power to provide for the buy out of a person's transferable interest in connection with the person's dissociation.

Sandra K. Miller, *What Buy-Out Rights, Fiduciary Duties, and Dissolution Remedies should Apply in the Case of the Minority Owner of a Limited Liability Company?*

38 Harv. J. on Legis. 413 (2001)

The difficulty a minority LLC investor may have in effectively negotiating buy-out rights and obtaining other contractual protections from majority overreaching cannot be over-emphasized. The observations of F. Hodge O'Neal were made in connection with the corporation but are equally applicable to the limited liability company:

> Statutory protection is needed for minority shareholders who fail to bargain for and obtain protective contractual arrangements. Although most state corporation statutes validate special charter and bylaw provisions and shareholder's agreements designed to protect minority shareholders, no statute—not even any of the separate, integrated close corporation statutes—furnishes adequate self-executing protection for minority shareholders who have failed to bargain for special charter provisions or for protective clauses in shareholders' agreements.... He (the minority shareholder) may be unaware of the risks involved, or his bargaining position may be so weak that he is unable to negotiate for protection.

Although some limited liability companies may be subject to detailed operating agreements that have been negotiated at [arm's length], others may not have extensive agreements that establish the parties' rights and responsibilities. Some limited liability companies may not have an agreement at all. Others, including some small limited liability companies, may be subject to boilerplate agreements that do not contain detailed provisions dealing with deadlocks or disputes among owners and/or managers. In fact, many small businesses are staffed by friends or family members who have such a close personal relationship that they may not consider that disputes could arise at a later time. To the extent that an LLC agreement is executed, it may not address the grievances that eventually develop between members. Despite the existence of a boilerplate LLC agreement, the understanding between the parties to small informal business ventures may be primarily oral, or at least not fully articulated in the operating agreement.

An assumption of a level contractual playing field may be unrealistic in the context of many family limited liability companies. In second-generation businesses, for example, children may join parents or relatives in a business enterprise. Minority interests may be inherited and the business may be operated by a variety of relatives or acquaintances over time. The original LLC operating agreement, however, may have been personal to those parties who initially formed the limited liability company and negotiated and drafted the agreement. Members who inherit an LLC interest or who join an LLC years after its formation may lack either the foresight or the leverage to renegotiate the fundamental workings of an existing LLC agreement. Those minority owners who inherit an LLC interest as assignees and are inactive may lack the sophistication or the bargaining power to modify the fundamental terms of the inherited LLC operating agreement.

Years of experience with the traditional corporate model illustrate that minority owners of closely held businesses require special statutory protections from fraudulent or opportunistic majority misconduct. The history of dispute resolution among business participants illustrates that there will be failures in contractual agreements as well as failures in human relationships in the context of LLCs, as in other private business entities. Difficulties between majority and minority LLC members, therefore, should be anticipated.

At a minimum, a default buy-out right should be made available to LLC owners who find themselves in a dispute with the majority without any operating agreement or with ineffectual contractual protection. Even if most LLC owners tend to have a contractual buy-out clause, default statutory protection should exist for those few who do not.

Further, a variety of statutory protections in addition to default buy-out rights are important to deter fraudulent and opportunistic majority conduct. Now that Check-the-Box regulations permit an LLC to have perpetual life, a growing number of LLC members will find themselves locked into the LLC for a specified term or indefinitely. Like corporate shareholders, members who are locked into an LLC should have the remedy of dissolution in cases where those in control have engaged in illegal, fraudulent, or unfairly prejudicial conduct. Most states provide shareholders the right to seek a corporate dissolution in the event of certain majority misconduct, and it is suggested that a similar remedy be provided to locked-in minority LLC members....

Although the primary motivation for eliminating the default buy-out rights of LLC members is to enable taxpayers to qualify for estate and gift tax valuation discounts, a substantial number of LLCs are not, in fact, formed for use as a family held investment. Indeed, the LLC was enacted to serve as the business entity of choice for a broad array of privately owned businesses.

Nationwide data suggest that use of the LLC form is increasing rapidly and that LLCs are housing a wide variety of business enterprises. It thus does not appear that LLCs are being used for the relatively narrow purpose of holding family investments.

According to a recent analysis of records of the individual secretaries of state compiled by the International Association of Corporation Administrators, new registrations of corporations and limited partnerships grew by 13 and 15% respectively between 1992 and 1996, whereas LLCs grew by over 2300% in the same time period. By 1996, nearly one in six new business registrations were LLCs. A sample of registration records show that a wide variety of industries are utilizing the LLC form. LLCs span a significant range of business classifications, including engineering and management support services, real estate, construction and general contracting, investments, retail, health services, amusement and recreation, agriculture, oil and gas, restaurants, and leasing services. Of the approximately 1200 LLCs analyzed, 26% were in engineering and management support, 19% were in real estate, 12% were in construction, and 9% were investment companies. The remaining one-third of the sample was spread over a number of different industries.

While the data do not indicate the LLCs used within the context of family estate planning, the diversity of LLC registrations suggests that the LLC is serving the needs of a broad base of the business community. In light of this apparent diverse use of LLCs, it may be more sensible to retain default buy-out rights in each state's LLC statute while removing default buy-out rights in a different statute such as the state's limited partnership statute. If, for example, it appears that most estate planners commonly use the family limited partnership as a means of obtaining minority discounts for estate tax purposes, it may make the most sense to eliminate default exit rights in the state's family limited partnership statute, while retaining default exit rights in the state's LLC and general partnership statutes.

3.3: Distributions of Assets and Profits After Dissolution

Revised Uniform Limited Liability Company Act (2006) § 708: Distribution of Assets in Winding Up Limited Liability Company's Activities

(a) In winding up its activities, a limited liability company must apply its assets to discharge its obligations to creditors, including members that are creditors.

(b) After a limited liability company complies with subsection (a), any surplus must be distributed in the following order, subject to any charging order in effect under Section 503:[3]

(1) to each person owning a transferable interest that reflects contributions[4] made by a member and not previously returned, an amount equal to the value of the unreturned contributions; and

(2) in equal shares among members and dissociated members, except to the extent necessary to comply with any transfer effective under Section 502.

(c) If a limited liability company does not have sufficient surplus to comply with subsection (b)(1), any surplus must be distributed among the owners of transferable interests in proportion to the value of their respective unreturned contributions.

(d) All distributions made under subsections (b) and (c) must be paid in money.

Comment

Subsection (a)—This section is mostly not a default rule. See Section 110(c)(11) (stating that "except as provided in Section 112(b), [the operating agreement may not] restrict the rights under this [act] of a person other than a member or manager"). However, if the creditors are willing, a dissolved limited liability company may certainly make agreements with them specifying the terms under which the LLC will "discharge its obligations to creditors."

Subsections (b), (c) and (d)—These subsection provide default rules. Distributions under these subsections (or otherwise under the operating agreement) are subject to Section 503 (charging orders).

Section 4: "Series" LLCs

Revised Uniform Limited Liability Company Act (2006): Prefatory Note

No Provision for "Series" LLCs

The new Act ... has a very noteworthy omission; it does not authorize "series LLCs." Under a series approach, a single limited liability company may establish and contain

---

3. A "charging order," as in partnership law, is an order effectively giving a creditor a lien on a member's transferrable interest in a business. [—ed.]

4. Under Re-ULLCA § 102(2), a "contribution" is defined as follows:

(2) "Contribution" means any benefit provided by a person to a limited liability company:
(A) in order to become a member upon formation of the company and in accordance with an agreement between or among the persons that have agreed to become the initial members of the company;
(B) in order to become a member after formation of the company and in accordance with an agreement between the person and the company; or
(C) in the person's capacity as a member and in accordance with the operating agreement or an agreement between the member and the company.

The comment to § 102 adds: "This definition serves to distinguish capital contributions from other circumstances under which a member or would-be member might provide benefits to a limited liability company (e.g., providing services to the LLC as an employee or independent contractor, leasing property to the LLC)." [—ed.]

within itself separate series. Each series is treated as an enterprise separate from each other and from the LLC itself. Each series has associated with it specified members, assets, and obligations, and—due to what have been called "internal shields"—the obligations of one series are not the obligation of any other series or of the LLC.

Delaware pioneered the series concept, and the concept has apparently been quite useful in structuring certain types of investment funds and in arranging complex financing. Other states have followed Delaware's lead, but a number of difficult and substantial questions remain unanswered, including:

- *conceptual*—How can a series be—and expect to be treated as—a separate legal person for liability and other purposes if the series is defined as part of another legal person?
- *bankruptcy*—Bankruptcy law has not recognized the series as a separate legal person. If a series becomes insolvent, will the entire LLC and the other series become part of the bankruptcy proceedings? Will a bankruptcy court consolidate the assets and liabilities of the separate series?
- *efficacy of the internal shields in the courts of other states*—Will the internal shields be respected in the courts of states whose LLC statutes do not recognize series? Most LLC statutes provide that "foreign law governs" the liability of members of a foreign LLC. However, those provisions do not apply to the series question, because those provisions pertain to the liability of a member for the obligations of the LLC. For a series LLC, the pivotal question is entirely different—namely, whether some assets of an LLC should be immune from some of the creditors of the LLC.
- *tax treatment*—Will the IRS and the states treat each series separately? Will separate returns be filed? May one series "check the box" for corporate tax classification and the others not?
- *securities law*—Given the panoply of unanswered questions, what types of disclosures must be made when a membership interest is subject to securities law?

The Drafting Committee considered a series proposal at its February 2006 meeting, but, after serious discussion, no one was willing to urge adoption of the proposal, even for the limited purposes of further discussion. Given the availability of well-established alternate structures (e.g., multiple single member LLCs, an LLC "holding company" with LLC subsidiaries), it made no sense for the Act to endorse the complexities and risks of a series approach.

Section 5: Litigation Procedure in LLCs

Revised Uniform Limited Liability Company Act (2006) § 901: Direct Action by Member

(a) Subject to subsection (b), a member may maintain a direct action against another member, a manager, or the limited liability company to enforce the member's rights and otherwise protect the member's interests, including rights and interests under the operating agreement or this [act] or arising independently of the membership relationship.

(b) A member maintaining a direct action under this section must plead and prove an actual or threatened injury that is not solely the result of an injury suffered or threatened to be suffered by the limited liability company.

Revised Uniform Limited Liability Company Act (2006) § 902: Derivative Action

A member may maintain a derivative action to enforce a right of a limited liability company if:

(1) the member first makes a demand on the other members in a member-managed limited liability company, or the managers of a manager-managed limited liability company, requesting that they cause the company to bring an action to enforce the right, and the managers or other members do not bring the action within a reasonable time; or

(2) a demand under paragraph (1) would be futile.

Revised Uniform Limited Liability Company Act (2006) § 903: Proper Plaintiff

(a) Except as otherwise provided in subsection (b), a derivative action under Section 902 may be maintained only by a person that is a member at the time the action is commenced and remains a member while the action continues.

(b) If the sole plaintiff in a derivative action dies while the action is pending, the court may permit another member of the limited liability company to be substituted as plaintiff.

Revised Uniform Limited Liability Company Act (2006) § 904: Pleading

In a derivative action under Section 902, the complaint must state with particularity:

(1) the date and content of the plaintiff's demand and the response to the demand by the managers or other members; or

(2) if a demand has not been made, the reasons a demand under Section 902(1) would be futile.

Revised Uniform Limited Liability Company Act (2006) § 903: Special Litigation Committee

(a) If a limited liability company is named as or made a party in a derivative proceeding, the company may appoint a special litigation committee to investigate the claims asserted in the proceeding and determine whether pursuing the action is in the best interests of the company. If the company appoints a special litigation committee, on motion by the committee made in the name of the company, except for good cause shown, the court shall stay discovery for the time reasonably necessary to permit the committee to make its investigation. This subsection does not prevent the court from enforcing a person's right to information under Section 410 or, for good cause shown, granting extraordinary relief in the form of a temporary restraining order or preliminary injunction.

(b) A special litigation committee may be composed of one or more disinterested and independent individuals, who may be members.

(c) A special litigation committee may be appointed:

(1) in a member-managed limited liability company:

(A) by the consent of a majority of the members not named as defendants or plaintiffs in the proceeding; and

(B) if all members are named as defendants or plaintiffs in the proceeding, by a majority of the members named as defendants; or

(2) in a manager-managed limited liability company:

(A) by a majority of the managers not named as defendants or plaintiffs in the proceeding; and

(B) if all managers are named as defendants or plaintiffs in the proceeding, by a majority of the managers named as defendants.

(d) After appropriate investigation, a special litigation committee may determine that it is in the best interests of the limited liability company that the proceeding:

(1) continue under the control of the plaintiff;

(2) continue under the control of the committee;

(3) be settled on terms approved by the committee; or

(4) be dismissed.

(e) After making a determination under subsection (d), a special litigation committee shall file with the court a statement of its determination and its report supporting its determination, giving notice to the plaintiff. The court shall determine whether the members of the committee were disinterested and independent and whether the committee conducted its investigation and made its recommendation in good faith, independently, and with reasonable care, with the committee having the burden of proof. If the court finds that the members of the committee were disinterested and independent and that the committee acted in good faith, independently, and with reasonable care, the court shall enforce the determination of the committee. Otherwise, the court shall dissolve the stay of discovery entered under subsection (a) and allow the action to proceed under the direction of the plaintiff.

Comment

Although special litigation committees are best known in the corporate field, they are no more inherently corporate than derivative litigation or the notion that an organization is a person distinct from its owners. An "SLC" can serve as an ADR mechanism, help protect an agreed upon arrangement from strike suits, protect the interests of members who are neither plaintiffs nor defendants (if any), and bring to any judicial decision the benefits of a specially tailored business judgment.

This section's approach corresponds to established law in most jurisdictions, modified to fit the typical governance structures of a limited liability company....

Chapter 7

Nonprofits and Related Organizational Forms

Section 1: Nonprofit Organizations: Nature, Theory, and Organization

Revised Uniform Limited Liability Company Act (2006) § 104: Nature, Purpose, and Duration of Limited Liability Company

[...]

(b) A limited liability company may have any lawful purpose, regardless of whether for profit....

Henry B. Hansmann, *The Role of the Nonprofit Enterprise*

89 YALE L.J. 835 (1980)

Private nonprofit institutions account for a sizable and growing share of our nation's economic activity. The sectors in which these institutions are most common—education, research, health care, the media, and the arts—are vital elements in the modern economy. Moreover, these are sectors that present particularly pressing and difficult problems of public policy. The existing literature in law and economics, however, has largely overlooked nonprofit institutions; while we are reasonably well supplied with positive and normative perspectives on both profit-seeking and governmental organizations, to date there has been extraordinarily little effort to understand the role of nonprofits.

This lack of understanding is reflected in the substantial confusion that characterizes policymaking concerning nonprofits. Nonprofit corporation law is poorly developed and varies in significant respects from one state to the next. Even the Model Nonprofit Corporation Act exhibits uncertainty about such basic issues as the purposes for which nonprofit corporations may be formed. Large classes of nonprofits receive special treatment in almost all areas in which federal legislation impinges upon them significantly, including corporate income taxation, Social Security, unemployment insurance, the minimum wage, securities regulation, bankruptcy, antitrust, unfair competition, copyright, and postal rates. Yet the principles on which such special treatment is based are nowhere clearly formulated. Similarly, there continues to be debate concerning the action of the National Labor Relations Board in shifting radically, over the past decade, from a policy of excluding nonprofits entirely from coverage under federal labor law to a policy of including them under the law on the same terms as profit-seeking enterprise....

I. The Essential Characteristics of Nonprofit Enterprise

Before examining the purposes served by nonprofit organizations, it is necessary to have a clear image of their essential structural features.

A. What Makes an Organization Nonprofit?

A nonprofit organization is, in essence, an organization that is barred from distributing its net earnings, if any, to individuals who exercise control over it, such as members, officers, directors, or trustees. By "net earnings" I mean here pure profits—that is, earnings in excess of the amount needed to pay for services rendered to the organization; in general, a nonprofit is free to pay reasonable compensation to any person for labor or capital that he provides, whether or not that person exercises some control over the organization. It should be noted that a nonprofit organization is not barred from earning a profit. Many nonprofits in fact consistently show an annual accounting surplus. It is only the distribution of the profits that is prohibited. Net earnings, if any, must be retained and devoted in their entirety to financing further production of the services that the organization was formed to provide. Since a good deal of the discussion that follows will focus upon this prohibition on the distribution of profits, it will be helpful to have a term for it; I shall call it the "nondistribution constraint."

Most nonprofits of any significance are incorporated. For these organizations, the nondistribution constraint is imposed, either explicitly or implicitly, as a condition under which the organization receives its corporate charter. Thus a nonprofit corporation is distinguished from a for-profit (or "business") corporation primarily by the absence of stock or other indicia of ownership that give their owners a simultaneous share in both profits and control.

In the corporation law of some states, the nondistribution constraint is accompanied or replaced by a simple statement to the effect that the organization must not be formed or operated for the purpose of pecuniary gain. Often such a condition as applied is equivalent to the nondistribution constraint. Occasionally, however, it is interpreted more restrictively to mean that an organization may not be incorporated as a nonprofit even if it is intended to assist in the pursuit of pecuniary gain in a more indirect manner.

Another restriction that was until recently quite common, and that still appears in the statutes of some states, is that an organization can incorporate as a nonprofit only if it is formed to serve one or more of a limited set of purposes. Today such explicit limitations are the exception rather than the rule. Many states now permit a nonprofit corporation to be formed "for any lawful purpose," which, like the similar language that is today nearly universal in business corporation statutes, means that it may be formed to engage in any activity that is not criminal—subject, of course, to the nondistribution constraint. There continues to be strong debate about the wisdom of restricting the purposes for which nonprofit corporations may be formed....

In most other respects, the nonprofit corporation statutes closely parallel the statutes that provide for business corporations. In fact, they are, if anything, even more permissive. Thus a nonprofit corporation may have a membership that, like the shareholders in a business corporation, is entitled to select the board of directors through elections held at regular intervals. But the statutes typically do not make this a requirement, so that the board of directors may, alternatively, simply be made an autonomous, self-perpetuating body....

B. A Categorization of Nonprofit Organizations

The flexibility of the corporation statutes permits nonprofit organizations to assume a wide variety of forms. Consequently, for the sake of simplifying exposition and analysis, it will help us to develop a basic subcategorization of nonprofits according to the manner in which they are financed and controlled.

1. Financing: Donative Versus Commercial Nonprofits

Nonprofits that receive most or all of their income in the form of grants or donations I shall call "donative" nonprofits. Organizations for the relief of the needy, such as the Salvation Army, the American Red Cross, and CARE, are perhaps the most obvious examples. Those nonprofits that, on the other hand, receive the bulk of their income from prices charged for their services I shall call "commercial" nonprofits. Many nursing homes, most hospitals, and the American Automobile Association would clearly fall within this latter category.

Of course, not all nonprofits fit neatly into one or the other of these two categories. For example, most universities rely heavily upon donations as well as upon income from the sale of services—i.e., tuition—and thus lie somewhere between the two. Consequently, donative and commercial nonprofits should be considered polar or ideal types rather than mutually exclusive and exhaustive categories....

2. Control; Mutual Versus Entrepreneurial Nonprofits

Nonprofits that are controlled by their patrons I shall call "mutual" nonprofits. Country clubs provide an example: generally their directors are elected by the membership, which comprises the organization's customers. Common Cause, the citizens' lobby, presents another example: the board of directors of that organization ultimately is selected by the membership, which consists of all individuals who donate at least fifteen dollars annually to the organization. On the other hand, nonprofits that are largely free from the exercise of formal control by their patrons I shall term "entrepreneurial" nonprofits. Such organizations are usually controlled by a self-perpetuating board of directors. Most hospitals and nursing homes, for example, belong within this latter category. Again, the two categories are really the ends of a continuum. For example, the board of trustees of some universities is structured so that roughly half is elected by the alumni—which constitutes the bulk of past customers and present donors—while the other half is self-perpetuating.

It is important to recognize that, while the organizations that I have termed "mutual" nonprofits may bear some resemblance to cooperatives, they are by no means the same thing. Cooperatives are generally formed under state cooperative corporation statutes that are quite distinct from both the nonprofit corporation statutes and the business corporation statutes. Cooperative corporation statutes typically permit a cooperative's net earnings to be distributed to its patrons or investors, who may in turn exercise control over the organization. Thus, cooperatives are not subject to the nondistribution constraint that is the defining characteristic of nonprofit organizations.

Section 2: Vicarious Liability in Nonprofit Organizations

Smith & Edwards v. Golden Spike Little League

577 P.2d 132 (Utah 1978)

CROCKETT, J.

Plaintiff Smith & Edwards, a dealer in sporting goods, sought to impose personal liability on twelve defendants who signed for and picked up various baseball equipment, including uniforms, from the plaintiff's store in Ogden. The defendants are a group of persons who joined together to sponsor and promote a little league baseball team, and who performed duties in promoting, managing, coaching, umpiring and doing secretarial work for that enterprise, which they called Golden Spike Little League. It was thus an unincorporated association. Upon a trial the court refused to impose personal liability upon the defendants, but stated that the unincorporated association, Golden Spike Little League should be held responsible. Plaintiff appeals.

In the spring of 1974 these defendants and other residents of Harrisville, a suburb of Ogden, met for the purpose of providing little league baseball for the youngsters of that town. They applied for and received a charter from the national association, Little League Baseball, Inc., which allowed them to organize and use the name of Golden Spike Little League.

The need for equipment was discussed at a meeting of the organizers, and it was agreed that defendant David Anderson would contact dealers to obtain the best possible price. Pursuant to that directive he talked to Albert Smith, owner of the plaintiff. Defendants do not question that Mr. Smith was motivated in substantial measure by a desire to cooperate in defendant's worthwhile project and offered a very favorable price for the needed merchandise. They did not discuss in detail just who nor how it would be paid for. Subsequently, various of the defendants would go into plaintiff's store and pick up and sign for different items of baseball equipment and uniforms. Mr. Smith was away from the business during much of this period. Upon his return late in the summer, he found that the defendants had obtained $3,900 worth of merchandise without making any payment thereon. He contacted defendants Anderson and Bloxham about payment. They arranged a fund-raising activity which produced only $149 to pay on this debt. Upon the refusal of the persons who had picked up and signed for the merchandise to pay for it, and their denial of any personal responsibility, plaintiff commenced this suit.

The trial court's ruling exempting the defendants from personal liability can only be predicated upon its view that the defendants were not acting on their own behalf, but were acting as agents of the national association, Little League Baseball, Inc., or of Golden Spike Little League. Analysis of that determination requires reference to the charter. In the provisions material here, it authorizes: the defendants to use "Little League," in their name; requires that certain types of equipment be used; that those participating wear little league approved patches and emblems, and provides for rules, guidebooks and an insurance program for the participants. It is particularly pertinent to note that it contained no provision authorizing the defendants, or Golden Spike Little League, to make any purchase or incur any obligations on its behalf, nor is there any evidence that the defendants had any apparent authority to do so. There is thus no basis for the defendants to escape responsibility by shifting it to the national association, Little League Baseball, Inc.

The difficulty with the other basis asserted for avoiding personal liability of the defendants: that they represented to the plaintiff that the merchandise was being purchased for Golden Spike Little League, is that the Golden Spike Little League is but a loosely formed voluntary association and is not a legal entity upon which liability can be imposed.

The principle of law which is controlling under the circumstances shown herein is that where a person enters into a contract with another, under a representation that he is acting as agent for a principal, when there is in fact no such principal, he renders himself personally liable upon the contract. This is equally true if the named principal is fictitious, or nonexistent, or is not a legal entity which can be subjected to liability; and it is also true, even though the purported agent had no wrongful intent. The reasoning in such circumstances is that the supposed agent's conduct results in damage to an innocent party, for which he should be held responsible.

The doing of justice in this case requires application of the just-stated principles of law to these essential facts: that the defendants associated themselves together in a common enterprise; that their chosen spokesman persuaded the plaintiff (Albert Smith) to furnish the merchandise; that this merchandise was picked up by the defendants who signed receipts acknowledging such delivery; that the plaintiff in good faith and in reliance upon representations made by the defendants (or those acting for them) fulfilled his part of the agreement and delivered the merchandise; and the defendants have not paid for it.

Though not involved in this action, we think it not amiss to observe that where a group of people become involved in an enterprise for a common purpose, and some of them, with the consent of the others, go forward and act for the group, so that they become personally liable as here, they have a right to apply any assets acquired by the association in payment of the obligation, and further, that they may well have a right of indemnity against anyone who was joined with them in the enterprise, and for whose collective benefit the purchases were made.

The judgment is reversed, and the case is remanded for such further proceedings as the parties may deem appropriate. Costs to plaintiff (appellant).

See Heims v. Hanke, *supra* Section 2.1

Revised Uniform Unincorporated Nonprofit Association Act (2008) § 2: Definitions

...

(8) "Unincorporated nonprofit association" means an unincorporated organization consisting of [two] or more members joined under an agreement that is oral, in a record, or implied from conduct, for one or more common, nonprofit purposes. The term does not include:

(A) a trust;

(B) a marriage, domestic partnership, common law domestic relationship, civil union, or other domestic living arrangement;

(C) an organization formed under any other statute that governs the organization and operation of unincorporated associations;

(D) a joint tenancy, tenancy in common, or tenancy by the entireties even if the co-owners share use of the property for a nonprofit purpose; or

(E) a relationship under an agreement in a record that expressly provides that the relationship between the parties does not create an unincorporated nonprofit association....

Revised Uniform Unincorporated Nonprofit Association Act (2008) § 8: Liability

(a) A debt, obligation, or other liability of an unincorporated nonprofit association, whether arising in contract, tort, or otherwise:

(1) is solely the debt, obligation, or other liability of the association; and

(2) does not become a debt, obligation, or other liability of a member or manager solely because the member acts as a member or the manager acts as a manager.

(b) A person's status as a member or manager does not prevent or restrict law other than this [act] from imposing liability on the person or the association because of the person's conduct.

Comment

1. The effect of section 8 is to provide members and managers of a UNA with the same protection against vicarious liability for the debts and obligations of the UNA and tort liability imposed on the UNA as the members and managers of a nonprofit corporation would have under the enacting jurisdiction's laws. These principles, taken together, constitute what is known as the limited liability doctrine under which a member or manager is personally liable for his or her own tortious conduct under all circumstances and is personally liable for contract liabilities incurred on behalf of the UNA if the member or manager guarantees or otherwise assumes personal liability for the contract or fails to disclose that he or she is acting as the agent for the UNA. A member or manager is not otherwise personally liable for the tort or contract liabilities imposed upon the UNA. A creditor with a judgment against the UNA must seek to satisfy the judgment out of the UNA's assets but cannot levy execution against the assets of a member or manager.

The one exception is the alter ego doctrine (also known as the veil piercing doctrine). Courts have pierced the corporate veil of nonprofit corporations.... The fact that members of nonprofit corporations for the most part do not have an expectation of financial gain, as compared to shareholders of a for profit corporation, should mean that there will be fewer types of cases than those involving for profit corporations where the veil piercing doctrine will be held to be applicable to nonprofit corporations. The same criteria that are applied to pierce the veil of nonprofit corporations should be applied in UNA veil piercing cases.

If the alter ego doctrine is found to be applicable, the separate entity status of a UNA would be disregarded and the assets of the UNA and its members and managers would be aggregated and subject to a UNA creditor's claims in the same manner that a judgment creditor collects a judgment against the assets of a general partner in a general partnership.

2. In recent years all states have enacted laws providing unpaid officers, board members and other volunteers some protection from liability for their own negligence (but generally not for conduct that is determined to constitute gross negligence or willful or reckless misconduct). The statutes vary greatly as to who is covered, for what conduct protection is given, and the conditions imposed for the freedom from liability. Some apply only to nonprofit corporations.... This means that members and volunteers involved with unincorporated nonprofit associations do not obtain protection under those state statutes. Others may cover the managers of UNAs but only if the UNA qualifies as a tax-exempt entity under federal or state law.... Some states have statutes that premise the insulation of liability upon the organizations having specified amounts of liability insurance....

3. "Solely" as used in section 8 is intended to make it clear that a member or manager is not vicariously liable for the liabilities of the UNA or the liabilities of another member or manager merely because of that person's status as a member or manager. A member or manager may, however, have personal liability as a result of his or her own actions. A member or manager will be personally liable, for example, for his or her own tortious acts, or for breach of a contract binding on the UNA which the member or manager is a party to or has guaranteed. This personal liability is imposed by other law ... and not because of his or her status as a member or manager.

Section 3: Fiduciary Duties in Nonprofit Organizations

Revised Uniform Unincorporated Nonprofit Association Act (2008) § 18: Duties of Member

(a) A member does not have a fiduciary duty to an unincorporated nonprofit association or to another member solely by being a member.

(b) A member shall discharge the duties to the unincorporated nonprofit association and the other members and exercise any rights under this [act] consistent with the governing principles and the obligation of good faith and fair dealing.

Revised Uniform Unincorporated Nonprofit Association Act (2008) § 23: Duties of Managers

(a) A manager owes to the unincorporated nonprofit association and to its members the fiduciary duties of loyalty and care.

(b) A manager shall manage the unincorporated nonprofit association in good faith, in a manner the manager reasonably believes to be in the best interests of the association, and with such care, including reasonable inquiry, as a prudent person would reasonably exercise in a similar position and under similar circumstances. A manager may rely in good faith upon any opinion, report, statement, or other information provided by another person that the manager reasonably believes is a competent and reliable source for the information.

(c) After full disclosure of all material facts, a specific act or transaction that would otherwise violate the duty of loyalty by a manager may be authorized or ratified by a majority of the members that are not interested directly or indirectly in the act or transaction.

(d) A manager that makes a business judgment in good faith satisfies the duties specified in subsection (a) if the manager:

(1) is not interested, directly or indirectly, in the subject of the business judgment and is otherwise able to exercise independent judgment;

(2) is informed with respect to the subject of the business judgment to the extent the manager reasonably believes to be appropriate under the circumstances; and

(3) believes that the business judgment is in the best interests of the unincorporated nonprofit association and in accordance with its purposes.

(e) The governing principles in a record may limit or eliminate the liability of a manager to the unincorporated nonprofit association or its members for damages for any action taken, or for failure to take any action, as a manager, except liability for:

(1) the amount of financial benefit improperly received by a manager;

(2) an intentional infliction of harm on the association or one or more of its members;

(3) an intentional violation of criminal law;

(4) breach of the duty of loyalty; or

(5) improper distributions.

Section 4: Hybrid Organizations

11 Vermont Stat. Ann. § 3001

(27) "L3C" or "low-profit limited liability company" means a person organized under [Vermont's LLC statutes] that is organized for a business purpose that satisfies and is at all times operated to satisfy each of the following requirements:

(A) The company:

(i) significantly furthers the accomplishment of one or more charitable or educational purposes within the meaning of Section 170(c)(2)(B) of the Internal Revenue Code of 1986, 26 U.S.C. § 170(c)(2)(B); and

(ii) would not have been formed but for the company's relationship to the accomplishment of charitable or educational purposes.

(B) No significant purpose of the company is the production of income or the appreciation of property; provided, however, that the fact that a person produces significant income or capital appreciation shall not, in the absence of other factors, be conclusive evidence of a significant purpose involving the production of income or the appreciation of property.

(C) No purpose of the company is to accomplish one or more political or legislative purposes within the meaning of Section 170(c)(2)(D) of the Internal Revenue Code of 1986, 26 U.S.C. § 170(c)(2)(D).

(D) If a company that met the definition of this subdivision (27) at its formation at any time ceases to satisfy any one of the requirements, it shall immediately cease to be a low-profit limited liability company, but by continuing to meet all the other requirements of this chapter, will continue to exist as a limited liability company. The name of the company must be changed to be in conformance with subsection 3005(a) of this title. (Added 1995, No. 179 (Adj. Sess.), § 4; amended 2007, No. 106 (Adj. Sess.), § 1, eff. April 30, 2008; No. 190 (Adj. Sess.), § 74, eff. June 6, 2008.)

Dana Brakman Reiser, *Governing and Financing Blended Enterprise*

85 Chi.-Kent L. Rev. 619 (2010)

...

I. New Hybrid Forms of Organization

Hybrid forms vary widely in their provenance and characteristics. Legislation here and abroad has spawned some of them; others are creatures of self-regulation. Although they are certainly novel, none of these hybrid forms have invented their features entirely of whole cloth. Rather, the creators of each form selected an existing form of organization as a core framework and then engrafted special hybrid features onto that basic form. These borrowed frameworks run the gamut. This [Article] describes the components of three quite different, currently available hybrid forms: the L3C ["Low-Profit Limited Liability Company"], the CIC, and the B corporation. In doing so, it focuses particularly on how the forms variously address governance, financing, and taxation to create a blended nonprofit/for-profit form.

A. Low-Profit Limited Liability Companies

Vermont was the first U.S. state to permit entities to form as low-profit limited liability companies, adopting legislation creating the form in April 2008. Since then, Michigan, Utah, Wyoming, the Crow and Oglala nations, and Illinois have followed Vermont's lead, enacting L3C legislation of their own. North Dakota and Maine have committed by legislation to studying this new form. Individuals and lawmakers in yet other states are engaged in more informal discussions about the L3C option. As entities can form in any state to do business throughout the United States, the L3C has quickly become a widely available choice of form. As a form of organization only in its infancy, much remains to be learned about how it will function in practice. This subpart uses the existing L3C law and some other materials produced by the form's promoters to (1) outline its basic approach to issues of taxation and (2) to discuss one option for L3C governance and financing.

The L3C takes the limited liability company form as its base, retains much of the LLC's inherently flexible nature, and adds features that hybridize nonprofit and for-profit elements. Each adopting jurisdiction has thus far followed a similar pattern, which engrafts the L3C option onto an existing LLC statute. The L3C enactments add language defining an L3C as organized for business purposes and operated to satisfy four core requirements. An L3C must "significantly further the accomplishment of one or more charitable or educational purposes" under the federal tax code. The enabling legislation typically also issues a kind of negative command, requiring that a company "would not have been formed but for the company's relationship to the accomplishment of" those purposes. Next, the statutes require that neither income production nor property appreciation may be a significant purpose of an L3C, and some require this to be stated in the L3C's formative documents. Yet the enactments generally clarify that producing "significant income or capital appreciation shall not, in the absence of other factors, be conclusive evidence" of such a prohibited purpose. Finally, each statute specifically disallows L3Cs from pursuing purposes that would disqualify an entity from exemption under I.R.C. § 501(c)(3)'s limitations on lobbying and political campaign activity.

This homogeneity among the various state enactments is, in large part, due to the genesis of the L3C's contours with its advocates, including the Mannweiler Foundation, its CEO Robert Lang, and attorney Marcus Owens (former head of the Internal Revenue Service Exempt Organizations Division). Along with other contributors, these advocates devised the basic L3C model. The model was intended to fit easily onto various states' LLC bases and provide sufficient limitations so that properly formed L3Cs would qualify to receive "program related investments" (PRIs) under existing Internal Revenue Service (IRS) rules.

PRIs are investments made by non-profit, tax-exempt private foundations that are entitled to two important forms of special treatment. First, like grants and most operating expenditures, PRIs qualify toward the required distribution percentage private foundations must expend for charitable purposes annually. This percentage is determined using a relatively complex formula, but generally it will fall close to 5% of the fair market value of a foundation's assets. Second, a PRI is sheltered from designation as a jeopardizing investment if its primary purpose "is to accomplish one or more of the [organization's exempt] purposes ... and no significant purpose of [it] is the production of income or the appreciation of property." Jeopardizing investments can subject private foundations to costly and potentially confiscatory excise taxes.

The desire of the L3C's inventors to define the entity to meet the PRI criteria explains much of the form's content. In order for an investment to qualify as a PRI, its primary purpose must be "to accomplish one or more of the purposes described in section 170(c)(2)(B)." Additionally, no significant purpose of a PRI may be "the production of income or the appreciation of property." Other sections of the tax code likewise preclude private foundations from expenditures for the political purposes forbidden to L3Cs. These mandates are reproduced in three of the four core requirements for forming as an L3C. The final requirement, that the entity would not have formed but for its charitable or educational purpose, reinforces the L3C's position as an entity created to meet the PRI requirements, helping to signal to private foundations and other investors that it is a predictable, consistent, and useful type—one that its boosters hope will establish a brand.

The L3C legislation includes virtually no additional content beyond the four core requirements, relying instead on existing LLC law to address any matters not covered by these spare enactments. LLC law is quite voluminous, covering myriad topics ranging from filing requirements to investor liability to derivative actions. Certainly, a [full] exploration of the subject is beyond the scope of this article. The pivotal issues for the current inquiry, though, relate to LLC taxation, governance, and financing.

Much has already been said about the L3C's position on issues of taxation. Its genesis was in large part to create a form for entities that would receive PRIs, a tax category; language from tax statutes defining that category provide much of the content of L3C enactments. In addition, however, the L3C relies heavily on the tax treatment of LLCs to produce its desired effects. Since 1997, LLCs have been [optionally] treated as partnerships under federal income tax law. That is, LLCs (and L3Cs by extension, it is assumed) [can be] treated as pass-through entities. The entity itself is[, then] not subject to taxation on its income; rather, profits and losses are allocated to the members, each of whom must pay tax accordingly to their own tax status. According to current IRS guidance, an LLC qualifies for entity-level exemption under § 501(c)(3) only if it is a single-member LLC with an exempt organization as its sole member or a multiple-member LLC in which all members are themselves exempt entities. An L3C would often not, therefore, itself be eligible for tax-exemption. But, for federal income tax purposes, pass-through treatment makes the entity-level exemption of precious little consequence. Because each member is credited profits and losses and then pays tax or not, depending on its own taxable or tax-exempt status, the profits a tax-exempt L3C member receives from its membership may avoid federal income tax liability. Whether and to what extent these profits will avoid federal income tax will depend on the type of exemption the tax-exempt member possesses (e.g., as a public charity or private foundation) and whether the profits are taxable as unrelated business income....

On the topic of governance, the hallmark of LLC law is flexibility.... Advocates of the L3C tout this flexibility as key to the value of this new hybrid form and have highlighted the L3C's ability to create a tranched membership structure. An equity tranche of members could be tax-exempt private foundations making program-related investments. Because the PRI regulations specifically bar foundations from contemplating a financial return as a motive for investment, this tranche of members would be given scant or very remote rights to distributions. A mezzanine tranche of individuals or entities could purchase L3C memberships as a type of socially-responsible investment. This tranche of investors would agree to operating agreement terms that provided them with some access to distributions, but at a rate lower than market return, presumably doing so in return for the social or psychic value produced by the entity. The L3C's operating agreement could then provide for a market-like return to a senior tranche of individuals and entities seeking such returns, presumably doing so in competition with other market-rate investment opportunities. The structure of these provisions might be more debt-like or equity-like (though if the latter, more like preferred than common stock), providing either a guaranteed return or a return keyed to the L3C's profits.

Despite their limited or attenuated financial rights, LLC law would permit an L3C using tranched membership to endow the equity tranche of tax-exempt entities with significant governance advantages. They could be granted overwhelming voting power, enhanced rights to vote on matters of management or policy, powers to select or monitor managers, or other rights that would vest significant control over the L3C's operations in this tranche. Likewise, LLC law permits a corresponding reduction or exclusion of governance rights in the other tranches. This technique assumes that governing rights in this tranche of investors without a profit motive or with only a limited one would safeguard the mission of the L3C to pursue charitable or educational purposes.

Of course, the question of transferability will crucially impact both governance and financing of L3Cs with tranched memberships. As noted above, LLC statutes default to placing significant limits on transfer of membership rights, generally permitting each member to voluntarily and unilaterally transfer her financial rights to another, but requiring the other LLC members to approve of the transferee's admission before the transferee will receive any rights in governance. L3C enactments thus far do not vary this pattern; however, since these are only default positions, operating agreements may vary them to some extent. If transfer limitations are left in the LLC default mode, the member interests of those tranches of investors with governing rights will not have a high degree of transferability, which may be the desired effect. These tranches will be locked into the L3C and will be unable to effectively sell to buyers intent on changing its mix of social and market goals. In contrast, those tranches of investors purchasing member interests that do not offer governance rights will see no additional loss in transferability, as they will not have governance rights to offer to buyers in the first place.

The extreme flexibility of the L3C form of course allows for variations beyond tranched membership structures. For example, an L3C might be used to structure an angel investment fund with a limited membership admitted only on consent of a gatekeeper foundation. Investors seeking a social and financial return could, therefore, be screened for a commitment to blended enterprise. The foundation could be empowered to mandate redemption of memberships in certain circumstances, making it the sole arbiter of entry and exit for the L3C's investors. Likewise, the foundation could be granted dominant governance rights, such as a veto to prevent the L3C from taking actions that could jeopardize its L3C status or the foundation's program-related investment in it. This type of structure is another way to deploy the flexible L3C framework to appeal to both foundations and some broader class of investors.

Ultimately, L3C status appears to be neither a permanent nor a publicly-guarded designation. Such entities might over time veer away from their charitable or educational purposes for various reasons. If this occurs, and the L3C no longer pursues primarily social purposes, the statutes provide that it would simply be converted to a standard LLC. The statutes do not say how this conversion would take place or who would monitor whether such a transformation has occurred in the first place. The L3C form thus boils down to a tremendously flexible financing and governance regime.

B. Community Interest Companies

Across the Atlantic, the United Kingdom recently initiated a hybrid form of organization that is now available in England, Wales, Scotland and Northern Ireland. The form is called a community interest company, or CIC. The CIC idea was first proposed in a report by the Prime Minister's Cabinet Office Strategy Unit in 2002, as part of a broader reform agenda for UK charity law. The report proposed the CIC to "improve access to finance, create a strong new brand, be legally protected from demutualization, and preserve assets and profits solely for social purposes." The CIC was officially created in a 2004 set of amendments to the UK company law—the analogue to corporate law in the U.S. Although CICs are still quite new, recent tallies show thousands of organizations have used the form.

The actual content of the CIC enactment is relatively thin, relying on company law as the basic framework for the new form, though supplying more details than do the L3C statutes. This enactment delegates continuing rulemaking and supervision for CICs to a light touch, dedicated CIC Regulator. The Regulator has been fairly active, issuing copious guidance materials for CICs as well as calls for comment on revising them toward improvement. Like other UK companies, CICs are required to register their existence and then must apply to the Regulator for their special community interest status. Once authorized, the CIC moniker must be incorporated into the entity's name, and special features of CIC status will apply to differentiate the entity from other companies. In reviewing the CIC's contours, this subpart will again focus on the paramount issues of taxation, governance, and financing.

In the area of taxation, CIC status does not confer any benefits beyond those available to other UK companies....

As under company law generally, CIC governance is primarily enshrined in the board of directors. CICs organized as private companies may have only one director; other companies must have two or more. All directors are fiduciaries who must exercise their management and supervisory duties with "reasonable care, skill and diligence" and avoid conflicts of interest or other situations of potential disloyalty. The goals and responsibilities of a company versus a CIC director, however, diverge considerably. In a typical company limited by shares, directors should pursue the interests of the shareholder members in good faith and need [not] consider other interests such as employees or the environment in their decision-making. In a CIC or other company with purposes other than solely to benefit shareholders (such as charities set up as companies limited by guarantee), these alternative stated purposes are to be the directors' primary goals.

CIC directors are also made responsible for preserving the CIC's ability to meet the community interest test. This test, which must be met in order to form as a CIC in the first place, requires that "a reasonable person might consider [the CIC's] activities are being carried on for the benefit of the community." The CIC must report its community interest achievements to the Regulator annually, and in this report, it must "confirm that access to the benefits it provides will not be confined to an unduly restricted group.

UK company law, and by extension CIC law, also provides a role for members in governance. In a CIC limited by shares, these members will generally be shareholders; in a CIC limited by guarantee, they will be donors or others admitted to membership by the terms of the CIC's organic documents. While members will not typically manage the company or oversee its operations on a regular basis, like US shareholders, they retain a few important rights in company governance, including election and removal of directors, amending the company's organic documents, and approving major transactions. Moreover, the Regulator asserts that members have especially important responsibilities in a CIC. As its Guidance explains:

In all companies, but more so with CICs, members should not regard delegation to directors as being the same as abdication of responsibility. It is important that the members should monitor the performance of the CIC and the directors, for example, to satisfy themselves that the company continues to meet the community interest test and fully involves the community in its activities and development.

Furthermore, the Regulator notes that it counts on members to be an important source of information revealing concerns about a CIC's activities that might merit regulatory action....

The CIC form also entails several important financing aspects. A CIC's assets are subject to an "asset lock." This asset lock prohibits a CIC from disposing of assets for consideration of less than their fair market value, except in pursuit of the community benefits the CIC is designed to pursue or in a transfer to a charity or another CIC. On dissolution, assets may not be paid out to directors, members, or equity holders; all assets must go to another entity whose assets are perpetually devoted to community benefit. The Regulator views the asset lock feature of a CIC's financial structure as its "fundamental feature."

In addition to locking assets into community benefit purposes, CICs are subject to important financial limits relating to dividends. The CIC statute permits dividends to be paid to members of a CIC limited by shares only if the Regulator authorizes such dividends by regulations; the statute also permits the Regulator to place limits on any such dividends....

When the dividend restrictions are viewed in conjunction with the asset lock, the CIC can be seen as offering investors a significantly altered form of equity investment. Investors may purchase shares and can participate in the profits of a CIC limited by shares. Yet, shares entitle investors only to capped dividends—not the full measure of the CIC's profits it might be prudent to disburse—and on dissolution, shares do not entitle their owners to residual earnings.

As compared with the L3C's virtually complete flexibility, CIC governance and financing interact in a relatively prescribed fashion. When equity-type shares are owned, shareholders are members and accordingly have governance rights to appoint and remove directors, amend the entity's organic documents, and approve major transactions. These control rights accompany their financial entitlements, which include the ability to receive (capped) dividends. However, shareholders are not be the only voice in CIC governance. The Regulator demands that stakeholders have input as well, though this involvement may be structured in various ways. Thus, the CIC statute and accompanying regulations impose a fairly rigid structural sense of how to finance and govern these blended enterprises, and empower both shareholders and a dedicated external regulator to enforce.

C. B Corporations

The final hybrid form to be canvassed here, the B corporation, is self-imposed and privately regulated, as opposed to the legislatively approved L3C and CIC forms. A B corporation, also sometimes called a "for-benefit" corporation, uses the traditional, state-law-governed corporate form as its base. This base is then varied through statements amending an individual corporation's organic documents to commit it to "use[] the power of business to solve social and environmental problems." So amended, the creators of the "B" idea envisioned the entity's documents as self-enforcing. A private, nonprofit organization, B Lab, vets the changes and the company's structure and operations as part of its certification system. Once B Lab certifies a company as meeting its requirements, the company may license the "certified B Corporation" trademark from B Lab.

As a private certification system, the B corporation designation offers no special tax treatment for corporations that obtain it. Ordinary federal and state income and property taxes will apply regardless of B certification, though it is possible that this situation may change over time. Commentators are currently debating whether and how tax benefits should be extended to for-profit companies pursuing social ends. Anup Malani and Eric Posner argue for uncoupling tax exemption from nonprofit form and its nondistribution constraint. They further assert that when for-profit entities engage in activities that benefit the community, they should receive the same tax benefits and other government subsidization as nonprofit charities. These claims are roundly criticized by James Hines, Jill Horwitz, and Austin Nichols, who argue that it is unnecessary and unwise to extend tax benefits for the community benefit activities undertaken by for-profits. First off, they explain that any profit losses taxable entities experience as a result of their community benefit activities already proportionally decrease their tax liability. In addition, they worry that Malani and Posner's proposal will encourage tax arbitrage and competition with traditional nonprofits that will negatively influence them away from their charitable missions.

My own view charts a middle course. I believe charity tax status and its attendant panoply of tax benefits should not be extended to wholesale hybrid organizations. These forms differ too significantly from traditional charities to match well with the incentives these benefits create. Yet, hybrid forms do offer promise of societal benefit. As we learn more about how they benefit communities, I believe that distinct, targeted tax incentives to encourage some or all of these forms will be warranted. These issues will no doubt be debated for years to come. Currently, though, "B" status will not confer any special tax treatment on those who adopt it.

In contrast, B corporations depart significantly from their strictly for-profit counterparts in terms of governance. Shareholders and directors both play important roles in B corporation governance, operating in much the same fashion as in any other for-profit corporation organized under state law. Shareholders must approve amendments to the corporate charter as well as other major transactions, including merger, sale of all or substantially all assets, and dissolution. They also compose the body that elects the board of directors and maintain certain rights to remove or recall directors from the board. Directors are empowered to manage the corporation or direct its management by officers and staff. In doing so, the directors are bound by fiduciary obligations, to act with due care, loyalty, and in good faith.

The B corporation concept, however, imposes an important gloss on directors' fiduciary obligations. As noted, to be eligible to license the "B" mark, corporations must amend their organic documents to include language instructing directors to consider interests beyond those of shareholders in carrying out their duties. More specifically, a New York B corporation would need to insert the following language into its articles of incorporation:

> In discharging his or her duties, and in determining what is in the best interests of the Company and its shareholders, a Director shall consider such factors as the Director deems relevant, including, but not limited to, the long-term prospects and interests of the Company and its shareholders, and the social, economic, legal, or other effects of any action on the current and retired employees, the suppliers and customers of the Company or its subsidiaries, and the communities and society in which the Company or its subsidiaries operate, (collectively, with the shareholders, the "Stakeholders"), together with the short-term, as well as long-term, interests of its shareholders and the effect of the Company's operations (and its subsidiaries' operations) on the environment and the economy of the state, the region and the nation.

To give these instructions the best chance of legal enforcement, B Lab requires applicants to incorporate in a state with an "other constituency" statute or to reincorporate in such a jurisdiction. "Other constituency" statutes expressly permit directors to consider constituencies other than shareholders in directorial decision-making, often particularly contemplating takeover situations. The quoted language above resonates with New York's relatively broad constituency statute, which allows directors to consider the interests of employees, retirees, creditors, customers, and the broader community when they make decisions in the context of changes of control or otherwise. Yet, under the required charter amendments, a New York B Corporation director would be obliged to go further, as she would be commanded to consider these outside interests. Moreover, the range of outside interests she must consider is even broader than that described by the statute, including abstract social and environmental concerns.

These changes impose unique and seemingly forceful obligations on B corporation directors. Yet, the charter language and statutes both explicitly decline to create new rights of action in individuals to assert that directors did not sufficiently consider these non-shareholder interests or constituencies. Nor do they suggest that these interests should or must predominate serving the interests of shareholders. Perhaps this is merely pragmatism on the part of the B corporation's creators. It seems likely that courts would enforce a mandate that directors consider social impact in their decisions, but even strong "other constituency" statutes frequently block enforcement rights expressly.

Perhaps shareholders who invest in a B corporation will do so because of its commitment to social impact, and these shareholders can serve as a proxy for the non--shareholder constituencies. B corporation shareholders do elect directors and have a statutory veto on at least some transactions. They could elect only director candidates who promise to heed this mission and cast aside those who do not; they could reject mergers or other actions that would imperil it. B corporation shareholders have significant rights to litigate, though of course they face substantial obstacles in challenging the directorial action—including the formidable business judgment rule, demand requirements, and other procedural hurdles involved in derivative litigation. They could attempt to use litigation to enforce the charter requirements explained above, possibly succeeding in requiring due consideration of social and environmental impact in the company's operations. On the other hand, shareholders might simply purchase for return, come to the position that return can be maximized by less consideration for society and the environment, or sell to those who would take such a position. Which type of shareholders a B corporation attracts, particularly if it is not closely-held and shareholder identity changes over time, will be far from certain.

The B Ratings survey does address the question of stakeholder involvement in governance, but does not demand it. In the section on governance, questions regarding accountability are split into "Board" and "Other" categories, which notably receive equivalent weightings. Within the "Other" category, however, are four questions, two of which ask whether the company has a policy on whistleblowing and maintains financial controls to enable it to prevent fraud and generate accurate reporting. The other two ask whether "the company has a forum to directly engage external stakeholders on a regular basis" and to "describe how [the] company engages stakeholders," to which applicants may respond that they offer annual meetings for stakeholders, fora for them on company websites, surveys of them, other means they may fill in, or that the question does not apply. The entire section is allocated between 1.6 and 3.3 out of 200 points in the B scale, depending upon whether the company operates in the manufacturing/wholesale, transportation/distri-bution or service sectors. Companies must achieve a score of 80 or higher in order to be eligible to license the "B" mark. Rather than relying upon stakeholders in governance, the B Ratings rely on their certification and auditing systems to ensure B corporations are pursuing and achieving their blended aims. The B Ratings heavily weight questions about how the applicant integrates its business and social goals, including relationships with employees, suppliers, local communities, and the environment.

Thus, the B corporation form realistically offers only moral, rather than legal, assurances to non-shareholder constituencies and social interests. Stakeholders have no structural rights in governance, and no additional parties are granted standing to litigate. B corporation directors are empowered to act in the interests of other constituencies; whether they do so will depend on their own desires or feelings of moral obligation.

Finance, too, tracks the standard for-profit menu. B corporations issue debt and may utilize equity investors by selling various classes of common or preferred stock. Dividends are uncapped and shareholders have rights to acquire any residual assets on dissolution, following the usual order of priority. B corporation shares may be kept closely-held or may be offered for sale to the wider public. Closely-held shares may be subject to de jure transferability limits under shareholder agreements or de facto ones due to their closely held nature. Publicly-held shares are freely transferable but offer much greater risk of changing the complexion of a B corporation's shareholding constituency. B corporation founders and leaders may well desire to keep the corporation closely-held in order to scrutinize potential shareholders and constrain them by agreement. Even if the financing capacity of public share ownership becomes attractive, those leaders committed to the "B" ideals may well adopt additional structures to limit shareholder power or avert takeovers by a less committed individual or group.

The B Corporation thus makes few changes from the traditional corporation, save branding. This branding may, of course, be an important contribution. It could draw in directors committed to a blended mission and investors willing to enforce it. It could become something consumers, employees, and business partners value. The brand also entails a private regulatory system to help enforce a blended enterprise's dual mission, but it remains to be seen whether this system will have strong teeth.

Index